The Edinburgh History of Reading:
Early Readers

THE EDINBURGH HISTORY OF READING

General Editors: Mary Hammond and Jonathan Rose

Bringing together the latest scholarship from all over the world on topics ranging from reading practices in ancient China to the workings of the twenty-first-century reading brain, the four volumes of *The Edinburgh History of Reading* demonstrate that reading is a deeply imbricated, socio-political practice, at once personal and public, defiant and obedient. It is often materially ephemeral, but it can also be emotionally and intellectually enduring.

Early Readers, edited by Mary Hammond
Modern Readers, edited by Mary Hammond
Common Readers, edited by Jonathan Rose
Subversive Readers, edited by Jonathan Rose

The Edinburgh History of Reading: Early Readers

Edited by Mary Hammond

EDINBURGH
University Press

Edinburgh University Press is one of the leading university presses in the UK. We publish academic books and journals in our selected subject areas across the humanities and social sciences, combining cutting-edge scholarship with high editorial and production values to produce academic works of lasting importance. For more information visit our website: edinburghuniversitypress.com

© editorial matter and organisation Mary Hammond, 2020, 2022
© the chapters their several authors, 2020, 2022

Edinburgh University Press Ltd
The Tun – Holyrood Road, 12(2f) Jackson's Entry, Edinburgh EH8 8PJ

First published in hardback by Edinburgh University Press 2020

Typeset in Sabon and Futura
by R. J. Footring Ltd, Derby, UK

A CIP record for this book is available from the British Library

ISBN 978 1 4744 4608 2 (hardback)
ISBN 978 1 4744 9485 4 (paperback)
ISBN 978 1 4744 4609 9 (webready PDF)
ISBN 978 1 4744 4610 5 (epub)

The right of Mary Hammond to be identified as the editor of this work has been asserted in accordance with the Copyright, Designs and Patents Act 1988, and the Copyright and Related Rights Regulations 2003 (SI No. 2498).

Published with the support of the University of Edinburgh Scholarly Publishing Initiatives Fund.

Contents

List of Figures, Plates and Tables   vii
List of Contributors   ix

Introduction   1
   Mary Hammond

1 The Move Towards Literacy Among Confucian Scholars in Ancient China   11
   Liqing Tao and David Reinking

2 Reading for Rule: Emperor Taizong of Tang and *Qunshu zhiyao*   31
   Fan Wang

3 Medieval Women Writers and What They Read, c. 1100–c. 1500   54
   Martha W. Driver

4 *Mi ritrovai per un poema sacro*. The Ideological Reading Subject in Dante's *Inferno 5*   74
   Glenn A. Steinberg

5 The Unreadable *Book of Margery Kempe*   98
   Ashley R. Ott

6 Between Reading and Doing: The Case of Medieval Manuscript Books of Practical Medicine   115
   Faith Wallis

7 Visual Form and Reading Communities: The Example of Early Modern Broadside Elegies   135
   Katherine Acheson

8 Ottomans Reading Persian Classics: Readers and Reading in the Ottoman Empire, 1500–1700   160
   Murat Umut Inan

9 Books, Readers and Reading Experiences in the Viceroyalties of New Spain and Peru in the Sixteenth to Eighteenth Centuries 182
Pedro M. Guibovich Pérez

10 'Read it o're and o're': *Eikon Basilike* and Sacramental Reading in the Seventeenth Century 206
Kyle Sebastian Vitale

11 Plurilingual Poetry and the Hinterland of Intertextuality: Europeanising Reading Culture in the Early Modern Iberian World 227
Maya Feile Tomes

12 Printed Private Library Catalogues as a Source for the History of Reading in Seventeenth- and Eighteenth-Century Europe 249
Helwi Blom, Rindert Jagersma and Juliette Reboul

13 Reading, Visual Literacy and the Illustrated Literary Text in Eighteenth-Century Britain 270
Sandro Jung

14 Reading Aloud, Past and Present 297
W. R. Owens

Select Bibliography 315
Index of Methods and Sources 355
General Index 356

Figures, Plates and Tables

Figures

6.1	Roger Frugard, *Cirurgia* (medieval French translation). A patient carries out a self-test for hairline cranial fracture under instruction from a surgeon	129
7.1	Thomas Philipot, 'AN ELEGIE OFFER'D UP TO THE Memory of His Excellencie Robert Earle of Essex and Ewe. . .' (1646)	139
7.2	Thomas Philipot, 'Englands sorrow for the losse of their late generall' (1646)	141
7.3	Anon., 'A Funerall Elegie upon the deplorable and much lamented Death of the Right Honourable Robert Devereux . . .' (1646)	142
7.4	Anon., 'A MITE from Three MOURNERS: In MEMORIAL of THOMAS GLASS . . .' (1666)	147
7.5	Anon., 'An Elegy, an Acrostick, and also an Anagram, On the Death of that Faithful and worthy Minister and Servant of GOD, Mr. JOSEPH CARYL' (1672)	148
7.6	Anon., 'An Elegie Upon the Truly Worthy, and ever-to-be-remembred Loyal Gentleman, Captain WILL. BEDLOW . . .' (1680)	151
9.1	General view of the library of the Palafox Seminary in Puebla, Mexico, by José de Nava (1771)	191
9.2	Portrait of Agustin Sarmiento in his study in Lima (1669)	194
10.1	Charles I and John Gauden, *Eikon Basilike* (1649)	214
12.1	Numbers of surviving editions of catalogues published between 1599 and 1800, as recorded by Gruys for the Dutch Republic, by Bléchet and then Marion for France, and by Munby and Coral for the British Isles	253
13.1	Frontispiece, *The Seasons* (1785)	274
13.2	Vignette for January, *Royal Engagement Pocket Atlas for 1793*	277
13.3	Woodcut vignette, *The Seasons* (1804)	277
13.4	Frontispiece, *The Seasons* (1804)	280

13.5	*The Curious Hieroglyphic Bible* (1788), p. 17	282
13.6	Title page, *The Death of Abel* (1799 reprinting of the 1765 illustration)	284
13.7	Woodcut vignette, *The Death of Abel* (1783)	284
13.8	Frontispiece, *The Death of Abel* (1790 reprinting of the 1787 illustration)	285
13.9	Frontispiece, *The Death of Abel* (1801 reprinting of the 1795 illustration)	287
13.10	Frontispiece, *The History of Pamela; or, Virtue Rewarded* (1775 reprint)	289
13.11	Frontispiece vignette, *The History of Pamela; or, Virtue Rewarded* (1799)	291
13.12	Frontispiece, *The History of Pamela; or, Virtue Rewarded* (c. 1820)	292
13.13	Frontispiece, *The Sugar Plumb* (1787)	294

Plates

1. 'La comtessa didia', portrait of the Countess of Dia, Chansonnier provençal, thirteenth century
2. 'Na Castelloza', portrait of Castelloza, Recueil des Poésies des Troubadours, 1201–1300
3. Marie de France at her desk, Paris, Recueil D'Anciennes Poésies Françaises, 1275–1300
4. Christine de Pizan presents her book to Isabeau of Bavaria
5. Charles I and John Gauden, *Eikon Basilike* (London: John Williams, 1649), A2 recto, title page
6. Charles I and John Gauden, *Eikon Basilike* (London: s.n., 1649), frontispiece

Tables

| 1.1 | Categories of textual autonomy | 12 |

Contributors

Katherine Acheson is Professor of English and Associate Dean of Arts at the University of Waterloo in Ontario, Canada. She is the editor of *Early Modern English Marginalia* (2019) and *The Memoir of 1603 and the Diary of 1616–1619 by Anne Clifford* (2008), and the author of *Visual Rhetoric and Early Modern English Literature* (2013) and *Writing Essays About Literature* (2011). Her chapter in this volume is part of her current research about the visual form of English seventeenth-century printed poetry.

Helwi Blom is a literary historian whose research focuses on early modern France. Her scholarly interests include popular literature (the 'Bibliothèque bleue'), book history and reception studies. In 2012 she earned her PhD in French studies from Utrecht University with a dissertation on the reception of medieval romances of chivalry in seventeenth-century France. She is currently a postdoctoral researcher in the MEDIATE (Measuring Enlightenment: Disseminating Ideas, Authors and Texts in Europe, 1665–1830) project at Radboud University Nijmegen (mediate18.nl). In the context of this project, she studies private library catalogues published in France between 1630 and 1830.

Martha W. Driver is Distinguished Professor of English and Women's and Gender Studies at Pace University in New York City. A co-founder of the Early Book Society for the study of manuscripts and printing history, she writes about illustration from manuscript to print, book production and the early history of publishing. Her books include *The Image in Print: Book Illustration in Late Medieval England* (2004), *An Index of Images in English Manuscripts*, Fascicle 4, with Michael Orr (2001), and, with Sid Ray, *The Medieval Hero on Screen* (2004) and *Shakespeare and the Middle Ages* (2009). She contributed to and edited *Preaching the Word in Manuscript and Print in Late Medieval England: Essays in Honour of Susan Powell*, with Veronica O'Mara (2013).

Maya Feile Tomes is Junior Research Fellow in Modern Languages and Classics at Christ's College, Cambridge, specialising in literary culture from the early modern Iberian context. Current projects include a translation of Domingo de Soto's *Aquí se contiene una disputa o controversia* . . . (1552) for Oxford University Press, a co-edited volume on classical reception in the Americas for Brill, and an edition of the Latin epic poem of José Manuel Peramás, discussed in her chapter in this volume. A revised version of her doctoral dissertation will be published by Támesis.

Mary Hammond is Professor of English and Book History at the University of Southampton, UK. She is the author of numerous works on nineteenth-century book, publishing and readership history, including *Reading, Publishing and the Formation of Literary Taste in England, 1880–1914* (2006) and *Charles Dickens's Great Expectations: A Cultural Life, 1860–2012* (2015).

Murat Umut Inan received his doctoral degree in Near and Middle Eastern studies from the University of Washington and is Assistant Professor of Ottoman and Turkish Studies at the Social Sciences University of Ankara, Turkey. His research and teaching interests focus on the interconnected literary, cultural and intellectual histories of the Ottoman Empire and the wider Islamic world. He is completing a book on the reception of Persian literary culture in the Ottoman Empire between 1400 and 1600.

Rindert Jagersma is a book historian at Radboud University in Nijmegen (The Netherlands), specialising in the book trade and print culture of the Dutch Republic around 1700. In the ERC-funded MEDIATE project (Measuring Enlightenment: Disseminating Ideas, Authors and Texts in Europe, 1665–1830) he focuses on Dutch-printed private library catalogues and the circulation of books.

Sandro Jung is Distinguished Professor of English and Comparative Literature at the Shanghai University of Finance and Economics, and Senior EURIAS Fellow at the Freiburg Institute of Advanced Studies. He is the author of *David Mallet, Anglo-Scot: Poetry, Politics, and Patronage in the Age of Union* (2008), *The Fragmentary Poetic: Eighteenth-Century Uses of an Experimental Mode* (2009), *James Thomson's 'The Seasons', Print Culture, and Visual Interpretation, 1730–1842* (2015), *The Publishing and Marketing of Illustrated*

Literature in Scotland, 1760–1825 (2017) and *Kleine artige Kupfer: Buchillustration im 18. Jahrhundert* (2018).

Ashley R. Ott has a PhD in English from Saint Louis University and is a cultural historian specialising in medieval and early sixteenth-century British literature, especially Chaucer, the history of the book and print culture. Her recent projects explore the intersection of codicological and literary evidence of the period to interpret how unreadability functions as an imaginative strategy.

W. R. Owens is Emeritus Professor of English Literature at the Open University and Visiting Professor at the University of Bedfordshire. He has published widely on John Bunyan and Daniel Defoe, and was Director of the Reading Experience Database (RED) project from 2005 to 2015. Recent publications include an edition of the Gospels for Oxford World's Classics (2011) and he is co-editor, with Michael Davies, of *The Oxford Handbook of John Bunyan* (2018).

Pedro M. Guibovich Pérez has a PhD in history from Columbia University, New York, and is Principal Professor at the Pontifical Catholic University of Peru and Associate Professor at the Universidad del Pacifico, in Lima. He has been Research Fellow at the John Carter Brown (Brown University), Beinecke Library (Yale University) and Center for the Study of Books and Media (Princeton University), among other institutions. He has published two books on Inquisitorial book censorship and several articles on ecclesiastical history, censorship and readership in colonial Peru.

Juliette Reboul is a historian specialising in the study of the transnational circulation of ideas in eighteenth-century Europe. In 2017, she published her first monograph, entitled *French Emigration to Great Britain in Response to the French Revolution*. She worked on the Mapping Trade, Charting Enlightenment project (Western Sydney) before joining the MEDIATE team at Radboud University Nijmegen in the Netherlands (see mediate18.nl). In this, she examines sales catalogues of private libraries from the British Isles.

David Reinking is Emeritus Distinguished Professor of Education, with an appointment in the Department of Language and Literacy Education at the University of Georgia, USA. He is a past president of the Literacy Research Association and has served as editor of *Reading Research Quarterly* and the *Journal of Literacy Research*. His extensive publications include a chapter in *The Enduring Book: Print Culture in Post-war America* (2014), the fifth volume of University of North Carolina Press's 'The History of the Book in America'.

Glenn A. Steinberg teaches courses in classical, medieval and Renaissance literature at The College of New Jersey. His research focuses on the reception of classical and medieval texts in England during the late Middle Ages and Renaissance, with a particular emphasis on the evolving reputations of Virgil, Dante and Chaucer from the fourteenth to the sixteenth centuries. He has published essays in *The Chaucer Review*, *Chung Wai Literary Monthly*, *English Literary Renaissance*, the Modern Language Association's *Approaches to Teaching Chaucer's Troilus and Criseyde and the Shorter Poems* and *Modern Philology*.

Liqing Tao is Professor of Literacy Education at College of Staten Island/CUNY, and serves as doctoral faculty at CUNY Graduate Center. His publications include a chapter on the Confucian concept of learning in *Constructive Education in an Age of Accountability* (2017) and two chapters on ancient Chinese literacy in *Perspectives on Teaching and Learning Chinese Literacy in China* (2012).

Kyle Sebastian Vitale is Assistant Director for Faculty Teaching Initiatives at Yale University's Poorvu Center for Teaching and Learning. He writes and publishes about teaching, higher education and the intersections of theology with early modern literature. His work appears in *Religion and Literature*, *Christianity and Literature*, *Notes and Queries* and *Pedagogy*. He is co-editor of *Shakespeare and Digital Pedagogy: Case Studies and Strategies* (2021).

Faith Wallis is jointly appointed in the Department of History and Classical Studies and the Department of Social Studies of Medicine at McGill University. Her research focuses on the transmission of medical and scientific knowledge in the Middle Ages. Her anthology of translated sources, *Medieval Medicine: A Reader*, was published by University of Toronto Press in 2010. She is presently editing the writings of Bartholomaeus of Salerno, a key figure in the emergence of academic medicine in the twelfth century.

Fan Wang is a PhD candidate in the Comparative Literature programme at the University of Massachusetts Amherst. Her research focuses on the history of reading and private libraries in pre-modern

China. She has published in the journal of *Late Imperial China* and *Private Libraries in Renaissance England: A Collection and Catalogue of Tudor and Early Stuart Book-lists*.

Introduction

Mary Hammond

As a reader of this book you are already engaging with a sophisticated set of ciphers, symbols and deeply embedded cultural practices, probably without being fully (or even at all) aware of them. The front cover of the book – part of what Gérard Genette designates the paratexts – may have caught your eye.[1] You may have flipped the book over and studied the blurb before opening it. You may have flicked through and looked at the illustrations first; or you may already have selected the chapter that interests you from the contents list, the indexes or the online descriptions, and started there. You may never read beyond that segment. Or you may read the whole volume cover to cover and then embark on another in the series. You may be reading with the book in your hand, on your desk or in your lap, on a train or bus or in bed, in photocopied fragments, or on a tablet or phone or other e-reader. You may be doing something else at the same time (eating, drinking, walking, conversing, listening to music, looking out of the window . . .). You may not be reading this introduction at all (most respondents to a 2015 Reddit poll said they habitually found introductions so annoying they skipped them altogether, or didn't read them until the end).[2] But whatever you do or don't do when you read, your actions, reactions or anticipated actions are part of a long and complex global history of social practices. Some of these are still with us in some form in some parts of the world; many have disappeared altogether, or shape-shifted, or faded from cultural memory as technologies, politics, national borders and priorities, and cultural needs and fads have changed. The belief underpinning the four volumes comprising *The Edinburgh History of Reading* is that reading is always a deeply imbricated, political and social practice, at once personal and public; defiant and obedient; sometimes materially ephemeral, often emotionally and intellectually enduring. The readers of these volumes, like the readers in them, are individuals – sometimes obedient, sometimes rebellious, often both at once. All bring to bear on their reading a unique individual tapestry of past knowledges and experiences of which these volumes (whether in fragments or as a whole) will become a part.

Both historians and theorists of reading have long suspected this to be the case. As long ago as the late 1970s and early 1980s Wolfgang Iser and Stanley Fish were slugging it out in print over whether or not readers interpreted texts individually and uniquely, as the former held, or were more influenced by their roles in 'interpretive communities', as Fish believed.[3] But more recent work by neuroscientists on the reading brain has suggested that Iser may have been partly right and that, as Maryanne Wolf puts it, 'Reading is a neuronally and intellectually circuitous act, enriched as much by the unpredictable indirections of a reader's inferences and thoughts, as by the direct message to the eye from the text'.[4] Further, it is becoming increasingly clear that the acts of learning to read, and of reading at different points in one's life, actually change our brains: 'Reading can be learned only because of the brain's plastic design, and when that reading takes place, that individual brain is forever changed, both physiologically and intellectually.'[5] This means it is highly likely not only that is the act of reading performed differently by different brains in different languages using different cipher systems, but that as the technologies of reading change, so do the activities and therefore the imprinted neural pathways of the reading brain. Reading in ancient China, that is, cannot – either culturally or physiologically – be the same thing as reading in the digital age.[6] A point each to Iser *and* Fish, then: we are beginning to understand that people read individually while also remaining part of a community, and that this community can be linguistic, social or historical – and is usually all three at once.

Of course, different periods, practices and technologies overlap (often within a single lifetime); yet brains and readers somehow manage to untangle the messy palimpsests of their own historical moments. We are somehow able to carve meaning out of messages whether they are heard (or overheard), remembered, deciphered in company or alone, wholly or in part, in translation or in a native language, on a cave wall, a pictographic tablet, a scroll, a codex page or a computer screen, or a combination of these things. We cannot, of course, hope to account in these volumes for all the vagaries of time, location and situation in which readers have encountered text since the first human made a series of decipherable marks on a surface in order to transmit a message about something to an absent person who needed to know about it. Those decipherable marks may or may not have begun with pictographic tablets in Mesopotamia in the fourth millennium BCE,[7] or with *Chia-ku-wen* script on the shell of a tortoise in China sometime between 1300 and 1100 BCE.[8] Both have been posited as possible beginning points (largely because we have evidence for them as contenders). But the undisputed fact remains that reading is plural, not singular, and that understanding its material properties, processes and significance in the past therefore requires a broader range of skills and methods than almost any other historical task facing us. Taking up the challenge, these volumes aim to map as many of those moments and cultures of reading over space and time as presently possible, so that more of the messiness of being a reading human in different places at different times can be inferred from those specifics that we have been able to capture.

In order to enable a more organic approach to the inevitable overlap of time, space and technologies, we have deliberately not ordered our volumes into sections with editorially draconian sub-headings that, we felt, might delimit their potential to be read freely, individually, randomly and/or relationally. This editorial decision will, we hope, encourage our readers to browse; to make connections and see synergies or ruptures that we haven't thought of; to feel free to discard or engage with chapters using patterns of their own choosing. What we hope to gain by this structure is the presentation of an account of reading history across the world that is free flowing, surprising, inviting and likely to open up new ways of thinking about historiography and methodology. As Anouk Lang has observed: 'it is important not to let an emphasis on structure and social context lead us to lose sight of individual agency, creativity, resistance, and freedom within the interaction between reader and text: the task must be to grasp both realities at the same time'.[9] Rather than imposing on each historical 'snapshot' a relationship with others that it may not have possessed, then, we invite our readers to browse, to cherry pick or to read methodically, at will. In order to facilitate the experience of the reader we have, though, named the volumes (for convenience, but also, of course, open to challenge) *Early Readers*, *Modern Readers*, *Common Readers* and *Subversive Readers*. We have also ordered the chapters within each of the volumes chronologically, and provided at the end of each not only the usual index (detailing occurrences of location, period, reader and text) but also an index of the diverse methodologies and types of sources utilised by our contributors. The aim here is not to reproduce the oft-anthologised and tired old cornerstones of theory and methodology that still cling to most histories of reading (Darnton, Iser, Fish and the rest appear here only in cameo, as time-served veterans) but to put them to work and showcase the results. We hope this structure will enable a deeper understanding of the approaches, resources and methods current scholars have found the most revealing and useful (and why), while also suggesting by omission what work remains to be done.

We are aware that we enter a crowded field: an impressive number of books have emerged in recent decades that attempt to explain how fragments of evidence can imply broader social practices in the past. Many of these, such as Steven R. Fischer's *A History of Reading* and Alberto Manguel's book of the same title, work on the principle that reading will always 'inspire and empower the world'[10] or that the individual's experience can be somehow generalised (for Manguel, 'Reading, almost as much as breathing, is our essential function').[11] For them, reading is a human right, and they assume we all share their fervent belief in its liberating potential. In this model, readers have always been ontological rebels, flying in the face of what D. A. Miller famously calls the 'police' of the oppressive ideologies potentially lurking in texts.[12] They may be right. Yet many readers in the past (and plenty in our own time) are neither empowered nor inspired by their reading, but undertake it as a duty or under threat of punishment. Many avoid reading anything but the news, or postings on Twitter or Instagram, because (and I include my students in this, based on a recent poll in class) reading for pleasure or instruction or 'empowerment' or 'inspiration' in one's leisure hours is seen as unmanly, or unfeminine, or overly intellectual, or old fashioned. Or, perhaps, one is simply tired of reading and wants to do something else for a while. Physical limitations are as important as ideological ones: while many avoid reading as a matter of choice, many millions more could (and can) not read at all, or were (and are) prevented from reading by the demands of their jobs or by cultures that deny them the right. For these people, the idea of reading being an 'essential function' like breathing is very wide of the mark, if not downright insulting.

These volumes attempt to capture reluctant, accidental, secretive and disadvantaged as well as eager readers. As Rachel Ablow has suggested, in many instances in history, 'text and world were commonly conceived as productively opposed to one another, rather than cognitively linked', and it can be enormously productive to approach reading from the point of view of 'feeling' rather than 'knowing'.[13] This approach goes some way towards ensuring that we are constantly and consistently aware of the particularity of reading and of the humanity of our historical subjects, though we also fully recognise the validity of bibliometric and other quantitative approaches more aligned with Franco Moretti's contentious concept of 'distant reading'.[14] We make no claims to universality (political, ideological or otherwise), or historical or geographical comprehensiveness (such a task would in any case be impossible) and we have not instructed our contributors to take any particular stance: their methods and arguments are as varied as their subjects, and in some cases they disagree with one another.

We are not particularly interested, either, in extrapolating the general from the particular (though we do include a number of single-reader case studies), or in providing a whistle-stop global tour of reading in history (though our global and temporal coverage is fuller than has ever been attempted before). Our focus is on how different modalities of reading arose, became embedded in and imbricated across various cultures, and changed over time in different locations, often simultaneously. Our contributors aim to explore what constitutes 'reading' in these disparate locations, and thus collectively offer some ideas about how, in the twenty-first century, we might understand reading as a social and cultural practice in all its varieties, while remaining open to future scholarship that may challenge epistemological assumptions about who historical readers were and what they experienced, thought and felt.

One problem dogs all historians (and theorists) of reading, and these volumes are no exception: how do we know what people in the past read, under what circumstances they read it, and what its effect on them might have been, since 'readings', as Cavallo and Chartier point out, 'are always of the order of the ephemeral'?[15] Archives get destroyed, memories fade and die, most readers leave no traces of their experiences (or lie about them when they do) and texts crumble to dust. Inevitably, historians of reading have always had to work with a limited dataset, particularly (though by no means exclusively) those working – as some of the contributors to this volume do – with readers from the earliest epochs of human civilisation, in locations whose traces have been altered or erased by wars, politics, weather, natural disasters or simply the passage of time.

Different readership historians – and different editors – have approached this problem differently, but none has yet done so as comprehensively as *The Edinburgh History*. Perhaps frustrated by the fact that scarcity of evidence has inevitably led to a scarcity of scholars willing to tackle the earlier periods, the excellent three-volume *History of Reading* edited by Rosalind Crone, Katie Halsey, W. R. Owens and Shafquat Towheed is delimited to scholarship on readers from the sixteenth to the twentieth century, though they do provide an excellent range of international perspectives.[16] A focus on specific locations has seemed like a sensible solution to Cavallo and Chartier, who – unlike us – confine their exploration to the West, although, like us, since they do range as far back as antiquity, they too must wrestle with a paucity of evidence. Jesper Svenbro's chapter on 'Archaic and Classical Greece' in their volume resolves this, ingeniously, by dint of tracing changes in word use and in the meaning of the word 'read' over time,[17] and this close-reading tactic is utilised by several of the contributors to the present volume, to persuasive effect.

In Chapter 1, for example, Liqing Tao and David Reinking, also faced with a serious evidentiary deficit, focus on the features of texts attributed to Confucius (551–479 BCE), Mencius (c. 372–289 BCE) and Xun Zi (c. 310–c. 235 BCE). They argue that moving 'from an oral tradition to literacy entails more than the change from illiteracy to literacy. It also involves a change in a mentality from the oral to the literate.' There are intriguing premonitions here of the findings of modern neuroscience, which has yet to address the idea that while reading might change the brain, those changes might in turn leave distinct traces in a text.

In Chapter 2, in a related vein, Fan Wang examines a range of Confucian texts specially commissioned for Emperor Taizong of Tang (598–649) in order to help him, a good soldier but a reluctant scholar, become a more effective ruler. Wang argues that 'The meaning of [this] poetry . . . resides not in the poem but in the dynamic interplay between poetic lines and the circumstances under which they are applied. Reading consequently becomes an act of creative appropriation that transforms and renews the significance of the original text for different purposes and times.' This particular close reading, reliant on knowledge of the reader and the politics of his particular moment, is subtly able to suggest that there is always a reader and a reading experience somewhere in the text, if we look hard enough.

To fast forward a thousand years and shift hemispheres is not necessarily to improve the readership historian's lot. In Chapter 3, Martha W. Driver is able to extrapolate from their writing what historically elusive medieval women – Marie de France, Julian of Norwich, Margery Kempe and Christine de Pizan – read. As she suggests, their 'writing is informed not only by their reading but also by their adept uses of rhetoric, by their cultural influences and by their expression of authentic emotions'. Driver is thus able to trace textual influences and techniques in Kempe's writings, in particular, to ascertain what she most likely read or heard read aloud.

Ashley Ott, on the other hand, focuses in Chapter 5 not on what Kempe herself read, but on how others came to read her. Tracing the 'unreadability' of Kempe's writing, she suggests, 'presents spiritual encounters both as readable events and as opportunities for decipherment'. She goes on to examine how a scribe or other reader might have used this process of decipherment as a test: 'the readability of the first draft is governed by extra-textual means, namely faith'. Reading, in this model, is not an intellectual competency so much as a spiritual one.

Between and beyond these two chapters, different versions of close textual reading take us in different directions, geographically and methodologically. We shift the focus to fourteenth-century Italy in Chapter 4, where Glenn A. Steinberg uses Louis Althusser's model of interpellation to suggest that 'Reading is one instance of . . . interpellation – a moment in which the reader encounters content that elicits ideological responses and subjectivity'. For Steinberg, tracing the text's indicators and contexts of interpellation 'helps us to flesh out a rough picture of Dante's readers, about whom otherwise little is known, and to reconstruct available ideological frameworks for reading in fourteenth-century Italy'.

Faith Wallis (Chapter 6) is interested in how we might determine the 'use' to which books were put in medieval Britain. Using two streams of materialist analysis – evidence of reading, and evidence of doing as a direct result of reading – she takes as her case study a range of medieval medical books and is able to demonstrate that *how* a book was read by a physician performing a medical procedure provides concrete evidence that it *was* read. As she points out, 'it is unlikely that a trained phlebotomist would prop a book open in front of him to guide him in executing . . . [a bloodletting] operation'; nonetheless, the fact that evidence exists of such an operation being performed in precisely the way the book describes demonstrates its enduring use, and its impact on the professional reader.

Equally – though differently – expressive of the usefulness of materialist analysis is Katherine Acheson in Chapter 7, where she offers a detailed reading of the paratextual features of early modern broadside funeral elegies. The illustrations, typefaces and layout, she suggests, 'help express and shape the commitments, interests and priorities of readers and, like words, have the power to join those readers together in networks and communities of shared values and understanding'.

In Chapter 8, Murat Umut Inan shows how texts travel across time and space as he close-reads extant reprinted copies of the thirteenth-century poet Hafiz for traces of how they were read by teachers and pupils in the Ottoman Empire. Teacher Süruri's preface to a collection of Hafiz's poems, he suggests, 'offers a glimpse into the world of a community of readers in sixteenth-century Istanbul' that would otherwise be lost to us.

Evidence is – perhaps surprisingly – less of a problem for Pedro M. Guibovich Pérez in Chapter 9; he is able to draw on extant booksellers' accounts, monastic records and shipping inventories. Tracing the import of reading material (especially forbidden material) through official channels and in travellers' luggage enables him to offer a persuasive overview of reading practices in the viceroyalties of New Spain (or Mexico) and Peru during the sixteenth, seventeenth and eighteenth centuries. Since it was so difficult and expensive to import books, he argues, they must surely have been wanted and most probably also read. This method has another advantage: it 'challenges understandings inherited from nineteenth-century historiography that tended to judge that period as backward and reactionary, [and] turns the book into a historical protagonist'. This is a powerful argument for the need to map the circulation of books and reading practices as closely as we can; it can help to shift our understanding of historical political structures and help us adjust our own historiographical prejudices.

Like Acheson, other contributors also offer ways to 'read' paratexts, including illustrations, that get to the heart of how texts were consumed. Kyle Sebastian Vitale (Chapter 10) alerts us to the need to read the material text in context. He warns us that the English Royalist pamphlet the *Eikon Basilike*, originally designed to deify and rescue the executed Charles I for posterity, has been 'at once overstated and understated by modern critics, in ways that blur rather than clarify seventeenth-century reading habits'. Without analysing the diverse published responses to the *Eikon*, he argues, we would be in danger of generalising Royalist support and eliding much of the political complexity of the period. For Maya Feiles Tomes (Chapter 11), too, critical *mis*reading can be partially addressed through a micro-history of reading that pays close attention to the invisible politics of historiography; and, like Guibovich Pérez, she performs this address through an examination of the impact of immigrant literatures alongside indigenous texts. For Tomes, to tell the full, complex story of reading in the Iberian Americas 'is to redress widespread misconceptions, themselves inherited from the early modern period, about the nature of literary culture in the early Iberian world. What at first sight might appear a Eurocentric story is in fact a corrective to an enduring anti-Ibero-American polemic.' The history of reading, clearly, is able in certain contexts to punch well beyond its long-assumed critical weight.

In Chapter 12, Helwi Blom, Rindert Jagersma and Juliette Reboul step into the hotly contested terrain of book ownership as evidence of reading practices using purpose-built digital tools that are able to map the details of book ownership across space and time in Europe in the seventeenth and eighteenth centuries. They argue that an exhaustive quantitative analysis of the movement of texts is instrumental in indicating markets for them driven by real readers, not merely because they are able to indicate social and professional patterns, but because, crucially, 'each discrepancy and deviation might indicate a personal reading interest'.

Sandro Jung (Chapter 13) then moves us back from the macro- to the micro-historical approach. He closely analyses a range of eighteenth-century British book illustrations to show that 'the non-typographical nature of the printed images necessitated a reflective engagement on the part of the reader' and that this 'relied on special skills to comprehend graphic representations that had their origins in the material culture and the relationships of readers' daily experience'.

The volume ends with a return to the macro and digital historical methods that nonetheless take account of the particularity of experience. W. R. Owens's analysis in Chapter 14 of the evidence for instances of reading aloud collected in the Reading Experience Database 1450–1945 offers the perhaps surprising suggestion that 'reading aloud is not just a thing of the past, but has a distinctive and valuable role to play in present-day society'. His claim, like many of the others encountered in this volume, serves to unsettle previous historiographies that have posited models of historical ruptures rather than continuities. And in so doing, he provides us with a thought-provoking bridge from the 'early' readers of this volume to the 'modern' readers who populate the pages of the next volume of *The Edinburgh History of Reading*, demonstrating that these divisions ought themselves to be continuously interrogated. It is our hope that these contributions will facilitate and encourage just such an interrogation.

Notes

1. Gérard Genette, *Paratexts: Thresholds of Interpretation (Literature, Culture, Theory)* (Cambridge: Cambridge University Press, 2010).
2. See <https://www.reddit.com/r/books/comments/30ooz8/do_you_read_the_introduction_of_a_book> (accessed 23 August 2018).
3. Wolfgang Iser, 'Interaction Between Text and Reader', in David Finkelstein and Alistair McCleery (eds), *The Book History Reader*, 2nd edition (London: Routledge, 2006), pp. 391–6; Stanley Fish, 'Interpreting the Variorum', ibid., pp. 450–8.

4. Maryanne Wolf, *Proust and the Squid: The Story and Science of the Reading Brain* (New York: Harper Perennial, 2007), p. 16.
5. Ibid., p. 5.
6. Ibid.
7. Denise Schmandt-Besserat, *Before Writing, Vol. I: From Counting to Cuneiform* (Austin: University of Texas Press, 1992), p. 1.
8. Alberto Manguel, *A History of Reading* (London: Penguin, 1997), p. 27.
9. Anouk Lang, *From Codex to Hypertext: Reading at the Turn of the Twenty-First Century* (Amherst: University of Massachusetts Press, 2012), p. 2.
10. Steven Roger Fischer, *A History of Reading* (London: Reaktion Books, 2003), p. 8.
11. Manguel, *A History of Reading*, p. 7.
12. D. A. Miller, *The Novel and the Police* (Berkeley: University of California Press, 1988).
13. Rachel Ablow (ed.), *The Feeling of Reading: Affective Experience and Victorian Literature* (Ann Arbor: University of Michigan Press, 2010), p. 2.
14. Franco Moretti, *Distant Reading* (London: Verso, 2013).
15. Guglielmo Cavallo and Roger Chartier (eds), *A History of Reading in the West*, trans. Lydia G. Cochrane (Cambridge: Polity, 1999), p. 1.
16. Rosalind Crone, Katie Halsey, W. R. Owens and Shafquat Towheed (eds), *The History of Reading* (Basingstoke: Palgrave, 2011).
17. Jesper Svenbro, 'Archaic and Classical Greece: The Invention of Silent Reading', in Cavallo and Chartier (eds), *A History of Reading in the West*, pp. 37–63.

Chapter 1

The Move Towards Literacy Among Confucian Scholars in Ancient China

Liqing Tao and David Reinking

The roots of literacy in China developed millennia ago. Arguably, as we suggest in this chapter, those roots can be traced to the centuries of unprecedented intellectual, cultural and social developments in China that started around the sixth century BCE. The impetus for these developments was the intellectual force of, among others, the teachings of Confucius (孔子) and the Daoist thinking of Lao Zi (老子), which remain influential today. They were followed in subsequent centuries by notable thinkers in various schools of thought, such as Mo Zi (墨子) in the fifth to fourth centuries BCE, Mencius (孟子) and Zhuang Zi (庄子) in the fourth to third centuries BCE and Xun Zi (荀子) and Han Fei Zi (韩非子) in the third century BCE. These centuries, encompassing the late Chun-qiu and Warring States periods in China (春秋末期与战国) (551–221 BCE),[1] have generally been regarded as the formative period of Chinese society and culture.[2] They also overlap with what the German philosopher Karl Jaspers[3] called the Axial Age, which saw important shifts in thinking emerge, not only in China, but independently in the ancient civilisations of India, Persia and the Greco-Roman world. Given the significant intellectual and social developments of that period, it would be logical to assume comparable developments in literacy across those diverse cultures during the same period of history.

This chapter, although it is focused on China, might represent a case study for parallel developments in other ancient cultures during this Axial Age. For the period under discussion, direct evidence from records for actual historical readers is not available.[4] Therefore, we examine the evidence of changing literacy practices as reflected in the structure and coherence of texts, much as scholars have done when studying shifts in reading practices by tracking the physical changes in texts and their production.[5] We focus particularly on the features of texts attributed to Confucius (551–479 BCE) as well as

Mencius (c. 372–289 BCE) and Xun Zi (c. 310–c. 235 BCE), the most prominent Confucian scholars of that period. We discuss a shift from orality to literacy as reflected in the writings of Confucian scholars in the historical setting that influenced and was influenced by a move towards literacy. Finally, we speculate about the implications of the move towards literacy in that period for subsequent social and educational developments in China.

Literacy and evidence of a literate culture

In our analysis of Confucian texts, we consider literacy as an ability to use reading and writing in response to specific social, cultural and technical demands and constraints. That definition treats literacy as a sociocultural practice, not only as a human ability to master the unique characteristics and specific linguistic conventions of a written language. To define 'being literate', we rely on Clanchy's definition of 'literate mentality', which refers to internalising sociocultural viewpoints precipitated by becoming literate.[6] Specifically, it refers to mental and attitudinal postures exercised in social practices that accrue from being fully literate. Literate mentality is typically contrasted with an 'oral mentality', associated with non-literate or pre-literate cultures, but which may persist to some extent after literacy has been achieved.

Table 1.1 Categories of textual autonomy

Category	Definition
Intra-paragraph or intra-section textual explicitness	A text that provides readers with contexts, support and other necessary information for its understanding
Intra-paragraph or intra-section textual ambiguity	A text that does not provide sufficient information for readers to convey its message
Inter-paragraph or inter-section coherence	A text that has a clear connection between paragraphs or sections
Inter-paragraph or inter-section incoherence	A text that has no clear connection between paragraphs or sections
Peritext features of clarity	A text that has chapter titles
Peritext features of ambiguity	A text that has no chapter titles
Sources of textual meaning or authority	A text that does not rely on an authority figure for its meaning; or a text does depend on an authority figure for meaning

Other scholars, such as Ong, Olson and Scribner and Cole,[7] using an anthropological perspective, have proffered similar distinctions.

Using these perspectives, we seek evidence of a literate or oral mentality in the Confucian texts analysed. Specifically, we seek evidence of a literate mentality in a text as reflected in the textual autonomy[8] that is captured in explicitness[9] and coherence, essential characteristics of texts in a literate culture that cater to the needs of readers. We operationalise this as follows: (1) explicit statements of shared knowledge as opposed to textual ambiguity at the intra-section and intra-paragraph level, which is more characteristic of an oral mentality; (2) paragraph- and section-level coherence as opposed to a disconnection between paragraphs and sections, an oral characteristic that emphasises additive rather than subordinative style;[10] and (3) textual autonomy as displayed in peritextual features and sources of text authority in texts. These categories with definitions are shown in Table 1.1.

The historical setting: China in the sixth through to the third century BCE

The sixth through to the third century BCE was one of the most intellectually active periods in China's history. It was initiated with the teachings of Confucius and Lao Zi and followed by various other philosophies, often referred to during this period as the Contention of Hundred Schools of Thought (百家争鸣).[11] Not coincidentally, the period saw the rise of a special group called Shi (士; scholars). The active intellectual landscape would have certainly been conducive to the use and development of shared texts and literacy: conditions were ripe for both.

Concurrently, education and schools moved beyond the exclusive circles of the ruling classes and the hereditary aristocrats, and became available to commoners.[12] Schools of various types provided elementary education to village children as well as to children of noble descent.[13] The number of book titles increased tremendously during the period. These books were usually produced on bamboos, wood strips and silk fabrics.[14] The Chinese orthography changed drastically in style at this time.[15] Different states showed more or less deviations in style, particularly in remote states.[16] For example, in Chu and other southern states, a picture-like style called *niao-chong* (鸟虫书; bird-worm) appeared, as did *Li* (隶书; cleric or scribal) in Qin.[17] Both differed from the style stipulated in a book devoted to character learning and standardisation called *Shizhou* (史籀), believed to have been composed around the ninth century BCE.[18] But the ideographic nature of Chinese orthography remained unchanged. The six principles of creating ideographic characters widely known at the time must have been familiar to anyone then learning to write Chinese.[19] In fact, most of these principles are still relevant to learning and understanding Chinese orthography today.[20]

Meanwhile, the period saw a rapid growth of new characters for ideological and scientific concepts, and a visible increase in double-syllable words,[21] which reflected the intellectual and scientific development of the time and the need for a flexible way to expand the writing system[22] to meet changing social needs. There are indications that officials 'published' laws on publicly displayed cast iron or bronze ritual vessels elaborately decorated and with the writing on the surface;[23] special orders and regulations were also posted in public places.[24] Thus, scribes and administrative officials exercised authority for writing[25] and it seems there was an expectation of literacy among the general public.

But this period of intellectual advancement, perhaps ironically, was one of the saddest periods in the social history of China. Social order crumbled within the loosely structured dynastic empire. The once central royal court of Zhou (周王室) lost its grip on its vassal states. The latter, moving to the centre of political power struggles and territorial encroachments, waged large-scale wars against their neighbours and conspired against each other; even within states, thrones were usurped. Although a potentially countervailing condition for fostering literacy, the chaos and wars that plagued this period nonetheless provided a fertile ground for intellectual talents and for participation in the unprecedented intellectual activities.[26] For example, to address the needs of rulers for ideological justifications of their power, for political and military strategising, and for the practical demands of the administration of these warring states, various intellectual schools of thought came into being. Literacy must have been a valuable tool that many of these intellectuals used to distribute their thoughts to followers, market their talents to the rulers, and to consolidate their thinking.

Three Confucian texts

It is in this historical context of increasing intellectual activities accompanied by social upheavals that we examine the literate mentality as exhibited in the degrees of autonomy of three Confucian works:

the *Analects* (论语) of Confucius himself and the eponymously known *Mencius* (孟子) and *Xun Zi* (荀子). We use these Confucian works not merely because the Confucian school of thought was the most widely known and the dominant one of the time, but also because the school's extensive use of written language was clearly intended to record and transmit Confucian thinking. Further, these three works, respectively, took their incipient forms at around the beginning, the middle and the end of the period in question. The *Analects*, a collection of quotations and conversations of Confucius and some of his top disciples, began to emerge only after Confucius's death around 479 BCE; *Mencius* was composed about a 170 years or so later; and *Xun Zi* was written some 50 years or so after *Mencius*.

Mainly due to the destruction of books during the Qin dynasty (秦朝),[27] authentication of pre-Qin books always poses a challenge to scholars, and these three works are no exception. Scholars of pre-Qin classics generally agree that *Mencius* and *Xun Zi* remain largely in the original, since Mencius and Xun Zi wrote or participated in writing the main parts of their works. There is more controversy about when Confucius's *Analects* appeared and about its authentication.[28]

However, we believe there are several justifications for our use of these works for the current study. First, despite disputes about when exactly these texts took their current forms, particularly the *Analects*, scholars have usually considered them to have originated with Confucius, Mencius and Xun Zi. While *Mencius* and *Xun Zi* were produced mostly in their lifetime, Confucius's *Analects* is generally considered to be the result of continuous compilation over several hundred years.[29] Yet, the *Analects* itself has evidence that some written records of Confucius's talks were made while he was teaching his students,[30] indicating the authenticity of a collection of sayings that served as a prototypical book before it was eventually compiled into its more stable textual form known today. In other words, some original sections were supplemented by additions over the years. However, there is little doubt that the core of each text can be attributed directly to Confucius, Mencius and Xun Zi. Second, in differentiating what is authentic in texts such as Confucius's *Analects*, scholars mainly rely on the consistency of the ideas expressed and the linguistic features used, the latter including grammar and word choices.[31] Therefore, we can be reasonably confident that any results obtained in the current study examining the textual features for literacy marks should not be severely affected by questions of authentication in relation to the lost originals. Third, the forms of these texts must have remained relatively stable over the years because of at least a residual commitment to an oral tradition of faithful reproduction. For example, teaching and learning among Confucian scholars relied on a close reading, if not memorisation, of a text, suggesting some degree of textual consistency over time. Fourth, even those who might have intentionally inserted their own ideas later into the books would have been motivated to feign consistency with the original, so any later additions would likely conform putatively to the Master's style in order to be credible.[32]

Evidence of literacy through analysis

Our analysis focuses on coherence within inter-sections and/or inter-paragraph coherence, the explicitness of the texts and coherence between and among sections, peritextual features, and sources of textual authority in these texts. Based on the unique physical and typographic features of each of the three texts, for our analysis we use: the first two sections, roughly equivalent to paragraphs in appearance, in the first chapter of the *Analects*; the first two sections, roughly similar to two complete narrative episodes, in the first chapter of *Mencius*; and the first two paragraphs in the first chapter of *Xun Zi*. As sub-units of chapters, these excerpts should be comparable as units of texts from these three books. Our analysis starts with the *Analects*, moves to *Mencius* and then ends with *Xun Zi*, in an attempt to provide a clear line of progression represented by these three works from an oral to a literate mentality.

Excerpts from the *Analects*

The Master said: 'Is it not pleasurable to learn and practise often? Is it not also delightful to receive friends from afar? Is he not also a gentleman who is not upset when not recognised?'[33]

Master You said: 'It is rare to find someone filial and loyal but enjoying defying his superiors. One who does not enjoy defying his superiors but likes to rebel has never existed. The gentleman attends to the foundations, which, when built, give birth to the Way. Filiality and loyalty are the foundations of benevolence!'[34]

These first two sections taken from the first chapter of the *Analects* are short and on two different topics: one on Confucius's view regarding learning, friends and a *Junzi*'s (君子; gentleman's) qualification, the other on the importance of *Xiao* (孝; filiality) and *Zhong* (忠; loyalty) to *Ren* (仁; benevolence). At the inter-section level, the relationship between the two sections is neither sequential nor subordinate, but additive: the two sections describe two separate events, presenting two different 'Master' figures and their respective quotations: one from Confucius, the other from his disciple You Zi (有子). Without a thematic connection between them, these two events form an incoherent and non-continuous text at this level.

This incoherence persists throughout the book. The sections in all the chapters are usually short and lean in description and elaboration, their organisation less than perfect, if not random, and quotations evidentially additive and aggregate, as is typical of oral transactions.[35] In short, at this level the *Analects* is not coherent in the sense that we would understand the term, and falls short of the textual autonomy that a modern Western reader, say, would generally expect of such a book.

At the intra-section level, also, these excerpts in the *Analects* display textual ambiguity. In the first excerpt, the context of the quotation is ambiguous. Aside from the fact that the quotation was supposed to be enunciated by Master Confucius, we are not informed as to why the quotation was uttered, and in relation to what specific context, event or person. In its current lean style, the quotation allows for different interpretations. Furthermore, a close look at the textual relations between the three terse claims shows the same ambiguity. The intra-section connection is not established through any signal words or phrases. We are not told why the delight of welcoming friends from far-away places in the second claim should follow or even parallel the pleasure one obtains from learning and practice in the first claim. Nor can we see any textual progression from the first two claims to the last one without stretching our imagination. From the standpoint of a fully literate culture, the text is inconsiderate of the reader because it assumes so much unstated (because commonly shared) knowledge that it becomes a challenge if not impossible for the text to be fully comprehended without it.

At this intra-section level, the second excerpt, You Zi's quotation, is less ambiguous; it has a clear argument. However, the logical relation between the concepts of benevolence and the Way (*Dao*; 道) is not explicitly stated; and the reason to use filiality and loyalty as the foundation for benevolence rather than the other way round is not clear. Similar to the first section, the current one also lacks context for You Zi's discourse. A reader's only recourse is to trust the Master's words.

Aside from the inter-section and intra-section lack of coherence and clarity, the *Analects* also does not offer a meaningful or thematic title for each of its twenty-two chapters, offering no peritextual support for a reader. In addition, the book has a prominent Master figure, as well as a strong Master voice, making it literally the only source for trust in any implied or arbitrary meaning, of which there are many.

Excerpts from Mencius

Mencius visited King Hui of Liang. 'Sir,' said the King, 'you've travelled from afar, undeterred by a thousand *li* distance. You must have ways to profit my state?'

'Your Majesty,' responded Mencius. 'Why talk about profits? Benevolence and righteousness would be sufficient. If Your Majesty says, "How to profit my state?" counsellors say, "How to profit my family?" and the gentlemen and commoners say, "How to profit myself?" then those above and below will rival each other for profits and put the state in danger. Regicide, in a state of ten thousand chariots, is certain to be committed by someone with a thousand chariots, and when in a state of a thousand chariots, it is certain by someone with a hundred chariots. A share of a thousand in ten thousand or a hundred in a thousand is by no means small, yet when profit is placed before righteousness, only complete possession of all will suffice. A benevolent man never abandons his parents; a righteous man never puts his superiors last. Your Majesty, it should be sufficient for you to talk about benevolence and righteousness. Why mention profit?'[36]

Mencius visited King Hui of Liang, who was standing by a pond. 'Does a virtuous man enjoy these things too?' asked the King, eyeing his wild geese and deer.

'Only if he's virtuous,' answered Mencius, 'can he take joy in them. A non-virtuous man could not. The *Odes* say,

> He surveyed and started the Sacred Platform.
> He surveyed and planned.
> People worked hard at it.
> They finished it promptly.
> He surveyed and said to his people 'No hurry'.
> People came in throngs.
> The King was in the Sacred Park.
> Doe lay down, plump and sleek;
> White birds glistened with beauty.
> The King was at the Sacred Pond.
> It was teeming with leaping fish!

King Wen built his platform and pond by labours from people, yet the latter were so delighted that they named his platform 'Sacred Platform' and his pond 'Sacred Pond', and were elated that there were many deer, fish and turtles. Kings in antiquity were happy because they shared their joys with people. Tang Shi says, 'O Sun, when wilt thou perish? We care not if we are to die with thee.' If people would rather die than live with him, how could that person still enjoy by himself the platform, pond, birds and animals?[37]

In comparison with the *Analects*, *Mencius* tends to be more explicit and coherent at the intra-section level. However, it, too, overlooks inter-section coherence. At the inter-section level, the excerpts from *Mencius* lack explicit textual signals and thematic connections. The first section is about a principle that a ruler should avoid using profit/ interest to measure success in state governance, and the second is about how a state ruler should value people. The stories told in the two sections occur in different settings and on different topics, as two different stories. A reader can infer conceptually that both sections are on the principles of benevolence and righteousness (*Yi;* 义) principles in statecraft, but textual links and clear thematic associations are absent to signal actual section connections. The episodic nature of the sections makes them flexible, capable of being moved around without disrupting their reading or reception. As a result, one can read either section first, as the text, at this level, is less connected and coherent than would be expected by a reader in a fully literate culture.

Within sections, *Mencius* has more coherent and explicit writing than at the inter-section level. The first section in *Mencius* is an example. It starts with a general but implicit setting of the dialogue: Mencius had an audience with the king at the royal court. The setting makes appropriate the king's opening question that concerns him and that could be answered by the wise Master: how his country could benefit from Mencius's visit. Mencius's response is elaborately worded, explicitly making use of the king's word *Li* (利; profit, interest) as his starting point, and turning it into an argument to advocate his core Confucian concepts of benevolence and righteousness in state governance, which he emphasises immediately thereafter. The argument of how to govern a state is then clearly laid out and supported throughout the dialogue through the consecutive uses of hypothetical negative examples of using only profit as the focus of governing. Reasons are given as follows. If profit is the only attraction to a king and his subjects in thinking about their country, families and themselves, then the country would be in danger. It further puts forth the worst-case scenario of everyone chasing after profit: the regicides and killing of one's superiors would occur because no one would be satisfied in their pursuit of profits until they got their hands on what they do not have already. Therefore, a king, as the argument goes, should not ask about profits, but instead about benevolence and righteousness. The whole argument is well supported and it ends by reiterating the beginning point about using benevolence and righteousness in governing a state. The text flows coherently, with a clearly structured argument. This approach, unlike the quotations in the *Analects*, is elaborate and complicated. And the dialogue, in its elaborate form and arguments, is unlikely to have occurred verbatim. It was either reconstructed through recall or constructed through imagination, perhaps a combination of both, at a later date. In short, within sections, this text is structured autonomously, catering well to a reader.

However, the Master in the text is figured prominently, providing support for textual ambiguity when needed. Here, the text itself does not take all the credit for the argument made. In other words, it is not totally autonomous, at least not sufficiently so to support an independent reading. It still relies, within sections, on the wisdom of the words of the Master and on the Master himself as an authoritative figure for the text's trustworthiness.

It is also insightful to consider how the argument is grounded, and the evidence supported. Underlying the flow of the argument in this section, the indispensable role of the Master still asserts authority. In fact, the argument by itself is somewhat arbitrary. The focus for Mencius's main argument is the moral high ground of governing through benevolence and righteousness. But aside from warning about the potentially disastrous outcomes of focusing exclusively on profits, there is only the voice of the Master on which this conclusive assertion is premised. This section itself has not proffered any reason as to why benevolence and righteousness would be the best alternative to a profit-focused motive in governing a state: rejecting one form of governing does not automatically justify another. In addition, the disastrous outcomes are stated as facts, without further explanations. The statements of regicides are not explicitly supported. Given a history of the horrific regicides in King Hui's state of Liang, it is apparently clear to Mencius and the king what Mencius was hinting at, a shared knowledge between the speaker and the listener. But as a text, this omission of the shared knowledge as support for the claim forces the reader to trust the authority of the speaker, a scenario more common in an oral culture. In short, without the explicit grounding of the argument and textual support for key claims in the section, the text lacks sufficient clarity to be an autonomous text, and therefore would create difficulty for an independent reader.

Excerpts from *Xun Zi*

The gentleman says: 'One should never stop learning/studying.' Colour Qing, coming from blue, is bluer than the colour blue; ice, coming from water, is colder than water. Wood can be straightened to measure up to a plumb-line or can be steam-bent into a wheel shape as round as if drawn by a compass. Once bent, the wood will keep bent without straightening back even when dried in the Sun; the steam-bending has made it that way. Therefore wood can be straightened to measure up to a plumb-line, metal sharpened when subject to the whetstone, and a gentleman intelligent and flawless in his comportment when he embraces broad learning and constant daily self-reflections. Therefore, without ascending a high mountain, one will not know the height of the Sky; without descending to a deep ravine, one will not know the depth of the Earth; and without hearing the words from the former Kings, one will not know the profundity of knowledge. The descendants of the states of Gan, Yue, Yi and Mo, all capable of making similar sounds when born, grow up with different customs. This is so because of what they have been taught. The *Odes* say:

Oh, you gentlemen,
Do not rest for too long.
Respectfully perform your duties,
Love those who are correct and upright,
The divinity will hear you,
And bestow on you great blessing.

There is nothing more divine than to be transformed with the Way, and nothing more blessed than to be misfortune-free.[38]

I once spent my whole day thinking, but it was not as useful as momentary learning. I once was on tiptoe to gaze into the distance, but I was not as far-seeing as when I climbed up high land. Climbing up to a high place to beckon, one has not lengthened one's arm, but people from afar can see it. Shouting with the wind, one has not raised one's voice, but people can hear clearly. Those who make use of carriages and horses have not become fleet-footed, but they are able to cover a thousand *li*. Those who make use of boats and oars have not become swimmers, but they can cross rivers. Gentlemen are not born different; they are just good at making use of things.[39]

Xun Zi, half a century later, is a very different text. The outline of the first paragraph gives us some idea of its explicit structure. It starts with a topic sentence for the whole essay: the importance of lifelong learning. It then enumerates the benefits of learning, ranging from effects on the learners, to the correct ways of learning, to the curriculum of correct learning, and to the closing lines that emphasise how a learned gentleman would display transformed dispositions, behaviours and mentality in every aspect of life until death. It highlights two features of composition that the *Analects* and *Mencius* do not have: a comprehensive theme-based discussion, and a subdued voice of the Master. It is no longer a collection of quotations or dialogical episodes. It centres on a theme of urging people to engage in learning, aptly captured in its title, Quan Xue (劝学 ; 'Exhortation to Learning') and thereafter allows a continued flow of subthemes through the essay: learning has importance, learning requires correct procedures, mind-sets, curriculum and teachers, correct learning should transform the learners, and learners should never stop until their lives end. This comprehensive argument for learning, particularly correct learning, is consistent with, but also gradual in building up, its anchoring theme, and provides sufficient contexts and clearly supported texts for a reader to follow. In addition, all is now realised more in the text itself than in the voice of a single master. While Xun Zi is the one who makes the argument, his figure or voice is no longer highlighted as Masters Confucius and Mencius are respectively in the *Analects* and *Mencius*, and there are no arbitrarily asserted claims. Its meaning or trustworthiness is no longer in the Master's presence: it now resides primarily in the text, capable of being read by readers who may weigh its arguments autonomously.

At the inter-paragraph level, the thematic coherence is clear. The first paragraph is about the effect of learning, both in transforming the learner for good and in letting the reader know what it is that is to be learned. Following this claim about the benefits that learning can bring, the second paragraph continues by stating the importance of adroit learning through capitalising on available resources. The benefit of learning therefore is connected to the methodological issue of how to learn in a general sense, providing a transition to the following paragraphs on how and what to learn, and what behaviours and practices to avoid in learning. The coherence between the two paragraphs is attained through their common theme and the sequential flow of subthemes.

At the intra-paragraph level, these two paragraphs offer explicit connections among the statements as an introduction to the thirteen-paragraph essay, thereby contributing to its comprehension for a reader. The first sentence uses a gentleman's words as a topic starter, a very similar opening strategy as in the *Analects* and *Mencius*. However, given the ambiguity regarding the identity of its supposed speaker, it does not play a role here similar to a master's. It is a topic sentence in an essay rather than a to-be-trusted quotation of a master. The position of its importance is now exclusively supported through what follows: parallel analogies, a lucid extension of an analogy to create a transition into one subtheme in this essay, and a continued elaboration to emphasise the author's central theme. The analogies are used to drive home the concept of self-transformation by enlisting the changes in nature and daily life that everyone can observe. Whereas the first two analogies occur in nature without human intervention, the third one, about steam-bending wood, occurs only when humans intervene in a specific way, a procedure that might not be clear to a reader. Therefore, the author goes on to explain the third analogy by highlighting the nature of such change: it changes through humans having precisely shaped it via a steam-bending process so that it stays that way thereafter. Here, Xun Zi has set up the connection between this analogy and what immediately follows. He has also prepared readers for what he will emphasise throughout the essay: the importance of using correct education to transform learners for good. This extra explanation of steam-bending makes these analogies unequal in sentence structure but renders the next statement more understandable to the reader: 'wood can be straightened to measure up to a plumb-line'. In addition, since all these changes highlight the fact that materials or matter can be transformed through imposed conditions, this statement about the wood and metal is not merely alluding to the preceding analogy of a wooden wheel, but also provides an explicit transition to the following comments as to why a gentleman should learn and reflect daily: it is only through the correct type of learning, and constancy in learning, that one can be transformed.

So, what is correct learning? Xun Zi uses two more analogies, one of climbing a mountain and another of looking into a ravine, to press home the message that correct learning comes from knowing what former sage kings have already said, or knowing that the greatness of knowledge is available for one to learn. The subsequent statement notes that people turn out to be what they have learned, echoing not merely the importance of correct learning in the preceding sentences, but also hearkening back to the first sentence of this whole paragraph, that learning should never stop. The ensuing quote from the *Odes* captures metaphorically how a learned gentleman would comport himself as a result of continuous learning. To reiterate the point that learning is of ultimate importance and therefore should not stop for a gentleman, Xun Zi capitalises on two Chinese characters in the poem, *shen* (神; divinity) and *fu* (福; blessing), to imply that these states come from learning. These two themes, of self-transformation with the Way and of keeping away from the misfortunes and evils of the world, are further elaborated in the second half of the essay, thus foreshadowing what is to come for a reader, creating an explicit inter-paragraph coherence at the same time.

The evolution of a literate mentality

Our analysis shows the *Analects* is not an autonomous text. It lacks inter- and intra-section clarity and coherence. It does not have thematic titles for its chapters and often figures an authoritative master image. It is consistent with a mainly oral community in which learning does not rely exclusively on texts but on the coexistence of the Master, the disciples and the texts[40] and on common knowledge they share as a community. The learners, in this sense, are not readers. What has been enunciated by the Master is to be trusted and accepted, or to be further interpreted by the Master later. The Master's enunciations recorded in the *Analects* are ambiguous about the context and lack textual signals, but can be understood by the disciples because they are listeners and participants interacting with their Master rather than readers engaging with an autonomous text.

The text of *Mencius* is intriguingly different, suggesting an increasingly literate mentality. It still retains the Master's enunciation, to some extent, in which the Master, Mencius himself, was making his own thoughts known. However, there is now an obvious tension in *Mencius* between this borrowed authority for meaning from the Master and a growing textual autonomy. While the Master in these enunciations still provides a major voice, the text becomes increasingly explicit and coherent. This tension is reflected metaphorically in the texts depicting the dialogues between the Master and kings and state officials. In such scenes, the Master is no longer the only prominent figure. Confronting a powerful figure such as a king, the Master has to resort to more elaborations and rhetorical forces such as analogies and examples to make his arguments subtly, but convincingly, in order for them to be acceptable. Such awareness of an outside audience who may not share implied common knowledge with the Master, as his disciples would have done, is a real as well as a metaphorical reflection of the need for textual explicitness, contributing to the salient increase in textual autonomy.

Therefore, *Mencius* does show a strong tendency for textual explicitness in that it has moved beyond terse and aphoristic quotations. At the intra-section level, it has also shown solid structural coherence in making its arguments. Further, this text usually provides contexts for dialogues, as well as cogent arguments with beginnings and ends. Its argument is vividly worded and forcefully and coherently presented. All this helps make the text itself more accessible to a broader audience. But the oral mentality is still evident, making it challenging for readers to approach it as a fully autonomous text. Chapters are not titled. At the inter-section level, it is not explicitly thematic, and there is no directional connection between the sections. More substantively, at the intra-section level, the Master still figures prominently, and his voice and authority can come to the rescue when arbitrary assertions are made and when claims are not explicitly supported. Oral mentality still plays a role, even when literate mentality shows up visibly in the increased autonomy of the text. Readers in this period are clearly not yet fully conscious consumers of autonomous texts: they are still dependent on an awareness of the Master's teachings and a separate exposition of them.

Towards the end of the period, *Xun Zi* has assumed a format that is textually explicit at both the inter-paragraph and the intra-paragraph levels, making it autonomous, that is, independent of a master. The textual authority comes from its clear explanations, its employment of multiple analogies, its use of thematic titles for its essays, its methodical introduction of subthemes, and its textual explicitness and coherence. Without the Master's strong voice, the text speaks on its own merit to its readers, revealing a literate mentality that favours autonomous texts and textual explicitness. The textual autonomy shown in *Xun Zi* favours an independent readership.

The three sources also use peritextual features differently. For example, each uses chapter titles differently to mediate the transaction between readers and texts. Their different treatments of this feature indicate their different considerations for readers: a relevant chapter title cues a reader to the focus of a chapter, and an irrelevant or absent one reveals an oral mentality.[41] The *Analects* uses the opening two or three characters of the chapters as chapter titles, providing little thematic indication about the nature of the quotations under the same chapter heading. *Mencius* follows the practice of the *Analects* in naming its chapters by using a chapter's opening two or three characters, with no commitment to abstracting the theme of the multiple sections in the chapters. In contrast to the nominal titles or non-titles in the *Analects* and *Mencius*, *Xun Zi* shows, through its thematically based titles, a conscious endeavour to provide clues to potential readers.

Our analysis shows a gradual move among the Confucian scholars of the period away from an oral mentality and towards an increasingly mature literate mentality. It coincides with some recorded observations among the Confucian community during this period. For example, learning with Confucius took various forms, including practising social rites, asking questions, thinking critically, visiting states and ancient temples, learning music, studying and discussing the *Odes* (诗经) and the *Book* (尚书) and learning to become a gentleman. The reading of books was recognised in the *Analects*, but only as preludes for understanding and discussing the books with the Master. Confucius's disciples and students, in such depictions, are mostly listeners and participants, rather than readers.

By Mencius's time, prominent thinkers emerged, such as Mo Zi and Zhuang Zi, and many others, articulating their thoughts increasingly through written texts. The reform movements (变法) across all of China's seven major states at that time facilitated the spread of these different schools of thought. The widely available literary products made Mencius issue the warning against blindly following books,[42] showing a Platonic argument about the adverse effects of literacy when compared with orality.[43] In spite of his own deft ability to use literacy, Mencius must have realised its possible pernicious effects on those gullible learners now turning into 'readers', as a literate mentality continued to permeate society. By Xun Zi's time, some half a century later, it is quite clear that a literate mentality had been firmly established. For example, for the first time, Xun Zi explicitly offered a Confucian curriculum, and set out the pros and cons of each of the Confucian classics, but he also urged learners to study personally with Master teachers, for fear that readers, on their own, might be lost in the multitude of relevant works. His concern in this regard indicates the cultural status afforded to books. By way of another example, Qin premier Lu Buwei (吕不韦), Xun Zi's younger contemporary, went so far as to challenge anyone who could alter a word of a book which, under his sponsorship, was put on public display for anyone to read, unwittingly highlighting the essential role of literacy in society. By then, a literate mentality was apparently firmly in place, and its prominence affirmed in the existence of a wide readership – just as Xun Zi assumed in his curricular advice and Lu in his arrogance.

Conclusions and implications

Our analysis in this chapter indicates that a fully literate mentality among Confucian scholars was slowly evolving in China during the Axial Age. Confucius, Mencius and Xun Zi displayed different degrees of textual autonomy in their eponymous works. Between the sixth and third centuries BCE, Confucian scholars evolved into a highly literate community, from being listeners to the Master's teachings (encapsulated in texts) to being readers of autonomous texts that made their own arguments, thus breaking the bounds of orality.

The development of literate mentality came at an intellectually pivotal time in China, consequently contributing to its ensuing evolution as a civilisation that became both wary of the power of literacy yet still reverent of its authority. For example, Qin Shi Huang (秦始皇) (259–210 BCE) expressed an extreme dread of the power of literacy in his notorious book-burning edict. He also recognised the importance of literacy by ordering an official effort to streamline Chinese orthographic style to enhance administrative efficiency.[44] Such responses mirror independent developments in other cultures during the Axial Age. For the following 2,000 years, literate mentality instilled a cultural reverence in China for books, writings, papers and those who read books (读书人). Civil service examinations (科举) became a partial embodiment of such a literate mentality, rewarding those who were devoted to the study of the classics.[45] A literate mentality, as in other cultures, became permanently embedded into the character of Chinese people and likewise became a mark of civilisation in China, where readers were often equated with scholars.

As we have demonstrated in our analysis, the cultural prominence of a literate mentality had its origins in ancient Chinese history. That history suggests that the development of literacy in a society and culture is not merely a process that spreads spontaneously from a highly educated or privileged few to the masses.[46] Instead, it can be seen as a complex process embedded in a cultural milieu that emerges gradually. For the community, that development is reflected in the increasing awareness of the need for autonomous texts aimed at independent readers. Moving from an oral tradition to literacy entails more than a change from illiteracy to literacy. It also involves a change in a mentality from the oral to the literate, which eventually marks the true maturity of a community's literacy. The community of Confucian scholars, with their school of thought dominant in China for the past 2,000 years, profoundly influenced Chinese culture not only through their teachings, but also in providing the foundation for the cultural prominence of literacy. In this complex picture of literacy, we are reminded of the importance of literacy not merely as an ability but also as a foundational element of society's value system and cultural characteristics. This view of literacy complexity can be useful in our efforts to understand literacy within any society, particularly at the critical point of social transitions that accompany a move from orality to literacy, or today, perhaps, from print to digital literacy.

Our analysis also illustrates how ancient texts may indirectly reflect a movement towards literacy, especially when more direct evidence of readerships from records and other artefacts is not available. Such analysis is one lens for documenting a transition from an oral to a literate mentality. As we have shown, researchers investigating historical readers can fruitfully examine the indicators of the development of a literate mentality in written artefacts to gain an understanding of literacy development in a particular culture. For ancient civilisations, such as China, this can be a viable approach for helping us understand the complexity of literacy and the rudiments of its role in contemporary culture.

Notes

1. We use 551 BCE, when Confucius was born, as the starting year for the period under discussion.
2. Y. S. Yu, 人文与理性的中国 [*A Humanitarian and Rational China*] (Taipei: Lianjing Press, 2008), pp. 1–22.
3. K. Jaspers, *The Origin and Goal of History* (New Haven: Yale University Press, 1953), pp. 1–21.
4. K. Yang, 战国史 [*A History of Warring States*] (Taibei: Taiwan Commerce Press, 1997), pp. 11–12.
5. On the effect of changes in word spacing on silent reading practice, see P. Saenger, *Space Between Words: The Origins of Silent Reading* (Stanford: Stanford University Press, 1997). On printing's influences on social changes, see E. L. Eisenstein, *The Printing Press as an Agent of Change* (Cambridge: Cambridge University Press, 1979). On written language's impact on human consciousness, see W. J. Ong, *Orality and Literacy: The Technologizing of the Word* (New York: Routledge, 2002).
6. M. T. Clanchy, *From Memory to Written Record: England 1066–1307* (Oxford: Blackwell, 1993), p. 185.
7. Ong, *Orality and Literacy*; D. R. Olson, 'From Utterance to Text: The Bias of Language in Speech and Writing', in S. W. Beck and L. N. Olah (eds), *Perspectives on Language and Literacy: Beyond the Here and Now* (Cambridge, MA: Harvard Educational Review, 2001), pp. 137–60; S. Scribner and Michael Cole, 'Unpackaging Literacy', in E. Cushman, E. R. Kintgen, B. M. Kroll and M. Rose (eds), *Literacy: A Critical Sourcebook* (Boston: Bedford/St Martin's, 2001), pp. 123–37.
8. Ong, *Orality and Literacy*, p. 77.
9. Olson, 'From Utterance to Text', p. 154.
10. Ong, *Orality and Literacy*, pp. 36–8.

11. Yang, *A History of Warring States*, pp. 498–585.
12. Ibid., p. 498.
13. X. Chi, 中国古代小学教育研究 [*A Study of Elementary Education in Ancient China*] (Shanghai: Shanghai Education Press, 1991), pp. 8–12.
14. E. Wilkinson, *Chinese History: A Manual* (Cambridge, MA: Harvard University Press, 1998), pp. 435–48, 457–63.
15. X. Qiu, 文字学概要 [*Chinese Grammatology: An Outline*] (Beijing: Commerce Press, 2009), pp. 51–64.
16. Ibid., p. 52.
17. Ibid., p. 48, pp. 68–72.
18. G. Ban, 汉书 [*History of Han*] (111 CE; Changsha: Yue Lu Press, 1991), p. 765.
19. Q. Hu, 中国小学史 [*A History of Chinese Grammatology*] (Shanghai: Shanghai People Press, 2005), pp. 45–6.
20. P. Chen, *Modern Chinese: History and Sociolinguistics* (New York: Cambridge University Press, 1999), pp. 132–41.
21. C. Xu, 上古汉语词汇史 [*A History of Archaic Chinese Words*] (Beijing: Commerce Press, 2003), p. 13.
22. Y. Chu, 'The Chinese Language', in John Meskill (ed.), *An Introduction to Chinese Civilisation* (New York: Columbia University Press, 1973), pp. 587–615.
23. C. Shen, 中国历史: 先秦史 [*China: A Pre-Qin History*] (Beijing: People's Press, 2006), p. 280.
24. R. D. S. Yates, 'Soldiers, Scribes, and Women: Literacy Among the Lower Orders in Early China', in F. Li and D. P. Branner (eds), *Writing and Literacy in Early China: Studies from the Columbia Early China Seminar* (Seattle: University of Washington Press, 2011), pp. 339–69.
25. M. E. Lewis, *Writing and Authority in Early China* (Albany: SUNY Press, 1999), pp. 13–51.
26. Yang, *A History of Warring States*, p. 501.
27. Q. Sima, 史记 [*The Records of the Historian*] (86 BCE; Zhengzhou: Zhongzhou Classic Press, 2003), pp. 39–40.
28. E. B. Brooks and A. Taeko Brooks, *The Original Analects: Sayings of Confucius and His Successors* (New York: Cambridge University Press, 1998), pp. 201–7, 249–56, 339; John Makeham, 'On the Formation of Lun Yu as a Book', *Monumenta Serica*, 44 (1996), p. 1.
29. John Makeham, *Transmitters and Creators: Chinese Commentators and Commentaries on the 'Analects'* (Cambridge, MA: Harvard University Press, 2003), pp. 17–18.
30. Confucius, *The Analects* (479 BCE?; Beijing: Zhonghua Press, 1980), p. 162. All translations here and below of excerpts from *The Analects*, *Mencius* and *Xun Zi* are our own.
31. Makeham, 'On the Formation of Lun Yu as a Book', pp. 1–25.
32. Brooks and Brooks, *The Original Analects*, p. 208, refer to an instance of interpolation in the *Analects* as keeping to its formal, but not necessarily linguistic, features.

33. Confucius, *The Analects*, p. 1.
34. Ibid., p. 2.
35. Ong, *Orality and Literacy*, pp. 36–9.
36. Mencius, 孟子 [*Mencius*] (300 BCE?; Beijing: Zhonghua Press, 2015), p. 2.
37. Ibid., pp. 3–4.
38. K. Xun, 荀子 [*Xun Zi*] (245 BCE?; Shanghai, Shanghai People's Press, 1974), p. 1.
39. Ibid., p. 2.
40. Lewis, *Writing and Authority in Early China*, pp. 58, 84.
41. G. Gennette, *Paratexts: Thresholds of Interpretation*, trans. Janee Lewin, foreword by R. Macksey (Cambridge: Cambridge University Press, 1997), p. 295.
42. Mencius, *Mencius*, p. 285.
43. Plato, *Phaedrus* (370 BCE; Indianapolis: Hackett Publishing, 1995), pp. 79–80.
44. Sima, *The Records of the Historian*, p. 36.
45. T. H. C. Lee, *Education in Traditional China: A History* (Boston: Brill, 2000), pp. 104–70.
46. R. Venezky, 'The Development of Literacy in the Industrialized Nations of the West', in R. Barr, M. L. Kamil, P. Mosenthal and P. D. Pearson (eds), *Handbook of Reading Research, Vol. II* (New York: Longman, 1991), pp. 46–67.

Chapter 2

Reading for Rule: Emperor Taizong of Tang and *Qunshu zhiyao*

Fan Wang

Compiled by a group of minister-scholars at the court of Emperor Taizong of Tang (598–649 CE), *Qunshu zhiyao* (*Collected Writings on the Essential Principles of Government*) was one of the earliest anthologies in China to be produced with the explicit aim of educating an emperor on governance. In this chapter, I discuss how the editors of *Qunshu zhiyao* prepared Emperor Taizong for Confucian rulership by instructing him in certain modes of reading, and how the fashioning of Taizong as a reader became intricately intertwined with the fashioning of him as a ruler. As Tao and Reinking suggest in Chapter 1 of the present volume, one of the many challenges facing studies of the history of reading in ancient and medieval China is the scarcity of evidence. No commonplace books, reading notes or catalogues of private libraries from this period survive, so scholars rely on paratextual materials, literary works, government records and occasional biographical sketches scattered across dynastic histories to shed light on contemporary reading practices or, more often, contemporary ideas about reading. Similarly, since Taizong's copy of *Qunshu zhiyao* no longer survives, this chapter draws upon imperial memorials regarding the purposes and intended uses of the anthology, the preface written by its editor-in-chief (dated 631) detailing the project's editorial principles and procedures, and, of course, the contents and organisational structure of the anthology itself to reconstruct the model of the ideal imperial reader as conceived and advocated by its compiler-courtiers.

The limitations of primary sources inevitably result in a skewed picture: we end up knowing more about how the Emperor was expected to read than about how he actually read. But in this case, the prescriptive and normative understandings of readers and reading prove illuminating in their own right. How should an imperial ruler read? And what kind of readerly attitudes and competencies, according to Taizong's courtiers, would be required of a good Confucian ruler? Focusing on their strategies in including in *Qunshu zhiyao* excerpts from the two major commentary editions of the *Classic of Poetry* (done in order to instruct him in reading), I argue that the editors persistently encouraged Taizong to assert readerly agency and initiative, to approach the text not as a source of authority but as a contested site where authority is mediated and negotiated in the ongoing process of textual reinterpretation and reappropriation. Foregrounding the role of the reader as an active participant in meaning-making calls attention to an inherent, though often neglected and misunderstood, aspect of Chinese intellectual tradition. Instead of imposing an all-encompassing, unifying influence on society (at least the educated section of it), classical Chinese texts invite revisions, transformations, expansions and even deviations effected by the reader. And this internal/intrinsic vibrancy challenges the conventional idea of classical Chinese texts as a static, monolithic body of knowledge that resists change and compels conformity. The astonishing capacity for self-perpetuation these texts have demonstrated, rather than being sustained by disciplinary mechanisms (rote memorisation, the imperial examination, etc.), derives from the interpretive licence of the reader, who constantly enriches and renews the original texts with his or her own experiences, values and, ultimately, historical situatedness.

A guidebook for an unprepared emperor

The reign of Emperor Taizong of Tang, spanning the years from 626 to 649, is historically known as the 'good government of Zhenguan' ('True Vision') – an era marked by political stability, economic prosperity and cultural brilliance.[1] Celebrated by posterity as an imperial paragon whose rule was emulated by succeeding generations of emperors and princes, Taizong, however, did not show much promise as an exemplary Confucian monarch when he first ascended the throne. Fighting alongside his father in military campaigns from the age of sixteen, he had had little opportunity to study the classical texts traditionally thought to prepare rulers to follow in the steps of the sage kings of antiquity. By the time he assumed power at the age of twenty-eight, Taizong was urgently aware of both his cultural inadequacy and the unfortunate implications this incompetence could have for his reign. In an elite culture deeply invested in the power of reading to shape character, behaviour and expertise, a ruler unfamiliar with these foundational texts might be considered capable of moral laxity and political ineptitude. To remedy the worrying readerly deficiencies that overshadowed his accession, Taizong commissioned a group of leading scholar-officials to compile an anthology, 'comprising quintessential extracts from an exhaustive range of books and purged of the redundant, the irrelevant, and the clichéd', that would furnish him with a 'highlighted and illuminated overview of the classics'.[2] The end product was *Qunshu zhiyao* (*Collected Writings on the Essential Principles of Government*), a compendium totalling more than 500,000 words and consisting of excerpts selected from more than sixty-five titles, among them the Six Confucian Classics, the Four Official Histories and philosophical works from various schools of thought. As Wei Zheng (580–643) – its chief editor and Taizong's most trusted minister – proudly stated in the preface (dated 631), *Qunshu zhiyao*, 'striking a delicate balance between depth and breadth, and between extensiveness and thoroughness', would help the emperor navigate the 'bewildering categories of books and myriad schools of thought'.[3] An effective ruler needed to be a trained reader, and this carefully curated anthology would guide the emperor through the daunting abundance of texts available to the privileged elite in seventh-century China.

As with any anthologising enterprise, the editorial team of *Qunshu zhiyao* confronted the vexed issue of what to include and what to exclude, of what counts as 'quintessential', what 'the redundant, the irrelevant, and the clichéd'. With the emperor as sole target reader, *Qunshu zhiyao* focuses on statecraft, and so contains primarily 'admonitions and counsels' regarding 'the art of governance'.[4] And the model of governance Taizong's courtiers-cum-editors sought to inculcate in their new emperor was Confucianism. Instead of offering pragmatic political advice along Machiavellian lines, *Qunshu zhiyao* emphasises the Confucian connection between ethics and politics, between good governance and the ruler's moral impeccability. But Confucianism by this period was already a complex tradition, with many strands. As with any anthology, to select is to make choices, to shape textual traditions in ways that best suit the editors' purposes. In this case, the decision was to pretend that there was no decision to make, no alternatives to choose among. *Qunshu zhiyao* presents a comprehensive image of a unified Confucianism, one without counter-narratives or internal tensions. The 'highlighted and illuminated overview of the classics'[5] Taizong required turned out to be unapologetically coloured by the Confucian orthodoxy endorsed by his ministers, at the expense of competing philosophical doctrines that complement, contradict and complicate Confucianism in interesting and enriching ways.

The anthology's skewed take on tradition is most notable in the extracts selected from *Han Feizi*, a collection of essays by the social and political theorist Han Fei (c. 280–233 BCE), whose work constituted the most cogent expression of pragmatism in ancient Chinese thought and a forceful rebuttal of the Confucian tradition.[6] Of the twenty fascicles and more than 100,000 words of *Han Feizi*, only eighteen passages totalling around 2,600 words are included in *Qunshu zhiyao*. In contrast, 124 passages totalling more than 3,800 words are excerpted from the *Analects*, a primary Confucian classic that contains fewer than 16,000 words altogether. Moreover, the few passages selected from *Han Feizi* largely ignore the distinctive legalist ideas central to Han Fei's philosophical and political system, and instead either complement Confucian beliefs or address issues dear to Confucian moralists. For instance, eight of the eighteen passages engage with the need to recognise talented officials, and four stress the importance of distinguishing treacherous ministers who employ flattering speech from faithful ones who bravely offer honest criticism – two subjects emphasised throughout the Confucian canon, and skills Taizong's courtiers not surprisingly sought to foster in their own emperor.[7] Similarly, all ten excerpts from *The Art of War* (c. fifth century BCE) focus on the notion of righteous warfare, the moral imperative for avoiding war and the superiority of leaders who conquer without bloodshed. All sections on crafty tactics and brilliant strategies – the book's main thrust and the source of its fame – are omitted.[8] Rather than shedding light on the 'bewildering categories of books and myriad schools of thought' as promised in the preface, *Qunshu zhiyao* offers a circumscribed version of the classics that reduces a complex body of nuanced ideas to a focused selection of Confucian tenets and principles. While the excerpts are selected from a wide range of sources representing different intellectual and ideological orientations, they are shaped in ways that repeat and reinforce the same essentially Confucian messages.

But *Qunshu zhiyao* was more than a teaching anthology in the 'mirrors for princes' style designed to inculcate the precepts of wise, Confucian-oriented rulership. Yes, the emperor's courtier-editors used the process of selection to articulate their political stances, ethical values and intellectual investments. At the same time, however, they were modelling rhetorical uses of classical texts, training the emperor in the sophisticated reading strategies that had developed in China by this period. To prepare Taizong for an intellectual world that privileged ingenious appropriation and manipulation of existing texts rather than original authorship, his courtier-scholars showcased the interpretive potential of excerpting and compiling, educating the emperor in the subtleties of a mode of textual production that centred on the repackaging and repurposing of materials already in circulation. Through strategies of inclusion and exclusion, *Qunshu zhiyao* not only conveys Confucian moral and political messages, it also instructs the imperial reader in the art of approaching these foundational texts as flexibly renewable sources of meaning generated in the processes of de- and re-contextualization.

When the anthology was finally presented to the emperor, what material form did *Qunshu zhiyao* take? Woodblock printing would not be common in China until the ninth century, when it was used primarily to print Buddhist charms and scriptures, calendars, household manuals, dictionaries and poetry collections (probably only of the most popular poets).[9] But woodblock printing did exist during Taizong's reign.[10] In 1974, a Dharani Sutra printed from woodblocks, dated around 650, was discovered in China. And as recorded in *Hongjian lu*, a magisterial historiographical work by Shao Jingbang (c. 1511–58), in 636, Taizong, in memory of his wife Queen Zhangsun, ordered the printing of a collection of stories of exemplary women she had compiled. However, manuscript remained the predominant and usually preferred means of textual transmission in the Tang Dynasty (and, some scholars argue, for many centuries afterwards). When *Qunshu zhiyao* was completed, Taizong ordered the imperial scriptorium to make more than ten copies of the book and distribute them among his sons, including the crown prince. Clearly, *Qunshu zhiyao* originally circulated in manuscript.

Paper had largely replaced bamboo and silk as the primary material for books in China by the third century. Though books were still written on silk (though rarely) during the Tang Dynasty, a multi-fascicle work such as *Qunshu zhiyao* was probably transcribed on paper.[11] The scroll format used for bamboo and silk documents, however, persisted long after the ascendancy of paper, and fell out of fashion only in the late ninth century, when accordion-folding, inspired by palm-leaf Buddhist scripture, became the dominant binding style.[12] As we know from Wei Zheng's preface, the copy of *Qunshu zhiyao* presented to Emperor Taizong consisted of fifty *juan*.[13] The term *juan* – literally meaning 'scroll' – originally referred to silk rolls, and later came to designate 'fascicle', 'chapter' or 'volume'. In this case, Emperor Taizong's copy of *Qunshu zhiyao* most likely consisted of fifty actual manuscript scrolls. According to contemporary practice, sheets of paper were pasted end to end to form a continuous scroll, with a roller made of wood, ivory or glazed glass attached to its left end. Individual scrolls were then wrapped in paper or silk, and bound with thin strings to prevent loosening. Depending on their length, every five to ten scrolls were put in a cloth bag, with an ivory label inscribed with the title of the book and the numbers of the chapters it contained affixed to the opening of each bag.[14] The fifty scrolls of *Qunshu zhiyao*, as Wei Zheng pointed out, were kept in five bags.[15]

How did Emperor Taizong read his *Qunshu zhiyao*? Did he read it in private, or with the guidance of courtiers? Did he read it himself, or have someone read it to him? If he read it himself, would he have done so aloud or silently? And how do we know if he even read it at all? As is generally the case with studies of reading history in medieval China, we have little evidence to draw upon. Taizong's copy of *Qunshu zhiyao* is no longer extant, so any material traces of his engagement with the book, if there were any, are forever lost. What we do have, however, are two brief accounts of him reading the book. These accounts, five years apart and composed by the emperor himself, shed light on his physical and intellectual interaction with the work he commissioned and, by extension, give us a glimpse into elite reading practices in seventh-century China. In his reply to Wei Zheng's memorial regarding the completion of *Qunshu zhiyao* in 1631, Taizong wrote that 'after reading [*lan*] the anthology, [I am] impressed by its comprehensiveness and conciseness'.[16] The word Taizong used for his act of reading, *lan*, literally means 'to look at' and is the same verb used to describe the viewing of landscapes or surveying of people. In contrast with *song*, a word that indicates oral enunciation, and especially intonation, *lan*, with its decided emphasis on visual engagement, strongly suggests silent reading instead of reading aloud or being read to by others. Interestingly, *lan* is often interchangeable with *guan*, a term that connotes sensory, artistic appreciation, and to look at something as a whole, in its entirety. Known as a calligraphy aficionado, Taizong established the first imperial calligraphy academy in the history of China, and recruited the sons of high- and middle-ranking officials as students. Calligraphy was even listed as one of the six subjects of the imperial examination (to select future officials). Probably not by coincidence, two of the most influential calligraphers of the time were also on the editorial team of *Qunshu zhiyao*. For Taizong, to *lan* the presentation copy of *Qunshu zhiyao*, which, in all likelihood, was meticulously prepared by the best scribes at court, might involve enjoying it as a total work of art, valued for its calligraphic beauty as well as its textual content.

In the second account (dated 636), Taizong invoked the phrase 'never without the book in one's hands' to indicate his avid reading of *Qunshu zhiyao*.[17] Though a figure of speech, the expression vividly conjures up the image of the emperor holding a manuscript scroll, an image that not only underscores Taizong's intellectual affinity with the text but also his bodily intimacy with the material book. If the first account, composed soon after the completion of *Qunshu zhiyao*, suggests a quick browse that gave the emperor an initial understanding of the anthology's structure, the second one, written five years later, implies sustained, intensive engagement. Drawing attention to Taizong's physical proximity to and frequent reading of the book, it gives the impression that reading *Qunshu zhiyao* played a role in his day-to-day life and, as his courtiers would have it, conditioned his day-to-day ruling.

Paper scrolls from the Tang Dynasty usually measure a foot in height but vary considerably in length. The number of characters in each column also differs from one manuscript to another, ranging from ten to several dozens.[18] With 500,000 words in fifty scrolls, each scroll of *Qunshu zhiyao* would have contained about 10,000 words. Intended for imperial use, the book would have featured a generous layout, with around twenty characters in each column and ample space between columns. To read a scroll one foot high and long enough to accommodate more than 500 amply spaced columns would involve the use of a support. In fact, instead of literally holding a scroll in his hands, Taizong likely put it on a long table, using the roller to unfold the book from right to left as he read. A medieval scroll could contain one or multiple complete chapters. In a typical Tang manuscript, the chapter heading and the book title appear at both the beginning and the end of the chapter, with the chapter heading in the upper part of the column and the book title in the lower part; the date on which the scroll was finished, the names of its scribes, proofreaders and binders; also, the quantity of paper used and the total number of words transcribed are placed at the end of some scrolls. By the early seventh century, double lines of interlinear comments in small characters (sometimes in red ink, to contrast against the black ink of the main text) had become a common scribal device to distinguish the main text visually from commentary. Of the sixty-five classics the editors of *Qunshu zhiyao* excerpted, thirty-three were accompanied by commentaries. It is tempting to speculate that the presentation copy Taizong read featured elaborately coloured, beautifully demarcated interlinear comments.

How to read the *Classic of Poetry*

Qunshu zhiyao was a high-stakes pedagogical project designed to educate the emperor such that he could be a competent Confucian ruler. And it did so not only by prescribing what he should read, but also how he should read, equipping him with certain readerly competencies in the process of acquainting him with certain texts. This section explores what kind of reader the courtiers-cum-compilers hoped to shape Emperor Taizong into, and how they instructed him in reading strategies by excerpting the *Classic of Poetry*.

A collection of folk poems compiled by Confucius and later canonised as one of the Five Classics, the *Classic of Poetry* is one of the most hermeneutically complex works in the Chinese textual tradition. The compilers of *Qunshu zhiyao* initiated Taizong into two distinct modes of reading by excerpting two versions of the *Poetry*, namely *The Classic of Poetry with the Mao Commentary* and *Exoteric Commentary on the Classic of Poetry by Master Han Ying* (henceforth the 'Mao edition' and 'Han edition', respectively). Representing different interpretive approaches to the *Poetry*, these two critical editions laid the foundation for the two rival hermeneutic systems in Chinese literary thought, and together they exerted a profound influence upon the ways educated elites in pre-modern China read the classics.

Composed by Han Ying (c. 150 BCE), the Han edition consists of 360 historical anecdotes and literary allegories, each concluding with a single stanza from the *Poetry* that often has no obvious bearing on the story to which it is attached.[19] Instead of explaining, amplifying, corroborating or even contradicting the prose narratives in telling counterpoint, the poetic quotations engage them in a dense intertextual dialogue, constructing a network of oblique significations, paradoxical references and rhetorical ambiguities. The open, fluid connections between the prose narratives and the poetic quotations train readers to regard the poems not as aesthetic creations in themselves but as decontextualised sources of infinite applicability. The meaning of poetry, the Han edition implies, resides not in the poem but in the dynamic interplay between poetic lines and the circumstances under which they are applied. Reading consequently becomes an act of creative appropriation that transforms and renews the significance of the original text for different purposes and times.

The application-oriented approach adopted in the Han commentary aligns well with the reading goals of an imperial ruler. Occupying a unique power position, the emperor engages with texts of the past for their relevance to the present. In his preface to *Qunshu zhiyao*, Wei

Zheng cautions Taizong against reading for 'elaborate, overwrought literary expressions', an indulgence that indicates intellectual triviality and that leads, he warns, to moral decay.[20] Similarly, reading 'for the display of erudition' is frowned upon when it comes to imperial readers.[21] While encyclopaedic knowledge of a comprehensive range of subjects might be appreciated in a courtier-minister, preoccupation with 'minor branches of learning' only distracts an emperor from 'fundamental ways and principles'.[22] For an imperial reader, apparently, studies serve neither for 'delight' nor 'ornament', as Francis Bacon would suggest, but only for 'ability', their chief use lying in the 'judgement and disposition of business'.[23] Instead of reading for information, contemplation and aesthetic pleasure, an imperial ruler reads with the aim of extracting historical lessons and practical wisdom for ruling – lessons and wisdom that would guide his day-to-day governance. In this respect, Taizong shared affinities with early modern English readers such as Gabriel Harvey and William Drake, who 'read for action' and for historically informed guidance to navigate contemporary realpolitik.[24] The value of the *Poetry* as a book of veiled political advice had been recognised since the Western Han Dynasty (206 BCE–9 CE). When Wang Shi (c. 74 BCE) was accused of dereliction of duty and faced the death penalty after his pupil, the infamous Emperor Fei (c. 92–59 BCE), was deposed for incompetence and debauchery after only twenty-seven days on the throne, he absolved himself by arguing that 'he instructed the emperor (then crown prince) in the interpretations of the *Poetry*'.[25] This line of defence proved successful, as it rested on the well established assumption that a politically informed, situation-oriented reading of this book should adequately prepare any prince for the challenges and demands of rule.

Privileging readerly licence over authorial authority and textual fluidity over determinacy, the hermeneutic tradition exemplified in the Han commentary originates in and derives its legitimacy from the Confucian notion of the ideal reader, a notion that emerged from two characteristically cryptic conversations about the *Poetry* between Confucius and his disciples:

> Zigong said, 'To be poor but never a flatterer; to be wealthy but never arrogant – what would you say to that?'
> The Master said, 'That's fine, but not so good as: To be poor but joyful; to be wealthy and love *li*'.
> Zigong said, 'In the *Poetry* it says "as though cut, as though chiselled, as though carved, as though polished". Is that what you mean?'

The Master said, 'Ah, Si [Zigong]! I can finally begin to talk about the *Poetry* with him. I tell him what came before and he understands what is coming next'.

...

Zixia asked, 'What is the meaning of the lines from the *Poetry*, "The fine smile dimples, the lovely eyes flashing, the plain ground brings out the colour?"

The Master said, 'Painting follows after plain silk'. Zixia said, 'Then is it that *li* comes after?'

The Master said, 'How Shang [Zixia] lifts me up! At last I have someone to discuss the *Poetry* with!'[26]

In the first conversation, Confucius observes that 'to be poor but never a flatterer; to be wealthy but never arrogant' is morally inferior to being 'poor but joyful; to be wealthy and love *li*'. Zigong, understanding that the Master is implying the imperative for continuous self-improvement, responds with a line from the *Poetry* that compares fine manners and learning to finely 'cut' bone, 'chiselled' ivory, 'carved' jade and 'polished' stone. Citing this poem in a conversation on moral progress, Zigong demonstrates bold readerly entrepreneurship on two counts. First, he expands the original metaphor to refer not only to scholarly accomplishments but also to moral cultivation. Second, with an ingenious interpretive sleight of hand, he shifts the semantic focus of the poetic expression from the quality of being 'cut', 'chiselled', 'carved' and 'polished' to the act of repeated cutting, chiselling, carving and polishing, implicitly highlighting the process of perfecting one's moral character over the attainment of moral perfection, which, as Confucius suggested at the beginning of the conversation, gives rise to complacency.

Along a similar line, Zixia in the second conversation performs an act of creative appropriation by drawing an analogy between the way the ivory skin of a beauty functions as 'the plain ground' that puts her 'fine smile dimples and lovely eyes flashing' into relief, and the way inner qualities serve as a moral foundation that takes precedence over their external manifestations in codified ceremonies and rituals.

The readerly initiative and imagination Zigong and Zixia display qualify them as worthy interlocutors with whom Confucius can 'discuss the *Poetry*', a high compliment coming from the Master, who considered the *Poetry* the textual embodiment of literary elegance and moral purity central to the cultural sphere of high antiquity (1047–772 BCE). The phrase 'someone to discuss the *Poetry* with' later becomes a shorthand for the Confucian notion of the ideal reader, who, unconstrained by the text's original meanings, actively participates in the constant reimagining and refashioning of its associative possibilities. Instead of being an object of interpretive attention in itself, the text is taken as a point of departure that prompts new ideas and serves new purposes by inspiring analogies and connections with other texts and experiences. Epitomising the creative responsiveness advocated by Confucius, the Han commentary was excerpted by the editors of *Qunshu zhiyao* to initiate Emperor Taizong into a free-associative model of reading and to steer him towards becoming a reader who 'understands what is coming next', that is, someone who appreciates not only what a text means but also what it can mean when read in different contexts. In fact, in the preface to *Qunshu zhiyao* Wei Zheng explicitly urges Taizong to 'expand the meanings of the words [in the anthology] by seeking out parallels, correspondences, and interactions [with contemporary politics]', a note that unmistakably resonates with the reading practices the Han edition sought to inculcate.[27]

If the Han commentary encourages readers to unleash the signifying possibilities of the *Poetry* by opening it up to an endless range of applications, the Mao commentary curbs readerly initiative by situating each poem within its context and pinning it down to a historically specific reading. For instance, a poem in which a young woman urges discretion on her lover, to protect her reputation, is read as a critique of a ruler of the state of Zheng who 'in 722 BCE failed to avert disaster by allowing his young brother to usurp ever greater power until he finally could be subdued only military force'.[28] Another poem, one celebrating the timely marriage of a young woman by evoking images of 'blazing peach blossoms', 'ripened fruits' and 'luxurious leaves', is construed as praise of the perfect moral and social order of the Western Zhou.[29] According to the Mao scheme of interpretation, poignant poetic expressions of romantic longing and frustration, pain and joy, express particular political and moral messages. The responsibility of the reader, then, is to decode the poems, regarded as elaborate allegories. While the Han edition empowers the reader to understand the text in order to use it, the Mao edition shifts exegetical attention back to the author and foregrounds the text. Rather than reading for action in the extra-textual world, the Mao-style reader is concerned with deciphering the hidden signification embedded in the words.

The allegorical hermeneutics of the Mao commentary are predicated upon the assumption that 'Poetry articulates *what is on the mind intently* [*zhi*]' (emphasis added).[30] First appearing in the *Book of Documents* (c. 11–3 BCE), this formulation constitutes the earliest definition of poetry in China and leads into fundamental issues of language and reading that underlie Chinese literary thought. The idea of poetry as an articulation of *zhi* is further developed in the general preface to the Mao commentary: 'The poem is where the *zhi* goes. In the heart it is *zhi*; sent forth in speech, it is the poem.'[31] So what precisely is *zhi*? As Stephen Owen observes, 'one of the most misleading translations from Chinese to English is the translation of *zhi* as "intention"'.[32] Instead of being the Chinese equivalent of 'authorial intention', *zhi* refers to the essential selfhood of the author, the ultimate subjectivity that inevitably, and often involuntarily, informs any writing. In other words, *zhi* encompasses both the self-conscious intentions conveyed in a specific text and all the unarticulated and sometimes unconscious passions, desires, motives and impulses that make up the writer's unique individuality. When engaging with a poem, the reader is expected to uncover not only the local, authorially intended meaning, but also, and more importantly, the author himself or herself and the broader *zhi* that imbues the words.

How does one capture this pervasive but elusive *zhi*? 'In the heart it is *zhi*; sent forth in speech, it is the poem.' A poem is conceptualised as the external manifestation of its author's *zhi*. Yet language, being an imperfect and inadequate medium, reveals as much as it conceals, and reflects as much as it distorts. The problematic correspondence between inner self and its linguistic expression poses a challenge but also provides an opportunity to readers of the *Poetry*. In fact, the model of reading illustrated in the Mao commentary revolves around the possibility and difficulty of gaining access to someone's *zhi* through their language, a paradoxical situation Mencius addresses in his dialogue with Gong Sunchou:

> Gong Sunchou: 'What, sir, is your excellence?'
> Mencius: 'I understand language and have mastered the fostering of boundless and surging *qi* [inner energy]'.
> 'What do you mean by "understanding language"?'
> 'When someone's words are one-sided, I understand how his mind is clouded. When someone's words are loose and extravagant, I understand the pitfalls into which that person has fallen. When someone's words are warped, I understand wherein the person has strayed. When someone's words are evasive, I understand how the person has been pushed to his limit.' (*Mencius* II.A.2.xi, xvii)[33]

For Mencius, language bespeaks character, and style denotes mentality. Authors cannot help but reveal themselves and communicate their *zhi* in some way in their writing. All it takes is a reader who 'understand[s] language' to recognise the person behind the words, to identify moral flaws, intellectual limitations and emotional vulnerabilities by parsing the silences, evasions, ambiguities and awkwardness that creep into writing. Mencius's model of reading depends on the assumption that a text never fails to manifest the author's *zhi* – even (or especially) through its lacunae, confusions and obscurities. The burden of perceiving and understanding authorial presence therefore resides entirely with the reader, who is expected to fathom not only what the author says, but also what the author attempts to say, pretends to say, fails to say, or deliberately avoids saying by unpicking the ways he or she appropriates generic conventions, manipulates literary devices and deploys rhetorical strategies.

Despite their shared author fixation, Mencius's notion of reading, exemplified in the Mao commentary, differs fundamentally from the traditional autobiographical-historical approach to literary criticism long prevalent in the West. Unlike their Western counterparts (until recent decades), Chinese readers working in this interpretative tradition aim to uncover what the author fails or refuses to reveal as well as what the author intends. Here Mencius does not so much negate the validity of authorial intention as bypass it: what is at issue is not how authors present, misrepresent or hide their *zhi*, but how the reader reconstructs this *zhi* by negotiating the gaps and inconsistencies between its outward expression and inner essence, by unpacking those 'one-sided', 'loose and extravagant', 'warped' and 'evasive' words. Instead of being the ultimate authority on the meaning of the text, the author becomes an object of interpretation, the recovery of whose *zhi* constitutes the ultimate goal of reading. The Mencian circumvention of authorial intention is also distinct from the Barthesian idea of 'the death of the author'. Though the text takes on a life of its own in Mencius's argument, performing independently of the author's will, it does not do so 'through a prerequisite impersonality' as Barthes suggests.[34] On the contrary, it is precisely the agency and dynamism of the text that allows the Mencian reader to fully realise the personality that pervades it. While the liberation of the text comes at the author's expense for Barthes, for Mencius its autonomy enables the dis/recovery of the author.

In short, the reading of the text implies the reading of the authorial person. Subscribing to this Mencian notion of 'understanding language', the Mao commentary is used to train Taizong to understand people through engagement with their words, an approach to reading particularly suitable for an imperial reader whose capacity to evaluate character, identify motives and recognise hidden agendas on the basis of what people write will affect the success of his reign. Operating in opposite hermeneutical directions, the Han commentary and the Mao commentary are nevertheless equally reader-oriented: while the former inspires creative responsiveness in the reader to translate ancient texts for contemporary purposes, the latter entails readerly discernment to realise authorial presence. In either case, the burden of meaning-making decidedly falls on the reader.

The *Classic of Poetry* and the tradition of implicit political critique

The 305 poems in the *Poetry* are divided into three sections: the 'airs of the states', the 'court hymns' and the 'eulogies'. Of the three, the 'airs of the states,' containing 160 poems, is the largest and most influential. Originating as folk songs, the 'airs of the states' were documented by royal officials at the court of the Western Zhou Dynasty (c. 1046–771 BCE), who were dispatched across the empire during the harvest season to collect local songs that reflected popular opinion and sentiment. The songs were then presented to the Zhou rulers to inform them of the condition of the common people, their difficulties and concerns, beliefs and aspirations, discontents and protests. Moreover, as the Mao commentator observes in the general preface:

> the poems of a well governed era are at ease and lead to joy; its rulership is harmonious. The poems of an era in turmoil are bitter and lead to anger; its rulership is perverse. The poems of a declining state are lamenting and lead to longing; its people are in difficulty.[35]

Embodying the tone and style of a cultural discourse, the 'airs of the states' were believed to communicate a particular ethos, the knowledge of which would help rulers gauge the success or failure of their reign.

The songs collected in the *Poetry* therefore originally functioned as a communication channel between the ruler and the ruled, a discursive vehicle through which the latter offered the former 'criticism and advice veiled in suggestive terms'.[36] Shrouding moral and political messages in extended conceits, analogies, imagery and allegories, they established the tradition of implicit political critique in imperial China, a tradition that for many centuries profoundly shaped the modes of political self-expression adopted by educated elites and, as a result, shaped the modes of reading expected of rulers in their day-to-day dealings with persuasive genres, ranging from imperial memorials to exam essays. As Wei Zheng indicates in the bibliographic entry for the *Poetry* included in the official history of the Sui Dynasty (581–618), the rhetoric of implicit political critique initiated in the *Poetry* was necessitated by the collapse of the utopian social order of high antiquity, and the consequent loss of the 'unclouded state of mind' that characterised its people.[37] With the emergence of hierarchical division between ruler and subjects, unmediated transparency between the two became impossible: suddenly, honest compliments ran the risk of being taken as self-interested flattery and genuine criticism as hostile slander. This rhetorical unease, inevitable in a 'fallen' world, found its resolution in the intricately figurative and subtly allusive language of the *Poetry*, which made it possible for 'the speaker/author to express opinions without incurring anger and blame' while for 'the listener/reader to still receive the admonition'.[38]

The delicate equilibrium between tact and efficacy relies as much on the rhetorical agility of the author as on the rhetorical perspicacity of the reader. Criticism and advice, 'veiled in suggestive terms' to avoid 'incurring anger and blame', can be recaptured only through the active efforts of a reader capable of unpacking the elaborate figures of speech within which it is embedded.[39] This model of rhetorical reading entails well orchestrated collaboration between author and the reader, whose shared familiarity with the forms and conventions of oblique persuasion is prerequisite for smooth communication. If the Han and Mao commentaries on the *Poetry* train Emperor Taizong to read for action and for truth respectively, the *Poetry* itself attunes him to the discourse of implicit political critique, and equips him with a rhetorical proficiency essential for an imperial ruler. After all, one of the defining qualities of the sage king is the ability to excavate admonitory meanings from cautiously couched metaphors, analogies, paradoxes and implications. By incorporating excerpts from the two commentaries on the *Poetry* into *Qunshu zhiyao*, the courtiers did not simply acquaint Taizong with a specific collection of poems and specific formulas of a poetic genre. More importantly, they inculcated him with a general approach to textuality, a way of reading and thinking oriented towards seeking out hidden significations and double meanings in expressions packed with ambiguities and overtones, allusions and innuendos.

Anxiety about causing offence and the assumption (or rather expectation) of readerly competence inform the entire tradition of political persuasion in imperial China. They constitute a mutually, if rarely openly, acknowledged rhetorical concern that pervades the exchanges and relationships between courtiers and rulers. And *Qunshu zhiyao*, itself a project intended to persuade, is no exception. In the preface, Wei Zheng calls for 'the speaker/author to express opinions without incurring anger and blame . . . [while for] the listener/reader to still receive the admonition' as both a rationale for his editorial decisions and a mode of reading recommended to the emperor.[40] When compiling *Qunshu zhiyao*, he deliberately rejected the model established by *Huang lan* ('imperial conspectus'), the first topically arranged encyclopaedia in China and also the earliest compendium intended for the use of an imperial reader. Instead of structuring excerpts with subject headings, he chose to group together the ones taken from the same text, under the title of the book and in the order as they originally appeared. *Qunshu zhiyao* deviates from *Huang lan* not only in the organisation of excerpts but also in the process of excerpting. The compilers of *Huang lan* aggressively fragmented the original texts, producing an anthology that consists of truncated sentences, half-sentences and phrases removed from their immediate contexts, whereas the editorial team of *Qunshu zhiyao* preferred self-contained passages that 'narrate stories in all their details' and 'propose ideas with all their nuances'.[41] Wei Zheng then proceeds to discuss the rhetorical implications of the two editorial models. In the case of *Huang lan*, the radical decontextualisation obscures the original meanings of the excerpts, leaving them hermeneutically indeterminate and sometimes even syntactically incomplete. Deprived of textual self-sufficiency, these excerpts are reinscribed and re-imagined through strategies of categorisation, acquiring specific valences and significations as they are entered under various subject headings. With the autonomy of the original works dissolved in the process of excerpting, the compilers of *Huang lan* in effect cannibalised the original texts to fashion a new work, a work markedly bearing the stamp of their own moral/political agenda.

In his preface, Wei Zheng denounced the aggressive editorial approach adopted in *Huang lan* and proposed the model of *Qunshu zhiyao* as a preferable alternative.[42] While the compilers of *Huang lan* dismembered the original texts, drawing attention to themselves as the organising intelligence that weaved heterogeneous textual fragments into a coherent moralistic narrative, *Qunshu zhiyao* foregrounded the coherence of the original works, its legitimacy derived from the authority of the classics per se. Furthermore, the categorical framework of *Huang lan* predisposed the reader to engage with the original texts from a specific perspective, whereas the editors of *Qunshu zhiyao*, refraining from explicit signposting, provided wide interpretive latitude. Their minimalist editorial intervention (beyond the broader rhetoric of selection itself), precisely designed to pre-empt anger and blame, invited the reader to exert rhetorical agency in order to excavate oblique admonitions. By training the emperor to read the *Poetry* in light of the imperative 'to express opinions without incurring anger and blame [while for] the listener/reader to still receive the admonition', the compilers of *Qunshu zhiyao* primed him to read their own rhetorically fraught work.

The *Classic of Poetry* and the art of quotation

Throughout the premodern period, the *Classic of Poetry* featured prominently as a shared repertoire of texts frequently quoted by the educated elites in their writings and conversations. The ability to cite a verse, or more often a single stanza of a verse, to fit specific circumstances and situations was considered a cultural competence essential for sophisticated engagement in polite discourse. The prestige attached to the command of the *Poetry* finds its most compelling expression in the recount of a 'teachable moment' between Bo Yu and his father Confucius:

> Chen Kang asked Bo Yu, saying, 'Have you heard any lessons from your father different from what we have all heard?' Bo Yu replied, 'No. He was standing alone once, when I passed below the hall with hasty steps, and said to me, "Have you learned the *Poetry*?" On my replying "Not yet," he added, "If you do not learn the *Poetry*, you will not be fit to converse with." I retired and studied the *Poetry*. Another day, he was in the same way standing alone, when I passed by below the hall with hasty steps, and said to me, "Have you learned the rules of Propriety?" On my replying "Not yet," he added, "If you do not learn the rules of Propriety, your character cannot be established." I then retired, and learned the rules of Propriety. I have heard only these two things from him.' Chen Kang retired, and, quite delighted, said, 'I asked one thing, and I have got three things. I have heard about the *Poetry*. I have heard about the rules of Propriety. I have also heard that the superior man maintains a distant reserve towards his son.'[43]

Confucius, the greatest teacher in ancient China, had personally taught his son only two things, one of them being the urgency to 'learn the *Poetry*' in order to become someone 'fit to converse with'. Tellingly enough, Confucius located the significance of the *Poetry* in its performative, dialogical potential, emphasising the social function of the text over its status as a work of art inspiring solitary contemplation. In fact, during the Zhou Dynasty, the *Poetry* was studied and used not so much as literature – at least not in the modern Western disciplinary sense – as a specialised mode of communication, an exalted, exclusive language adopted by aristocrats and the rising class of educated administrators in their day-to-day interactions with one another. According to the *Zuo Tradition* and the *Discourses of the States*,[44] single stanzas of the *Poetry* were routinely quoted in diplomatic missions during the Spring and Autumn period (771–476 BCE) as a means to convey nuanced political messages. And this elite cultural practice was known as *fushi duanzhang* – literally, 'reciting single stanzas from the *Poetry*' to express one's own intentions. Sometimes entire diplomatic conversations were conducted in quotations from the *Poetry*.[45] For instance, after having sealed an alliance with the powerful kingdom of Jin, Duke Wen of the kingdom of Lu met with Duke Bo of the kingdom of Zheng on his way home. The latter, in equally dire need of a strong ally, requested Duke Wen to return to Jin and negotiate a similar alliance between Jin and Zheng on his behalf. To persuade the already exhausted Duke Wen to make another trip, Zijia, a senior official at the court of Zheng, recited part of 'Swan Geese' from the *Poetry*, a poem that laments the miseries of homeless migrants, especially the helpless widowed among them. By way of reply, Ji Wenzi, a courtier on the side of Lu, quoted a stanza from 'April' which depicts the hardships and hazards of life in exile. Zijia subsequently responded with the fourth stanza from 'Winged Chariot'. Conventionally attributed to Madame Xumu, princess of the kingdom of Wei and wife of the Duke Mu of the kingdom of Xu, 'Winged Chariot' registers her frustrations with the indifference and naked self-interest displayed by the ministers of Xu when her homeland was under attack and on the verge of collapse. The fourth stanza of the poem is a famously poignant expression of her determination to seek support from powerful neighbouring countries by herself, despite the disapproval, doubt and ridicule of Xu ministers.

Ji Wenzi then answered Zijia by reciting the fourth stanza of 'Collecting Weeds', a poem that catalogues the pains and sufferings inflicted by war on the common soldiers, with its fourth stanza deploring their rootless, restless existence constantly on the move. After Wenzi's citation, Duke Bo, without another word, 'bowed to Duke Wen in gratitude', and the latter bowed in return.[46]

For a modern reader untrained in the special language of the *Classic of Poetry*, the aforementioned episode presents a hermeneutical riddle. Indeed, to carry out this diplomatic exchange smoothly, all the participants needed to have not only an intimate knowledge of the poems and a thorough understanding of their original meanings, but also, more importantly, the good judgement to select the apt passages that most eloquently conveyed their intentions, and the ability to fathom why the other party had selected a particular poem, and what they intended it to mean on this specific occasion. When Zijia recited 'Swan Geese', Ji Wenzi at once understood that he was appealing to the sympathy of Duke Wen by comparing the vulnerable kingdom of Zheng to the homeless, defenceless widowed portrayed in the poem. To indicate Duke Wen's reluctance to serve as Duke Bo's go-between and thus prolong his travels, Ji Wenzi in turn invoked 'April', drawing a parallel between the difficulties of life in exile and the hardships of life on the road. If this first round of verbal exchange required little interpretive imagination on either side, the second round was shot through with ambiguities and resonances that illustrate the peculiar power of *fushi duanzhang*. On the face of it, by reciting the fourth stanza of 'Winged Chariot', a passage in which the narrator expressed the urgent need to win the patronage of powerful neighbours, Zijia was merely acknowledging Zheng's reliance upon strong allies, and thus indirectly enlisting Duke Wen's assistance. But, with all the participants on this occasion intimately familiar with the entire poem, its literal meaning and historical reference alike, one is tempted to think that Zijia's invocation of 'Winged Chariot' could well be interpreted as signalling not only Zheng's dependence on external support, but also its determination to secure that support with or without the help of Duke Wen, just as Madame Xumu was ready to fight for her homeland without the help of the kingdom of Xu. Furthermore, Zijia's selection of this particular poem put Duke Wen in an awkward position: if he refused Duke Bo's request, he would run the risk of being implicitly compared to the selfish, cowardly ministers of Xu, and thus joining the ranks of nonchalant onlookers who offered nothing but ridicule and suspicion when their friends were in need. Zijia's recitation of 'Winged Chariot' was nothing short of a brilliant verbal checkmate that rhetorically cornered Duke Wen. In this case, the stanzas that remained absent from the conversation loomed large in the background, their absence speaking as eloquently as the presence of the one stanza that Zijia did recite. As expected, Ji Wenzi gave in right away by reciting a stanza from 'Collecting Weeds', basically pledging that Duke Wen would not rest until an alliance was formed between Jin and Zheng.

Though the tradition of *fushi duanzhang* fell into decline after the Zhou Dynasty, the practice of quoting passages from the *Poetry* to convey one's intentions continued in more diffuse forms throughout the premodern period. *Poetry* recitation, for its allusive subtlety and evocative resonance, particularly appealed to courtiers and ministers, who routinely adopted it as a means to admonish imperial rulers. For instance, Wei Zheng himself made references to the *Poetry* in more than 200 of his memorials to Emperor Taizong. Once, he cited a line from 'Hatchet Handle', a poem that addresses the necessity of adhering to proper marriage rituals and procedures, to advise Taizong of the urgency to learn from the mistakes of the fallen Sui Dynasty (581–618) and follow the principles of good rule.[47] As apparent from the conversation between Zijia and Ji Wenzi and Wei Zheng's memorial, the quoted poems did not always match the situations in which they were quoted. Rather, reciters often took liberties with the original meanings of the poems, selecting isolated stanzas as a vehicle for their own thoughts and intentions. This mode of communication, similar to the Han and Mao commentaries, places great demands upon the listener/reader. On top of a deep familiarity with the individual verses in the *Poetry*, the listener/reader needs to grasp the motivations behind the choice of a specific stanza, to understand in what ways the reciter appropriated the original, and to decode the intended messages communicated through quotation of that specific stanza on that specific occasion. By instructing Emperor Taizong in the reading of the *Poetry*, the compilers of *Qunshu zhiyao* introduced him to a repository of ready-made quotations, a collective medium through which the educated elites conducted nuanced political conversations. And the ability to identify allusions to the *Poetry*, to decipher intentions embodied in poetic quotations, would enable Taizong to engage intelligently in courtly dialogues and to comprehend courtly memorials. Once again, readerly competence became intricately imbricated with ruling capacity.

Conclusion

We do not know to what extent or in what ways *Qunshu zhiyao* contributed to the success of Emperor Taizong's reign, or if his courtiers actually succeeded in training him into the kind of reader they hoped to create. But the emperor and his courtiers, in their writings and recorded conversations, insistently associated the reading of this anthology with the ruling of the empire, so much so that *Qunshu zhiyao* went down in history as the book that created a brilliant ruler and ushered in a brilliant era.[48] Little wonder that succeeding generations of emperors, princes and officials, in China and later in Japan, turned to *Qunshu zhiyao* for wisdom of good governance.

In order to ascend the throne, Taizong killed his brothers and forced his father into abdication. From the outset, his rise to power was haunted by the taint of illegitimacy.[49] The commission of *Qunshu zhiyao*, along with other propagandistic measures, helped transform his image from a martially oriented and fratricidal prince-general involved in bloody court intrigues and power struggles into a benign sovereign who ruled according to the Mandate of Heaven, in effect converting a Macbeth into a Duncan. To those who were suspicious of the moral legitimacy and cultural authority of his reign, Taizong's carefully crafted self-presentation as an avid reader of *Qunshu zhiyao* sounded a reassuring note: whether or not his rule was actually shaped by his reading of the anthology, the effort at self-fashioning alone bespoke endorsement of the Confucian ethical-political system, and a willingness to read himself into wise rulership.

Notes

1. Denis Twitchett (ed.), *The Cambridge History of China* (Cambridge: Cambridge University Press, 1979), vol. III, pp. 589–906.
2. Yunwu Wang (comp.), 叢書集成初編 [*A Compendium of Miscellaneous Books*] (Beijing: Zhonghua shuju, 1985), vol. X, p. 226.
3. Ibid., p. 227.
4. Ibid.
5. Ibid., p. 226.
6. Xunchu Zhou (ed. and annot.), 韓非子校注 [*An Annotated Edition of Hanfei zi*] (Nanjing: Fenghuang chuban she, 2009).
7. Wang, *A Compendium of Miscellaneous Books*, vol. X, pp. 389–418.
8. Ibid., pp. 477–92.
9. Xiumin Zhang, 中國印刷史 [*A History of Printing in China*] (Hangzhou: Zhejiang guji chubanshe, 2006), p. 305.
10. Ibid., p. 298.
11. Tsuen Hsuin Tsien, *Written on Bamboo and Silk: The Beginning of Chinese Books and Inscriptions* (Chicago: Chicago University Press, 2004), pp. 145–52.
12. Tsuen Hsuin Tsien, *Science and Civilisation in China, Volume V: Chemistry and Chemical Technology. Part 1, Paper and Printing* (Cambridge: Cambridge University Press, 1985).
13. Wang, *A Compendium of Miscellaneous Books*, vol. X, p. 227.
14. Tsien, *Written on Bamboo and Silk*, pp. 169–74.
15. Wang, *A Compendium of Miscellaneous Books*, vol. X, p. 227.
16. Wu Yun and Ji Yu (eds and annots), 唐太宗集 [*Collected Writings of Emperor Taizong*] (Xi'an: Shaanxi renmin chubanshe, 1986), p. 285.
17. Ibid., p. 434.
18. Tsien, *Written on Bamboo and Silk*, p. 161.
19. Yanyuan Lai (annot. and trans.), 韓詩外傳今注今譯 [*An Annotated*

Edition of Hanshi Waizhuan with Modern Translation] (Taipei: Taiwan shangwu yinshuguan, 1972).
20. Wang, *A Compendium of Miscellaneous Books*, vol. X, p. 227.
21. Ibid.
22. Ibid.
23. Francis Bacon, 'Of Studies', in Brian Vickers (ed.), *The Oxford Authors: Francis Bacon*, (Oxford: Oxford University Press, 1996), p. 439.
24. Kevin Sharpe, *Reading Revolutions: The Politics of Reading in Early Modern England* (New Haven: Yale University Press, 2000); Lisa Jardine and Anthony Grafton, '"Studied for Action": How Gabriel Harvey Read His Livy', *Past and Present*, 129 (November 1990), pp. 30–78.
25. Gu Ban (comp.), 汉书 [*The History of the Former Han Dynasty*] (Beijing: Zhonghua shuju, 1962), vol. V, p. 254.
26. Xi Zhu (ed. and annot.), 四書章句集注 [*An Annotated Edition of the Four Books*] (Beijing: Zhonghua shuju, 1983), p. 83.
27. Wang, *A Compendium of Miscellaneous Books*, vol. X, p. 228.
28. Kang-I Sun Chang and Stephen Owen (eds), *The Cambridge History of Chinese Literature, Vol. I: To 1375* (Cambridge: Cambridge University Press, 2014), pp. 28–39.
29. Ibid.
30. 毛詩正義 [*Mao Commentary Edition of the Classic of Poetry*], in Ruan Yuan (ed. and annot.), 十三经注疏 [*Annotated Editions of the Thirteen Classics*] (Beijing: Zhonghua shuju, 2009), vol. VII, p. 184.
31. Ibid.
32. Stephen Owen, *Readings in Chinese Literary Thought* (Cambridge, MA: Council on East Asian Studies, Harvard University Press, 1992), p. 28.
33. Jiao Xun (ed. and annot.), 孟子正義 [*Commentary on Mencius*] (Beijing: Zhonghua shuju, 1987), p. 157.
34. Roland Barthes, 'The Death of the Author', in *Image–Music–Text* (London: Fontana Press, 1977), pp. 142–8.
35. 毛詩正義 [*Mao Commentary Edition of the Classic of Poetry*], in Yuan (ed. and annot.), *Annotated Editions of the Thirteen Classics*, vol. VII, p. 83.
36. Ibid.
37. Zheng Wei (comp.), 隋書 [*The History of Sui*] (Beijing: Zhonghua shuju, 1973), vol. V, p. 519
38. *Mao Commentary*, p. 83.
39. Ibid.
40. Wang, *A Compendium of Miscellaneous Books*, vol. X, p. 228.
41. Ibid., p. 229.
42. Ibid.
43. Xi Zhu, *An Annotated Edition of the Four Books*, p. 64.
44. *Zuo Tradition*, trans. Stephen Durrant, Wai-yee Li and David Schaberg (Seattle: University of Washington Press, 2016); *Discourses of the States* (Shanghai: Shanghai guji chubanshe, 1998).

45. Bojun Yang (ed. and annot.), 春秋左傳注 [*An Annotated Edition of Spring and Autumn*] (Beijing: Zhonghua shuju, 1990), passim.
46. Ibid., pp. 263–5.
47. Jing Wu (comp.), 貞觀政要 [*The Essentials of the Reign of Zhenguan*] (Shanghai: Shanghai guji chubanshe, 1978), pp. 305–6.
48. Ibid., passim.
49. Jack W. Chen, *The Poetics of Sovereignty: On Emperor Taizong of the Tang Dynasty* (Cambridge, MA: Harvard University Asia Center for the Harvard–Yenching Institute, 2010), pp. 13–47.

Chapter 3

Medieval Women Writers and What They Read, c. 1100–c. 1500

Martha W. Driver

Medieval women writers practised several kinds of reading. These were: first and most commonly, heard reading, that is listening to texts read aloud or performed; silent reading, which was thought to be much rarer in the Middle Ages; reading through the process of translation; and finally, reading through writing, or copying out manuscripts. While we may not always know precisely which manuscripts women read (though some of these survive today) or which libraries they may have accessed, we can reconstruct their milieu to some extent and extrapolate their reading from their allusions to texts, whether to the Bible or to Ovid's *Heroides*, an epistolary collection purportedly penned by classical women to their lovers. This chapter surveys sources and analogues known to women writers over several centuries, including Heloise, the women troubadours, Marie de France, Julian of Norwich, Margery Kempe and Christine de Pizan. Remarkably, all of these women writers still speak to us across time from hundreds of years ago – their writing is informed not only by their reading but by their adept uses of rhetoric, by their cultural influences and by their expression of authentic emotions.

The early twelfth-century abbess Heloise was perhaps the most traditionally learned of all the women writers considered here; her letters to Abelard show her classical training. While women troubadours sometimes wrote in answer to the poetry of male troubadours (to whom they were often married or related, if their *vidas* are to be believed), there are also connections with Arabic love poetry and ideas about courtly love current in later twelfth-century society and fiction. Writing in about the same period, Marie de France in her *Lais* emphasises literacy and written correspondence, while recording in verse tales she has heard. Through her work as a translator from Latin to French, Marie also knew Aesop's *Fables*, among other sources, and a Latin text of *St Patrick's Purgatory*, from which she made a translation.

In some historical periods, learned women were encouraged, but in other eras women's education and literacy were suppressed, and much of their writing was lost. Women's writing flourished in the twelfth century, but thereafter there were few outstanding woman writers until the fourteenth century, when another cluster of learned ladies appeared. Julian of Norwich, for example, was a fourteenth-century spiritual writer whose knowledge of the Bible and mystical texts is incorporated in her *Revelations of Divine Love*. Julian's contemporary Margery Kempe was a wife, a businesswoman and a would-be saint, as well as the author of the first autobiography in English. (Note the many 'firsts' among the women discussed here.) Julian likely read some of the texts that were influential in her writing; Margery says she was illiterate but she was familiar with scripture and the writings of the Church fathers, as well as those of English and other mystics (see Ashley Ott, Chapter 5 in this volume, for further discussion of Kempe). Finally, the fifteenth-century writer Christine de Pizan, a student of a wide variety of literature, first made her literary reputation by criticising the well known medieval allegory the *Romance of the Rose*, which she read and absorbed nonetheless. She oversaw her own scriptorium, producing manuscripts for noble and royal patrons; many of these manuscripts survive today. These case studies provide some insight into the reading practices of various classes, with examples of aristocratic reading, religious reading and lay literacy in the preprint age.

Heloise (c. 1101–1164), the earliest of our writers, was the famous participant in the epistolary exchange with her teacher, lover, husband and fellow monastic Peter Abelard. Three of her personal letters to him survive in nine manuscripts; these were translated later from Latin into French by the popular and controversial thirteenth-century poet Jean de Meun. We have, further, the *Problemata Heloissae*, which appears in only one manuscript, copied close to 1400, which shows Heloise's command of the writings of St Jerome and the Bible, particularly the Gospels and the Pauline letters.[1] Another surviving letter, from Heloise to Peter the Venerable, thanks him for bringing Abelard's body to her for burial and asks for a Church position for their son, Astralabe. There is also an anonymous epistolary collection that has recently been tentatively ascribed to Heloise and Abelard.[2] Constant Mews further attributes two Easter plays to Heloise, 'modeled on the so-called *Sponsus* drama from Limoges'.[3]

Before her studies began with Abelard, Heloise had been educated by the nuns at the prestigious convent of Argenteuil to read four languages, Abelard says: Latin, Greek, Hebrew and French. (He himself 'had little or no Greek and no Hebrew beyond an occasional quoted word'.[4]) By the twelfth century, convents often had their own scriptoria to produce books for their libraries; Heloise's education at Argenteuil was remarkable by any standard. In her writing, she shows a formidable and well honed intelligence, gained through not only her religious reading but also her profound study of classical writers, including Ovid, particularly his *Heroides*, Seneca, her personal favourite, and Cicero, whom she often quotes. Michael Clanchy comments on her 'imaginative understanding of the classics and, in particular, her passionate feelings about the pagan sages. She actually cared about the moral standing of Socrates or the Stoics and this is what she conveyed [in her letters] to Abelard.'[5] Peter Dronke traces her style to 'that chosen and diffused by a leading Italian teacher of letter-writing in the first years of the twelfth century, Adalbertus'.[6] Heloise's letters share with the model letters in Adalbertus's handbook not only 'their choice of sentence-endings' but the 'use of elaborate rhythmic parallelism in phrases and clauses, a parallelism that, especially when intense emotion is to be expressed, is heightened by frequent, almost regular, rhymes'.[7] Dronke further points out, however, that 'we cannot identify with certainty a precise treatise or teacher that Heloise knew'.[8]

Other classical writers whom Heloise alludes to or cites by name include Lucan and Horace. She further refers to Boethius, Augustine, Gregory the Great and Ambrose, and knows texts from the Hebrew Bible, including Job, Isaiah, Ezekiel and Solomon. How did Heloise become so learned? Heloise says she read books at Argenteuil more than once, presumably in the convent library, where she 'had the freedom to devote [herself] to prayer and meditation on sacred books'.[9] One might further surmise that Heloise had access to books in the Notre Dame Cathedral Library through her uncle Fulbert, who was a canon there, and through Abelard, a professor at the University of Paris. Heloise was a brilliant student, already famed for her learning before she met Abelard, and later a revered abbess who built Abelard's foundation, the Paraclete, into a distinguished religious house, creating six further daughter houses.[10] The scope of her learning is breathtaking, remarkable for any age, as is her passion, which leaps off the pages of her prose. But how she learned so much remains a mystery, as does her social class. Though Heloise was illegitimate, the name of her father unknown, she received a first-class education.

Among aristocratic writers (and readers) are twenty named women troubadours (or *trobairitz*), though music survives for only one of their songs.[11] The best-known of these are the Countess of Dia and

Castelloza. Others include Bieiris de Romans, who wrote a love poem to another woman, Maria; and Lady Carenza, who, when asked by two young sisters about love and marriage, advised them to turn their desires instead towards the Crown of Wisdom ('Coronat de Scienza').[12] These aristocratic women wrote in Occitan, also called Provençal, a language spoken in southern France, and their poetry appears to have been written for performance. Their songs were part of the courtly game of love, played by both women and men.

The four songs that survive of the Countess of Dia (c. 1150–c. 1215) evoke the vivid presence of a self-assured writer who assimilates 'the realm of the *Heroides* freely and creatively, at Ovid's own imaginative level'.[13] They also by turns mock and emulate the poetry of male troubadours, another source with which the Countess was clearly familiar, either from witnessing work in performance or by reading it, or likely both. Music for one of her verses, 'A chanter m'er de so qu'ieu no volria' ('I must sing of things I would rather keep silent about'), is recorded in a thirteenth-century manuscript. Portraits of her, indicating her popularity with her audiences, appear in Bibliothèque Nationale de France, MS Fr. 12473 (Plate 1) and elsewhere.

Her songs show her familiarity with medieval romance: at one point she mentions Floris and Blancaflor, whose love story has survived to this day in both French and Middle English versions, and she also alludes to the lovers Seguin and Valensa, from a romance now lost, which the Countess may have heard or read.[14]

Her *vida*, or 'life' (which is not reliable, as *vidas* are often fictions), describes her as 'the wife of En Guillem de Poitiers, a lady beautiful and good. And she fell in love with En Raimbaut d'Orange, and wrote many good chansons in his honor.'[15] Raimbaut III d'Orange or d'Aurenga was 'a great troubadour himself, who lived from roughly 1146 to 1173'.[16] Two other women troubadours are associated with Raimbaut: his older sister Tibors, from whom we have a fragmentary lyric, and Azalais de Porcairagues, whose one surviving poem was written in response to verse by Raimbaut.[17]

While the Countess's *vida* may be fictional, it suggests a world of poets in which writers interacted and responded to each other's work, in which women engaged with men on the same footing, and where the *trobairitz* 'were relatives, friends, colleagues, and lovers of the male poets'.[18] Though her poetry is artful, the Countess writes directly and frankly. Dronke notes that she 'sees herself in the man's role, not the woman's: she is the one who chooses actively, and who, by being more fervent, is also more vulnerable'.[19] In her poetry, she is self-assured, in complete command of rhetorical forms: she manipulates and reshapes troubadour conventions, with which she was directly familiar, to suit her themes.

Castelloza (early thirteenth century) writes in a different vein. Her work explores love when it is no longer requited yet that same work simultaneously celebrates the transformative act of creation. Writing her songs allows her to triumph over the loss of her (fictional?) lover. Like the Countess of Dia, she may have known Ovid's *Heroides*, though both poets seem more directly influenced by their courtly milieu and by other poets in their circle. Like that of the Countess, Castelloza's *vida* is rather vague, but it does say she was married to Turc de Mairona, lived in Auvergne and loved a man named Arman de Beon; she was also 'very joyful and very well-schooled and very beautiful'.[20] Three of her songs appear in five surviving manuscripts, and a fourth anonymous song ('Per ioi que d'amor m'avegna') that is probably hers is included in Morgan M. 819, a collection of *Chansonniers* dating from between 1285 and 1300. Castelloza was clearly aware of other troubadour poetry. She addresses one verse to her fellow *trobairitz* Almois de Castelnou; another of her songs seems related to poetry composed by Peirol (fl. c. 1185–1221), a troubadour who mentions Castelloza's husband in one of his compositions.[21] Surviving portraits of Castelloza (Plate 2) indicate her prestige and fame.

In their verses, both the Countess of Dia and Castelloza upend and exploit tropes familiar in troubadour lyric, effectively inscribing 'their own voices in a highly conventional lyric system'.[22] As Matilda Bruckner writes, both show 'how a woman poet can (re)invent troubadour lyric; together they offer an excellent illustration of how complex and varied these transformations can be'.[23] Both were readers of and participants in producing sophisticated work that responded to the writing of other poets, often inverting the expectations of that perhaps more conventional poetry. They flourished in a period when literate women writers were encouraged, as did their near contemporary Marie de France.

Marie (twelfth century) is the first named woman writer of vernacular narrative poetry in Europe. She remains unidentified, though she mentions herself by name in all three of her surviving works, which were composed between 1160 and 1215. These are written in Marie's preferred form of octosyllabic rhymed couplets. Marie was clearly an aristocrat who inhabited a literate and literary world of stories, letter writing and translation, but it is easier to trace Marie's sources, the stories she heard and the books she read, than to identify who she was. (Various identities have been proposed, from Marie de Champagne, daughter of Eleanor of Aquitaine, to Marie, Countess of Boulogne, daughter of Stephen of Blois and Matilda of Boulogne.²⁴) Marie's work was clearly popular in her own day and beyond; portraits of her (Plate 3) attest to her authorship while simultaneously creating 'an impressive visualization of the ambiguous world of oral and written culture in the thirteenth century'.²⁵

Marie's *Espurgatoire Seint Patriz* (*St Patrick's Purgatory*), a 2,300-line poem that mixes Christian belief with Celtic folklore, is a fairly close French translation of the *Tractatus de purgatorio scanti Patricii* (*Treatise on St Patrick's Purgatory*), composed in the 1180s in Latin by the English Cistercian Henry of Saltrey. Marie tends to amplify her original source, a practice that typified medieval translation, which was looser than modern translation practice. The *Espurgatoire* retells the story of the knight Owein, who follows the example of St Patrick, an earlier visitor to Purgatory. Owein enters Purgatory as people sometimes entered fairyland (through a cave), witnesses various torments and then reforms. Despite the prodigious feats of memory sometimes attributed to pre- and early literate cultures, this is not the sort of story one can simply hear and retain, so Marie must have been working from a copy or copies of the text.²⁶

The main manuscript collection of Marie's works is found in British Library MS Harley 978, a miscellany copied in the third quarter of the thirteenth century (c. 1261–1265). This includes Marie's *Fables* (of which there are 102), also called *Isopet*, which exists in twenty-two other manuscripts. Here Marie identifies herself with Aesop, who translated the fables from Greek to Latin for Emperor Romulus. In this case, like that of the *Espurgatoire*, the act of translation is the impetus for reading and understanding as well as expanding upon an extant text or texts. The *Romulus* (not actually written by Emperor Romulus) is a medieval collection that derives in part from the prose paraphrases of Aesop by the Roman poet Phaedrus; the *Romulus* collections began to circulate in the tenth century and accrued various other tales as they were copied.²⁷ The first forty of Marie's fables derive from *Romulus*, though even these are adapted and extended, presumably to speak to Marie's audience. In her Epilogue, Marie claims further that her French version of the *Fables* was based on an English version made by King Alfred the Great (ninth century; 'li reis Alfrez'), a work no longer extant, if indeed it ever existed.²⁸ Her *Fables* also show Marie's knowledge of the *Roman de Renart*, the famous medieval collection of stories about the trickster fox Reynard, as well as medieval versions of Statius and Virgil, stories deriving from Ovid, and popular folktales.²⁹

Marie's most famous and enduring work is the *Lais*, a collection of short narrative poems. In its preface, Marie describes her writing process: she says that at first she considered 'translating a Latin text into French, but this would scarcely have been worthwhile, for others have undertaken a similar task'.[30] So she turned to Breton lays she 'had heard' that were written to 'perpetuate the memory of adventures'.[31] She says she has made these into French verse, working on them 'late into the night'.[32] Twelve lays then follow, with various themes: shape-shifting, adultery (perhaps justified given the practice of arranged marriage at the time), even the first werewolf story, the stuff of medieval romance or fairy tale. Some stories emphasise the liberating power of the imagination or allude to the benefits of women's education (the attractiveness of Le Fresne, for example, is partially based on her convent education). Others centre on exchanges of letters between lovers, likely reflections of the literate courtly environment in which Marie wrote. Marie also retells a brief allusive episode from Tristan and Isolt, a story she knows well, which she places into the mouth of Tristan as the original teller: 'Tristran, a skilful harpist, in order to record his words (as the queen had said he should), used them to create a new lay . . . I have told you the truth of the lay I have related here', an early and effective experiment in first-person narration.[33] Her *Lais* were influential: 'there are translations or other versions of the *Lais* clearly dependent on hers in Old Norse (nine in a thirteenth-century manuscript), Middle English, Middle High German, Italian, French and even Latin'.[34] The *Lais* in French are extant in five manuscripts and are included, like her *Fables*, in BL MS Harley 978.

Marie wrote a range of works, and imposed her stamp on each of them, and seems to have heard as well as read some of her sources, even, in writing her *Lais*, preferring sources she has heard to making a translation from Latin. That is, while Marie consulted written exemplars for both the *Purgatory* and *Fables*, the *Lais* came mainly from oral tradition, which Marie mentions several times: they were originally meant to be performed as songs, not written down, as she tells us.

We can reconstruct some forms of reading in the twelfth century. One might learn to compose lyrics and songs from the courtly world one inhabited, from a brother, husband, lover, or father, from other women, from stories one had heard, or from a written text. How Heloise knew so many classical works is uncertain, though she was located in Paris, a centre for books even in the twelfth century, and Argenteuil, the convent just outside Paris in which she began her education, was clearly rigorous in the teaching of languages. The women troubadours learned their craft from listening to public performance, along with reading or hearing stories of medieval romance. Marie seems to have practised two forms of reading: she wrote heard stories down in order to preserve them and the adventures they told about, and she translated texts from Latin, sometimes adding other sources to her translations that were not taken from her main exemplar.

While the twelfth and thirteenth centuries produced women writers from the aristocratic class, by the fourteenth century women writers from an increasingly affluent middle class began to write books – and they too practised several types of reading. Julian of Norwich (1342–c. 1416) was an anchoress who, after vowing to live apart from the world, was walled up in a funeral service, indicating her rejection of earthly values and her choice to live away from society. Her anchorhold was in the graveyard of St Julian's Church in Norwich, from which Julian took her name, part of the Carrow Priory which itself was part of the Norwich Cathedral Priory. Julian's Norwich had three grammar schools, in addition to the convent school at Carrow, and four secular colleges for priests: the College of St Mary in the Fields, the Carnary College, the College of the Chantry Priests in the bishop's palace, and the college attached to St Giles Hospital.[35] Norwich Cathedral had one of the finest libraries of the period, with 1,350 volumes prior to the Dissolution, and just down the road from Julian's church was an Austin friary with an excellent library to which Julian may have had access.[36] It is unclear how isolated Julian actually was: the anchoress lived in a little house attached to a church with three windows – one for her maid, one through which to observe the mass, and a third through which to give spiritual advice to seekers. There are four surviving bequests to Julian, from 1393 to 1416; two of these also leave money to her maid, who could conceivably have brought Julian books, as could her priest or confessor.[37]

Julian is another 'first': the first woman to write a book in English. In May 1373, at age thirty and a half, as she tells us, Julian became ill and had a vivid vision of the crucified Christ, along with sixteen revelations about God's love for humanity. Over the rest of her life, she wrote about this experience in two versions, short and long, called the *Revelations of Divine Love*. Her main theological contribution was to posit the Holy Spirit, the third part of the Trinity, as a female figure, identifying God as Mother as well as Father and Son. Her work was particularly influential among Carthusians and Bridgettines and survives because it was copied in those religious houses. Four manuscripts of her work are extant, two written before the Dissolution.

What kind of reading did Julian practise? While reading aloud at convent meals was typical in many religious orders, Julian lived much of her life separately (and may not have been a nun at all), but she would have heard sermons and conversed with a spiritual adviser, and she seems also to have read many books, as we understand reading today, in preparation for writing her own. At the time of her vision, Julian says, she was 'one who could not read a letter' and describes herself as 'a simple creature that cowde [knew] no letter[s]'.[38] If we believe her, she was at first illiterate but over the years, after her divine 'shewings', in her effort to write them down accurately, she developed a powerful command of both scripture and the theology of St Augustine, among other texts. She adopted Augustine's vision of the Trinity (God as power, Son as wisdom and the Holy Spirit as love), as well as his belief that God's love is inherent in human beings, no matter how far they may stray. She was especially familiar with the Pauline and Johannine epistles, the Psalms, the four Gospels and Second Isaiah, some of which she may have learned through memorisation, hearing or her daily recitation from the Psalter, perhaps in addition to more conventional reading. Her work shows the influence of many other sources, some of them originally in Latin, but these had been translated into English by the fourteenth century (as had been the Bible, in the heretical but popular translations of John Wycliffe, which circulated widely). It is unclear whether Julian knew much Latin; she does seem to have preferred English to Latin texts, though she sometimes uses her own translations from Latin as references in her *Revelations*.[39]

Several other sources inform her work. In the long version of her *Revelations*, Julian cites two authors directly, 'Saint Dionyse of France', whose work in English is called *Hid Divinite*, and St Gregory the Great, from his *Life of Saint Benedict*.[40] In her formulation of the Holy Spirit as maternal love, Julian shows she may have also known St Anselm's Prayer to St Paul: 'And you, Jesus, are you not also a mother? / Are you not the mother who, like a hen, / Gathers her chickens under her wings?'[41] In addition, Julian seems to make allusion to late medieval English spiritual works. These include *The Cloud of Unknowing* and *The Scale of Perfection* (written for a 'ghostly sister in Jesus Christ') and possibly also Geoffrey Chaucer's translation of Boethius's *The Consolation of Philosophy*.[42] As Vincent Gillespie comments, 'Julian's writing exists in a complex, polyphonic, and intertextual relationship with many other works of catechesis and penitential theology, devotion, Passion meditation, contemplation and escatology'.[43]

Gillespie adds other works to Julian's reading list, including the English translations of the mystical and contemplative work by Heinrich Suso *Horologium saptientiae* (in English known as the *Seven Points of True Wisdom*), William Fleet's *Remedies against Tribulations*, and *The Prickynge of Love*, a guide to contemplation.[44] Julian seems to have absorbed these works wholesale, but she rarely provides references to the source material with which she shaped her description of her visions. Her prose shows her rhetorical techniques, possibly learned aurally (from sermons?) or perhaps from a book of rhetoric, perhaps both: she uses alliteration, rhyme, repetition and *complexio*, repetition of the same word at the start and end of a sentence for emphasis, among other devices. Like many of the other women under consideration here, we do not know a great deal about Julian's life, but if her *Revelations* are to be believed, she seems to have moved from aural literacy to becoming a more active reader (and writer) in order to communicate her visions of God's divine love to the world.

Julian has one important eyewitness to her kindness, generosity and theological perspectives. Margery Kempe (c. 1373–1439) recorded in her *Book* that she visited Julian in her cell for several days sometime between 1413 and 1415. Julian counselled Margery to 'Set all [her] trust in God and fear not the language of the world', and Margery quotes Julian at some length.[45] And, perhaps like Julian, whose social class we do not know but whose language is marked by its homely, unpretentious style, Margery came from the mercantile elite. Though illiterate in the modern sense, Margery produced the first autobiography in English, dictating her experiences to two scribes, one a priest and one who did not have good command of English, sometimes said to have been her son.[46] The surviving manuscript (London, British Library, MS Additional 61823) is a copy of the lost original put together by an efficient scribe named Salthows or Salthouse, perhaps a Richard Salthouse (fl. 1443), who was a monk at Norwich's Cathedral Priory.

In her *Book*, Margery expresses her yearnings for God, describes her visions of Jesus, Mary and sometimes demons, and often cites people important in her day (for example, Thomas Arundel, Archbishop of Canterbury; Philip Repingdon, Bishop of Lincoln; William Alnick, Bishop of Norwich; Alan of Lynn, who urged Margery to write her *Book*, and William Sowthfeld, both Carmelites; and her confessor, Robert Spryngolde). She also frankly reveals her divinely inspired behaviours, which included excessive weeping in public, proclaiming while in company that she had heard the voice of God or was more blessed than others, and being rescued from various hair-raising situations by handsome young men, whom Margery apparently considered angels (they always turn up in the nick of time). Margery retained a healthy interest in men, even after fourteen children and even after she declared herself chaste and refused to sleep with her husband. Despite this human foible, Margery was very committed to her religious beliefs and answered the Archbishop of York quite boldly when he questioned her about them. Her self-portrait is (unintentionally) humorous even as it documents her many trials and tribulations, some of which evoke compassion as well as laughter. Her *Book* also details her several pilgrimages to holy places. She travelled through England, as well as to Spain, Italy, Norway, Germany and the Holy Land, seeking out religious sites (and was, on occasion, left behind by her fellow travellers).

Most importantly for this study, Margery discusses what 'the creature' (she consistently refers to herself in the third person) heard being read aloud, including the foremost devotional and religious texts of her day. In addition to her regular attendance at church, where she heard Bible passages, she explained that whenever she received word from the Trinity, it was spoken 'so excellently that she heard never a book, neither Hilton's book, nor Bridget's book, nor *Stimulus Amoris*, nor *Incendium Amoris*, nor any other that she had heard read that spoke so highly of the love of God'.[47] These were central devotional texts of the later Middle Ages: Walter Hilton's *Scale of Perfection*, a work of spiritual counsel originally composed for an anchoress; St Bridget's *Revelations*, influential in its vivid visionary depictions of the sufferings of Christ; the fourteenth-century mystical work *Stimulus amoris* (*The Prick of Love*), a devotional poem on the Passion, attributed in some manuscripts to Walter Hilton; and the *Incendium amoris* (*The Fire of Love*), a guide to spiritual life written by the fourteenth-century English mystic Richard Rolle of Hampole.

Later Margery describes hearing a priest read to her in Lynn: 'He read to her many a good book of high contemplation, and other books, such as the Bible with doctors thereupon, St. Bride's book, Hilton's book, Bonaventura, *Stimulus Amoris*, *Incendium Amoris*, and such other.' The priest continued to read to her 'the most part of seven years or eight years', to which, being Margery, she cannot help but add that this reading did him a lot of good.[48]

Margery's retentive memory is evident in her Passion narrative, much of which seems to have been drawn from Nicholas Love's *Meditationes vita Christi* (*Meditations on the Life of Christ*). She also knew the lives of the saints and holy women. Two were particularly influential role models. In Part II, Chapter 10, Margery describes her visit to Syon, the English foundation of the Bridgettine Order, dedicated to St

Bridget of Sweden, a widowed saint with eight children who also made numerous pilgrimages and whose writings were popular in England at the time.[49] Transcription of Margery's *Book* began on St Bridget's Day in 1436, and there are a number of other parallels between the two women, consciously echoed by Margery and absorbed, no doubt, from hearing Bridget's book read to her.[50] Margery's holy (and loud) weeping had a religious precedent in Jacques de Vitry's biography of Marie d'Oignies, a late twelfth-century woman mystic who also experienced ecstasy and who, like Margery, wept uncontrollably when meditating on the Passion of Christ.[51] This work, mentioned in Margery's *Book*, had been translated into Middle English by the fourteenth century.[52] So, despite her repeated claims of illiteracy, Margery was able not only to imbibe the major spiritual works of her day but also to dictate a book incorporating those references.[53] There is much emphasis here on reading aloud, whether Margery is listening to her priest, hearing her own text read back to her, or incorporating scripture and other passages learned by memory into her text.

Last, but hardly least, Christine de Pizan (1364/5–c. 1430) was the first French writer to earn a living by her pen. This statement may be read both literally and figuratively, as Christine not only wrote books but also sometimes copied them out in her own hand, including copies of her own writings made for noble or wealthy patrons.[54] Christine shared with Heloise fluency in several languages (in Christine's case, French, Italian and Latin); with the troubadour poets, a love of lyric poetry; with Marie, pleasure in retelling stories; and with Julian and Margery, profound religious belief.

Much of Christine's biography can be reconstructed from her writing. After the death of both her father and her husband, Christine was left, at the age of twenty-five, with her mother, three children and a niece to support. On the basis of manuscript copies of Christine's works that have been identified as autographs, it is sometimes surmised that Christine at first supported herself and her family as a scribe employed in the manuscript trade.[55] It is further thought that Christine read sources that later appear in her work while copying them for patrons or for the Paris bookdealers.[56] It is known that Christine oversaw a scriptorium that produced copies of her own works for royal and noble patrons. The most magnificent of these is British Library Harley MS 4431 (Plate 4), with its lavish frontispiece showing Christine offering her book to Queen Isabeau of Bavaria, which was completed after 1410, partially copied by Christine herself.[57]

Christine's reading was wide ranging and encouraged by her father, Thomas de Pizan. Originally from Bologna, he served Charles V as a physician, astronomer and counsellor, and moved his family with him to Paris. Charles V was an avid book collector, known for his library, which was partially housed in the Louvre. Christine described the king's collection of books as 'all the notable volumes that had been compiled by sovereign authors, either of Holy Scriptures, of theology, philosophy, and all the sciences, very well written and decorated, always by the best scribes occupied by his order at this work'; Charity Cannon Willard agrees that it 'was unequalled by anything in Europe except the Visconti Library in Pavia'.[58] Christine knew (and apparently used) the reading room above the king's library, which Christine wrote of 'as if from personal knowledge. Desks and benches were provided, the walls were paneled in Irish wood, . . . and the ceilings had inlays of cypress wood'.[59] It is thought Christine had access to the royal library through its librarian, Gilles Malet, and that she may also have borrowed books from some of her patrons, including the dukes of Berry and Burgundy and possibly even from Jean Gerson, the chancellor of the University of Paris. Certainly, Christine often describes herself as 'a literate laywoman' or 'as a learned writer impassioned with study'.[60] As we will see from a brief sample of her work, as a reader, Christine had apparently boundless curiosity about many subjects and an intellectual command that was truly astonishing.

Christine produced ten surviving works in verse (collections of either lyrics or narrative poetry), her final poem a celebration of the triumphs of Joan of Arc, and eleven prose works, showing her extraordinary versatility and many interests, from love poetry to the details of warfare.[61] Her first foray into the world of French letters began with a salvo against the *Roman de la Rose* (*Romance of the Rose*), the famous thirteenth-century allegorical work that considers love from the sacred to the profane, begun by Guillaume de Lorris and completed by Jean de Meun. Christine's criticism of the *Rose* in 1400 made her early literary reputation, yet the *Rose* influenced virtually all her subsequent writings. In her famous correspondence with Jean de Montreuil, the provost of Lille, Christine says the work 'would be better shrouded in flames than crowned with laurel'.[62] Here Christine takes exception to the words of Genius, who 'makes great attacks on women, saying, in fact, "Flee, flee, flee from the deadly serpent." Then he declares that men should pursue them unremittingly.'[63] In 1405, when Christine was completing the *Book of the City of Ladies*, she includes Genius's words again, upended, this time warning women against the duplicities of men: 'Oh my ladies, flee, flee the foolish love they urge on you! . . . Flee, flee, my ladies, and avoid their company – under their smiles are hidden deadly and painful poisons.'[64] This, as

Renate Blumenfeld-Kosinski has pointed out, 'is a sarcastic echo of Genius' warning against women'.[65]

In some cases, Christine agrees with La Vieille, the corrupt old woman who features in the *Rose*. Both conclude that men are untrustworthy. According to La Vieille, 'all men betray and deceive women; all are sensualists, taking their pleasure anywhere'.[66] In *The Book of the Three Virtues* (1405), Christine similarly warns women against developing friendships with men: 'For women do not suspect that before these men have frequented them for very long, some or most of them will try to seduce them if they can', while verse 53 of her *One Hundred Ballades* advises, 'Wise are those who know how to guard against false lovers who have the habit of ceaselessly betraying women with their words'.[67]

Christine's most famous work, *Le livre de la cité des dames* (*The Book of the City of Ladies*, 1404–5), was inspired not only by St Augustine's *Civitate Dei* (*City of God*) but also by Boccaccio's *De claris mulieribus* (*On Famous Women*), which by that point had been translated into French as *Des cleres et noble femmes*. Dante figures as a main inspiration for Christine's *Livre du chemin de long estude* (*Book of the Path of Long Study*, 1402–3), in which Christine is guided by the Cumaean sibyl, a journey drawn from the *Divine Comedy*, which Christine may have been the first writer to read in France. The influence of the poetry of Petrarch, along with her reading of the Psalms, is seen in her *Sept psaumes allegorisés* (*Seven Allegorised Psalms*, 1409) and elsewhere.

Christine's popular *Epître d'Othea* (*Letter of Othea to Hector*, c. 1401) is a collection of moralised mythological stories drawn from Ovid, or more specifically from the *Ovide moralisé*, a popular medieval compilation of Ovid's *Metamorphoses* written in 72,000 lines of verse with various (often Christianising) additions. The earliest known surviving manuscript of Christine's *Epître* (Paris, BN fr. 848) is copied in Christine's hand, as are the copy of her *Mutacion de fortune* presented to the Duke of Burgundy (Brussels, Bibliothèque Royale 9508) and two manuscripts of her *Debat des deux amans* (BN fr. 1740 and Brussels, Bibliothèque Royale 11034). In the *Avision-Christine*, she cites some of her reading, including ancient history, Boethius's *Consolation of Philosophy* (probably read in the French translation of Jean de Meun) and again the *Ovide moralisé*. For her biography of Charles V, *Le livre des fais et bonnes meurs du sage Roy Charles V* (1404), Christine's first long work in prose, a genre that had not been previously attempted in French, she consulted the *Grandes chroniques de France* (*The Great Chronicles of France*) and Bernard Gui's *Flores chronicorum* (*Flowers of the Chronicles*), translated into French in the fourteenth century; she also read moral treatises and contemporary political theory. In her *Faits d'armes et de chevalerie* (*Feats of Arms and Chivalry*), a book about conducting warfare possibly commissioned for the French dauphin by the Duke of Burgundy, Christine shows her knowledge of the works of the classical writers Vegetius and Frontinus, also drawing on the late fourteenth-century *Arbre des batailles* by Honoré Bouvet. This brief overview is able only to touch on some of Christine's sources but indicates something of the range and diversity of her reading.

This chapter has examined the ways in which medieval women's reading influenced their writing, speculated about women's access to books and libraries, and discussed their reading practices. Some of the claims made by or about these women writers may be fabricated or misleading: the *vidas* of the women troubadours, for example, do not offer much about their reading habits or tell us who they actually were. Was Heloise actually fluent in four languages, as Abelard boasts? Did Marie de France base her *Fables* on a ninth-century Anglo-Saxon translation by King Alfred, as she claims? Did Julian learn to read only after receiving her visions? Was Margery, in fact, entirely illiterate? Their writing, on the other hand, reveals the texts they knew, and also read or heard. These case studies present a variety of types of reading as cited in their work, described by the women themselves, or found more allusively in their texts. By letting primary sources tell the story, we see a whole range of reading practices over a span of 300 years or more, whether 'heard reading', silent reading (which seems to have been more prevalent than perhaps previously thought – for more on this see W. R. Owens, Chapter 14 in this volume), or reading through writing, copying or translating texts.

Notes

1. Available in recent translation by Joan Ferrante, Columbia University, at <https://epistolae.ctl.columbia.edu/letter/178.html> (accessed 5 August 2019).
2. Constant J. Mews with Neville Chiavaroli (ed. and trans.), *The Lost Love Letters of Heloise and Abelard: Perceptions of Dialogue in Twelfth-Century France* (New York: St Martin's Press, 1999); Barbara Newman, *Making Love in the Twelfth Century: 'Letters of Two Lovers' in Context* (Philadelphia: University of Pennsylvania Press, 2016).
3. Constant J. Mews, *Abelard and Heloise* (Oxford: Oxford University Press, 2005), pp. 146–7.

4. Betty Radice, 'The French Scholar-Lover Heloise', in Katharina M. Wilson (ed.), *Medieval Women Writers* (Athens: University of Georgia Press, 1984), pp. 90–108 (p. 98). Abelard's claims about Heloise's linguistic achievements may be exaggerated. See Betty Radice, *The Letters of Abelard and Heloise* (New York: Penguin, 1974): 'no one else has said she knew any Hebrew except the monk William Godel, writing in 1173. . . . She probably had enough Greek for liturgical purposes' (p. 32).
5. Michael T. Clanchy, *Abelard: A Medieval Life* (Cambridge: Blackwell, 1997), p. 277.
6. Peter Dronke, *Women Writers of the Middle Ages: A Critical Study of Texts from Perpetua (203) to Marguerite Porete (1310)* (Cambridge: Cambridge University Press, 1984), p. 111. For a general study, see Peter Dronke, *Abelard and Heloise in Medieval Testimonies* (Glasgow: University of Glasgow Press, 1976).
7. Dronke, *Women Writers of the Middle Ages*, p. 111.
8. Ibid.
9. Clanchy, *Abelard*, p. 192.
10. Clanchy notes, 'Even before Abelard taught her, she was reputed to be the most learned lady in France' (ibid., p. 12), which echoes Abelard's famous description of Heloise in his *Historia Calamitatum*: 'In looks she did not rank lowest, while in the extent of her learning she stood supreme. A gift for letters is so rare in women that it added greatly to her charm and had won her renown throughout the realm' (quoted in Radice, 'The French Scholar-Lover Heloise', p. 91).
11. Matilda Bruckner suggests that the works of other anonymous women troubadours survive as well, thus 'the tally is up to thirty-some poems in the trobairitz corpus'. Matilda Bruckner, 'Fictions of the Female Voice: The Women Troubadours', in Anne L. Klinck and Ann Marie Rasmussen (eds), *Medieval Woman's Song* (Philadelphia: University of Pennsylvania Press, 2002), pp. 127–51 (p. 134).
12. Meg Bogin, *The Women Troubadours* (New York: Norton, 1980), pp. 144–5.
13. Dronke, *Women Writers of the Middle Age*, p. 105.
14. Bogin, *The Women Troubadours*, pp. 84–5, 88–9.
15. Ibid., p. 163.
16. Ibid., p. 164.
17. Sarah Kay, *Subjectivity in Troubadour Poetry* (Cambridge: Cambridge University Press, 1990), p. 104; Marcelle Thiébaux, *The Writings of Medieval Women* (New York: Routledge, 1994), p. 254.
18. Thiébaux, *The Writings of Medieval Women*, p. 242.
19. Dronke, *Women Writers of the Middle Age*, p. 105.
20. William D. Paden, Jr, 'The Poems of the Trobairitz Na Castelloza', *Romance Philology*, 35 (1981), pp. 158–82 (p. 159). See also Peter Dronke, 'The Provençal Troubairitz Castelloza', in Wilson (ed.), *Medieval Women Writers*, pp. 131–52 (p. 134).

21. Paden, 'The Poems of the Trobairitz', pp. 162–3.
22. Bruckner, 'Fictions of the Female Voice', p. 128.
23. Ibid., p. 137.
24. See variously Joan M. Ferrante, 'The Education of Women in the Middle Ages in Theory, Fact, and Fantasy', in Patricia H. Labalme (ed.), *Beyond Their Sex: Learned Women of the European Past* (New York: New York University Press, 1984), pp. 9–42 (p. 27, p. 41 n. 80); Glyn S. Burgess and Keith Busby (trans. and eds), *The Lais of Marie de France* (New York: Penguin, 1986), pp. 17–19; Thiébaux, *The Writings of Medieval Women*, p. 277.
25. Sandra Hindman, 'Aesop's Cock and Marie's Hen: Gendered Authorship in Text and Image in Manuscripts of Marie's Fables', in Jane H. M. Taylor and Lesley Smith (eds), *Women and the Book: Assessing the Visual Evidence* (London: British Library, 1996), pp. 45–56 (p. 52). Hindman comments further that multiple portraits of Marie that occur particularly in two manuscripts (Paris, BN, MS Fr. 2173, Paris, BN, MS Arsenal 3142) were 'designed to convey pictorially a translatio studii' (ibid., p. 52). See also Susan L. Ward, 'Fables for the Court: Illustrations of Marie de France's Fables in Paris, BN, MS Arsenal 3142', in Taylor and Smith (eds), *Women and the Book*, pp. 190–203.
26. For discussions of memory in the Middle Ages, see M. T. Clanchy, *From Memory to Written Record: England 1066–1307* (Oxford: Blackwell, 1979, reprinted 1993), especially pp. 172–7, 295–7; Frances A. Yates, *The Art of Memory* (Chicago: University of Chicago Press, 1966), pp. 50–81, particularly contemporary descriptions of Thomas Aquinas's eidetic memory (p. 70 and following); Walter J. Ong, *Orality and Literacy: The Technologizing of the Word* (New York: Methuen, 1982), pp. 57–68.
27. Laura Gibbs (trans. and ed.), *Aesop's Fables* (Oxford: Oxford University Press, 2002), pp. xxi–xxiii.
28. Harriet Speigel (ed. and trans.), *Marie de France: Fables* (Toronto: University of Toronto Press, 1987), p. 258, l. 16, p. 259, l. 16.
29. Karl Warnke, *Die Fabeln der Marie de France, mit Benutzung des von Ed. Mall hinterlassenen Materials* (Halle: M. Niemeyer, 1898). See also Karl Warnke, *Die Quellen des Esope de Marie de France* (Halle: M. Niemeyer, 1900). For a more recent analysis, see Jayshree Sethuraman, 'The Impact of the Indo-Arabic Fable Tradition on the "Esope" of Marie de France: A Literary, Historical, and Folkloristic Study', PhD dissertation (Tulane University, 1998), who argues that Marie's *Fables* introduced stories from non-Western sources to European readers for the first time.
30. Burgess and Busby, *The Lais of Marie de France*, p. 42.
31. Ibid., p. 42.
32. Ibid.
33. Ibid., pp. 109–10.
34. Ferrante, 'The Education of Women', p. 27.
35. Edmund Colledge and James Walsh (eds), *A Book of Showings to the*

Anchoress Julian of Norwich (Toronto: University of Toronto Press, 1978), part 1, pp. 39–40.
36. Ibid., p. 40.
37. Ibid., pp. 33–4.
38. Marion Glasscoe (ed.), *Julian of Norwich, Revelation of Love* (Exeter: University of Exeter, 1976, revised edition 1986), pp. 1, 2.
39. Julian's command of Latin is debated. Colledge and Walsh, her editors, say Julian had a complete understanding of the Vulgate Bible (though many of her sources, the majority, were available in one English form or another). See Colledge and Walsh, *A Book of Showings*, part 1, pp. 45–6; see also Edmund Colledge and James Walsh, 'Editing Julian of Norwich's Revelations: A Progress Report', *Medieval Studies*, 38 (1976), pp. 407–10 (p. 410). She would have had some Latin in order to follow the mass and to pray, but her choice to write in English suggests that this is her stronger language.
40. Her reference to the conversion of 'Saint Dionyse of France' occurs in Part 18. See Glasscoe, *Julian of Norwich*, p. 21. See also Clifton Wolters (trans. and ed.), *Julian of Norwich: Revelations of Divine Love* (New York: Penguin, 1966), pp. 18–19.
41. For more on Anselm, see Caroline Walker Bynum, *Jesus as Mother: Studies in Spirituality of the High Middle Ages* (Berkeley: University of California Press, 1982), pp. 112–15, 124, 129. Jesus is described as a hen gathering her chicks under her protective wings in Matthew 23: 37, and Luke 13: 34–5.
42. Colledge and Walsh, *A Book of Showings*, part 1, pp. 47–8.
43. Vincent Gillespie, 'Seek, Suffer, and Trust: "Ese" and "Disese" in Julian of Norwich', in Sarah Salih (ed.), *Studies in the Age of Chaucer* (London: New Chaucer Society, 2017), vol. XXXIX, pp. 129–58 (p. 131).
44. Ibid., pp. 132, 133.
45. Lynn Staley (trans. and ed.), *The Book of Margery Kempe* (New York: Norton: 2001), chapter 18, pp. 32–3. The lengthy quotation that Margery supplies sounds very much like Julian's writing and appears to have been verbatim.
46. William Provost, 'The English Religious Enthusiast Margery Kempe', in Wilson (ed.), *Medieval Women Writers*, p. 301; Barry Windeatt (ed.), *The Book of Margery Kempe* (Cambridge: D. S. Brewer, 2004), pp. 5–6. For an opposing (and probably accurate) view, see Marion Glasscoe, *English Medieval Mystics: Games of Faith* (London: Longman, 1993), pp. 285–7.
47. Staley, *The Book of Margery Kempe*, p. 30.
48. Ibid., p. 106.
49. Ibid., pp. 179, 229. Margery's text actually says she visited Sheen for Lammas Day (1 August) to receive the Syon Pardon, but the word 'Sheen' is crossed out in the manuscript and 'Syon' supplied.
50. Margery describes the badly transcribed work of one scribe 'who could neither write good English nor German' (sometimes and probably

erroneously identified as her son: see note 46), then talks of a priest who undertakes to write down her book at 'compulsion of his own conscience . . . in the year of our Lord 1436, on the day after Mary Magdalene according to the information of this creature', that is, 23 July, celebrated as the feast of the death of St Bridget. See Staley, *The Book of Margery Kempe*, p. 6.

51. Ibid., pp. 112–13. Margery describes her priest's (relieved) discovery of the biography of Marie d'Oignies 'of the plenteous tears that she wept', and even mentions the two chapters in the book where these are most fully described: 'Of the plenteous grace of her tears he treats specially in . . . the eighteenth chapter . . . and also in the nineteenth chapter'.
52. Bodleian Library MS Douce 114.
53. Staley doubts Margery's claims of complete illiteracy and playfully suggests that Margery may have invented the scribe or scribes in order to mediate her material. See Staley, *The Book of Margery Kempe*, pp. 236–42.
54. Charity Cannon Willard, 'An Autograph Manuscript of Christine de Pizan?', *Studi Francesi*, 27 (1965), pp. 452–7; Gilbert Ouy and Christine M. Reno, 'Identification des autographes de Christine de Pizan', *Scriptorium*, 34 (1980), pp. 221–38; James Laidlaw, 'Christine de Pizan as Publisher', *Modern Language Review*, 82 (1987), pp. 35–75; James Laidlaw, 'Christine and the Manuscript Tradition', in Barbara K. Altmann and Deborah L. McGrady (eds), *Christine de Pizan: A Casebook* (New York: Routledge, 2003), pp. 119–21. See also: the Christine de Pizan Project overseen by James Laidlaw, University of Edinburgh, at <http://www.pizan.lib.ed.ac.uk/aims.html> (accessed 5 August 2019), which contains a list of presentation copies prepared by Christine; Olivier Delsaux, *Manuscrits et practiques autographes chez les écrivains français de la fin du Moyen Âge: l'exemple de Christine de Pizan* (Geneva: Droz, 2013), a study of fifty-four manuscripts of Christine's work, twenty-five of which are written or partially written by Christine herself. Tracy Adams comments, 'Of the roughly two hundred manuscripts containing works by Christine, about fifty were produced in her own scriptorium, under her own supervision'; Tracy Adams, 'État Présent: Christine de Pizan', *French Studies*, 71:3 (July 2017), pp. 388–400 (p. 390).
55. Charity Cannon Willard, *Christine de Pizan: Her Life and Works* (New York: Persea, 1984), p. 45.
56. Charity Cannon Willard, 'The Franco-Italian Professional Writer Christine de Pizan', in Wilson (ed.), *Medieval Women Writers*, pp. 333–63 (p. 335).
57. Laidlaw, 'Christine de Pizan as Publisher', p. 66.
58. Willard, *Christine de Pizan*, p. 28.
59. Ibid., p. 29.
60. Deborah McGrady, 'Reading for Authority: Portraits of Christine de Pizan and Her Readers', in Stephen Partridge and Erik Kwakkel (eds),

Author, Reader, Book: Medieval Authorship in Theory and Practice (Toronto: University of Toronto Press, 2012), pp. 154–77 (p. 159).
61. A descriptive list of Christine's publications may be found in Christine de Pizan, *The Book of the City of Ladies*, Earl Jeffrey Richards (trans.) (New York: Persea, 1982), pp. xxii–xxvi.
62. Willard, 'The Franco-Italian Professional', p. 345. See also Joseph L. Baird and John R. Kane (eds and trans.), *La Querelle de la Rose: Letters and Documents* (Chapel Hill: University of North Carolina, Department of Romance Languages, 1978), p. 55; Eric Hicks (ed.), *Le débat sure le Roman de la Rose*, Bibliothèque du XVe siècle 43 (Paris: Champion, 1977); Willard, *Christine de Pizan*, pp. 73–90.
63. Baird and Kane, *La Querelle*, p. 51.
64. De Pizan, *The Book of the City of Ladies*, Richards (trans.), pp. 256–7.
65. Renate Blumenfeld-Kosinski, 'Christine de Pizan and the Misogynistic Tradition', in Renate Blumenfeld-Kosinski (ed.), *The Selected Writings of Christine de Pizan*, Renate Blumenfeld-Kosinski and Kevin Brownlee (trans.) (New York: Norton, 1997), p. 302.
66. V. A. Kolve and Glending Olson (eds), *Geoffrey Chaucer: The Canterbury Tales* (New York: Norton, 1989), p. 315.
67. Sarah Lawson, *Treasure of the City of Ladies* (New York: Penguin, 2003), pp. 150–1; Blumenfeld-Kosinski (ed.), *The Selected Writings*, p. 8.

Chapter 4

Mi ritrovai per un poema sacro. The Ideological Reading Subject in Dante's *Inferno* 5

Glenn A. Steinberg

According to Louis Althusser, 'all ideology hails or interpellates concrete individuals as concrete subjects'.[1] Reading is one instance of this kind of interpellation – a moment in which the reader encounters content that elicits ideological responses and subjectivity. The traces of the reader's interpellation should therefore be visible within the text's pages. In the imagery, characters and plot of a text, we should be able to identify likely ideological triggers, reconstruct the ideological contexts of those triggers and characterise the subjects whom such triggers might recruit. As a test case, this chapter examines the episode of Paolo and Francesca in Dante's *Inferno* 5 and considers what kind of subjects this famous canto interpellates, as well as what kind of ideologies function in that interpellation. Tracing the text's indicators and contexts of interpellation in this way helps us to flesh out a rough picture of Dante's readers, about whom otherwise little is known, and to reconstruct available ideological frameworks for reading in fourteenth-century Italy.

When Dante begins the *Commedia*, from the very first line, he draws attention to the implied presence of his reader through the poem's very language, using a first-person plural pronoun: 'Nel mezzo del cammin di *nostra* vita' (*Inf.* 1.1; 'In the middle of *our* life's path'; emphasis added).[2] Again and again in the early lines of the poem, Dante draws attention to his act of 'saying' the poem's words and 'recounting' its story, presumably to a living, breathing audience of readers: 'Ahi quanto a dir qual era è cosa dura. . . . Io non so ben ridir com' i' v'intrai' (*Inf.* 1.4, 10; 'Oh, how to say how it was is a hard thing. . . . I do not know how to recount rightly how I entered there'). Throughout the *Commedia*, moreover, Dante repeatedly apostrophises his 'lettore' ('reader'), addresses a 'voi' ('you') and uses inclusive first-person pronouns (e.g., *Inf.* 7, 8, 9, 16, 20, 22, 25, 34; *Purg.* 8, 9,

10, 12, 17, 29, 31, 33; *Par.* 2, 5, 9, 10, 22). Throughout the poem as well, texts and reading feature prominently – from the written words above the gate of Hell in *Inferno* 3 to the divine book of *Paradiso* 33, from the romance-reading Francesca in *Inferno* 5 to the Virgil-reading Statius of *Purgatorio* 22, from the Virgil- and Bible-quoting angels of *Purgatorio* 30 to the letter-forming souls in *Paradiso* 18. Even beyond the *Commedia*, Dante's preoccupation with his readers, explicit and insistent, spans his entire career. As Justin Steinberg observes, 'Is there any medieval poet more concerned than Dante with the public circulation and reception of his works?'[3]

The actual identity of Dante's readers is, however, difficult to establish because of 'the fundamental problem of a lack of primary sources for tracing a history of reading'.[4] For the bulk of medieval literature, material evidence of actual, historical readers is tantalisingly scant, lost over time or never recorded in the first place in an age long before the advent of personal reading journals, professional literary criticism or online reader reviews. Most of our knowledge about the audiences of specific medieval texts and authors comes from studies that trace manuscript ownership and circulation, such as recent studies of the manuscripts of the *Roman de la Rose* or of Boccaccio's works. Material and textual evidence of patronage also provides critical information about medieval readership, indicating, for example, the importance of female patrons to vernacular literature in the Middle Ages. But even when we have evidence of actual medieval readers, we have little evidence of how they read – whether 'alone or in groups, silently or out loud . . . [or] having the text read to them by others'.[5] From documentary evidence, we can deduce sundry modes of reading, as well as various levels of literacy,[6] but we have scant evidence for reading practices or strategies of interpretation with particular texts.

For Dante's readers specifically, our knowledge of the *Commedia*'s early circulation is complicated by the lack of a surviving manuscript of his poem before 1336 (fifteen years after Dante's death) and by the sheer range of Dante's early reception: 'In Rome, Siena, Gubbio, Arezzo, Florence, Bologna, Ravenna, Venice, and Verona the poem circulated widely, crossing divisions between Guelph and Ghibelline, lay and clerical, Dominican and Franciscan, Christian and Jew, often in surprising ways.'[7] John Ahern has provided a useful catalogue of known readers of the *Commedia* before the first surviving manuscript (as evidenced by quotations, allusions and other concrete references before 1336), as well as a persuasive argument for widespread, popular oral performances of the poem.[8] Justin Steinberg has examined two of the earliest manuscript anthologisations of Dante's lyric poems (in the *Memoriali bolognesi* and Vaticano 3793) and has situated the anthologisers of these early manuscripts – 'the upwardly mobile and newly educated notaries of Bologna' and 'the Florentine mercantile elite' – within their social and political context.[9] Nevertheless, Ahern's catalogue of pre-1336 Dante readers, though valuable, is inevitably riddled with gaps and peppered with qualification and conjecture, and Steinberg's analyses of the *Memoriali bolognesi* and Vatican anthology, while provocative, focus narrowly on just two manuscripts and on the reception of Dante's lyric poetry rather than on that of the *Commedia*. We are left in the end without solid, comprehensive evidence of who the first readers of the *Commedia* were or how they read the poem.

We have, however, one source of information that we do not have for most other medieval authors: the texts of at least twelve extant fourteenth-century commentaries on all or part of the *Commedia*. These commentaries present a snapshot of how twelve readers – from Dante's own sons to Giovanni Boccaccio and Filippo Villani – read the poem. But even Dante's earliest commentators are decidedly unreliable as evidence of Dante's contemporary readership more generally. The commentators themselves are hardly a representative lot: 'all male, all educated, all members of the learned professions (clergy, jurists, notaries, public officials), all demonstrably or presumably Latinate'.[10] In addition, as Saverio Bellomo has noted, the very practice of textual commentary in the Middle Ages leads to especially conservative readings, 'softening [a text's] most innovative elements, in order to carry it back into the crib of tradition and thus into contexts familiar to the reader'.[11] As Simon Gilson observes, moreover, medieval commentators make 'extensive use of *compilatio*', copying earlier commentaries, 'often verbatim and without attribution' – so that '[s]ome modes of reading, which were widely practiced between the early Trecento and the late Cinquecento, are not found in the exegesis upon Dante'.[12] In essence, because of their near identical social backgrounds, their interpretive conservatism (typical of medieval commentary), and their dependence on each other (recycling the same safe material in their agglutinative *compilationes*), we cannot regard the early commentators on the *Commedia* as broadly representative of Dante's readers or as indicative of the range of possible reactions and interpretations for Dante's poem. In addition, 'Dante commentaries often resist speaking directly about their historical juncture and cultural milieu', making them poor indicators of the social and political contexts of Dante's readers as well.[13]

But I propose that Dante's text itself, within its own pages, reveals a great deal about its reading public – especially the social and political contexts of that public – through the operation of ideology in the text. As Althusser describes it,

> ideology 'acts' or 'functions' in such a way that it 'recruits' subjects among the individuals (it recruits them all), or 'transforms' the individuals into subjects (it transforms them all) by that very precise operation which I have called *interpellation* or hailing, and which can be imagined along the lines of the most commonplace everyday police (or other) hailing: 'Hey, you there!'[14]

In other words, a stimulus confronts an individual with a moment of subjective self-awareness and (apparent) agency. In that moment, the individual is transformed into (or confirmed as) a subject of a particular sort and responds accordingly. In a similar way, a text, such as Dante's *Commedia*, hails its readers – calling out to them (or calling them out) as subjects and demanding from them an ideological response in the form of a new or renewed self-consciousness as subject and, in line with that new or renewed self-consciousness, some form of material action. In the concrete triggers of this hailing, Dante's text inevitably contains evidence of the ideological reading subjects that it hails, inscribed within the imagery, form and content that provokes the subject's moment of interpellation. The ideological cues within the text indicate both the type of audience that Dante expects or seeks to address and the kind of reader who likely responds favourably to the text and consumes it. Ideological traces in the text become bread crumbs that allow us to track, at least hypothetically, the text's readership.

I am certainly not the first to suggest that readers of a text can be found inscribed within the text's own pages. Peter Rabinowitz, for example, has advanced the concept of what he calls the 'authorial audience'. Rabinowitz argues that authors 'design their books rhetorically for some more or less specified *hypothetical* audience. Artistic choices are based upon these assumptions – conscious or unconscious – about readers.'[15] The text's form and content inevitably derive from and reveal these readerly assumptions on the author's part. As Rabinowitz observes,

> Some assumptions are quite specific. William Denby's *Catacombs*, for instance, takes place in the early 1960s, and it achieves its sense of impending doom only if the reader already knows that John F. Kennedy will be assassinated when the events of the novel reach November 22, 1963. . . . Other assumptions are more general.[16]

Some assumptions are about the reader's knowledge of historical fact or information (as in Rabinowitz's example from *Catacombs*); others are about the reader's knowledge of literary conventions. In either case, the authorial audience is implied in the generic, rhetorical, cultural and stylistic literacies presupposed by the text – an indication of the audience that the author wanted or imagined (but, admittedly, may or may not in fact have reached).

In a vein similar to Rabinowitz, a special forum in the journal *Dante Studies* has analysed the projected audiences in and for Dante's minor works – in effect examining Dante's authorial audiences in those texts.[17] Looking at '[s]ubject matter and rhetorical style, not to mention direct addresses to the reader', the contributions to this forum tease out 'the image of the audience that the writer provides within the text itself'.[18] These projected images of Dante's audiences, while they vary from text to text and account for 'the great diversity of voices with which Dante wrote',[19] are nonetheless consistent in many respects. According to the contributors to the *Dante Studies* forum, Dante envisions 'a universal audience', extending far beyond his limited circle of family and friends, to every corner of Italy.[20] But at the same time, Dante anticipates a small, elite audience that is 'subtle' and 'noble at heart',[21] composed of the 'very few' who are 'qualified readers' of sophisticated writing.[22] In essence, Dante seeks a specialised, educated audience but casts his net widely in order to capture 'as many as are fit to receive his presentation of learning in the vernacular'.[23]

But as the *Dante Studies* forum itself concludes, Dante's desired audience here – a fourteenth-century audience uniquely 'fit to receive' his poetry – 'does not in fact exist' and did not in fact read his works.[24] Focusing on Dante's desired audience, then, fails to illuminate who Dante's real readers might have been. For this reason, both Rabinowitz's authorial audience and the projected images of Dante's readers explored in the *Dante Studies* forum are of limited usefulness. The concept of audiences envisioned by an author is fundamentally author-centred, focused on the author's assumptions, artistic choices, projections and intent. My focus is not on the author but instead on the text and reader. Rather than reconstruct the imaginary audiences that the author seeks in a text, I want to reconstruct the reader's experience of being hailed by the text, and I want to situate the reader's hailing in the context of the ideological frameworks within which readers likely experienced their subjectivity as they read. For such an endeavour, the author's knowledge and intent are insignificant. Whatever audience the author seeks or projects, the text interpellates any number of other readers whose subjective ideological responses may vary markedly from the author's expectations.

I suspect, however, that Dante himself understands readerly interpellation rather well. In the Statius episode of *Purgatorio* 21–2, Dante fictionalises Statius's reading of Virgil in terms that suggest something very like the interpellative process. Dante's Statius explicitly describes his subjectivity as developed through his reading of Virgil: 'Per te poeta fui, per te cristiano' (*Purg.* 22.73; 'Through you I was a poet, through you, a Christian'). More specifically, a particular moment in his reading of Virgil crucially hails Statius and recruits him to recognise and assert his subjectivity, making his eternal salvation possible: 'io drizzai mia cura, / quand'io intesi là dove tu chiame, / crucciato quasi a l'umana natura: / "Per che non reggi tu, o sacra fame / de l'oro, l'appetito de' mortali?"' (*Purg.* 22.37–41; 'I set right my focus, when I understood where you cried, as if vexed by human nature: "Where do you not rule, O accursed hunger for gold, the appetite of mortals?"'). As William Franke has noted, 'the phenomenon experienced by Statius – the reality that comes over him – in his encounter with Virgil's text is that of being personally addressed . . . highlighted through the personal pronoun . . . literally calling to him in his own existential situation with its specific risks'.[25] In essence, Statius is interpellated by Virgil's text and, as a result, is recruited as a repentant, Christian subject, whose ideological response to his interpellation is to change his sinful ways and be saved ('io drizzai mia cura').

Because of this portrayal of Statius's experience of reading, I credit Dante with considerable agency and awareness with respect to the interpellation that takes place in his poem. But Dante himself portrays an author's participation in his reader's interpellation as irrelevant. Virgil's text may be the site of Statius's salvific interpellation, but Virgil himself is wholly ignorant of the redemptive action of his poem. As Dante's Statius describes Virgil, 'Facesti come quei che va di notte, / che porta il lume dietro e sé non giova, / ma dopo sé fa le persone dotte' (*Purg.* 22.67–9; 'You did as the one who goes by night, who carries the light behind and does not benefit himself, but after himself makes the people wise'). Virgil's text has the power to interpellate Dante's Statius, but the author Virgil plays no conscious role in that interpellation and does not benefit from it himself. Similarly, by Dante's tacit admission, Dante's text may interpellate its reader without Dante's knowledge or intent, working mysteriously through the reader's own subjectivity and idiosyncratic ideological frameworks. So, even Dante himself seems to indicate that our focus should be on his text's hailing rather than on him as author.

As a specific test case for how Dante's poem interpellates its readers, then, I would like to focus on canto 5 of the *Inferno*. In a sense, canto 5 itself draws attention to hailing. The characters implicitly and explicitly hail each other throughout the canto. Minos explicitly hails Dante the Pilgrim: '"O tu che vieni al doloroso ospizio," / . . . "guarda com' entri e di cui tu ti fide"' (*Inf.* 5.16–19; '"O you who come to the grievous almshouse . . . watch how you enter and whom you trust"'). Dante the Pilgrim in turn hails Paolo and Francesca: '"O anime affannate / venite a noi parlar, s'altri nol niega!"' (*Inf.* 5.80–1; '"O breathless souls, come to speak to us, if no other denies it"'). Most importantly, the figure of Minos, we are told, hails all the sinners who enter hell and compels them to confess their sins and submit to judgement (that is, to acknowledge their subjectivity and take their proper place within hell's social hierarchy): 'quando l'anima mal nata / li vien dinanzi, tutta si confessa; / e quel conoscitor de le peccata / vede qual loco d'inferno è da essa; / cignesi con la coda tante volte / quantunque gradi vuol che giù sia messa' (*Inf.* 5.7–12; 'when the ill-born soul comes before him, all is confessed; and that expert on sin sees which place in hell is [proper] for the soul; he belts himself with his tail as many times as levels he wishes that the soul be placed below'). Essentially, all the sinners in hell are interpellated as subjects by Minos – almost perfect images of Althusser's 'free subjectivity, a center of initiatives, author of and responsible for its actions', and at the same time 'a subjected being, who submits to a higher authority, and is therefore stripped of all freedom except that of freely accepting his submission'.[26]

Dante's poem does not directly address or explicitly hail its reader in canto 5, but readers' imaginations have long been captured by the alluring image of the canto's lovers, Paolo and Francesca. Canto 5 is perhaps the most remembered – and scrutinised – canto of the entire *Commedia* and has been subject to a range of conflicting interpretations.[27] Within the canto, many images, events and characters no doubt have served as triggers for the interpellation of readers, but I would like to focus here on three bird images that occur within fifty lines of one another. Significantly for our purposes, birds are multivalent in fourteenth-century Italy – accruing sundry meanings within contexts ranging from bestiaries and scriptural exegesis to the poetry of Virgil and Guido Guinizelli.[28] While few of Dante's first readers are likely to have approached his bird images from the perspective of a naturalist (since birds for Dante's largely urban audience would have had primarily symbolic rather than biological value), Dante's readers, depending on their ideological framework, might interpret Dante's bird images in any number of different – even contradictory – ways. For at least two important groups in particular, the symbolic value of birds resonates particularly strongly – that is, for those educated in the tradition of Scholasticism and for devotees of the *dolce stil novo*. As a result, the bird images of *Inferno 5* are especially apt as touchstones for a discussion of the ideological reading subject in the *Commedia*.

The first bird image is that of 'li stornei' ('starlings') that fly away in winter 'a schiera larga e piena' (*Inf.* 5.40–1; 'in a long, full crowd'). Just five lines later, the second image is that of 'i gru' ('cranes'), which fly 'cantando lor lai, / faccendo in aere di sé lunga riga' (*Inf.* 5.46–7; 'singing their lays, making of themselves a long line in the air'). Dante uses both these images to describe the whirling swarm of 'i peccator carnali, / che la ragion sommettono al talento' (*Inf.* 5.38–9; 'carnal sinners, who submit reason to inclination'). And then forty-three lines later, Dante uses the third and final bird image to describe Paolo and Francesca as they leave the swarm of lustful souls to speak to Dante and Virgil: 'Quali colombe dal disio chiamate / con l'ali alzate e ferme al dolce nido / vegnon per l'aere, dal voler portate; / cotali uscir de la schiera ov' è Dido' (*Inf.* 5.82–5; 'As doves called by desire, with wings raised and steady, come to the sweet nest through the air, conducted by their will, so these exited the multitude where Dido is'). The presence of these three bird images, so close together, demands a response of readerly subjectivity and interpretation, which necessarily derives from and confirms the reader's larger subjectivity and interpellation.

Given the dominance of Scholasticism in medieval education, Dante's readers are all in a sense inevitably Scholastic readers, and the bird images of *Inferno 5* hail a Scholastic reader by inviting engagement in Scholastic allegorical interpretation. Because Dante's text is plainly philosophical in scope, all elements of the text accrue philosophical significance that a Scholastic reader is impelled, simply by the presence of a suggestive word or image, to identify and construe. In Scholastic allegorical interpretation, '[t]here are many methods, some of which are handed down in fixed patterns', but in all cases 'the images and metaphors used are generally intended to reveal something hidden, to open up a new dimension of understanding'.[29] Dante's birds hail the Scholastic reader to allegorise the concrete elements of the avian images to '"mean" something else above and beyond the historical [or literal] context'.[30] Significantly, this method of reading is precisely the method that Dante himself describes and endorses in the *Convivio* as relevant to his earlier poetry: 'E con ciò sia cosa che la vera intenzione mia fosse altra che quella che di fuori mostrano le canzoni predette, per allegorica esposizione quelle intendo mostrare, appresso la litterale istoria ragionata' (*Conv.* 1.1.18; 'And since my true intention was other than that which the aforementioned *canzoni* reveal from the outside, I intend to show these [true intentions] through allegorical exposition, after the literal story is discussed'; cf. *Conv.* 1.2.17).

Scholastic allegorical interpretation generally takes the form of 'commentary on normative texts'.[31] Not surprisingly, then, given the centrality of commentary to Scholastic interpretive practice, the fourteenth-century commentaries on Dante's poem (like Dante's self-commentary in the *Convivio*) tend to exhibit the interpretive and ideological assumptions of Scholasticism when contemplating the bird images of *Inferno* 5, seeing the birds as allegorically reflecting and reinforcing the moral purpose of Dante's depiction of the lustful souls in hell. Benvenuto da Imola, for example, describes the starlings as

> animalia gregalia, et ita amantes semper incedunt sociati. Sturni sunt luxuriosi, sicut naturaliter aves; sturni sunt leves, et tales sunt amorosi; sturni transeunt ad partes calidas quo calor libidinis vocat eos, et fugiunt frigidas, ubi non sunt mulieres pulcrae, et si inveniunt vineam plenam dulcibus uvis sine custode, male populantur eam. (*ad Inf.* 5.40–3)
>
> sociable animals, and similarly lovers always approach friends. Starlings are lustful, like birds naturally; starlings are light, and such are the amorous; starlings cross to warm parts to which the heat of their lust calls them, and flee cold places, where pretty females are not, and if they discover a bower full of sweet grapes without a guard, they wickedly plunder it.[32]

Similarly, of the cranes, L'Ottimo Commento writes that they 'sono molt[o] lussuriosi; e nota che generalmente ogni uccello e lussurioso; pero la loro carne accende il fuoco della libidine' (*ad Inf.* 5.46–51; 'are very lustful; and note that generally every bird is lustful; hence their flesh lights the fire of the libido'). Of the doves, the Codice cassinese notes, 'Columba est avis dedicata veneri que sublatis pullis a loco etiam in eodem nidificat non ostante damno propter luxuriam suam ita amorosi non ostantibus damnis proprie infamie iterum ad eamdem amasiam revertuntur' (*ad Inf.* 5.82; 'The dove is a bird dedicated to Venus that, having raised its young from a place, yet nests in that self-same place despite condemnation for its lustfulness; so amorous ones, despite being damned by their own infamy, go back again to the self-same lover'). Likewise, Benvenuto da Imola observes that

> columbae sunt dedicatae Veneri, quae est mater Amoris, et Dea luxuriae, quoniam sunt aves luxuriosissimae. . . . Adhuc columba est nuncia pacis, societatis amica, mansueta, blanda, humilis, tractabilis et tales requirit

amor. Imo tanta est vis amoris, qui reddit serpentes blandos, sicut scribit Ambrosius in Exameron de Murena, quae effundit venendum. (*ad Inf.* 5.82–7)

doves are dedicated to Venus, who is mother of Love, and Goddess of Lust, because birds are most lustful . . . . Hitherto, the dove is messenger of peace, friend of fellowship, gentle, appealing, humble, tractable – and love asks for such qualities. But such is love, which renders serpents appealing (as Ambrosius writes in the *Exameron de Murena*), the power of which spews poison.

The uniformly moralistic tone in these commentaries is not coincidental. Ideologically, orthodoxy – both religious and social – is central to Scholasticism. Despite the occasional unorthodox individual among the Schoolmen (e.g., William of Okham, Ubertino da Casale and John Wycliffe), orthodoxy is so central to Scholastic thinking that, when an author seems to stray from received orthodox truth, 'one then resorts to the technique of *exponere reverenter*: One pays the necessary respect to the authority . . . by looking for a good meaning of the text, by advocating another opinion'[33] – often with 'recourse to allegorical interpretation . . . in order to avoid the problem of a factual error at the literal level'.[34] No reliable authority can deviate from truth, because truth is clear, singular and invariable. Within Scholastic philosophy and theology,

> factual questions are assumed to be answerable. Originally it was most often a matter of harmonizing discrepancies between authorities. Given the many different opinions, this is increasingly replaced by the question about the truth of a matter. Wherever the decisive method is logical-rational examination, optimism prevails that the truth can be found, even in the multiplicity of opinions.[35]

But if truth can be found, even in the multiplicity of opinions (that is, if truth's uniformity is assumed as a fundamental tenet), its uniformity can – and must – also be enforced as orthodoxy. Indeed, Scholasticism's focus on disputation as a pedagogical method not only served 'to find truth' but also 'to eliminate error'.[36]

Given the institutional Church's recognised role in determining and safeguarding orthodoxy in the Middle Ages, Scholasticism's ideology of orthodoxy inextricably links the Schoolmen to the maintenance of the institutional Church's authority and interests. Indeed, the institutional Church seems to have seen and exploited Scholasticism in exactly this way. According to Dante's contemporary Marsilius of Padua, bishops . . . subject to themselves colleges of learned men, taking them away from the secular rulers, and use them as no slight but rather very powerful instruments for perpetrating and defending their usurpations against the secular rulers. For since these learned men are unwilling to lose their professional titles, desiring the ease and glory resulting from possession of them, and believing that they have been obtained only by the authority of the Roman or other bishops, they carry out the bishops' wishes and oppose any persons, whether secular rulers or subjects, who contradict what they consider to be the authority of these bishops.[37]

Scholastic orthodoxy becomes a stick with which to enforce the institutional Church's power against perceived encroachments by secular authorities, the very encroachments that had been one of the sources of conflict between Guelphs and Ghibellines in Dante's Italy.

Yet, the readers hailed by Dante's bird images in *Inferno* 5 are not homogeneous, adhering to a single, monolithic ideology. A second kind of ideological reading subject who is interpellated by Dante's birds is the devotee of the *dolce stil novo*, a school of thought that advocated '[t]he identification of gentility not with wealth and feudal right but with a refined capacity for love'.[38] Parallel to Scholasticism's support of the institutional Church against encroachments by secular rulers, the *stil novo* defined itself in opposition to secular Ghibelline aristocrats, who identified gentility with feudal right, as well as to Italy's old mercantile elites, who identified gentility with family wealth. As Justin Steinberg notes, for the Ghibelline poet Guittone d'Arezzo,

> there exists a natural vertical ordering to the universe, expressed in the inviolable divisions between heaven and earth, sacred and profane, the Virgin and the beloved, man and woman, animate and inanimate. In the historical period in question, it is not difficult to imagine how such unassailable categories might serve to legitimize by analogy other 'natural' hierarchies, such as those between ruler and ruled or even noble and notary.[39]

In opposition, stilnovistic writers, such as Guido Guinizelli, defy this 'natural' ordering of society. Indeed, 'Guinizelli's defense in "Al cor gentil" of philosophical [that is, stilnovistic] love poetry . . . is tied to a critique of those who claim an inherited right to rule by lineage, "per sclatta"'.[40] In the *canzone* explicated in the fourth book of the *Convivio*, Dante similarly speaks at length 'del valore / per lo qual veramente omo è gentile / riprovando 'l giudicio falso e vile / di quei che voglion che di gentilezza / sia principio ricchezza' ('Le dolci rime d'amor ch'i' solia', lines 13–17; 'of the quality through which truly a man is noble, refuting the false and base judgement of those who would that the origin of gentility is wealth'). Understandably, stilnovistic poetry and its ideology of gentility appeal to 'the cultural independence and newly achieved intellectual and political status of the upwardly mobile and newly educated' in Dante's Italy.[41]

Significantly for *Inferno* 5, stilnovistic poetry and its ideology of gentility are specifically associated with birds. As Robert Durling and Ronald Martinez point out, poetry had, by Dante's day, long associated birds with love: 'In the *Commedia* as in troubadour and *stilnuovo* lyrics the song and movement of birds is a canonical metaphor for desire, and especially desire in poetry'.[42] But more specifically, Guido Guinizelli, in what is universally acknowledged to be one of the most important manifestos of the *stil novo*, likens love in the gentle heart to birds in a forest, using a bird image to suggest the naturalness and fundamental equivalence of love and gentility: 'Al cor gentil rempaira sempre amore / come l'ausello in selva a la verdura; / né fe' amor anti che gentil core, / né gentil core anti ch'amor, natura' ('Al cor gentil', lines 1–4; 'Love repairs always to the gentle heart, like the bird in the forest to greenery; neither did nature make love before the gentle heart, nor the gentle heart before love').[43] In 'Omo ch'è saggio non corre leggero', moreover, Guinizelli responds to criticism of the *stil novo* by Bonagiunta da Lucca with a bird image, refuting Bonagiunta's reliance on social class and convention as arbiters of taste and morality, because 'Volan ausel' per air di straine guise / ed han diversi loro operamenti, / né tutti d'un volar né d'un ardire. / Dëo natura e 'l mondo in grado mise, / e fe' despari senni e intendimenti' (lines 9–13; 'Birds fly through the air in eccentric manners and have their various actions, neither all of one flight nor of one desire. God set nature and the world in rank, and created disparate judgements and intentions'). Birds are thus associated with unconventional virtue, innate refinement and social mobility.

To the stilnovistic reader, then, Dante's bird images elicit strong sympathetic associations, exalting refined sensibilities over social elites. Dante's birds hail the stilnovistic reader to identify strongly with refined feelings of tenderness and love and, by doing so, encourage a sense that love and refinement trump religious and political power. In their adultery, Paolo and Francesca defy orthodox social norms in favour of love, and the dove image that Dante associates with these adulterous lovers seems, in its stilnovistic associations, to validate their defiance. Dante's stilnovistic reader is thus hailed as a subject who believes in the ennobling power of love and is interpellated in an ideology that places love – and refined sensibilities – above all, but most especially above wealth, birth and religious orthodoxy. This ideological symbolism appeals to the very same audiences who admire Guinizelli's philosophical love poetry – audiences like the notaries of the *popolo* government in Bologna, a social group at odds with both Ghibelline aristocrats and the emerging merchant-banker elites, who, entrenched in Florence, were responsible for Dante's exile.

Boccaccio is an actual fourteenth-century reader whom Dante's poem interpellates in just this way. In response to Dante's portrayal of the lovers, Boccaccio creates an entire romance narrative, complete with deception and injustice, to exonerate Francesca. Francesca is used by her family and Gianciotto's to cement ties between the political elites of Ravenna and Rimini. But in Boccaccio's story (a complete fiction, born of Boccaccio's vivid stilnovistic imagination), Francesca refuses to submit to the powers that be. Boccaccio characterises Paolo as 'bello e piacevole uomo e costumato molto' ('a handsome and pleasing man and very well-mannered'), one who associates 'con altri gentili uomini' (*ad Inf.* 5.97–9; 'with other noble men'). Francesca, having been told by a 'buona femina' ('good woman') that the noble Paolo 'è colui che dee esser vostro marito' ('is the one who is to be your husband'), is unjustly tricked into marrying Gianciotto:

> E fatto poi artificiosamente il contratto delle sponsalizie e andatone la donna a Rimino, non s'avvide prima dello 'nganno che essa vide la mattina seguente al dì delle noze levare da lato a sé Gian Ciotto; di che si dee credere che ella, vedendosi ingannata, isdegnasse, né perciò rimovesse dell'animo suo l'amore già postovi verso Polo. (*ad Inf.* 5.97–9)

> And after the marriage contract was cunningly made and the lady went to Rimini, she was not first aware of the deception until she saw, on the morning of the day following the wedding, Gianciotto rise at her side; from which it may be seen that she, seeing herself deceived, was furious, nor for this reason would she remove the love of her soul already placed in Paolo.

While the lovers suffer for their defiance of authority, Boccaccio's portrayal clearly sympathises with Francesca's priorities. Love and refined sensibilities are pure and decent; aristocratic authority and economic power are corrupt and unjust.

The difference here between the stilnovistic reader's sympathetic perception of the Francesca episode and the moralistic orthodoxy of Scholastic commentators, actively juxtaposed by the contrasting interpellations triggered by Dante's bird images, serves to unsettle both Scholasticism and the *stil novo* as ideological frameworks for approaching *Inferno* 5. Dante himself, by the time that he writes the *Commedia*, has little reason to espouse or advance the ideologies of either Scholasticism or the *stil novo*. Dante, an exile from Florence as a result of the machinations of papal allies among the Florentine Guelphs, hardly has reason to celebrate the institutional Church or its orthodox, clerical Scholasticism, for example. Sounding very much like Marsilius of Padua (who opined that 'learned men are unwilling to lose their professional titles, desiring the ease and glory resulting from possession of them'[44]) Dante in the *Convivio* has few kind words for Scholastics or Scholastic-trained public officials in Italy (precisely the educators, notaries and jurists who were Dante's early Scholastic commentators):

> tanto sono pronti ad avarizia, che da ogni nobilitate d'animo li rimuove. . . . E a vituperio di loro dico che non si deono chiamare litterati, però che non acquistano la lettera per lo suo uso, ma in quanto per quella guadagnano denari o dignitate. (1.9.2–3)

> they are so prone to avarice that it removes all nobility of soul. . . . And to the shame of them, I say that they should not be called lettered, because they do not acquire the knowledge of letters for its own use but insofar as through letters they gain money and dignities.

While Dante may appreciate Scholastic allegorical interpretation as a hermeneutic practice (e.g. *Convivio* 1.1.18 and 1.2.17), he has little truck with Scholastics (or their pupils) as a social class.

For Scholastic readers, *Inferno* 5 calls for allegorical interpretation of its bird (and other) images, but Dante's final bird image flagrantly flaunts orthodoxy, undermining the very foundations of Scholastic ideology. Dante specifically draws attention to the figure of Dido in the dove image that characterises Paolo and Francesca: 'Quali colombe dal disio chiamate / con l'ali alzate e ferme al dolce nido / vegnon per l'aere, dal voler portate; / cotali uscir de la schiera ov' è Dido' (*Inf.* 5.82–5; 'As doves called by desire, with wings raised and steady, come to the sweet nest through the air, conducted by their will, so these exited the multitude where Dido is'). But the presence of Virgil's Dido in the canto – 'colei che s'ancise amorosa, / e ruppe fede al cener di Sicheo' (*Inf.* 5.61–2; 'she who killed herself for love, and broke faith with the ashes of Sichaeus') – flies in the face of accepted Scholastic orthodoxy (based on the authority of the likes of Jerome, Augustine and Eusebius) that Dido and Aeneas did not live in the same time period, and so could never have met, as Virgil's poem falsely claims. Benvenuto da Imola, like most of Dante's early

Scholastic commentators (including Guido da Pisa, Pietro di Dante and Boccaccio), notes the problem of Dido's fictitious history with Aeneas and Dante's heterodoxy here:

> Quomodo autem Dido fuerit amorata de Enea, et quomodo se occiderit propter eius recessum, patet eleganter apud Virgilium, et quotidie vulgi ore celebratur. Sed hic est attente notandum quod istud, quod fingit Virgilius, nunquam fuit factum, neque possibile fieri. . . . Nunc ad propositum autor ponit Didonem amorosam, quia sequitur Virgilium, et fingit Virgilium hoc dicere. (*ad Inf.* 5.61)

> How Dido fell in love with Aeneas and how she killed herself because of his slipping away is told elegantly by Virgil and is discussed every day in the mouth of the vulgar. But it is to be carefully observed that these events, which Virgil feigns, were never accomplished, nor could be possible. . . . But now to the purpose, our author posits an amorous Dido, because he follows Virgil, and Virgil lied to say this.

Francesco da Buti condemns Dante soundly for his apostasy:

> Virgilio fece molto male a dare tale infamia a si onesta donna, per fare bella la sua poesia; e lo nostro autore Dante fece peggio a seguitarlo in questo, che credo che avesse veduto Geronimo e li altri che di cio parlano: potrebbesi scusare; ma le scuse non sono sofficienti. (*ad Inf.* 5.52–69)

> Virgil does great wrong in giving such dishonour to so honest a lady, in order to make his poetry beautiful; and our author Dante does worse in following in this, for I believe that he had seen Jerome and the others that spoke of this: he could be excused; but the excuses are not sufficient.

To Francesco and Benvenuto, Dante is dishonest and blameworthy for following the lies of a poet rather than the truth of orthodox Scholastic authorities. Dante's poem thus hails Scholastic readers to read allegorically but then frustrates their ideology of censorious orthodoxy.

Interestingly, given his stilnovistic sympathy for Francesca, Boccaccio does not share the censorious orthodoxy of Benvenuto da Imola and Francesco da Buti when it comes to Dante's portrayal of Dido:

> Fu adunque Dido onesta donna e, per non romper fede al cener di Siccheo, s'uccise. Ma l'autore seguita qui, come in assai cose fa, l'oppinion di Virgilio, e per questo si convien sostenere. (*ad Inf.* 5.61–2)

> So Dido was an honest woman and, in order not to break faith with the ashes of Sichaeus, killed herself. But our author follows here, as he does

in many things, the opinion of Virgil, and for this reason it behoofs us to be supportive.

Boccaccio's sanguine support for Dante's inaccurate portrayal of Dido does not, however, vindicate a stilnovistic reading of the canto. Dante's poem unsettles stilnovistic readers as readily as Scholastics, and Dante himself has little reason by the time of the *Commedia*'s composition for continued loyalty to the *stil novo*. Lino Pertile and others have traced the signs of Dante's growing disillusionment with the ideology of the *stil novo* and his rapprochement with the Ghibellines during his lifetime.[45] Dante's own poem, however, perhaps most authoritatively undermines a sympathetic stilnovistic reading of Francesca; as Saverio Bellomo notes, 'after all, Francesca is in hell'.[46]

To a refined, stilnovistic reader, in fact, Dante's portrayal of Francesca is problematic, to say the least. When Francesca says that she and Paolo met to read a French romance and 'soli eravamo e sanza alcun sospetto' (*Inf.* 5.129; 'alone we were and without any suspicion'), even sympathetic Boccaccio somewhat cuttingly observes, 'Scrive l'autore tre cose, ciascuna per se medesima potente ad inducere a disonestamente adoperare un uomo e una femina che insieme sieno: cioè leggere gli amori d'alcuni, l'esser soli e l'esser senza sospetto d'alcuno impedimento' (*ad Inf.* 5.129; 'Our author writes three things, each by itself sufficient to induce a man and a woman together to behave dishonestly: that is, reading the loves of others, being alone, and being without suspicion of any impediment'). More importantly, the use of the image of doves in connection with the lovers raises serious questions for a refined, non-Scholastic reader, since, according to popular medieval bestiaries, doves are icons of genteel behaviour – in sharp contrast to Francesca herself:

> Columba pro cantu utitur gemitu, quia quod libens fecit, plangendo gemit. Caret felle, id est irascibilitatis amaritudine. Instat osculis, quia delectatur in multitudine pacis. Gregatim volat, quia conventus amat. Non vivit ex raptu, quia non detrahit proximo. . . . Qui igitur has naturas habet, assumat sibi contemplationis alas, quibus ad cœlum volet.
>
> The dove uses a sigh for its song, because it mourns by lamenting what it did gladly. It lacks bile, that is, the bitterness of anger. It pursues kisses, because it delights in an abundance of peace. It flies in flocks, because it loves community. It does not live by theft, because it does not take away from its neighbour. . . . Who therefore has these qualities, let him assume for himself the wings of contemplation, with which he may fly to heaven.[47]

Where the dove lacks 'irascibilitatis amaritudine' ('the bitterness of anger'), for example, Francesca bitterly condemns her husband in anger (*Inf.* 5.107), and where the dove laments 'quod libens fecit' ('what it did gladly'), Francesca laments not what she did but 'ricordarsi del tempo felice / ne la miseria' (*Inf.* 5.122–3; 'remembering the time of happiness in misery') and ''l modo' of her death, which 'ancor m'offende' (*Inf.* 5.102; 'the manner still offends me'). In essence, the dove is refined gentility itself, but Francesca, despite her stilnovistic rhetoric, is entirely un-dove-like at every turn.

Dante's poem, then, hails both stilnovistic and Scholastic readers but, in the same breath, frustrates the smooth interpellation of those readers. The poem itself contradicts their expectations and inclinations as subjects – whether with respect to genteel refinement or to moral orthodoxy. From a Scholastic or stilnovistic perspective, the text is difficult and problematic to interpret, forcing the reading subject to struggle and reconsider or, alternatively, to misconstrue and condemn. We should not be surprised that some misconstrue, since Dante himself suggests that few readers possess the necessary capacity or the right disposition to read his writing productively. Already in his stilnovistic days, Dante says of one of his most important *canzoni* that 'chi non è di tanto ingegno che . . . la possa intendere, a me non dispiace se la mi lascia stare' (*Vita Nuova* 19.22; 'whoever does not have sufficient wit to be able to understand it . . . would not displease me if he let [the poem] be on my behalf'). In the *Paradiso*, Dante similarly advises his less capable readers: 'O voi che siete in piccioletta barca, / desiderosi d'ascoltar, sequiti / dietro al mio legno che cantando varca, / tornate a riveder li vostri liti: / non vi mettete in pelago, ché forse, / perdendo me, rimarreste smarriti' (*Par.* 2.1–6; 'O you who are in a tiny little boat, eager to hear, having followed after my bark that singing crosses, turn to see your shores again: don't put yourself in danger, because perhaps, losing me, you may remain forever lost'). In this sense, Dante's poem seems to hail its readers in a different vein entirely, interpellating what we might call an elite, discerning reader – one who reflects rather than simply reacts and who pilots an analytical boat that is sufficiently big and deft (a reader, as it happens, who is not unlike the projected reader in Dante's minor works).

Francesca perhaps gives, by way of negative example, an indication of the precise nature of the 'ingegno' required of a properly discerning reader, for she is a bad reader whose 'piccioletta barca' has apparently capsized. Francesca's poor reading skills have become something of a commonplace among Dante scholars today.[48] Elena Lombardi, in contrast to most scholars, argues that Francesca is no worse a reader than Statius, since both engage in misreading and 'misreading is not a crime in Dante and medieval culture'.[49] But Francesca's poor skills as a reader are not simply a matter of misreading but of taking away entirely the wrong lesson from her reading. Lombardi rightly points out that 'One must, according to Dante, misread potentially perilous texts such as pagan poetry and romance, in order to find one's own direction'.[50] But for Dante, the direction that one finds must be a good one – one that leads away from error and towards salvation. As Martin Eisner observes, 'the responsibility for determining the moral value of a work ultimately lies with the reader'.[51] When Statius misreads Virgil, the direction and moral value that he finds initiate his faith and repentance, allowing him to right himself (*Purg.* 22.38). In contrast, Francesca's misreading of stilnovistic poetry and French romance leads her in quite the opposite direction – away from faith and repentance and towards delusion, manipulation and error: 'Per più fïate li occhi ci sospinse / quella lettura, e scolorocci il viso' (*Inf.* 5.130–1; 'Many times that reading urged our eyes together and drained our face of colour'), until 'quel giorno più non vi leggemmo avante' (*Inf.* 5.138; 'that day we read there no further').

The success of a discerning reader, then, is primarily a matter of right disposition – that is, of sufficient 'ingegno', with proper moral perspective so as to be able to glean from one's reading the right lesson, whether or not that lesson is intended by the text's author. In this characterisation of successful reading, Dante seems to be following Augustine. According to Augustine, an author's intentions do not matter:

> Dum ergo quisque conatur id sentire in Scripturis sanctis, quod in eis sensit ille qui scripsit; quid mali est si hoc sentiat, quod tu, lux omnium veridicarum mentium, ostendis verum esse, etiamsi hoc non sensit ille quem legit; cum et ille verum, nec tamen hoc senserit? (*Confessions* 12.18.27)

> Provided, therefore, that each person tries to ascertain in the holy scriptures the meaning the author intended, what harm is there if a reader holds an opinion which you, the light of all truthful minds, show to be true, even though it is not what was intended by the author, who himself meant something true, but not exactly that?[52]

Neither does rigid orthodoxy matter, since as long as different interpretations do not contradict core truths or lead the reader astray from proper moral foundations, all interpretations are equally valid:

> Ita cum alius dixerit, Hoc sensit quod ego; et alius, Imo illud quod ego; religiosius me arbitror dicere, Cur non utrumque potius, si utrumque

> verum est? Et si quid tertium, et si quid quartum, et si quid omnino aliud verum quispiam in his verbis videt; cur non illa omnia vidisse credatur? (*Confessions* 12.31.42)
>
> Accordingly when anyone claims, 'He meant what I say,' and another retorts, 'No, rather what I find there,' I think that I will be answering in a more religious spirit if I say, 'Why not both, if both are true? And if there is a third possibility, and a fourth, and if someone else sees an entirely different meaning in these words, why should we not think that he was aware of all of them?'

As in Dante's portrayal of Statius, what matters to Augustine is what will have greatest effect on the reader's moral development:

> Ego certe, quod interpidus de corde meo pronuntio, si ad culmen auctoritatis aliquid scriberem; sic mallem scribere, ut quod veri quisque de his rebus capere posset, mea verba resonarent, quam ut unam veram sententiam ad hoc apertius ponerem, ut excluderem cæteras, quarum falsitas me non posset offendere. (*Confessions* 12.31.42)
>
> Of this I am certain, and I am not afraid to declare it from my heart, that if I had to write something to which the highest authority would be attributed, I would rather write it in such a way that my words would reinforce for each reader whatever truth he was able to grasp about these matters, than express a single idea so unambiguously as to exclude others, provided these did not offend me by their falsehood.

But each reader's grasp of truth depends upon that reader's disposition:

> This is the epiphany of 8.12.29 where [Augustine] recognizes God in himself, knowing that he would not be able to recognize Him if He had not been within Augustine already. This epiphany is triggered by a book, Augustine opening the Bible to a random passage and finding the passage's meaning originating inside him (the answer that all his questions presumed).[53]

For Augustine, as for Dante, one must be properly disposed – already have God within – in order to be able to interpret one's reading productively. Only when one is so disposed does one construe rightly.

In aligning himself with Augustine in this way, Dante is in company with the Franciscan reformers of his day. As an antidote to the new Aristotelianism that dominated Scholastic philosophy in the thirteenth century (with its focus on precise philosophical method and 'scientific' orthodoxy), Franciscan reformers such as Bonaventure sought to preserve and revive the Neoplatonic tradition of Augustine.⁵⁴ In that vein, early Franciscan theology emphasises the role of proper disposition – and the individual's susceptibility to right influences – in the process of conversion and salvation:

> Humans cannot dispose themselves adequately for grace, so the required disposition must be effected by God. God will, however, effect this disposition, if humans do *quod in se est*. John [of La Rochelle] uses Alan of Lille's analogy of the opening of a shutter to illustrate this point: the opening of the shutter permits the light of the sun to dispel darkness, just as the act of doing *quod in se est* permits the grace of God to dispel sin. Although humans do not have the power to dispel darkness, they do have the power to initiate a course of action which has this effect, by opening a shutter and thus removing the obstacle to the sun's rays.⁵⁵

Given this understanding of proper disposition (as a matter of 'opening a shutter'), the Franciscan reformers, in their dedication to an ideology of poverty, saw the corruption of medieval society and the Church as a matter of a wilful disposition to greed: 'Charity as the right order of love is against the perverse form of love, cupidity, which is rooted in a sinful disposition of the will and occasions obstacles to good'.⁵⁶

The reformers, especially the Spiritual Franciscans, soon found themselves at odds with the papacy because of this ideology. Many of the Spiritual Franciscans opposed the rise of Boniface VIII, Dante's own great papal enemy,⁵⁷ and, as Nick Havely notes, 'both Spirituals and "Michaelists" (like William of Ockham) were quite ready to affirm that [Pope John XXII] was not a Catholic'.⁵⁸ Tensions between the papacy and the Franciscan order arose out of the reformers' increasingly ideological preoccupation with

> the role of religious orders (especially the Franciscans), the leadership of the Church, and 'a desire to return the clergy to the rigorous discipline of early monastic founders or of the early apostolic Church itself, with particular emphasis on poverty and simplicity of life.'⁵⁹

These same concerns preoccupy Dante and underlie his criticism of both papacy and clergy throughout the *Commedia*; for example, 'la vostra avarizia il mondo attrista, / calcando i buoni e sollevando i pravi. / Di voi pastor s'accorse il Vangelista, / quando colei che siede sopra l'acque / puttaneggiar coi regi a lui fu vista' (*Inf.* 19.104–8; 'your greed saddens the world, treading on the good and raising the depraved. The Evangelist had you shepherds in mind when he saw the one who sits upon the water whore herself with kings').

Dante's poem, then, also hails its readers as elite, discerning subjects with proper disposition, interpellating its audience within an ideology of Augustinian Neoplatonism and Franciscan reformism. In this respect, Dante's bird images in *Inferno* 5 are once again pivotal, because birds, especially doves, hold a special place in Franciscan narrative and art – as symbols precisely of right disposition and poverty. Francis himself once famously preached to 'a very great number of birds of various kinds ... namely, doves, crows, and some others popularly called daws'.[60] This episode in Francis's life was so central to Franciscan hagiography that '[t]he earliest extant mural paintings' of the life of Saint Francis in 'the lower church of San Francesco in Assisi' included Francis's sermon to the birds as one of just five scenes depicted in the nave frescoes.[61] The thirteenth-century Bardi dossal in Florence similarly includes the preaching to the birds among twenty episodes from the life of Francis.[62] In all these narrative and visual depictions, moreover, the birds embody Franciscan ideals of innocence and poverty, serving as models of the humility and apostolic discipline that Franciscans called on the Church as a whole to embrace. According to Thomas of Celano's Francis, the birds 'neither sow nor reap' but God 'nevertheless protects and governs you without any solicitude on your part'.[63]

Dante's invocation of doves in *Inferno* 5, then, recruits the elite, properly disposed, discerning reader to recognise the secular paltriness of the stilnovistic ideology of gentility, as well as the reductive rigidity of Scholasticism's ideology of orthodoxy. Francesca's stilnovistic pretensions to the refinement and genteel sensitivity of doves pale in comparison with Francis's simple concern for simple birds to whom he preaches so simply and feelingly of poverty. But the smug, unyielding morality of Dante's Scholastic commentators equally pales in comparison with Francis's genuine humility and 'great fervor and great tenderness toward lower and irrational creatures'.[64] In hailing but frustrating stilnovistic and Scholastic readers as subjects, Dante's poem interpellates its reader to open the shutter to right subjectivity and adopt a Franciscan ideology of social and religious reform.

Notes

1. Louis Althusser, *Lenin and Philosophy and Other Essays*, trans. Ben Brewster (New York: Monthly Review, 1971), p. 173.
2. All quotations from Dante's works are taken from the Princeton Dante

Project <http://etcweb.princeton.edu/dante/pdp> (last accessed 5 August 2019). All English translations from Dante's Italian or Latin are my own.
3. Justin Steinberg, *Accounting for Dante: Urban Readers and Writers in Late Medieval Italy* (Notre Dame: University of Notre Dame Press, 2007), p. 1.
4. Rhiannon Daniels, *Boccaccio and the Book: Production and Reading in Italy 1340–1520* (London: Legenda, 2009), p. 1.
5. Ibid.
6. Elena Lombardi, *The Wings of the Doves: Love and Desire in Dante and Medieval Culture* (Montreal: McGill-Queen's University Press, 2012), pp. 212–13.
7. John Ahern, 'What Did the First Copies of the *Comedy* Look Like?', in Teodolinda Barolini and H. Wayne Storey (eds), *Dante for the New Millennium* (New York: Fordham University Press, 2003), p. 9.
8. Ibid., pp. 1–15, and John Ahern, 'Singing the Book: Orality in the Reception of Dante's *Comedy*', in Amilcare A. Iannucci (ed.), *Dante: Contemporary Perspectives* (Toronto: University of Toronto Press, 1997), pp. 214–39.
9. Steinberg, *Accounting for Dante*, p. 5.
10. Steven Botterill, 'Reading, Writing, and Speech in the Fourteenth- and Fifteenth-Century Commentaries on Dante's *Comedy*', in Paola Nasti and Claudia Rossignoli (eds), *Interpreting Dante: Essays on the Traditions of Dante Commentary* (Notre Dame: University of Notre Dame Press, 2013), p. 26.
11. Saverio Bellomo, 'How to Read the Early Commentaries', in Nasti and Rossignoli (eds), *Interpreting Dante*, pp. 84–5.
12. Simon Gilson, 'Modes of Reading in Boccaccio's *Esposizioni sopra la Commedia*', in Nasti and Rossignoli (eds), *Interpreting Dante*, p. 251.
13. Ibid.
14. Althusser, *Lenin and Philosophy and Other Essays*, p. 174.
15. Peter J. Rabinowitz, *Before Reading: Narrative Conventions and the Politics of Interpretation* (Ithaca: Cornell University Press, 1987), p. 21, original emphasis.
16. Ibid.
17. John Ahern, 'The New Life of the Book: The Implied Reader of the *Vita Nuova*', *Dante Studies*, 110 (1992), pp. 1–16; Richard Lansing, 'Dante's Intended Audience in the *Convivio*', *Dante Studies*, 110 (1992), pp. 17–24; Robert Durling, 'The Audience(s) of the *De vulgari eloquentia* and the *Petrose*', *Dante Studies*, 110 (1992), pp. 25–35; and Richard Kay, 'The Intended Readers of Dante's *Monarchia*', *Dante Studies*, 110 (1992), pp. 37–44.
18. Lansing, 'Dante's Intended Audience in the *Convivio*', p. 17.
19. Kay, 'The Intended Readers of Dante's *Monarchia*', p. 37.
20. Durling, 'The Audience(s) of the *De vulgari eloquentia* and the *Petrose*', p. 29; see also Ahern, 'The New Life of the Book', p. 8.

21. Ahern, 'The New Life of the Book', p. 10; Durling, 'The Audience(s) of the *De vulgari eloquentia* and the *Petrose*', p. 30.
22. Durling, 'The Audience(s) of the *De vulgari eloquentia* and the *Petrose*', p. 29.
23. Lansing, 'Dante's Intended Audience in the *Convivio*', p. 20.
24. Durling, 'The Audience(s) of the *De vulgari eloquentia* and the *Petrose*', p. 29.
25. William Franke, *Dante's Interpretive Journey* (Chicago: University of Chicago Press, 1996), p. 201.
26. Althusser, *Lenin and Philosophy and Other Essays*, p. 182.
27. Lombardi, *The Wings of the Doves*, p. 9.
28. Ibid., pp. 90–6.
29. Ulrich G. Leinsle, *Introduction to Scholastic Theology*, trans. Michael J. Miller (Washington, DC: Catholic University of American Press, 2010), p. 50.
30. Ibid.
31. Ibid., p. 12.
32. All quotations from Dante's early commentators are taken from the Dartmouth Dante Project <http://dante.dartmouth.edu> (lasted accessed 5 August 2019). All English translations of the commentators' Italian or Latin are my own.
33. Leinsle, *Introduction to Scholastic Theology*, p. 40.
34. Robert Wilson, 'Allegory as Avoidance in Dante's Early Commentators: "bella menzogna" to "roza corteccia"', in Nasti and Rossignoli (eds), *Interpreting Dante*, p. 30.
35. Leinsle, *Introduction to Scholastic Theology*, p. 40.
36. Alex J. Novikoff, *The Medieval Culture of Disputation: Pedagogy, Practice, and Performance* (Philadelphia: University of Pennsylvania Press, 2013), p. 170.
37. Marsilius of Padua, *The Defender of Peace*, trans. Alan Gewirth (New York: Columbia University Press, 1956), vol. II, p. 298.
38. Alison Cornish, 'A Lady Asks: The Gender of Vulgarization in Late Medieval Italy', *PMLA*, 115 (2000), p. 173.
39. Steinberg, *Accounting for Dante*, p. 43.
40. Ibid.
41. Ibid., p. 5.
42. Robert M. Durling and Ronald L. Martinez, *Time and the Crystal: Studies in Dante's* Rime Petrose (Berkeley: University of California Press, 1990), p. 203.
43. My text for Guinizelli's poems is *Poeti del duecento*, 2 vols, ed. Gianfranco Contini (Milan: Ricciardi, 1960). All English translations of Guinizelli's Italian are my own.
44. Marsilius of Padua, *The Defender of Peace*, vol. II, p. 298.
45. Lino Pertile, 'Does the *Stilnovo* Go to Heaven?', in Barolini and Storey (eds), *Dante for the New Millennium*, pp. 104, 113; Robert Hollander,

'Dante and Cino da Pistoia', *Dante Studies*, 110 (1992), p. 201; Marco Santagata, *Dante: The Story of His Life*, trans. Richard Dixon (Cambridge, MA: Belknap Press, 2016), pp. 274–5.
46. Bellomo, 'How to Read the Early Commentators', p. 106.
47. Pseudo-Hugh of Saint Victor, *De Bestiis et Aliis Rebus*, in Jacques-Paul Migne (ed.), *Patrologia Latina* (Paris: Migne, 1844–55), vol. CLXXVII, cols 19–20. The English translation of the original Latin is my own.
48. For example, Christoph Irmscher, 'Reading for Our Delight', *Dante Studies*, 128 (2010), pp. 49–50.
49. Lombardi, *The Wings of the Doves*, p. 215.
50. Ibid.
51. Martin Eisner, 'The Word Made Flesh in *Inferno* 5: Francesca Reading and the Figure of the Annunciation', *Dante Studies*, 131 (2013), p. 62.
52. My text for Augustine's *Confessions* is Migne (ed.), *Patrologia Latina*, vol. XXXII, cols 659–868. English translations are from *The Works of Saint Augustine: A Translation for the 21st Century*, ed. John E. Rotelle (Hyde Park: New City Press, 1990–), part 1, vol. I.
53. Stanley W. Levers, 'From Revelation to Dilation in Dante's *Studio*', *Dante Studies*, 134 (2016), pp. 11–12.
54. Zygmunt G. Barański, 'Dante's Signs: An Introduction to Medieval Semiotics and Dante', in John C. Barnes and Cormac Ó Cuilleanáin (eds), *Dante and the Middle Ages: Literary and Historical Essays* (Dublin: Irish Academic Press, 1995), pp. 150–1.
55. Alister E. McGrath, *Iustitia Dei: A History of the Christian Doctrine of Justification*, 3rd edition (Cambridge: Cambridge University Press, 2005), p. 109.
56. Virpi Mäkinen, *Property Rights in the Late Medieval Discussion of Franciscan Poverty* (Leuven: Peeters, 2001), p. 88.
57. Dabney G. Park, 'The Good, the Bad, and the Ugly: What Dante Says about Bonaventure of Bagnoregio, Matthew of Acquasparta, and Ubertino da Casale', *Dante Studies*, 132 (2014), p. 275.
58. Nick Havely, *Dante and the Franciscans: Poverty and the Papacy in the 'Commedia'* (Cambridge: Cambridge University Press, 2004), p. 42.
59. Ibid., pp. 184–5. Havely is quoting K. Kerny-Fulton, *Reformist Apocalypticism and 'Piers Plowman'* (Cambridge: Cambridge University Press, 1990), p. 9.
60. Thomas of Celano, *Vita Beati Francisci* 21.58, in *Saint Francis of Assisi*, trans. Placid Hermann (Chicago: Franciscan Herald Press, 1963), p. 53.
61. Louise Bourdua, *The Franciscans and Art Patronage in Late Medieval Italy* (Cambridge: Cambridge University Press, 2004), p. 2.
62. John Tolan, 'Mendicants and Muslims in Dante's Florence', *Dante Studies*, 125 (2007), pp. 234–8.
63. Thomas of Celano, *Vita Beati Francisci* 21.58, in *Saint Francis of Assisi*, p. 54.
64. Ibid., p. 53.

Chapter 5

The Unreadable *Book of Margery Kempe*

Ashley R. Ott

> With my grace I sometimes act with you as I do with the sun. Sometimes, as you know, the sun shines broadly so that many people can see it, and sometimes it is hidden under a cloud so that people cannot see it, and yet it is the sun nevertheless in its heat and in its brightness. And this is how I act with you and with my chosen souls.[1]

The *Book of Margery Kempe* (British Library, MS Additional 61823), which retrospectively acquired its name from Wynkyn de Worde's 1501 printed version, *A schorte treatyse of contemplacyon taught by our lorde Ihesu cryste, or taken out of the boke of Margerie kempe of Lynn*, is a text whose author is deeply concerned with its readability. The *Book* presents spiritual encounters as both readable events and as opportunities for decipherment. Though Kempe certainly did not intend that her words should prove difficult to read, Christ's analogy quoted at the start of this chapter, which places the visibility or hiddenness of the sun in equal stride with how Christ interacts with his 'chosen souls', proves how divine interaction may sometimes be cloaked, hidden and difficult to interpret: this interaction vacillates between visibility and invisibility – the sun may shine so as to be visible to many or be clouded, though its 'heat' and its 'brightness' may still be sensed.

The lambent grace of Christ is cause for Margery's concern when an outpouring of tears or spiritual dialogue suddenly erupts or ceases (are these feelings divinely motivated? can she withstand the scorn and contempt of others?); moments of uncertainly and doubt are also analogous to one's ability to read Margery's *Book*, which is sometimes readable and sometimes unreadable to the second priest-scribe responsible for its completion. Unreadability, as I define it, includes any writing rendered illegible as a condition of the physical manuscript (through erasure, crossings out, deliberate textual effacing or edits), as well as any writing not easily comprehensible (because the letters are badly formed; or because the reader is spiritually lacking). The literary and the material substrate on which the text is written work together in the formation of these unreadabilities.

Unreadability becomes an obvious problem for Margery's scribe in the two proems to the *Book*. Each outlines what Sarah Beckwith calls the 'difficult genesis'[2] of the *Book*, and provides a detailed account of the second scribe's struggle to read the unreadable ('vn-able for to be red' (6/14))[3] script. The problem of readability is pressed when the second scribe, presumed by some scholars to be also her confessor, Robert Spryngolde, continues the project of the first scribe. When approached with the book, this second scribe claims that her text is unreadable:

> The book was so ill-written that he could make little sense of it, for it was in neither good English nor German, nor was the handwriting shaped or formed as is other handwriting. Therefore the priest utterly believed that nobody could ever read it, unless it were by special grace. Nevertheless, he promised her that if he could read it he would willingly copy it out and write it better. Then there was so much evil talk about this creature and her weeping that, out of cowardice, the priest dared not speak with her but seldom, and he would not write as he had promised the said creature. And so he avoided and deferred the writing of this book for almost four years or perhaps more, even though this creature often called on him to do it. In the end he said that he could not read it, for which reason he would not do it. (5–6)

The phrase 'special grace' marks moments of miraculous literary abilities throughout the *Book* and offers that the readability of the first draft is governed by extra-textual means, namely faith. The role of special grace in marking moments of unexplained literary or poetic inspiration is frequent in medieval spiritual accounts. One instance is in Caedmon's *Hymn*, recounted in Bede's *Ecclesiastic History of the English People*. Book 4, chapter 24 introduces a brother named Caedmon who is specially marked by the grace of God (*diuina gratia specialiter insignis*[4]). In the account, Caedmon becomes embarrassed by his inability to sing at a feast and promptly leaves. While asleep he dreams that, through God's grace, he is given the gift of song: 'Thereupon Caedmon began to sing verses which he had never heard before [*uersus quos numquam audierat*] in praise of God the Creator' (417). *Diuina gratia* inspires Caedmon to become a zealous monk who teaches sacred history through song. Bede's story confirms the transformation of Caedmon's inarticulacy into poetic eloquence through divine grace. Special grace works in a similar way in Kempe's *Book* for her second scribe who charts the draft's readability. This shift is ultimately meant to demonstrate the workings of divine grace on the processes of reading and writing in this treatise, and perhaps more largely in medieval visionary texts.

Though the ability to write and the ability to read were not necessarily linked skills in the Middle Ages, in the *Book* Margery's scribe actively engages in both. Thus for her scribal reader to have doubts or disbelief in Margery and her text is tantamount to misreading or obfuscating her account. The Latin term *legibilis* (from the Latin verb to read, *lego, legere*) refers to the ability of a letter to be read, clearly formed and clearly visible. This ability of the letter to be read is different from a text being readable, meaning that the text is comprehensible and straightforward. For the purposes of this chapter, the types of unreadability in the *Book* encompass both unreadable and illegible moments and describe the following: the physical script of the first (missing) version of the book, written between 1436 and 1438; and the unreadable script of its first drafting, as indicated in the above citation, 'nobody could ever read it, unless it were by special grace' (5) as well as later, where the second scribe reiterates that 'it could not be read except by special grace, as there was so much calumny and infamy about this creature that few people would believe her' (7). Throughout the *Book*, Kempe refers to herself as 'creature', a word Anthony Bale explains is frequently 'used to describe mankind in fifteenth-century religious texts' (270). Importantly, the story of the creature is not the same as the story of Margery Kempe; the creature comes into being in the account of her giving birth for the first time, and Kempe's life began when she was born.

Further examination of the *Book*'s unreadability might include the deliberate over-markings of later readers, especially the Carthusian monk of Mount Grace Priory in Yorkshire known as the Red Ink Annotator, the jottings of a recipe later added to folio 124v,[5] and the truncated adaptation of the *Book* printed by Wynkyn de Worde (1501) and anthologised by Henry Pepwell (1531).

Reading by special grace

How can one understand the *Book*'s unreadability as both a physical feature of its writing and as affected by 'special grace'? Bringing literary and textual criticism together in his discussion of Ovid's tale of Narcissus, Shane Butler draws upon such an analogy between the literary and material texts. Speaking about the physical book page, he comments that 'far from flat, the page is a terrain, a tissue', and that in the image of Narcissus's reflecting pool we may understand how 'a pool, like a page, is never just a mirror, never fully reducible to its surface. Even when entirely flat (or seemingly so) and fully reflective, its guarantees what no ordinary mirror can, namely, that *there really is something down here*'.[6] Butler's analogy of the book page as a 'terrain, a tissue' works well to capture the thickness of real animal flesh, textiles and pulps that constitute such leaves. Additional MS 61823 is itself a paper codex with parchment flyleaves, and in the text it is this dimensionality, of writing on pulps and skins, that casts unreadability as both a physical written problem, and a test of spirituality, an experience that is not fully reducible to its material surface.

The idea that both forces can and do work in tandem for a fifteenth-century reader of religious texts is exemplified by the so-called Red Ink Annotator's emblem of the Passion detailed inside the large rubricated T on folio 31r (the beginning of chapter 27) and by a similar textual moment in Richard Rolle's *Meditations on the Passion*. Kelly Parsons notes that this T, one of several large rubricated Ts made by the Red Ink Annotator, is like no other in the manuscript. It has been closed in to look like a shield or the trunk of a body, and bears the five wounds of Christ (namely the two hands and two feet and the larger slit-like side wound, which is usually vertical).[7] In John Friedman's assessment, 'Christ's torment was often expressed by various metaphors in which the body was likened to a parchment book, a scroll, a deed, or even a shield bearing a "coat of arms" that could be read by the pious mediator.'[8] This annotator's depiction of Christ's wounds reveals that he is interested in the larger metaphorical tradition of sensory devotion, which often also included renditions of Christ as parchment, book, scroll, deed or charter; the distinction between wound and word commingle within the boundaries of the manuscript page, especially in the 'Charters of Christ' tradition.

The Charters of Christ is an allegorical trope that figures Christ's redemptive act as a legal charter, perhaps tracing its source from Hebrews 9: 15–18.[9] George Shuffelton, in his discussion of the fifteenth-century manuscript MS Ashmole 61 Bodleian Library, Oxford, locates the Charter of Christ tradition in a 'family' of related Middle English poems, the *Carta dei* and *The Long Charter of Christ*, which were widely circulated and survive in a large number of manuscripts.[10] This tradition entangles law with the Passion in order to authorise its poetry. Legal charters being the most authoritative document in English law and land tenure, Shuffelton identifies *The Short Charter of Christ* as imitative of a legal charter, which translates 'many Latin phrases with scrupulous precision to capture the same sense of grave authority possessed by royal charters'.[11] Medieval scribes of the *Short Charter* have even, in some cases, written the lyric 'on the back of legal charters and affix[ed] drawn seals that imitate the form of royal seals'.[12] This document signifies Christ's body and wounds also as a sealed charter to effect the authenticity of the text's legal and divine import.

Though images of the Sacred Heart and side wound can be found in Mechtild of Hackeborn's Latin *Liber Specialis Gratiae*, Julian of Norwich's *A Book of Showings* and Catherine of Siena's *Vita*, it is Richard Rolle's *Meditations* which represents Christ's bodily passion in terms of a spiritual book that must be read correctly. In this longer meditation, Rolle likens Christ's body to a book that demands to be understood, and he entreats Christ to help him read and understand the words more clearly:

> Yet another [comparison], sweet Jesus: Your body is like a book entirely inscribed in red ink, [which is] compared to your body because that is entirely inscribed with red wounds. Now, sweet Jesu, send me the grace to read this book again and again, and to understand something of the sweetness of that reading; and allow me the grace to grasp something of the matchless love of Jesus Christ.[13]

For Rolle to liken Christ's body to a book is to situate both body and page in a doubly readable context. What Rolle is asking for is the grace to understand the sweetness of its meaning, rather than help in being able to decipher its words. Unreadability for Rolle is made manifest through the simile 'Your body is like a book entirely inscribed in red ink'. The central plea in this meditation, that Rolle be granted grace to 'read this book again and again', requires that the 'red ink' and 'red wounds' – the consonance of 'red' (rede) and 'read' (reed) themselves reinforcing this connection – are also unreadable wounds. Christ is both the redeemer covered in 'red wounds' incurred because of human sin and a book 'written' with these wounds, aptly mimicking the rubrics of medieval manuscripts. Thus Rolle prays through this text-God in order that he be able to read and understand His body-text better, as a reward of diligent study. To redouble Christ as book is to extend the definition of readability to include the legibility of script as wound, or wound as script. Rolle's book is, in places, 'inscribed in red ink', and the body of Christ is 'inscribed with red wounds', a singular metaphorical construct in the Charters of Christ tradition.

Legibility of text is also legibility of Christ for his subjects, both requiring the intervention of what Rolle claims as grace. His emphasis on special grace to make legible visionary experience in writing, and writing as legible visionary experience, is similar to that in Margery's *Book*, as this same invocation is twice written in the proem at the very moment that unreadability surfaces. 'Special grace' refers to God's favour, miracle or 'charism', defined as a supernatural gift or power (*MED grace* 1c).[14] In John Audelay's 'Pope John's Passion of Our Lord', a poem this poet assembles from Pope John's apparent pre-death meditation, the apostle Paul asks God to give rest to souls in hell: 'And he prayed devoutly [*hylé*] to God's own son / For the souls in Hell, that they have some rest there'.[15] God responds by telling Paul, his 'beloved' [*leve*] and 'dear' apostle, that this 'special grace' will be granted to them. Special grace in medieval literature refers to one's favouring by God, especially those devout and beloved to him. Rolle, as a diligent reader of Christ, is not dissimilar to the priest-scribe who also requires special grace to read the illegible first draft of Margery's dialogue with Christ. The readability of the *Book* is thus dependent upon the scribe's faith in the work, and the problem of unreadability conflates this spiritual disposition with the physical writtenness of the work.

Despite the emphasis in each text that grace is also the prelude to legibility, scholars have generally made conjectures attendant to the physical writing of this unreadable draft. Sebastian Sobecki identifies Margery's son as this first 'priest-scribe', as he is called in the *Book*, based on his being in Lynn to settle business at the time her first draft was written.[16] Yet questions such as 'What did the writing of this unreadable draft look like?' and 'Why might the first scribe have written it so poorly?' bypass and play down the *Book*'s emphasis on the miraculous occurrence of legibility at its centre. The previous passage from the *Book*'s proem does, after all, describe this unreadable language in terms that might suggest a real physical precedence for such illegibility. The draft is neither good English nor good German, and the handwriting is not 'shaped or formed as is other handwriting' (5). What is more, this priest-scribe advises Margery to take this writing to a man in Germany, a man 'who had been very intimate with he who first wrote the book, supposing that he should know how best to read the book because he had formerly read letters in the other man's handwriting, sent from abroad while he was in Germany' (6). That the writing might be legible to a man in Germany presupposes that the work was not beyond the scope of standard writerly convention. The illegibility of this draft is then confirmed on two accounts, by the second scribe and this third party.

Yet, this illegibility never makes the priest-scribe hostile or dismissive of the first scribe or Margery; instead, the *Book* describes the interiorisation of his frustrations and inability. We are told that the priest becomes 'vexed in his conscience' (6) because he has broken his promise to Margery to complete the book for her. That the *Book* includes this moment of scribal reflection, rather than letting it be forgotten or minimised in what becomes the longer second proem, augments and marks his failure to read as a condition of the very genesis of the *Book*. His doubt in Margery's accounts, influenced by the surrounding community's slander and evil-speaking of her, is surely a factor in her scribe's ability to read this text. And it is the very inability to transcribe her text which becomes not a personal struggle that takes place outside of the text, but the very stuff of this treatise.

In the *Book*, readability is less a concern about legibility than it is about access. Instead of taking literally the claim that the first draft was unreadable – which I will not discount – it is perhaps more productive to focus on what function this second scribe might have served by belabouring the details of such unreadability. Sarah Beckwith supports a reading that seeks to examine the circumstances of readability in relationship to the spiritual directive of the *Book*. In Beckwith's words, Margery's voice is a frame for God himself:

> This is dramatized at numerous points in the text in those instances where difficulties of mediation miraculously disappear. Thus for example the second scribe, who attempts to transcribe the foreign, badly written text of the first scribe, is suddenly granted clarity of understanding. Such clarity of understanding is always a gift from God: it restores the truth by wiping over the traces of its construction.[17]

For Beckwith, this moment of the text's readability appears 'suddenly' and works as a frame for the action of God himself; she interprets such clarity of understanding as 'always a gift from God', a feature in the *Book* I locate in the phrase 'special grace'. Beckwith then understands this illegibility as important to the *Book*'s spiritual programme, a construction that can be wiped over, but is nevertheless importantly there.

In Karma Lochrie's assessment, the illegibility of the text is both a physical imposition and a symptom of disbelief:

> The first written text was a disaster. Not only did it suffer from a mutilated syntax and grammar, but it was incomprehensible at the level of the letters. The 'evilly' written letters with their queer shapes must have wreaked havoc with the most basic level of language, that is, the literal meaning [. . .]. The second scribe's dyslexia becomes apparent after he agrees to try to read the text for a second time and finds that 'hys eyes missed so that he might not see to make his letters nor could he see to

> mend his pen.' His vexation is caused by his own doubts about Kempe, which prevented him from reading in the first place and which invite the devil's interference. It is only through Kempe's intercession and his reliance on God's grace that his eyesight is repaired. More importantly, his ability to read, and hence to write, has been brought about through Kempe's interdiction, that is, her insertion of her own voice between text and reader. [. . .] Charity enables the profitable reading of mystical texts, just as lack of charity leads to misreading, perhaps even incomprehension, such as the scribe's. Doubt, fear, and cowardice all condition the priest's inability to read as much as any physical disability does.[18]

For Lochrie, the *Book*'s unreadability is and is not a feature of its writtenness; '[d]oubt, fear, and cowardice' are as much a condition of the priest's inability to read as any 'physical disability' would be (Lochrie cites dyslexia). When copying a text, a scribe borrows the words from one manuscript and adapts it to another; when authoring a text, a scribe becomes, in Alastair Minnis's words, 'at once a writer and an authority, someone not merely to be read but also to be respected and believed'.[19] Lochrie thus implies that Margery acts as *auctor* through 'interdiction', a go-between for text and reader that shapes what the scribe copies down. Margery's 'interdiction' therefore allows for her *Book*'s legibility, and unreadability sits astride the camps of poorly written prose and a lack of charity in the reader whose '[d]oubt, fear, and cowardice' condition this script. The legibility of the emerging text is then directly helped or hindered by psychological forces exterior to the moving, recording scribal hand, a phenomenon that presents unreadability as a condition of physical writing and narrative alike.

A 'more open' text

That the reader's troubled conscience impacts a text's readability is a theologically grounded trope in the Middle Ages. Saint Augustine's *Confessions*, for example, uses reading as a model for self-reflection. Augustine believed that scripture 'offers the reader – either the private reader or the audience at a reading – a privileged medium, through which God's will, framed in narrative, can be internalised and directed outwards as ethically informed action'.[20] It is in this way that conversion moments happen by reading in the *Confessions*. After weeping about his impure life, Augustine returns to a book he had earlier set down. In a moment of miraculous coincidence Augustine opened it and read 'the first passage on which [his] eyes lit'.[21] That passage was from Romans, and it condemns the sins of the flesh and calls the reader to 'put on the Lord Jesus Christ'. Not until Augustine's expression of guilt does this passage appear to him, offering him a 'relief from all anxiety'.[22] It is as if Augustine's expression of guilt makes possible the appearance of this passage from Romans. Instead of an unreadable text, then, Augustine presents his reader with a book that is readable and emphatically prescient. The manifestation of readable passages for Augustine occurs at moments when he is in need of reassurance or direction and it foreshadows Augustine's subsequent conversion. The sudden readableness of Margery's *Book* to her confessor offers a similar moment of textual readability by means of special grace and faithful conversion.

What is so striking about the nature of the *Book*'s unreadability is not the fixation over what type of letters Kempe's son drew, or the way in which he organised his writing on the page – 'it was in neither good English nor German, nor was the handwriting shaped or formed as is other handwriting' (5); 'the book was so poorly composed and so unintelligibly written' (6) – but, instead, the way in which Kempe's reputation figures as a major component of the text's illegibility. Towards the end of the longer proem, the second scribe recalls the process by which the text transforms into a readable text for him as he is miraculously moved to read:

> Then the priest was vexed in his conscience, because he had promised her that he would write this book if he might manage to read it, and he was not doing his part as well as he might have done, and asked this creature to fetch the book again, if she could do so graciously. Then she got the book back and brought it very contentedly to the priest, asking him to do it with good will, and she would pray to God for him and gain grace for him to read it and write it too. The priest, trusting in her prayers, began to read this book and, he thought, it was much easier than it had been before [. . .]. When the priest first began to write this book his eyesight failed so much that he could not see to form his letters, and he could not see to mend his pen. He was able to see all other things well enough. He set a pair of spectacles on his nose but then it was much worse than it was before. He complained to the creature about his illness. She said that his enemy envied his good deed and would hinder him if he could, and she urged him to do as well as God would give him grace and to not leave off. When the priest came back to this book, he could see as well (he thought) as he ever had before, both by daylight and by candlelight. And it is for this reason, when he had written a quire, he added a leaf to it and then he wrote this proem, to express more openly than the one following does, which was written before this *Anno Domini* 1436. (6–7)

It is not until the priest is 'vexed in his conscience' and believes in Margery's assurances that she will acquire grace from him that he can begin reading the book with ease and, later, that he can see as clearly as he used to be able. This miracle of readability and vision brought to a previously illegible text becomes the cause for writing this later (1436), more detailed proem. The readability of the *Book* is not limited to the clarity of its physical writing, but importantly extends to include a need for 'special grace' mediated by Margery to ensure its legibility. This explanation of unreadability expresses a central concern of the *Book* that entangles legibility with Christ's special grace. In repetitive fashion, this later proem insists that scribal belief directly constructs textual legibility. It is only when the priest begins to trust in her prayers that he begins to read the book, and later when Margery reassures him that the envy of his enemy cannot overcome the grace of God, his eyesight is reinstated. In the movement from opacity to clarity the second scribe casts Margery's proem 'more openly'.

The writings of Blessed Angela of Foligno's *Memorial*, a text that also charts radical spiritual encounters and transcribed by a confessor, describes a similar scribal hurdle overcome in the genesis of her book. Though much of Angela's life parallels Margery's, what is most interesting is the way that Angela's scribe and confessor (sometimes named Brother Arnaldo by scholars) discusses his scribal process as that of reader, of translating Angela's visionary experience from her vernacular into Latin. B. A. Windeatt explains that there is evidence that the story Angela of Foligno's life was known in England, and that when Margery went on her pilgrimages she would have visited the areas where this mystic lived and where she had some of her experiences at Assisi.[23] Angela's *Memorial* contains many scribal reflections upon its composition. For example, the scribe details the process of his reading and writing multiple drafts. Angela would dictate to her scribe in an Umbrian dialect, and Arnaldo would rapidly jot down notes from which he would later work when translating those Umbrian dictations into Latin. One example of how Arnaldo's disbelief and hesitation to write for her directly affected the legibility of her text appears in the way he writes down her experience in Chapter 2 of the *Memorial*:

> I began by briefly and carelessly jotting down notes on a small sheet of paper as a sort of 'memorial' for myself, because I thought I would have little to write. Later, after I had compelled [Angela] to talk, it was revealed to Christ's faithful one that I should use a large copy book, not a small sheet of paper. Because I only half believed her, I wrote on two or three blank pages I found in my book. Later, of necessity, I made a copy book of quality paper.[24]

Little effort and expense went into the first writing of Angela's *Memorial*, according to Arnaldo. He explains that he thought he would have little to write and, only half believing her, used makeshift notes and leftover writing materials to complete the task. In this moment, the quality of both writing and paper insists that belief directly impacts the readability and motivations to preserve this translation. The contrast between the 'small sheet of paper' he originally uses and the large 'copy book' and 'quality paper' later required by Angela elevates her work to a more serious and readable material format, and redoubles the inner conversion of her confessor, who comes to take great care in expressing her visionary encounters by using suitable parchment.

Later, in Chapter 7, the presentation of an unreadable text is corroborated by an inability of Angela's new scribe to understand the spiritual dimension of her account:

> At my request, the revelation of the passion of the Lord related here at the beginning of the fifth step [which deals with divine union and love] was written down first in the vernacular by a young boy. I had to proceed in this fashion because during this period I had been forbidden by my brothers to speak with Christ's faithful one to take down what she said. As a consequence, it was so badly written that when Christ's faithful one heard it reread to her, she told me that I should destroy it rather than transcribe it in such a state. But since I did not have time to go over it with her and to correct it, I translated it just as it was into Latin, adding nothing, somewhat like a painter painting, because I did not understand it. What follows, therefore, was initially written in the vernacular.[25]

The stages of reading Arnaldo goes through to produce a written account of this text are many. Firstly, there is a vernacular account recorded by a young (presumably less-than-qualified) boy. As a consequence, this 'badly written' draft mis-records Angela's account, but nonetheless it is set into Latin. Thus the degradation of this initial draft is literally duplicated in his translation: 'like a painter painting', Arnaldo adds nothing, fixes nothing, because he cannot understand it. This proviso serves as a model for thinking about the role of the visionary needed for crafting a readable text by her scribe. In Angela's *Memorial* it is through the careful dynamic between speaker and writer that the text is clarified, understood and made readable. In Margery's *Book* it is the miracle of readability for the second scribe, who similarly requires the help of Margery to read through this text (5: 11–12; 6).

Perhaps this is why the priest constructs the unreadability of the first draft as a problem of spiritual disposition. In the first proem it is because of the 'evil talk [evel spekyng] about this creature and her weeping [wepyng] that, out of cowardice, the priest dared not speak with her but seldom, and he would not write as he had promised the said creature' (5). In the first, shorter proem, the scribe defers his writing because there was 'so much calumny [obloquie] and infamy [slawndyr] about this creature that few men would believe her' (7). The evil talk, excessive weeping, calumny and slander of this creature are forces which hinder the readability of the first draft indefinitely. And it is perhaps in these foreboding contexts that the scribe describes the book's unreadable writing as 'evel' – a word that defines something both poorly written and sinful. Of the four times 'evel' is used in the *Book*, it is notable that three of them occur in the proems to represent the *Book*'s being badly written ('evel wretyn' and 'evel sett') and the public's evil talk surrounding Margery.

It is the ecclesiastical doctrine of *discretio spirituum* (the discerning of spirits) that helps contextualise this passage. *Discretio spirituum* authorises visionary writing through the practised discernment of divine and evil visions. According to Rosalynn Voaden:

> *discretio spirituum* supplied a pattern for self-fashioning which extended to behaviour, demeanour and modes of expression. Familiarity with, and skill in, the discourse was a vital factor in the textual – and physical – survival of the visionary. Facility with *discretio spirituum* empowered medieval women visionaries and enabled them to fulfil their divine mandate to communicate revelation.[26]

Yet moments of public distrust, here framed in terms of the public's rebuke, slander and evil-speaking of Margery, convey her precarious position as a model of this discourse. Though the ideal visionary 'is meek and submissive, a channel, an instrument of God's will', Margery's authority is frequently compromised according to *discretio spirituum* because her revelation is 'always in flux, never stable, always open to question'.[27] This reviling of Margery by the public haunts the wavering hand of her priest-scribe, leaving traces of unreadable text. The repetition of 'evil' hints not only that there is something more getting in the way of the text's readability for the priest, but also that in his inability lies his own disbelief. Perhaps this is why the priest believes that the *Book* will be readable only by the intervention of 'special grace', and why his promise to transcribe this book is conditional rather than certain: '*if* he cowd redyn it', he would write it. Here readability is extra-textually shackled to belief, somewhere in the spectrum between legibility and illegibility rather than as a feature immediately deducible from the writing on the page.

'Neither priest nor beast': the problem of disbelief

The conditions of readability in the *Book* are meaningful only through the faithful disposition of its speaker and writer. Indeed, that a readership is directly implicated in the correct reading of a visionary text at all is a primary concern for the author of the late fourteenth-century mystical text *The Cloud of Unknowing*. The author frames the text's unreadability as dependent upon the faithful disposition of his audience – only the most spiritually devout readers are allowed to enjoy its contents:

> whoever you may be that have this book in your possession, whether by owning it or being in charge of it, whether by carrying it as a messenger or borrowing it, that so far as you are able you do not willingly and deliberately read it, copy it, speak of it, or allow it to be read, copied, or spoken of, by anyone or to anyone, except by or to a person who, in your opinion, has undertaken truly and without reservation to be a perfect follower of Christ.[28]

Though this despotic tone may be, in part, a ploy to engage readers to read on – the exclusivity of the text invites further enquiry – the concern is not only about the spiritual fitness of its readers, but also about the control of reading practices. The author explains that error may ensue when this contemplation is not read in its entirety ('readers' extend to mean all those who read, copy or speak about *The Cloud*):

> For it may perhaps contain some material at the beginning or in the middle which is left incomplete and not fully explained where it stands; and if not there, it is explained soon afterwards, or else at the end. So, if someone saw one part of the material and not another, he might perhaps be easily led into error.[29]

Readers of *The Cloud* are always implicated in its meaning being legible, the fear being that one's reading may become interrupted ('left incomplete'), rendering its message 'hanging and not fully declared'. It is in this moment of partiality that a reader may 'be led into errour'. A reader of *The Cloud* is involved in a demanding task both spiritually and scholastically. To be an impious reader is to be reading a text off limits, and to leave off or skip parts of the text in its reading is to be led into error. Though the model of reading espoused in *The Cloud* envisions that the clarity of the contemplation is achieved through the piety of its readers and thoroughness of their reading practices, the question remains to what extent all visionary writing (and the reading of it) is always involved in the construction of its legibility.

In chapter 24 of the *Book*, it is the very impiety of Margery's confessor that compels the circumstances of his testing her, and under which the circumstances of his promising to write for her are first raised. In chapter 62 Margery's priest-scribe experiences a conversion that, he confides, directly impacts the thoroughness of his memory and accuracy of writing in the *Book*. It is on St James's Day that a friar preaching in St James's Chapel yard, Lynn, indirectly condemns Margery and warns that his people distance themselves from her. Among these people is the same priest who later composed her book; at the time, however, he had doubts about Margery's visions [neuyr to a leuyd hir felyngys] (152: 33–4). It is not until this same priest reads the account of Mary of Oignies, and of her manner of life (the abundant tears she wept), that he is convinced by means of comparison that Margery's weeping, sobbing and crying are similar pillars of grace. He thus acknowledges that Margery's grace surpasses his own, without any comparison ('meche mor plente of grace' (153: 25–6)). The seeing and reading of Mary of Oignies's account serves as a foil for reading the *Book*. Both female figures share affective visionary experiences, and it is in this parallel account that the priest-scribe associates clarity of mind and writing with belief and trust.

Disbelief as a recognisable hurdle for the priest-scribe is also craftily assimilated in the early exploits of Margery's horse-mill: the description of her insubordinate horse echoes the failure of the priest-scribe to read Margery's first draft. In each account (in the proem and horse-mill account in chapter 2) belief and reluctance are corroborated in the refusal of the horse to draw his load, and in the priest to read Margery's first draft. In the proem, the priest-scribe admits on four separate occasions that he cannot read the text: 'The book was so ill-written that he could make little sense of it [. . .] nobody could ever read it'; 'he would not write as he had promised the said creature'; 'he avoided and deferred the writing of this book for almost four years or more perhaps'; 'he could not read it, for which reason he would not do it' (5–6). In a similar act of reluctance, Margery's horse refuses to draw its load in the mill, perhaps indicative of Margery's sins of covetousness and pride in this entrepreneurial endeavour. On the eve of Corpus Christi the horse refuses to draw its load. In as recursive a manner as the details are in the refusal of the scribe to read the first draft, readers are told that this horse also refuses to do its job – the horse would not pull in the mill; the horse would rather go backwards than forwards; the horse would not pull for anything that the man might do (10: 19–32). These moments of equine volition speak to the larger movement in the *Book* that presents disbelief or, in this instance, the shortcomings of Margery; they enact a framework of refusal by horse hooves and human hands. It is perhaps not inconsequential that the idea of ploughing, or, in the *Book*'s instance, drawing or pulling, has been historically metaphorised in an ancient Greek and Latin style of writing that compares the left-to-right trajectory of pen-to-page with the image of an ox ploughing back and forth through a field. Boustrophedon writing, literally ox-turning, provocatively supports my contention that the failed horse-mill constructs unreadability as a recurring trope of spiritual belief and conversion throughout the *Book*. Shane Butler, moreover, supports connections between our understanding of writing on a 'page' and agricultural work. He explains that the word page

> is cognate with *pango*, which means 'to fix by driving in,' as in boundary stones or the trees of a planned grove . . . Latin uses other agricultural terms, like *exarare*, for writing, and the phrase *pangere versus*, probably 'to plant some verses,' i.e., to write them (in wax) is common . . . a *pagina* is a bounded space set out for writing – a leaf in a waxed tablet, a single sheet of papyrus or parchment, or a column in a book-roll. Garden or enclosure, the page is, ironically enough, from its very origin, a plot available for plots (to play on our own not unrelated double sense of the word 'plot').[30]

The idea that the page is also a plot exemplifies the overlap between prose and plough, writing and readability.

Unreadability in the *Book of Margery Kempe* cannot be adequately explained through historical evidence or codicological data alone; that is, the indecipherability of the text is not purely the result of the ravages of time or of human carelessness, but of a variety of changes that a text is subject to because of human agency. Further, these moments of unreadability may induce a response or a shift in response for scribes, authors and their audiences, paradoxically both as a risk in the process of meaning-making and as a literary strategy. My examination of the *Book* has centred on its ability to respond to and restructure a readable experience in terms of this paradox. The *Book* thus offers its readers an expansive tissue of unreadabilities. These unreadable moments in this literature and across these manuscripts reinforce 'special grace' – the *Book*'s repeated term for spiritual inspiration and change – as the condition by which one is guided when reading this treatise. The inability of Margery's priest-scribe to transcribe the first draft is not a personal struggle that takes place outside of the *Book*, but is instead deliberately recorded as the central struggle of the *Book*'s transmission as a visionary text. Reading within this framework indeed guarantees that in Margery's *Book* '*there really is something down here*' to newly explore: namely that unreadability shapes and is shaped by attitudes to spirituality and grace.

Notes

1. *The Book of Margery Kempe*, trans. Anthony Bale (Oxford: Oxford University Press, 2015), p. 32. Subsequent references are cited parenthetically.
2. Sarah Beckwith, 'A Very Material Mysticism', in David Aers (ed.), *Medieval Literature: Criticism, Ideology, and History* (New York: St Martin's Press, 1986), p. 37.
3. *The Book of Margery Kempe*, ed. Sanford Brown Meech and Hope Emily Allen (New York: Oxford University Press, 1940), p. 31: 14–20. Subsequent references are cited parenthetically and give page number: line number. Middle English citations from texts other than *The Book* are presented in modern English only.
4. *Bede's Ecclesiastical History of the English People*, trans. and ed. Bertram Colgrave and R. A. B. Mynors (Oxford: Clarendon Press, 1969), p. 414. Subsequent references are cited parenthetically.
5. Laura Kalas Williams, 'The *Swetenesse* of Confection', *Studies in the Age of Chauce* 40 (2018), pp. 155–90.
6. Shane Butler, *The Matter of the Page: Essays in Search of Ancient and Medieval Authors* (Madison: University of Wisconsin Press, 2011), p. 83.
7. Kelly Parsons, 'The Red Ink Annotator', in Kathryn Kerby-Fulton and Maidie Hilmo (eds), *The Medieval Professional Reader at Work: Evidence from Manuscripts of Chaucer, Langland, Kempe, and Gower* (Victoria: University of Victoria, 2001), pp. 143–216 (p. 152).
8. John B. Friedman, *Northern English Books, Owners, and Makers in the Late Middle Ages* (Syracuse: Syracuse University Press, 1995), p. 162.
9. Mary Caroline Spalding, 'The Middle English Charters of Christ', dissertation (Bryn Mawr College, 1912), p. 42.
10. George Shuffelton, *Codex Ashmole 61: A Compilation of Popular Middle English Verse* (Kalamazoo: Medieval Institute Publications, 2008).
11. Ibid.
12. Ibid.
13. *Richard Rolle: The English Writings*, ed. Allen S. Rosamund (New York: Paulist Press, 1988), p. 114.
14. *Middle English Dictionary*, ed. Robert E. Lewis et al. Ann Arbor (University of Michigan Press, 1952–2001). Online edition in Middle English Compendium, ed. Frances McSparran et al. (Ann Arbor: University of Michigan Library, 2000–18).
15. *Poems and Carols: Oxford, Bodleian Library MS Douce 302, John the Blind Audelay*, ed. Susanna Fein (Kalamazoo: Medieval Institute Publications, 2009). Modern English translation mine.

16. Sebastian Sobecki, '"The writyng of this tretys": Margery Kempe's Son and the Authorship of Her Book', *Studies in the Age of Chaucer*, 37 (2015), pp. 257–83.
17. Beckwith, 'A Very Material Mysticism', p. 190.
18. Karma Lochrie, *Margery Kempe and Translations of the Flesh* (Philadelphia: University of Pennsylvania Press, 1991), pp. 100–1.
19. A. J. Minnis, *Medieval Theory of Authorship: Scholastic Literary Attitudes in the Later Middle Ages* (Philadelphia: University of Pennsylvania Press, [1984] 1988), p. 10.
20. Brian Stock, *Augustine the Reader: Meditation, Self-Knowledge, and the Ethics of Interpretation* (Cambridge, MA: Harvard University Press, 1996), p. 12.
21. *Saint Augustine's Confessions*, trans. Henry Chadwick (Oxford: Oxford University Press, 2008), p. 153.
22. Ibid., p. 153,
23. *The Book of Margery Kempe*, trans. B. A. Windeatt (London: Penguin Books, [1985] 1994), p. 20.
24. *Angela of Foligno: Complete Works*, trans. Paul Lachance (New York: Paulist Press, 1993), p. 136.
25. Ibid., p. 179.
26. Rosalynn Voaden, *God's Words, Women's Voices: The Discernment of Spirits in the Writing of Late-Medieval Women Visionaries* (Rochester: York Medieval Press, 1999), p. 4.
27. Ibid., p. 132.
28. *The Cloud of Unknowing and Other Works*, trans. A. C. Spearing (London: Penguin, 2001), p. 11.
29. Ibid., pp. 11–12.
30. Butler, *The Matter of the Page*, pp. 7–8.

Plate 1 'La comtessa didia', portrait of the Countess of Dia, Chansonnier provençal, thirteenth century. Paris, Bibliothèque Nationale de France, MS Fr. 12473, fol. 126v. By permission of the Bibliothèque Nationale de France

Plate 2 'Na Castelloza', portrait of Castelloza, Recueil des Poésies des Troubadours, 1201–1300. Paris, Bibliothèque Nationale de France MS Fr. 854, fol. 125r. By permission of the Bibliothèque Nationale de France

Plate 3 Marie de France at her desk, Paris, Recueil D'Anciennes Poésies Françaises, 1275–1300. Bibliothèque Nationale de France, MS Arsenal 3142, fol. 256r (frontispiece of Fables). By permission of the Bibliothèque Nationale de France

Plate 4 Christine de Pizan presents her book to Isabeau of Bavaria. London, British Library, Harley MS 4431, fol. 3r. By permission of the British Library

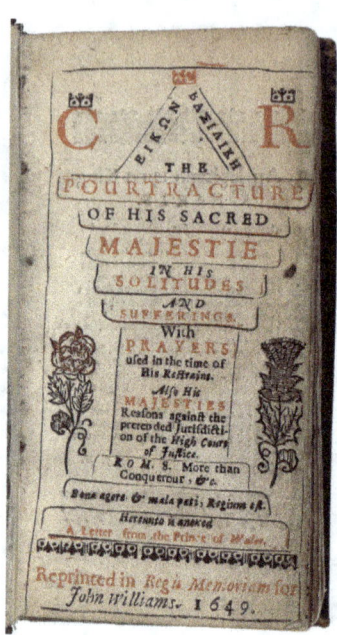

Plate 5 Charles I and John Gauden, *Eikon Basilike* (London: John Williams, 1649), A2 recto, title page. Call #: 266- 313.1q. Reproduced by permission of the Folger Shakespeare Library under a Creative Commons Attribution-ShareAlike 4.0 International License

Plate 6 Charles I and John Gauden, *Eikon Basilike* (London: s.n., 1649), frontispiece. Call #: E311. Reproduced by permission of the Folger Shakespeare Library under a Creative Commons Attribution-ShareAlike 4.0 International License

Chapter 6

Between Reading and Doing: The Case of Medieval Manuscript Books of Practical Medicine

Faith Wallis

Three manuscripts, one puzzle

Recent scholarship on medieval reading and literacy has stressed the relationship between the materiality of the book and the act of reading, whether that reading be for instruction and study, for solitary or collective entertainment, or for devotion and edification. Attention to the material book acknowledges the special conditions of reading in a manuscript culture, where no text, even one that existed in many copies, could be encountered apart from a particular physical support – a unique and irreproducible artefact. The art of making books was developed to amplify the unique materiality of each codex through decoration, illustration and, in some cases, exceptional bindings. But medieval arts of reading also exploited the physicality of the book, notably by using its individual features to support techniques of memory.[1] The unique physicality of the written word also allowed the non-literate or marginally literate to deploy written documents of various kinds in their daily lives, even if in some cases they could not read the words inscribed upon them.[2]

The goal of this chapter is to bring these two streams of materialist analysis to bear on the way we think about how medieval readers 'used' their books, particularly books that contained knowledge that was supposed to be put to use above and beyond the act of reading itself. It will use as its laboratory three fifteenth-century manuscripts on practical medicine. Their contents touch on diagnosis and prognosis, and the treatment of disease by regimen, drugs and surgery, and more specifically the treatment of wounds, ulcers and skin conditions, and the reduction of fractures and dislocations. Surgery also incorporated bloodletting, cautery and cupping as means to evacuate corrupt humours. Diagnosis and prognosis could be based on examination of clinical signs (notably pulse and urine) or on astrological criteria. A manuscript of practical medicine (*medicina practica*) is thus one whose textual contents were supposed to guide actions in the world. Hence 'using' such a book seems almost self-evidently to mean translating its instructions into clinical action. By closely examining these three manuscripts in the light of the new materialist approaches to medieval reading, however, I will demonstrate that 'use' of a manuscript book on practical medicine is more elusive and more complex than this instrumental approach implies. Looking at the diverse ways in which these books were used reveals numerous layers and dimensions of reading a medical text – for technical guidance, intellectual enrichment, commemoration, persuasion and even devotion.

The first of our exemplary manuscripts is British Library MS Harley 2558, a book partly acquired by, and partly made by, Thomas Fayreford, a medical practitioner who lived and worked in Somerset, Devon and Cornwall in the first half of the fifteenth century. About half of the book (folios 1r–8v and 152r–227v) consists of materials written in the previous century: this was the part Fayreford acquired.[3] These older materials include botanical vocabularies, recipes, tracts on diagnosis from urine, texts on anatomy, prognosis, medical astrology, the medical properties of plants, and the regimen of health. Most are in Latin, but some are in Middle English and in French. The block of material beginning on folio 9r (the first page of gathering 3) and ending with folio 151r was composed by Fayreford himself. Fayreford's contributions include a list of over 100 persons whom he had treated, naming their condition and sometimes describing what he did for them.[4] In addition, there is an alphabetical herbal with an index prepared by Fayreford, and arranged by the medical condition treated. Finally, there are two 'commonplace books' assembled by Fayreford, one on medicine and one on surgery, both furnished with indexes.

Fayreford's name is blazoned on these works: 'De curis factis per T. Ffayreford in diuersis locis' (folio 9r), 'Tabula super practicam . . . per Thomam Ffayreford collectam' (folio 12r); 'De chirurgia collecta secundum Ffayreford' (the index of the surgical collection, folio 12v); 'Chirurgia secundum Ffayreforde' (folio 125r) and, most spectacularly, 'Ffayreforde' in gold letters at the head of the medical commonplace book on folio 72v. The term 'medical commonplace book' captures the distinctive format of this text and its surgical counterpart. The text is laid out under topical headings, arranged roughly in head-to-toe sequence, with each heading beginning a new page. Fayreford entered recipes and extracts under the appropriate heading. If he did not fill the page with his initial entry, he left the remainder blank, so that he could add fresh material at a later date. The commonplace book cites a number of Scholastic medical sources, and since Fayreford once studied at Oxford, we can surmise that he copied much of his medical florilegium from books that he had had access to there. The whole ensemble is knitted together by various *tabulae* (indexes or tables of contents) and cross-references. It is also equipped with navigational devices such as marginal index notes and images, both explanatory and mnemonic.

It is natural to assume that the commonplace books and the other materials, like the alphabetical herbal, were for Fayreford's immediate use in his practice of medicine. They record and enable him to retrieve therapeutic information and instructions that he could translate into action – indeed, he often tells us that he actually did so, even providing cross-references to his commonplace book in his record of cases he had treated. But other aspects of the book complicate this utilitarian picture. The list of patients is neither an account book nor a diary. Instead, it seems to be a memoir, for 'it begins with cases [Fayreford] has reason to remember best'.[5] At the very top of the list ('In primis') is Lady Poynings, whom he cured of frenzy, fainting, quinsy and suffocation of the womb – probably separate interventions over time. There follow named patients (all male), and various *homines* (men), *mulieres* (women), *uxores* (wives), *pueri* (sons) and *filie* (daughters) identified by place of residence or the name of their husband or father. Sometimes they are identified collectively: three women cured of swollen breasts, or many people (*quamplures*) relieved of toothache. Interestingly, 'dominus ponynges' (Robert, 4th Baron Poynings) is well down on the list, between the 'rector of Spaxton' and a 'woman in London'. Lady Poynings appears again on fol. 77v, in the medical commonplace book, this time as the source for a remedy for migraine.[6] One gets the impression that Fayreford's relationship with Lady Poynings was socially and professionally valuable, and worth recording in his book in ways that would cause it to be noticed by a reader other than himself.

Fayreford also took pains to establish his identity and importance by recording his own special tried-and-true cures (*experimenta, secreta*), including one for removing a sore tooth with a tree frog, for which the barbers of London paid him much silver.[7] This self-promotion in a book apparently created for personal use suggests to Peter Murray Jones that one of the important functions of the manuscript was as 'a means of advertising Fayreford's prowess in general, and in particular as a warrant of professional experience, evidence that Fayreford knows what he is talking about when he gives a specific remedy for a disease'.[8]

This fits in with what we can reconstruct of his career. Fayreford studied theology at Oxford, but had no medical degree. He was apparently an itinerant clerical practitioner and probably depended on referrals from local gentry like Lady Poynings. Though a man of learning, his livelihood hinged on his reputation. Hence he used his book in a number of ways: as a repository of information for his practice, as an archive of that practice, and as a way of displaying to others his credentials, his connections and his dignity. If the book was useful to him during his lifetime, it was not exactly a private memorandum; rather, its formal arrangement and apparatus of reference aids bespeak an intention to pass the book on to a successor – and the repeated blazoning of the compiler's name may have been intended to ensure his memory in future time.

The second manuscript under consideration is Stockholm, National Library of Sweden MS X 188 (c. 1425–35), an unusual copy of the *Practica* or treatise on surgery by the English surgeon John of Arderne (composed in 1376). This work survives in over forty manuscripts, of which thirty-six are illustrated with a remarkably consistent programme of images devised by the author himself. Most take the form of marginal drawings set against the text to which they refer; the text in turn frequently alludes to the illustrations. Only the Stockholm manuscript of Arderne disregards this programme. It is exceptional in other ways as well. It is not a codex, but a roll, composed of twelve skins of parchment sewn together, and measuring 542.5 × 36 centimetres (17 feet 8 inches × 15 inches). The dimensions merit notice: this is not a compact *rotulus* for hand or pocket. It would not have been easy to read, because the text is written in two columns down the full length of the roll. There are illustrations in the outer margins of each column, as well as in the intercolumnal space. These intercolumnal illustrations include some of the images devised by Arderne to illustrate the stages of his signature operation for fistula in ano. But they also include pictures not found in any other Arderne manuscript, notably anatomical figures reminiscent of those illustrating Henri de Mondeville's *Surgery*, including a dramatic sagittal view of the whole body.[9] Another notable addition is the image of a woman in childbirth, together with fifteen drawings of fetal presentations derived from ancient prototypes in the *Gynecia* ascribed to Muscio (fl. c. 500).[10] The back of the scroll includes more anatomical figures and an image showing another stage of the fistula operation.

The margins of the roll contain ninety-nine figures exhibiting the most important symptom or consequence of the conditions discussed in the adjacent text – a veritable gallery of pathology. But as Peter

Murray Jones has observed, the Stockholm images 'do not seem to have any relation to [the programme] devised by Arderne for the other manuscripts [of his work], though some of the same subject matter is covered'.[11] The text in the Stockholm scroll is also anomalous: a mixture of Arderne's original Latin text with an epitome of Bernard of Gordon's *Lilium medicine*, a famous Scholastic manual of therapeutics that was also one of Arderne's principal sources.[12]

Perhaps the most puzzling aspect of the Stockholm roll is its genesis and ownership. It was made in England, probably London, around 1425–35. The claim that it was commissioned by or for Princess Philippa of England, who married the king of Norway and Sweden, Eric of Pomerania, in 1406, has never been proven, but as Kathleen Scott observes, whoever commissioned it commanded considerable financial resources and was likely 'no ordinary medical man'.[13] The layout of the scroll is expertly planned: for example, its centre column, calibrated to hold the anatomical, surgical and obstetrical images at the beginning of the scroll, was skilfully compressed after this material was copied, allowing for the two columns of text to occupy the entire writing space. The professional scribe added rubrics and paragraph marks, small capitals in blue and larger capitals at the beginning of each topical section in gold against a red and blue background. The images are well drawn and brightly coloured, and the dorsal anatomical views are traced directly over the frontal views on the recto of the scroll, so that the back of the scroll represents the back of the body.

The last of the three manuscripts in our sample is Number 7586 in the library of Sir William Osler (1849–1919), physician, educator and book collector. It is a fifteenth-century codex from Germany comprising two booklets within their original medieval binding. The first is Nicholas of Lyra's *Postilla in Iob* (*Commentary on the Book of Job*) (folios 1–56); the second (folios 57–92) is a medical handbook.[14] The medieval owner left his signature on the final page: 'Hi sexternuli sunt Johannis Regli plebani in Lengruch. Patientiam habe in me et omnia reddam tibi. Math 18' ('These gatherings of twelve belong to Johannes Reglus of Lengerich. Have patience with me, and I will repay you everything. Matthew 18'). Father Johannes identifies himself as the rector (or perhaps rural dean or archdeacon) of Lengruch (modern Lengerich), which could refer to either the town in Westphalia or the one in Niedersachsen of this name. The quotation from Matthew 18 is the incipit of the *Postilla in Iob*, which proves that the two works were together when they were in his possession. That a cleric should have owned a copy of Nicholas of Lyra's famous commentary comes as no surprise, but the medical handbook is less easy to account for, and their unusual pairing strongly favours the hypothesis that Father Johannes himself arranged for these two works to be bound together.

The medical text consists of excerpts from an unidentified Latin manual of therapeutics. It was evidently a Scholastic *practica*, because it cites Galen, Avicenna, Rhazes and other authorities. Traces of the parent treatise are preserved in the wording of its chapter headings and rubrics, which reveal that the original work was divided into *sermones* ('addresses'), *portiones* (parts), *tractatus* (tractates) and finally *capitula* (chapters). Only the first *sermo* is represented in the Osler manuscript: the one concerning conditions affecting the head. Moreover, a selection has been made from this *sermo*, because the internal divisions are not continuous. The decision to include only the *sermo* on the head, and to omit sections of the parent treatise, was therefore deliberate. The scribe closes his work with the statement 'Explicit et restant adhuc plura que hic deficiunt' ('Here it ends; and there are still many things which are not included here'). Moreover, while Scholastic manuals typically covered the definition, symptoms, prognosis and treatment of diseases, this abbreviation contains only treatments. For the most part, the ingredients are commonplace and cheap, though blind cross-references reveal that the parent treatise included more sophisticated and expensive compound remedies like theriac. This suggests that the designer of this compilation favoured remedies that non-specialists could prepare for themselves or on behalf of people of limited means, or could at least advise them how to do so.

'Using' manuscript books: assumptions and questions

These three manuscripts challenge the ways in which we understand how books were 'used' in the Middle Ages. The functionality of Fayreford's book is ambiguous, because the knowledge Fayreford produces and re-produces seems to be also for the eyes of readers other than himself. The Stockholm roll, at once unwieldy and visually spectacular, would be very difficult to read or study, let alone to consult for reference. And why did a clergyman own a carefully edited extract from a Scholastic *practica* that dealt only with diseases of the head? The practical content of these books exposes two larger problems: whether we can determine if and how *any* medieval book was 'used' in any sense, and what the relationship of books of practical medicine to the business of treating and curing might have been.

These two problems are closely intertwined, because if we were dealing with almost any subject other than practical medicine, 'use' could be documented in a reasonably satisfactory manner.[15] For example, were the contents of our three examples medical theory, we would be able to detect how they were used by looking for indicators of whether the book was read *in extenso*, referred to, used as a record, or functioned as a representation. Each reading style or intention assigns the physical codex a different performative role, and this role can be discerned in traces left by the scribes, artists or readers. For example, a scribe can 'score' the text for reading comprehension by punctuating it; but a reader can also 'score' a Latin text for oral reading by marking accents. And, of course, marginal *maniculae* and *nota* signs are vestiges of the readers' attention, marking locations for re-reading or flagging items for future reference.[16]

Using books for reference has been studied particularly in relation to Scholastic styles of learning in theology, law and medicine. These placed a premium on locating specific or topical information within the integral texts of authoritative works. An enabling infrastructure of tables of contents, subject indexes, concordances and navigational aids (e.g. running titles) could be added by either scribe or reader. But the most basic trace of reference use long pre-dated the academic turn of the twelfth century: the rubric which guides the reader to the desired textual selection, such as that indicating the object of a blessing within a benedictional ('To protect cattle'), or the target condition of a medical recipe ('For headache').[17] Apart from reference, manuscript books are also used as archives to store records of various kinds: obits of a monastic community are recorded in liturgical calendars, annals in the margins of Easter tables, legal documents on the flyleaves of cartularies or service books, and medical recipes almost everywhere, including the margins of medical manuscripts.[18] Finally, the book can be used to represent some value external to the acts of reading, referring and recording. The Lindisfarne Gospels manuscript, for instance, was created as an act of devotion – a 'shrine' for scripture to rest beside the shrine of St Cuthbert. Being a book was essential to its function as a representation, because it represented the word of God which it contained; and yet it was never meant to be read from during the liturgy:[19] being a book is separate from being used as a book.

Inflections of 'use' in medical manuscripts

Historians of medieval practical medicine, on the other hand, are seldom content to accept reading, reference, recording and representing as criteria of use, because these categories refer only to what takes place within the covers of the book itself. Practical medicine, by contrast, takes place in the 'real world'. In the view of these historians, to 'use' a medical manuscript thus means (implicitly, and sometimes explicitly) more than reading the text it contains: it connotes deploying the book to guide some action that lies over and above the act of reading. While this view is manifested more as a silent assumption than an explicit thesis, its logic is straightforward: a medical recipe or surgical protocol tells the reader what to do, but the doing takes place entirely outside the framework of reading words on a page. At the same time, it is assumed or explicitly claimed that a manuscript book on practical medicine is physically present and being read when it is put to 'use'.

To complicate matters, there is also the relationship of medical practice to the written word. Medicine's 'academic turn' over the long twelfth century was spurred by the arrival in the West of substantial works on ancient Greek and Arabic medicine, and the emergence of formal classroom instruction based on these texts. With the translation from Arabic into Latin of the *Isagoge* of 'Joannitius' (Hunayn ibn Isḥāq, 809–89) by Constantine the African at the end of the eleventh century, the term *practica* entered the lexicon as the counterpart of *medicina theorica*.[20] Diagnostic techniques like pulse taking and urine inspection are abundantly represented in medical manuscripts made both before and after the academic turn: the difference is that post-twelfth-century texts on urine inspection, for example, theorise the colours of urine in relation to the physiology of the humours and of digestion. The earlier texts simply equate the colour, texture and quality of precipitates with a diagnosis, without explaining why the sign indicates the symptom.[21] In both the pre-Scholastic and the Scholastic era, the position of the heavenly bodies was used to predict the outcome of an illness. The change, again, lay in the degree of theorisation. The older materials provided coarse equivalencies between the phase of the moon and the outcome of the disease. The post-twelfth-century style was a more sophisticated medical astrology that theorised the effect of the motion of the heavens on the human body and offered explanations why certain zones of the body, or humours, would be affected.[22]

The relationship between the Scholastic theory taught in the universities and bedside practice is a matter of continuing controversy.[23] The important thing to bear in mind is that the new academic style of diagnosis and prognosis did not drive out the older materials. This further complicates the question of 'use': would the owner of a manuscript containing both ancient divination devices and up-to-date medical astrology 'use' (in the sense of 'apply') only one or the other? Was one for use, the other for study, or even for show?[24]

Minimalists and motivationists

Medievalists who have tackled the problem of how manuscripts on practical medicine were used fall broadly into two camps. Some are minimalists, in that they are highly selective about the evidence which indicates that a book was 'used': only documented ownership and physical signs of wear qualify. In the opposite camp are the motivationists, who take the view that every book is in some sense 'used', and that the task of scholarship is to excavate motives for different kinds of use.

Minimalists argue that use can only be established by two criteria: first, the owner of the manuscript must be someone who could reasonably apply the information it contains for the purpose of medical intervention in the 'real world'; and secondly, the manuscript must exhibit physical evidence of such 'real world' use. Linne Mooney provides a lucid exposition of this approach. Taking as her domain manuscripts on practical medicine, applied mathematics, agriculture and animal husbandry, prognostication and divination, magic, and alchemy, Mooney begins by setting aside what she calls 'pseudo-utilitarian texts' or 'lore', because the aim of acquiring lore is 'adding to knowledge', not application.[25] A utilitarian text by contrast is 'instructive and straightforward': it tells the reader how to do things and, by implication, is used when, and only when, those instructions are translated into action. Utilitarian texts are conveyed in utilitarian manuscript forms: the quire or booklet; the 'collection', of which the premier example is the medical miscellany 'used by members of the medical profession' and varying in content 'with the practice and skills of the leech'. Any manuscript which looks like it cost a lot to produce, or retains its original good looks, is dismissed as neither 'intended for daily use' nor ever so used. In sum, the manuscript had to be owned by a health-care practitioner, and only modest volumes exhibiting clear signs of wear congruent with the manuscript being physically present and open during the medical intervention can actually be said to have been used. To distinguish 'the merely useful from the actually used', then, requires checking several boxes: the owner's occupation; the form of the manuscript; additions or annotations by the owner; physical wear and evidence of use. The mere fact that a book was read does not suffice to prove that it was 'used'.[26]

Applying Mooney's tests, however, is not easy. A parson and part-time practitioner named John Reed owned Bodleian Library MS Rawlinson A.393. Mooney claims that we know he 'used' his book, because he recorded his cures in the margins. But that merely proves that he 'used' his book as an archive, not that he applied all or even any of the book's contents in his practice. Information certainly went into the book, but it did not necessarily come out of it. Recipes added by a reader in the margins of medical manuscripts are said to 'attest to use by a reader in the performance of operations described therein'.[27] In fact they attest only to the reader's desire to record information. We might infer that the recipe added in the margin was at least recorded with the intention of one day using it, but such inferences cannot automatically be extended to the contents of the host manuscript which supplied the space for the record.

The prime example of 'practical' form is the folding medical almanac, 'designed to be carried in a pocket or worn in a leather carrying case hung from the physician's belt and taken out for quick bedside diagnosis'.[28] Worn from a belt they very likely were; but whether they were consulted at the bedside is another question.[29] We have to take into account what medieval sources tell us about how doctors visited their patients, and the role of books in their practice. Folding almanacs sometimes contain urine charts, but in the advice for doctors about how to examine urine at the bedside, nothing is said about consulting a manuscript. Arnau of Vilanova is even more explicit: patients will despise you if you appear to be dependent on books, and you should never give the impression that you are reading from a script. For a doctor to consult a manuscript at the bedside might actually damage his credibility: the learned physician is supposed to 'read' the urine, not a text.[30]

The criterion of wear and tear lends a literal connotation to the term 'use'. A medical book that is 'used' in Mooney's sense of the term is a book that is actually carried to the bedside and consulted there as the treatment is being carried out. Mooney points to British Library Sloane 100, whose verses on bloodletting on folio 34r are stained with rust-coloured fingerprints, which 'may be prints of fingers bloodied in the course of performing the bloodletting instructions that begin on this page'.[31] But it is unlikely that a trained phlebotomist would prop a book open in front of him to guide him in executing this operation; furthermore, the passage on folio 34r does not tell one how to perform phlebotomy; rather, it is a survey of the veins and the conditions that bloodletting from each of them is supposed to alleviate.

The weakest element in the minimalist argument is that it cannot explain why a handsome medical book like Fayreford's manuscript or the Stockholm roll would be made at all, or why it would be preserved. Indeed, survival is often invoked as an argument that a book was never 'used', because books that are used fall apart. But for those of the motivationist school, the act of preserving a book is as intentional as that of creating one. Peregrine Horden points out that the very question 'how was this manuscript used?' presupposes 'a certain vision of the texts' *Sitz in Leben* as providing the sole criterion. In effect, if the text did not sit in the consulting room, and it was not frequently in the doctor's hand, at least between patients and perhaps during the consultation, it was not practical or useful.'[32] Horden argues instead that because manuscripts were so costly to produce, there is no such thing as a medical manuscript that was not useful in some sense. Otherwise, it would not even exist. Moreover, a manuscript which has contrived to survive must have possessed some perceived value that encouraged preservation.[33] The uses and values that justify creation and preservation can include reverence for authority, display (of wealth, culture or taste), scientific reflection (including reflection by non-practitioners), study and instruction, as well as therapeutic guidance. Therefore a medical book in mint condition without any marginal notes could still have been 'useful' to its owner.[34] This approach has the advantage of opening up the prospect that the same book might be used in a number of ways, by more than one person, either simultaneously or at various times.

The historian's task is therefore to map features of surviving manuscripts onto this range of possibilities. However, this is inevitably imprecise and raises as many questions as it answers. How much medical theory needs to be present before we conclude that a book was used for school instruction rather than practical reference? What size of manuscript is 'portable'? How do we factor in the presence of non-medical materials in medical manuscripts? What can prefaces tell us? What is the significance of linguistic reworkings?[35]

Beyond the mirage of 'use'

Of course, neither approach is fully satisfactory: the minimalist defines 'use' in an unrealistically restricted and literal way; the motivationist is right that every book is in some sense 'used', but offers few criteria for recognising what kind of use, and by whom, any given manuscript might have been put to.

It might help to think about ways in which a manuscript book of practical medicine could be 'useless'. Two possibilities spring to mind: either the makers, owners and/or readers are not competent to put the information into practice in any sense of the term; or the information may not be relevant to the medical realities of the reader's world. Already, however, we run into difficulties. First, it is far from easy to determine 'competence'. In the late fourteenth century, the English Dominican Henry Daniel composed a treatise on uroscopy in Middle English based on the most authoritative Scholastic literature on the subject. Daniel's *Liber uricrisiarum* was certainly 'used' in the motivationist sense: it was often reproduced, and survives in thirty-seven manuscripts, representing twenty-two versions of the text, and it finally found its way into print in the sixteenth century. An encyclopaedic work that typically covers 100–200 manuscript leaves, it was an investment to copy, but one which many were ready to make. Daniel says that he undertook its composition to disseminate the benefits of uroscopic knowledge and yet openly confesses in his prologue that he had no experience in the practice of uroscopy. He claims to have learned the science from the Holy Spirit; in fact, he learned it from books.[36] Daniel's readers nonetheless thought him competent to say something about uroscopy, and neither he nor they considered it a problem that he was by his own admission not 'competent' to do uroscopy. To write about medical practice and to practise it were two distinct competencies. As Peter Murray Jones points out, these books are 'witnesses to practice' even if they were not literally, always, or by everyone used in practice.[37]

Relevance is also an elusive category. What 'relevance' did treatments for gynaecological disorders have for the cloistered Carolingian monks who carefully compiled, copied, diffused and read the *Liber Passionalis*? It is hard to imagine monks directly carrying out these instructions but, as Horden observes, the *Liber Passionalis* was not 'useless'. For monks, the womb may have been 'a focus of learned discussion or a means of moral edification'. This is by no means to claim that the monks never put any of the other kinds of instruction in the *Liber Passionalis* into 'real world' practice; to the contrary, it alerts us that monks were 'capable of a great range of medical interests, philosophical as well as practical'. In short, the same practical text could be 'used' in different senses, by different communities or individuals.[38]

To move beyond the mirage of use, it also pays to think about medieval manuscript books as leading social lives.[39] Both minimalists and motivationists tacitly assume that only one pair of eyes is trained on the manuscript: that of the owner/reader. Of course, books were also read by and to others, and were given, loaned, bequeathed, stolen and sold. More pertinent here, however, is to think about how, at a single moment in time, a book might 'belong' to more than one individual or group, and be simultaneously used in different ways. If we think of our three representative manuscripts as leading social lives, and not merely as the exclusive possessions of individuals, some important dimensions of 'use' emerge.

Fayreford's manuscript is the easiest to read in this light. Both its contents and its presentation proclaim that it was meant to be seen, studied and eventually owned by others. Fayreford saw the book as advocating for his skill in the eyes both of his present clientele and of future owners, who would add to his commonplace book. It was designed to be looked at as well as consulted, and to speak well of its owner even when he was not present.

The Stockholm scroll is a more challenging case, as the context of its creation is less evident. What stands out is its unusual format, size and decoration. Unlike Fayreford's book, this manuscript is not equipped for reference, nor does it name its maker or owner. Would a surgeon even want a manuscript of this kind? And if not a surgeon, who? Although the connection to the wedding of Princess Philippa referred to above remains speculative, I would argue that it is a theory worth pursuing, precisely because this manuscript of Arderne incorporates a birth scene and the images of fetal presentations of Muscio. We can compare it to another prominent surgical text that also picked up pictures of this type, namely Gerard of Cremona's twelfth-century translation of the *Surgery* of al-Zahrāwī (Albucasis), a work composed in Umayyad Spain around the year 1000. Like Arderne's book, Albucasis's *Surgery* had its own iconographic tradition, notably the illustration of surgical instruments. To these were added three other suites of images: (1) cautery figures; (2) the depiction of an apparatus for traction of the spine; and (3) the Muscio *foetus in utero* images. The Muscio images were added because Albucasis, uniquely among surgical authorities, addressed childbirth.

Another feature of these illustrated Albucasis manuscripts is that many were owned by members of the aristocracy. Layfolk of high rank routinely acquired medical works on regimen or herbals, but a manual of surgery cannot be constructed as a self-help manual, nor does it fall into the domain of 'collector science' like a star catalogue or a bestiary. Monica Green suggests instead that the Albucasis manuscripts might have been commissioned by 'the better class of practitioners', who 'might have seen Albucasis's text as a way of advertising their knowledge in order to attract the attention of powerful patrons' and, in particular, of advertising the special expertise of surgeons in resolving difficult childbirth.[40] They could then be offered to a prince as a suitable gift. A case in point is the manuscript in Budapest owned by Conversino da Frignano, a Bologna-trained physician and sometime professor at Siena who became court physician to Louis of Anjou, King of Hungary, in 1342. It includes the Muscio images, but adds novel obstetrical scenes, including what is perhaps a representation of the extraction of the afterbirth from a richly robed and crowned woman. The physician in this picture does not do the work himself, but instructs an assistant, who turns to face him; nonetheless, the doctor is conspicuously holding a book. Green argues that the image was not primarily for the surgeon's eyes, but for the royal client to inspect and admire. It 'shows a social scenario in which Albucasis's obstetrical chapters were already being used – or were *imagined* that they could be used: as a *reference tool* for the learned male physician or surgeon to use when called to aid an important female patient lying near death in childbirth'.[41] If the Budapest manuscript was 'used' by the potential patient (or her husband) as well as read by the practitioner, it is not difficult to imaging the Stockholm scroll leading a similar social life, perhaps at the court of Eric of Pomerania and his English bride.

On the other hand, the social life of Father Johannes's booklet concerning conditions affecting the head is manifested in the manner in which the text was compiled from its parent treatise – what was chosen and, just as importantly, what was not chosen. Though the sections on the head in most *practicae* include treatments for problems of the nose, mouth, ears and teeth, Father Johannes's compendium leaves these out. What was retained was, first, treatments involving the *visible* head – the face, hair and scalp – and, secondly, cures for the more alarming ailments of the brain, including headaches, insomnia, epilepsy, paralysis, insanity and stupor. Even the section on the eyes has been edited to include only conditions affecting the 'look' of the eyes – notably the state of the brows and lashes. The only chapter excerpted from *portio* 4, *tractatus* 4, on discoloration of the eyes, concerns black eyes that result of a fight or a fall.

This exclusive focus on the visible head and the brain unlocks the manuscript's social life. Any facial defect, even something as medically non-threatening as dandruff in the eyebrows, can have social consequences. In medieval Latin, *facies* denoted 'character' as well as 'face' and 'appearance', and the popularity of treatises on physiognomy confirms the face's enormous cultural salience.[42] As one of the arbiters of community harmony, the priest might have a special interest in cosmetic conditions that could exert a negative impact on the social dignity of a parishioner or patron. The head is also the seat of imagination, reasoning and memory, and therefore closely aligned with the immortal soul. Diseases like epilepsy and paralysis, so prominently represented in the booklet on the head, were also particular targets of Christ's healing ministry. Finally, we must consider that Father Johannes bound this booklet together with a commentary on the Book of Job, and Job's physical sufferings took the form of a visible and repulsive skin disease. Father Johannes's codex therefore spoke to his condition as a cleric who probably advised and tended the sick, but who also meditated on the sufferings of Job.

Conclusion

The representation of the doctor holding a book in the Budapest manuscript of Albucasis supports a reading of 'use' in terms of the social life of this manuscript book, even if its content concerned procedures to be carried out in the real world. The book in the Budapest Albucasis image is neither read nor consulted, and yet it participates in the complex social encounter between doctor, assistant and patient. It serves to triangulate the doctor's knowledge, the assistant's skill and the patient's confidence. An equally eloquent image (Figure 6.1)

Figure 6.1 Roger Frugard, *Cirurgia* (medieval French translation). A patient carries out a self-test for hairline cranial fracture under instruction from a surgeon. Cambridge, Trinity College O.1.20, folio 243r (detail). Reproduced by permission of the Master and Fellows of Trinity College Cambridge

reinforces this point. This drawing from the French translation of Roger Frugard's *Surgery*, preserved in Cambridge, Trinity College, depicts a test for the presence of a hairline cranial fracture.

The patient on the right side of the image actually performs the test by holding his nose, ears and mouth and blowing hard. The seated surgeon on the left tells the patient what to do (his hand is lifted in a gesture of address and command), but he does so with a book open on the lectern before him. As Tony Hunt astutely observes, we should not imagine that the practitioner needs actually to read out the instructions to the patient; after all, no book is present at the complicated cranial operations depicted on the preceding page. For Hunt, the book is 'propaganda by the artist for the sort of medical treatise which he is himself illustrating'.[43] I would add that the book is also part of a social encounter; it literally mediates – it sits between – the surgeon and the patient, and it is being 'used' by both of them. Indeed, in the minimalist sense of 'applying the instructions' it is actually used more by the patient than by the doctor. But, of course, the doctor is also putting its directives into action by conveying them to the patient and interpreting the results, thereby mediating between the book and the patient – a more motivationist reading of 'use'. Moreover, the drawing illustrates the Trinity College manuscript itself in action, since the instructions being conveyed and carried out in the picture, and implicitly contained in the book depicted in the picture, are actually written out in the real book, in the text above the drawing. The reader of the manuscript thus joins the community of 'users'. This book-within-a-book stands as an emblem of how using a manuscript on practical medicine needs to be read as a social transaction in which books are not an inert resource accessed by the practitioner alone, but objects charged with 'an agency in reserve of their function in conveying words' that empowers them to speak, move and interact with their worlds.[44]

Notes

1. See Armando Petrucci, *Writers and Readers in Medieval Italy*, ed. and trans. Charles Radding (New Haven: Yale University Press, 1995), especially ch. 7; Faith Wallis, 'The Experience of the Book: Manuscripts, Texts, and the Role of Epistemology in Early Medieval Medicine', in Don G. Bates (ed.), *Knowledge and the Scholarly Medical Traditions* (Cambridge: Cambridge University Press, 1995), pp. 102–26.

2. See M. T. Clanchy, *From Memory to Written Record: England, 1066–1307*, 3rd edition (Chichester: Wiley, 2013), especially chs 7 and 8; Rosamond McKitterick (ed.), *The Uses of Literacy in Early Mediaeval Europe* (Cambridge: Cambridge University Press, 1990); Petra Schulte, Marco Mostert and Irene van Renswoude (eds), *Strategies of Writing: Studies on Text and Trust in the Middle Ages. Papers from 'Trust in Writing in the Middle Ages' (Utrecht 28–29 November 2002)* (Turnhout: Brepols, 2008).
3. Digitised at <http://www.bl.uk/manuscripts/FullDisplay.aspx?ref=Harley_MS_2558> (last accessed 5 August 2019).
4. Peter Murray Jones, 'Thomas Fayreford: An English Fifteenth-Century Practitioner', in Roger French, Jon Arrizabalaga, Andrew Cunningham and Luis Garcís Ballester (eds), *Medicine from the Black Death to the French Disease* (Cambridge: Cambridge University Press, 1998), pp. 156–7, 159–63.
5. Jones, 'Thomas Fayreford', p. 159.
6. Ibid., p. 176.
7. Peter Murray Jones, 'Harley MS 2558: A Fifteenth Century Medical Commonplace Book', in Margaret Schleissner (ed.), *Manuscript Sources of Medieval Medicine* (New York: Garland, 1995), pp. 37–40, 50–1.
8. Ibid., p. 45.
9. R. Herrlinger, *History of Medical Illustration from Antiquity to A.D. 1600* (London: Medicina Rara, 1970), pp. 12, 41–2 and plate XVII.
10. On the Muscio images, see Monica H. Green, *Making Women's Medicine Masculine: The Rise of Male Authority in Pre-modern Gynaecology* (Oxford: Oxford University Press, 2008), pp. 150–9.
11. Peter Murray Jones, 'Staying with the Programme: Illustrated Manuscripts of John of Arderne, c. 1380–c. 1550', *English Manuscript Studies*, 10 (2002), p. 210.
12. Ibid., pp. 209–10. D'Arcy Power translated the text as *De arte phisicali et de cirurgia of Master John Arderne, surgeon of Newark, dated 1412* (London: John Bale, Sons & Danielsson, 1922).
13. Kathleen L. Scott, *Later Gothic Manuscripts 1390–1490*, A Survey of Manuscripts Illuminated in the British Isles 6 (London: Harvey Miller, 1998), vol. I, plates 261–2; vol. II, cat. no. 66, pp. 197–9 at p. 199; see also Kathleen L. Scott, *Illuminated Manuscripts and Other Remarkable Documents from the Collections of the Royal Library, Stockholm*, Catalogue of an Exhibition, June–September 1963, Kungl. Biblioteket utställningskatalog nr. 35 (Stockholm: A. B. Björkmans Eftr, 1963), p. 31. The Stockholm roll has been digitised at <https://www.wdl.org/en/item/11631> (last accessed 5 August 2019).
14. W. W. Francis, R. H. Hill and Archibald Malloch (eds), *Bibliotheca Osleriana: A Catalogue of Books Illustrating the History of Medicine and Science Collected, Arranged and Annotates by Sir William Osler, Bt., and Bequeathed to McGill University*, 2nd edition (Montreal:

McGill-Queen's University Press, 1969), p. 678 (no. 7,586). See also Faith Wallis, 'The Book of the Head in Osler Library MS 7586', in William Stoneman and Jacqueline Brown (eds), *A Distinct Voice: Medieval Essays in Honor of Leonard E. Boyle, O.P.* (Notre Dame: University of Notre Dame Press, 1997), pp. 121–54; and Faith Wallis, 'The Book of the Head and the Book of Skin: Compilation and Decompilation in Two Medieval Manuscripts of Practical Medicine in the Osler Library, McGill University', *Florilegium*, 33 (2016), pp. 15–44.

15. Eva Nyström, 'Looking for the Purpose Behind a Multitext Book: The Miscellany as a Personal "One-Volume Library"', in L. Doležalová and K. Rivers (eds), *Medieval Manuscript Miscellanies: Composition, Authorship, Use* (Krems: Institut für Realienkunde des Mittelalters und der frühen Neuzeit, 2013), pp. 70–81. 'Use' is left undefined in Julia C. Crick and Alexandra Walsham (eds), *The Uses of Script and Print, 1300–1700* (Cambridge: Cambridge University Press, 2004), and in Henry Ansgar Kelly and Christopher Baswell (eds), *Medieval Manuscripts: Their Makers and Users. A Special Issue of* Viator *in Honor of Richard and Mary Rouse* (Turnhout: Brepols, 2011).

16. On 'scoring', see Malcolm B. Parkes, *Pause and Effect: Punctuation in the West* (Berkeley: University of California Press, 1993).

17. See, for example, Richard and Mary Rouse, '*Statim invenire*: Schools, Preachers, and New Attitudes to the Page', in Robert L. Benson and Giles Constable (eds), *Renaissance and Renewal in the Twelfth Century* (Cambridge, MA: Harvard University Press, 1982), pp. 201–25.

18. Danielle Jacquart and Charles Burnett (eds), *Scientia in margine: Études sur les marginalia scientifiques du moyen âge à la Renaissance* (Geneva: Droz, 2005); Susan L'Engle, 'The Pro-Active Reader: Learning to Learn the Law', in Kelly and Baswell (eds), *Medieval Manuscripts*, pp. 51–75.

19. Michelle P. Brown, *The Lindisfarne Gospels: Society, Spirituality and the Scribe* (Toronto: University of Toronto Press, 2003), especially chs 2 and 3. For symbolic 'use' of the impractically huge Codex Amiatinus of the Bible, see Celia Chazelle, 'Painting the Voice of God: Wearmouth-Jarrow, Rome and the Tabernacle Miniature in the Codex Amiatinus', *Quintana*, 8 (2009), pp. 15–59.

20. *Isagoge* 1, trans. Faith Wallis, in *Medieval Medicine: A Reader* (Toronto: University of Toronto Press, 2010), p. 140 (slightly modified); see edition by Gregor Maurach, 'Johannicius. *Isagoge ad Techne Galieni*', *Sudhoffs Archiv*, 62:2 (1978), pp. 148–74 (p. 151).

21. Faith Wallis, 'Signs and Senses: Diagnosis and Prognosis in Early Medieval Pulse and Urine Texts', *Social History of Medicine*, 13 (2000), pp. 265–78; 'Inventing Diagnosis: Theophilus' *De urinis* in the Classroom', *Dynamis*, 20 (2000), pp. 31–73.

22. See for example Ernest Wickersheimer, 'Figures médico-astrologiques des IXe, Xe et XIe siècles', *Janus*, 19 (1914), pp. 157–77.

23. For a negative assessment of the impact of Scholastic medical theory on

practice see John Riddle, 'Theory and Practice in Medieval Medicine', *Viator*, 5 (1974), pp. 157–70; for a positive assessment see the work of Luke Demaitre, for example 'Scholasticism in Compendia of Practical Medicine, 1250–1450', *Manuscripta*, 20 (1976), pp. 81–95.

24. For example, astrology material in the manuscript associated with the farm steward and part-time healer John Crophill. |See James K. Mustain, 'A Rural Medical Practitioner in Fifteenth-Century England', *Bulletin of the History of Medicine*, 45:5 (1972), pp. 469–76.

25. Linne Mooney, 'Manuscript Evidence for the Use of Utilitarian Writings in Late Medieval England', in Richard Firth Green and Linne R. Mooney (eds), *Interstices: Studies in Middle English and Anglo-Latin Texts in Honour of A. G. Rigg* (Toronto: University of Toronto Press, 2004), pp. 184–202 (p. 189).

26. Ibid., pp. 185–7.
27. Ibid., p. 188.
28. Ibid., p. 189.
29. On folding almanacs see C. H. Talbot, 'A Mediaeval Physician's Vade Mecum', *Journal of the History of Medicine and Allied Sciences*, 16 (1961), pp. 213–33; Hilary Carey, 'What Is a Folded Almanac? The Form and Function of a Key Manuscript Source for Astro-Medical Practice in Later Medieval England', *Social History of Medicine*, 16 (2003), pp. 481–509; Hilary Carey, 'Astrological Medicine and the Medieval English Folded Almanac', *Social History of Medicine*, 17:3 (2004), pp. 345–63. See also Pamela Robinson, 'A "Very Curious Almanac": The Gift of Sir Robert Moray FRS, 1668' (a non-medical folding almanac), at <https://royalsocietypublishing.org/doi/full/10.1098/rsnr.2007.0017> (last accessed 5 August 2019).

30. Henry E. Sigerist, 'Bedside Manners in the Middle Ages: The Treatise *De cautelis medicorum* Attributed to Arnold of Villanova', in *Henry E. Sigerist on the History of Medicine*, ed. Féliz Marti-Albañez (New York: MD Publications, 1960), pp. 134–40.

31. Mooney, 'Manuscript Evidence', p. 195.
32. Peregrine Horden, 'Prefatory Note: The Uses of Medical Manuscripts', in Barbara Zipser (ed.), *Medical Books in the Byzantine World* (Bologna: Eikasmós Online, 2013), p. 1.

33. Ibid., pp. 2–4.
34. Ibid., p. 5.
35. A non-academic reading public does not account for the 'use' of all translations of medical works into the vernacular. For example, a translation of a Scholastic manual of therapeutics was created by a student as an aid to studying the Latin original. See Luke Demaitre, 'Medical Writing in Transition: Between Ars and Vulgus', *Early Science and Medicine*, 3:2 (1998), pp. 88–102.

36. Faye Marie Getz, 'Charity, Translation, and Language of Medical Learning in Medieval England', *Bulletin of the History of Medicine*,

64 (1990), p. 15, quoting the Latin prologue in London, British Library Royal 17.D.1, fol. 1r. An edition of the *Liber uricrisiarum* edited by M. Teresa Tavormina and Nicholas Everett is forthcoming in 2020 from University of Toronto Press: see <https://henrydaniel.utoronto.ca> (last accessed 5 August 2019).
37. Peter Murray Jones, 'Witnesses to Medieval Medical Practice in the Harley Collection', *Electronic British Library Journal* (2008), p. 2, at <http://www.bl.uk/eblj/2008articles/articles.html> (last accessed 5 August 2019).
38. Peregrine Horden, 'The Millennium Bug: Health and Medicine Around the Year 1000', *Social History of Medicine*, 13:2 (2000), pp. 207–8.
39. A. Appadurai, *The Social Life of Things: Commodities in Cultural Perspective* (Cambridge: Cambridge University Press, 1996).
40. Monica H. Green, 'Moving from Philology to Social History: The Circulation and Uses of Albucasis's Latin *Surgery* in the Middle Ages', in Florence Eliza Glaze and Brian Nance (eds), *Between Text and Patient: The Medical Enterprise in Medieval and Early Modern Europe* (Florence: SISMEL/Edizioni del Galluzzo), pp. 331–72.
41. Ibid., p. 355. The manuscript is Budapest, Eötvös Loránd Tudomány Egyetem Könyvtára, Department of Manuscripts and Rare Books, Cod. Lat. 15, s. xiii ex., and is digitised at <https://v2.manuscriptorium.com/apps/main/en/index.php> (last accessed 5 August 2019).
42. Joseph Ziegler, 'Skin and Character in Medieval and Early Renaissance Physiognomy', in *La pelle umana: The Human Skin*, Micrologus 13 (Florence: SISMEL – Edizioni del Galluzzo, 2005), pp. 511–35.
43. Tony Hunt, *The Medieval Surgery* (Woodbridge: Boydell, 1992), p. 13.
44. Martha Dana Rust, *Imaginary Worlds in Medieval Books: Exploring the Manuscript Matrix* (New York: Palgrave Macmillan, 2007), pp. 33–4.

Chapter 7

Visual Form and Reading Communities: The Example of Early Modern Broadside Elegies

Katherine Acheson

In a 1982 essay, Robert Darnton writes that the object of study of book history is the 'communications circuit that runs from the author to the publisher ... the printer, the shipper, the bookseller, and the reader'.[1] Darnton refers to 'the reader' here, but as the roots of book history in the Annales school of social historiography suggest, what is meant is *readers*, in the plural, social beings who compose communities of interpretation in which shared values, beliefs and interests are mediated by textual objects and their circulation. These textual objects are material and are, therefore, as Maureen Bell writes, 'constrained by the currently available technologies of paper, ink, print, illustration and binding'. In early modern print, these material texts participate in, imitate and challenge 'a set of typographical conventions shared and understood by the text's producers, buyers and readers'.[2] While we know that both verbal and visual components of typographical conventions impact readers and affect their understanding of and identification with material texts, our methodologies – rooted as they are in verbal disciplines which long considered books to be strictly verbal artefacts – are more suited for analysing verbal, rather than visual, effects. This chapter proposes that we recognise that the visual qualities of texts help express and shape the commitments, interests and priorities of readers and, like words, have the power to join those readers together in networks and communities of shared values and understanding.

Broadside funeral elegies

Broadside funeral elegies were increasingly popular in the course of the seventeenth century in Britain. These occasional poems offered 'a flexible way of addressing the occasion of a death, mourning, the endurance of traditional communal values, and topical concerns'.[3] They celebrated (or mocked) the lives of a wide range of public figures, including military men, jurists, and kings and queens, an astrologer, a philosopher, a poet or two, a couple of notorious thieves and several traitors, and 'Old Maddam Gwinn', Nell's mother, said to have drowned, drunk, 'in her own Fishpond'.[4] These poems could also serve to express political or theological allegiance, especially in times of conflict, such as during the Civil Wars (1641–52), in the aftermath of the Great Ejection in 1662, and around and about the Popish Plot (1678–81) and the Exclusion Crisis (1679–81). The genre was also well suited for satirical social commentary. The diction of these poems tends to be rough and ready, and in them there is much 'snatching' by 'cruel' Death, many 'horrid wounds' and vast floods of weeping. Hyperbole is the most common rhetorical device: as the (anonymous) poet writes in a 1643 elegy for Robert Greville, Baron Brooke, 'Out of that honour and love we owe to thee, / We lose our selves in an Hyperbole'.[5] An elegy for George Sonds, who was killed by his brother in 1655, expresses a common predicament for the speakers of these poems in its opening: 'Reach me a Handcerchiff, Another yet, / And yet another, for the last is wett'.[6] The poems are riddled with hackneyed tropes of heroism – the Rubicon is crossed anew, Hercules's labours are re-enacted endlessly, the afflictions of the saints are ladled on top of the sufferings of Christ on the cross, even though 'Antient and Moderne *Hero's* seeme, / Compar'd to ours, a poor low barren Theme'.[7] Two words will never do when ten or twenty are available and conceits are extended beyond all patience. In each and all of these respects, the broadside funeral elegy, then, provides a useful verbal context for other occasional and satirical works from the century, from Donne's more classical elegies to poems about the Anglo-Dutch wars and late Stuart society by Marvell and his contemporaries – and, indeed, any poems that feature death decked out in glorious hyperbole and cheered on by a teeming cast of deities and superpowers, past and present.

Broadside funeral elegies printed in the seventeenth century have distinctive visual features and therefore provide a significant archive for the assessment of the role of visual aspects of print in creating meaning for early modern readers. As a publication genre, broadside funeral elegies stand beside ballads and emblems: each has particular and conventional visual characteristics that are capable of signifying the genre *before* the viewer has a chance to read any of the words. For broadside funeral elegies, these conventions include a vertical layout on the page and Roman type, which distinguishes them from many ballads; the title always appears centred at the top of the page, and there is often a colophon – a brief informative statement giving publication details of the book – at the bottom. There are usually two columns (sometimes more), and wide black borders frame the poem, sometimes separating the columns, the title from the body of the poem and additional features such as an acrostic poem, anagram, epitaph or the authorial signature and colophon (see Figure 7.5 for examples of all of these features). Of the additional poetic forms integrated in single-page elegies, the epitaph is the most common, and the acrostic is not far behind; both have distinctive formats that coach and guide the reader's path through the matter of the page. The black borders occasionally reveal their origin as blocks of wood, which adds a rustic urgency to the composition of the verse (see Figures 7.1 and 7.3); the borders are sometimes shaped as a tomb or headstone, and are often embellished with thematically fitting illustrations, such as skeletons, fallen angels, skulls and crossbones, bones, flags, arrows, hourglasses, crowns, castle gates, banners (usually emblazoned 'memento mori') and picks and shovels (see Figure 7.6). For notorious or highly celebrated political or national figures, the elegy might be adorned with an illustration of a hearse, a monumental tomb, a funeral procession or even a portrait (see Figure 7.3). The visual presentation of these works is also distinguished by the bristling of italics, and the liberal scatterings of exclamation marks, apostrophic line openings and capitalised personifications; these features identify the works as *poems*, rather than as ballads or songs, or prose works such as petitions, grievances or declarations, which were all also printed on single sheets.

An early modern browser, therefore, could spot an elegy from afar; the visual codes constitute a promise of emotional, intellectual and aesthetic experience embodied in the elegy, its paratexts and its illustrative elements. As publicly displayed works about publicly recognised figures, the visual aspects of these elegies invite browsers and readers to join others in sharing the experience of them: they signal, that is, a community of the like-minded, or at least the conviction of printers and booksellers that such communities are imaginable and desirable to their audiences.

Elegies for Robert Devereux (d. 1646)

Robert Devereux, third earl of Essex, was, at the time of his death in 1646, a semi-retired Parliamentary general of mixed record and reputation. When he died suddenly of a stroke in 1646, however, he was given a lavish state funeral, modelled on that of Prince Henry, and was buried in Westminster Abbey. The scale of Essex's funeral is reflected in the fact that more than ten broadside funeral elegies about him survive (at least four longer elegies, formatted as pamphlets, were also printed), all produced in the year of his death. Most of the broadside elegies for Essex are illustrated, and their illustrations are distinctive and unusual, a mark of both the celebrity of the subject and of the dramatic and public ceremony of his funeral rites. The texts are all the things that elegies should be – hyperbolic in the extreme, larded with rhetorical questions, pathetically fallacious, but also political, as is so often the case. One offers, in part, 'A briefe Recitement of his valour and fidelity in the Kingdomes just Cause, against the Enemies of Religion, Parliament and Kingdome';[8] another decries the fact that heroic Essex did not face down the coward Death this one last time, and others mention particular battles, struggles, allies and enemies. Essex is persistently characterised as a moderate who sought to protect the rights and entitlements of Parliament, while respecting the security of person and the ancient responsibilities of the sovereign. The community of mourners, then, is also a community of ideological need and desire. The First Civil War had ended only months earlier and the funeral took place in London, heart of Parliamentary loyalty and the named addressee of one of the poems. The funeral was one of the first major public spectacles or pageants after the Parliament's victory in the First Civil War; Charles I had been under house arrest since May, and Oliver Cromwell had returned to Westminster in July.

The visual tropes of the Essex elegies express the topoi on which the printers imagine interested readers and buyers will want to meet others. There are two main sets of visual motifs that distinguish the Essex elegies from other examples of the genre. Two of the elegies are illustrated with a portrait of Essex, flanked by black blocks of ink, patterned with wood.[9] One of the portraits (Figure 7.1) is shaped as an oval, and bordered with an inscription identifying the subject; it resembles frontispiece illustrations of authors or famous subjects of printed works, which in turn echo painted portraits, commemorative medals and coins;[10] the inscription calls him 'The most noble Robert Earle of Essex and Lo[rd] Gen of the Forces for K[ing] & Parl[iament]', emphasising his mediating and moderate position even as a Parliamentary general. Both it and the other portrait represent Essex in armour and with the regalia of his rank (a sash, a baton and decorative cords) and with the collar that typically signals adherence to the

Figure 7.1 Thomas Philipot, 'AN ELEGIE OFFER'D UP TO THE Memory of His Excellencie Robert Earle of Essex and Ewe. . .' (London: Printed for William Ley at his shop, 1646). Call number EB65 P5377 646e, Houghton Library, Harvard University

reformed religion. These images depict Essex as a heroic military leader, an individual who embodies both longstanding tradition (in his numerous titles and the conservative and traditional outfit) and the needs and values of the present, someone distinguished by his longstanding relationships with Cromwell and Parliament, but duly aristocratic in mien, lineage and office. This portrait, then, imagines a community of readers for the elegy who want to collectively endorse the kind of leadership – military and governmental – that Essex embodies:

> London, thou know'st with what a willing mind,
> This Peere adventur'd, when thy men did find
> Such rare encouragements from their Generall,
> With resolutions, being inflamed all,
> To live and die with him, they were all bent,
> In maint'nance of just Lawes, and Parliament. [11]

The portrait also connects the funeral elegy with that other emergent mode of public discourse, the news. 'A Perfect Table of Three hundred fourty and three Victories obtained since the Kings attempt to enter into *Hull* at the begining of these VVars', for example, a newssheet printed in 1646 before Essex's death, is decorated with engraved portraits of Essex and the Parliamentary General Thomas Fairfax, both depicted in armour and with the regalia of warrior princes. The audience's familiarity with images of Essex as martial hero was enhanced by their ubiquity. The clearest example of the confluence of the visual styles of the broadside funeral elegy and the broadside news-sheet is 'Englands sorrow for the losse of their late Generall: An Epitaph upon his Excellencie ROBERT Earle of Essex' (Figure 7.2). This elegy combines an epitaph by Thomas Philipot (also the author of the poem shown in Figure 7.1) and the image of the hearse set in front of a map of England and below a stormy cloud, with a prose account of the 'severall Victories in which his Excellency was ingaged in person', 'A perfect List of 150. Castles, Garrisons, and Townes that were taken from the King by his Excellence the Earle of Essex' and another 'perfect List' of 48 'gallant Victories' led by forces under Essex's command. This elegy, like the news-sheet referred to above, is arranged in columns, with printer's flowers, straight lines and fine borders organising the content. The Essex elegies, then, are continuous with the circulation of information for mass consumption about current events: Essex was, himself, a key figure within the news circuits, and the elegies are marketed in part because of their appeal to readers of the other genres in which he features.

Figure 7.2 Thomas Philipot, 'Englands sorrow for the losse of their late Generall' (London, 1646). Call number 669.f.10.(88.), British Library. © The British Library Board

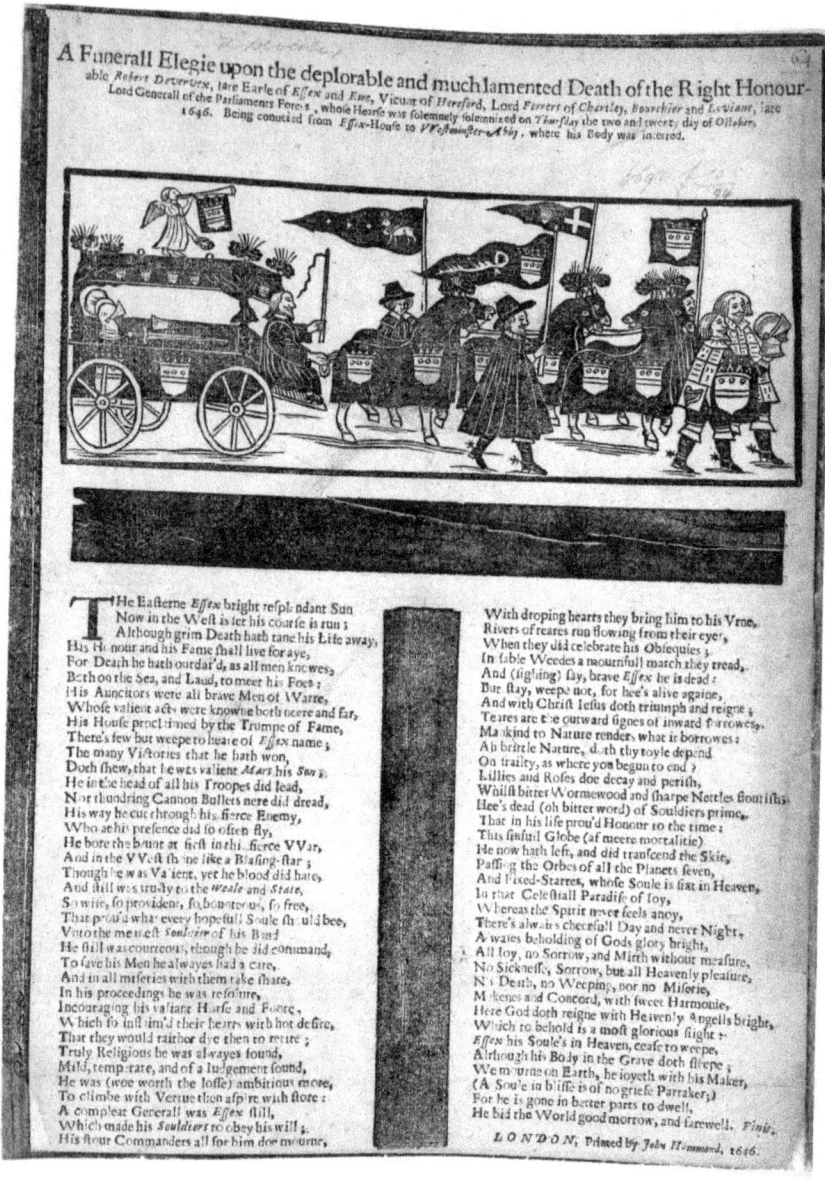

Figure 7.3 Anon., 'A Funerall Elegie upon the deplorable and much lamented Death of the Right Honourable Robert Devereux . . .' (London: Printed by John Hammond, 1646). Call number 669.f.10.(94.), British Library. © The British Library Board

The other visual trope that is used in the Essex elegies is the funeral procession or the hearse itself (see Figure 7.3). These poems celebrate the same values as the others; in addition to his military accomplishments (and with no mention of his several humiliations in that department), he is described as he 'That kept us safe from hostile Tyrannie' and 'Though he's extinct [a reference to the fact that Essex had no male heir, and thus the earldom of Essex fell into abeyance], yet let Posterity / Keep up his name, that did (our Liberty / Safely for us and them to keep) expose / Himselfe, unsafely, to the rage of Foes').[12] The pageantry of the funeral procession and its elaborate and costly furniture, trappings and hearse itself serve to represent a state that honours its heroes, respects the values they represent and joins with its people to celebrate those things. Significantly, the illustrations characterise the elegies themselves as monuments[13] and imagine the elegies as places where people will gather to remember and to mythologise in order to collect themselves at the ready for the future. If the readers of the elegies are figuratively gathering in honour of Essex as his hearse passes before them, or as he lies in state, then the visual aspects are drawing together a community of shared values around the values, ideas and feelings represented by the dead Essex.

Elegies for dissenting ministers, 1663–99

As a consequence of the Act of Uniformity of 1662, about 2,500 ministers were ejected from the Church of England, and therefore their livings, for refusing to conform to the prescriptions of the *Book of Common Prayer* and the liturgy. Elegies about ejected ministers and other non-conforming and dissenting ministers are one of several kinds of publications occasioned by their deaths; the sermons preached at their funerals were often printed and their wills were sometimes published.[14] These works joined the published sermons, commentaries and other theological discourses printed during the lifetimes of these figures, sometimes collected into multi-author volumes, such as *The Farewell sermons of the late London Ministers* (1662), which features those of twelve ejected ministers, collected by Edmund Calamy. Sharon Achinstein writes that after the 1662 Act, 'funerals were rare occasions when nonconformists did meet in large numbers in public'.[15] These events were affirmations of their community and its values, as well as recognition of the passing of an individual: 'Through funerals, nonconformists placed their individual experiences of suffering into a common fund; they assimilated collective trauma into a positive framework; they presented a memory for the future'.[16] The use of print to express their collectivity is evident in the full titles of collections of funeral sermons and tributes for dissenting ministers, such as *The second volumne of the farewel se[r]mons, preached by some London and country ministers* (1663), which contains sermons about or delivered by twenty ministers. In the funeral elegy, the powerful collective event of the funeral itself was brought together with the rich and diverse print networks of the dissenting community: like the elegies for Essex, then, these poems speak to their readers as members of a community of shared understanding, values, experience and desires.

The number and chronological range of my examples of elegies for dissenting and ejected ministers – twenty elegies printed between 1663 and 1699[17] – means it is unlikely that they will conform to a single template. Nonetheless, there are aspects of the visual design that do bring these together as a group, and would do so for prospective buyers. First, they almost never have illustrations that are unique to that elegy or that person, as we see in the Essex group. In elegies for dissenting ministers the incidence of illustration is considerably lower than in the average of the Essex group, in terms of both generic illustrations belonging to elegies in general, and unique or particular illustrations that express the character or value of one individual. Second, all but one of these elegies have black borders around the page and between the columns, making that feature more common than is average to the Essex group. Third, all of these elegies have at least two columns. Fourth, they share a distinctive typographic layout, and particular components typically occupy specific regions of the page: epitaphs are usually in the lower right-hand corner, separated from the body of the elegy by white space and the upper-case, often italicised, title; acrostics and anagrams are likewise shorter than the elegiac poem proper, and are set off with titles and with the arrangement or rearrangement of the letterforms to meet their generic requirements; marginalia are set in smaller type and run down the edges of the columns. In these respects, the dissenter's elegy might be easy to distinguish at a bookseller's stall from elegies about members of other groups or distinguished individuals, and attract readers and buyers who identified with the values and experiences of the elegiac subjects.

The elegies for dissenting ministers also make distinctive use of the play between verbal and visual modes of communication. Take, for example, the epitaph, which features in most of these poems. Our use of the term 'epitaph' to refer to a poetic genre – in which a brief, metrical and conventionally witty statement is made expressing the miracle of life after death – was derived from the use of the term to describe an inscription on a tomb. In these elegies, the epitaphs refer to this origin and figure themselves as part of a material tomb. 'Here Lyeth One' begins the 1663 epitaph for Henry Iesse (Jessey);[18] for Edmund Calamy in 1667, 'Here a poor Minister of Christ doth lie';[19] for Joseph Caryl in 1672, 'Judicious *Caryl* here at rest does lye';[20] for Thomas Wadsworth in 1676, 'Reader, stand off, and thy due distance keep, / For in this bed a Friend of Christ doth sleep! / His body here's interred, being Dead; / But his blest Soul to Abraham's bosom's fled!';[21] for John Wells in 1676, 'A Minister under this Tombstone lies';[22] for Christopher Fowler in 1677, 'Reader stand off, and thy due distance keep, / For in this Grave a Friend of Christ doth sleep';[23] for Richard Baxter in 1691, 'Consider, Reader, who lies here, / And for thy Loss them Drop a Tear';[24] and so on. The deictic 'here' in these lines points to the corpse and the grave: as Lorna Clymer writes, 'Unlike other poetical meditations on mortality that remain relatively restrained and meditative . . . the funeral elegy typically explores the meaning of death urgently, as if near an open grave, and relatively briefly, as if the devastating focus could not be sustained indefinitely'.[25] But these statements also refer to the visual conventions of the broadside funeral elegy, in which the page is figured as a tombstone, with a curved and sometimes decorated top, or a coffin – a box of wood enclosing the 'remains' of the subject. According to Achinstein, nonconforming ministers often asked to be buried privately (and therefore in ground unconsecrated by the official Church) and without the rites prescribed in the *Book of Common Prayer*.[26]

The epitaph, then, contributes to the complex and sharply tendentious sense of the material, social and theological displacement or 'ejection', even in death, of the nonconforming ministers and their congregations. The elegies are one of the several ways in which rhetorical and media forms provide virtual images for ejected and dissenting ministers of the spaces of pastoral care and spiritual guidance. For them, more so than other subjects of elegies, then, the poems perform the functions usually carried out by material memorials and ceremonies.

The layout of acrostics and anagrams, on which '[s]eventeenth-century writers expended great effort and ingenuity', is another feature of broadside funeral elegies for dissenting ministers that draws on the interplay of visual and verbal modes of representation.[27] They were particularly prevalent in religious verse, where they express spiritual paradoxes: if Christ is the word, then the incarnation, crucifixion and ascension can be understood metaphorically through the acts of deconstitution and reconstitution that anagrams and acrostics require, expressing the ways in which death transforms not only the individual but also our understanding of what is true and good. For instance, in the 1666 elegy for Nathanael Strange, the acrostic begins 'New Griefs, new Sorrows now are come' and it goes on to describe the event of Strange's death in paradoxes, such as 'Thiss World too low, for thee so High, so Heavenly divine' and 'Now unto us great Loss, to thee great Gain: most happy Change! / All Earthly Joys contemn disdst thou, because thou wert Sublime'.[28] Anagrams and acrostics are genres that instantiate the activity of interpretation: anagrams rearrange existing letters to produce new meanings, and acrostics spin lines out of letters that themselves compose words. Adele Davidson writes that George Herbert's acrostics in *The Temple* 'generate a material yet mystical surplus symbolizing divine bounty through an overdetermined and palimpsestic layering of plural signification'.[29] While broadside funeral elegies are surely poor cousins to Herbert's poetry, the anagrams and acrostics built into this genre, especially for dissenting and ejected clerics, signal religion based on reading, interpretation, the vernacular, and textually-mediated knowledge of the divine.

Early modern anagrams and acrostics are visually compelling and distinctive in elegies for dissenting ministers, as the rearrangement of letters is represented in variations on a standard typography and layout. 'A MITE from Three MOURNERS', a memorial for Thomas Glass, has 'An ACROSTICK' on the left side and 'An ANAGRAM' on the right (Figure 7.4). The acrostic spells the subject's name vertically, in upper-case letters, while each line expands upon his virtues. The anagram proved challenging (Thomas Glass becomes 'Glass as Moth'[30]), but the arrangement of the anagrammatic type is standard (small caps for the title, 'An ANAGRAM', and italics for the name and its anagram). The elegy for Nathaneal Strange mentioned above begins with the anagram '(Satan then all Anger)' and then offers another acrostic poem on this theme, the letters this time reading up the margin, rather than down, to spell Nathanael Strange. The second acrostic poem starts, as it were, at the bottom: 'Enrag'd was Satan; (*Satan then all* in his *Anger*) Why? / God by such Evangelick means, will make his Power dye'; Satan is superseded by Christ, in whose service Strange died. Both acrostic poems pun relentlessly on the minister's names: 'A las! *Strange*, thou art gone, to whom the World was very strange' for example, or 'This Doctrine strange unto the World, *Strange* to the World made'. The elegy for Thomas Glass takes similar liberties with the subject's name in both the acrostic and the poem that is headed by the anagram: the acrostic begins

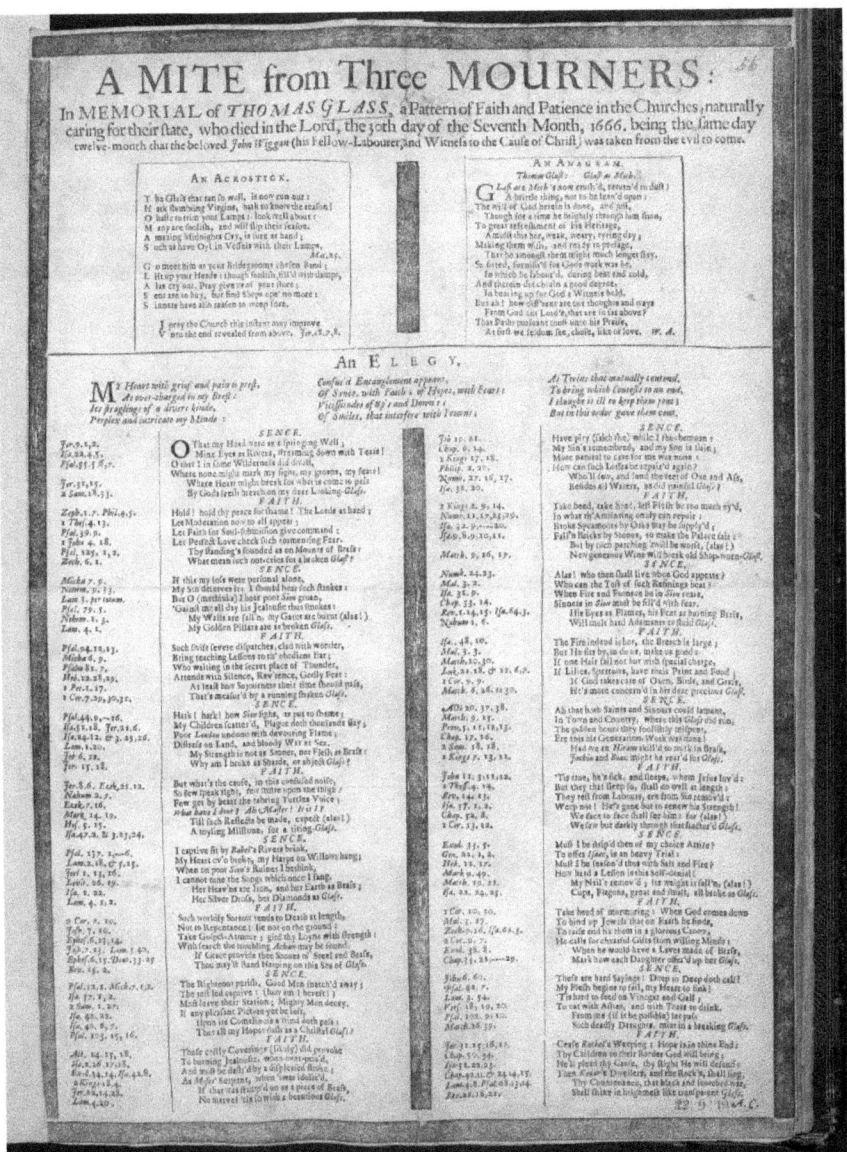

Figure 7.4 Anon., 'A MITE from Three MOURNERS: In MEMORIAL of THOMAS GLASS . . .' (London: 1666). Call number, Early English books tract supplement interim guide C.20.f.3[56], British Library. © The British Library Board

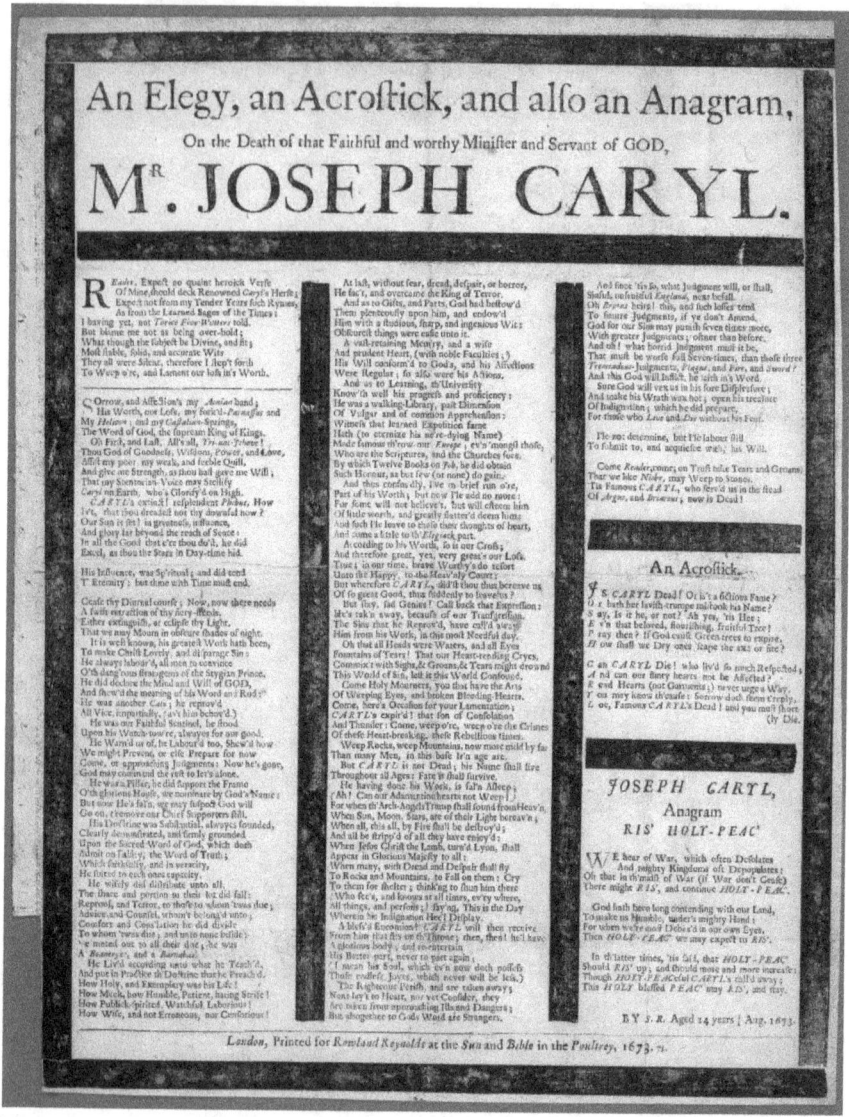

Figure 7.5 Anon., 'An Elegy, an Acrostick, and also an Anagram, On the Death of that Faithful and worthy Minister and Servant of GOD, Mr. JOSEPH CARYL' (London: Printed for R. Reynolds, 1672). Call number EB65 R100 673e, Houghton Library, Harvard University

'The Glass that ran so well, is now run out', and the other poem says that 'Glass' is 'return'd to dust'. In one of the several elegies for Joseph Caryl, 'An Elegy, an Acrostick, and also an Anagram, On the Death of that Faithful and worthy Minister and Servant of God, Mr. JOSEPH CARYL' (Figure 7.5), within the anagram the phrase 'RIS' HOLY-PEAC' is chopped and sorted in the poem below the anagrammatic title, which ends as follows:

> In th'latter times, 'tis said, that *HOLY-PEAC'*
> Should *RIS'* up; and should more and more increase:
> Though *HOLY-PEAC*eful *CARYL's* call'd away;
> This *HOLY* blessed *PEAC'* may *RIS'* and stay.

The reader perceives the integration of the subject with the thoughts expressed in the poem and the poetic modes used to express them, in part because the anagram of the name is picked out in upper-case italics. Simultaneously expressions of theological values, personal tributes and verbal wit, the anagram and the acrostic are significant features — both visual and verbal — of the elegies for nonconforming ministers.

The final graphical feature of early modern broadside elegies for dissenting ministers that I wish to discuss here is marginalia. A select few of the elegies for nonconforming ministers have marginalia. Most common of these are biblical citations and cross-references, such as those in 'A MITE from Three MOURNERS' (Figure 7.4). The main elegy on this broadside takes the form of a dialogue between faith and sense. The stanzas are bountifully annotated with references to biblical verses: next to 'Sence' only Old Testament verses are cited, while 'Faith' is supported by both Old and New, and therefore all Christian covenants. These marginalia, then, trace the triumph of faith over sense in terms of the collapse of the dialogic in Christian faith. In another example, the marginalia around the title of 'A MEMORIAL on the Death of that faithful Servant of Jesus Christ, NATHANAEL STRANGE' encode a story available to those with intimate knowledge of the scriptures, or the patience to research the references: they move from topical statements about memory and memorials — such as Matthew 26: 13 ('Wheresoever this gospel be preached in the whole world, there shall also this, that this woman have done, be told for a memorial of her') and Proverbs 10: 7 ('The memory of the just is blessed: but the name of the wicked shall rot') — through statements of allegiance to Christ and fellow dissenters which verge on antinomianism — Isaiah 26: 13 and Esther 3: 8, which reads 'There is a certain people scattered abroad and dispersed among the people in all the provinces of thy kingdom; and their laws are diverse from all people; neither keep they the king's laws: therefore it is not for the king's profit to suffer them' – to references to the Last Judgement and the triumph of Christ – 'Behold, a king shall reign in righteousness, and princes shall rule in judgment. Then the moon shall be confounded, and the sun ashamed, when the LORD of hosts shall reign in mount Zion, and in Jerusalem, and before his ancients gloriously' (Isaiah 32: 1) and 'He shall judge among the heathen, he shall fill the places with the dead bodies; he shall wound the heads over many countries' (Psalm 110: 6).

In both these examples, then, the marginalia articulate a set of theological statements and precepts. In visual terms, the marginalia act as a citation of the genres in which such glosses are typically found, especially in texts and paratexts of the Bible, such as the *Book of Common Prayer*. In these ways, the marginalia provide both a visual and a verbal subtext uniting readers in common faith and commitment. Two of the surviving elegies for dissenting ministers include marginalia which refer to other works by the deceased. For example, 'AN ELEGY On the Death of the Reverend and Pious Mr. Thomas Wadsworth', quoted above, cites the titles of one of Wadsworth's works, *His Exhortation to a holy Life*, in the elegy proper, and elaborates in the margin, saying 'His serious Exhortation to a holy Life, Written not long after his entrance on the ministry'. The poem makes reference to one other work by Wadsworth, which is likewise identified in the margin, and the remaining two annotations add biographical detail to the poem: where the poem reads 'Nor needs he * Stone or Collick for to fear', the margin adds, '* Of which he had sore Fits'. We are used to thinking of marginalia (both printed and manuscript) as extensions of the book at hand – glosses, intertextual references, finding devices, aides memoires – but these examples illustrate how they might signal genre, subject matter and intellectual status to the reading public, both visually and verbally.[31]

Elegies featuring a skull-and-crossbones headpiece, 1675–83

This group of elegies, printed between 1675 and 1683, shares an illustrated headpiece – either the actual woodblock or a copy. The illustration is shaped like a headstone, and features a skull in the centre, superimposed on crossbones, with more bones to the left and right; on either side are crossed pick-and-shovel combinations; an hourglass

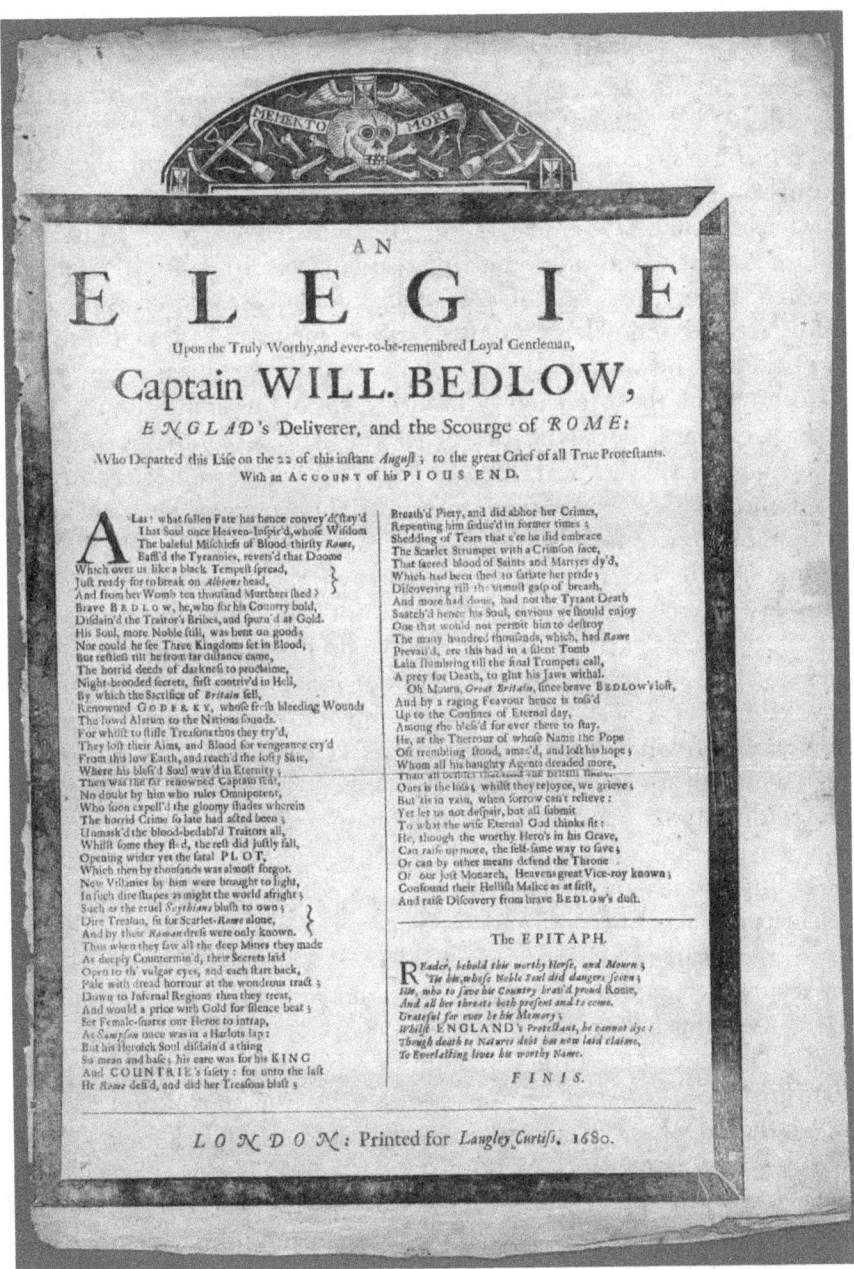

Figure 7.6 Anon., 'An Elegie Upon the Truly Worthy, and ever-to-be-remembred Loyal Gentleman, Captain WILL. BEDLOW . . .' (London: Printed for Langley Curtiss, 1680). Call number EB65 A100 680e2, Houghton Library, Harvard University

sits in each lower corner; atop the skull sits a third hourglass, this one with wings (see Figure 7.6 for an example). These bear similarities to other broadside elegies, as many of the genre have a decorative headpiece, a handful of which are repeated enough times in surviving examples to suggest they were both popular and recognisable. The group of subjects featured in this particular collection is diverse. Lazarus Seaman, a member of the Westminster Assembly, Master of Peterhouse at Cambridge and long-serving minister at All Hallows in Bread Street, was one of the better-known of the nonconforming ministers. Edmund Berry Godfrey was a magistrate drawn into the Popish Plot who was murdered in 1678. Richard Ford was a merchant, a governor of the Merchant Adventurers, commissioner of the East India Company, deputy governor of the Africa Company, and MP, alderman, sheriff, Lord Mayor and Fellow of the Royal Society. Robert Wild (died 1679) was a nonconformist minister and satirical poet, author of nonconformist tracts, elegies and satirical verse. William Bedloe (1680) was a figure at the centre of the Popish Plot. Colonel Thomas Blood (died 1680) was a notorious conspirator and spy infamous for his participation in the Dublin Plot to seize James Butler, Duke of Ormond, the Lord Lieutenant of Ireland, and his seat, Dublin Castle, in 1663, as well as an attempt to steal the crown jewels from the Tower of London in 1671, and a dirty tricks campaign launched in the year of his death to bring down the Duke of Buckingham. Heneage Finch (died 1682), first earl of Nottingham and Lord Chancellor, was a career politician who clung firmly to the middle of the road during this tempestuous and polarised era. Prince Rupert (died 1682) was a celebrity royal, army and navy officer, and a notable cavalier. James Cecil, third earl of Salisbury (died 1683), was a frenemy of Charles II, prosecutor of Stafford of Popish Plot fame, and a possible participant in the Rye House Plot.

These figures have little in common ideologically, politically or in terms of the factions of various sorts in British Restoration society. What they do have in common is that they are well known public figures whose reputations might attract attention to their elegies from a broad reading public. From figures involved in the Popish Plot, to notorious criminals, to respected magistrates and military figures, the subjects of this group of elegies are all public figures with established reputations in print. William Bedloe, Edmund Berry Godfrey, Thomas ('Colonel' or 'Captain') Blood and James Cecil, the Earl of Salisbury, are all familiar names to students of Restoration history because of their connections to the Popish Plot or because of their sensational criminal careers. But most of the other subjects of these elegies had significant reputations bolstered by printed materials by them or about them. Robert Wild is said by Sharon Achinstein to be 'perhaps the most widely read topical Dissenting poet, his works repeatedly attracting satirical response and also surviving in commonplace books and verse miscellanies of the period';[32] more than 100 printed works associated with his name survive. Thomas Butler, sixth earl of Ossory, Irish peer, Royalist, politician and naval officer, died as Governor of Tangiers and was also well known: 'Ossory's death', writes J. D. Davies, 'triggered a remarkable and genuine outpouring of popular grief. His modesty, affability, courtesy, and loyalty were well known, as was his unwillingness simply to follow the herd in a notoriously cynical and faction-ridden court'.[33] In fact, it becomes clear in this group that one of the functions that elegies could provide, especially at this point in history when their visual and verbal motifs are well established for the bookseller's audience, was to advertise for print itself: the colophon for the elegy for John Micklethwaite, a physician who died in 1682, for instance, serves to promote the business of its printer:

> Printed for William Miller, at the Guilded Acorn in St. Paul's Church-Yard, where you may be furnished with most sorts of Bound or Stitched Books as Acts of Parliament, Proclamations, Speeches, Declarations, Letters, Orders, Commissions, Articles of War or Peace; As also Books of Divinity, Church-Government, Sermons on most occasions, and most sorts of Histories, Poetry, and such like &c.[34]

The columns, the variations in type size and fount, the perfect disposition of the matter on the single page, the integration of dropped capitals and the generosity of the ink itself all speak to the quality of the printing in elegies such as these.

About half of these elegies were printed for the publisher-bookseller Langley Curtis by diverse printers.[35] Curtis, according to the English Short Title Catalogue, is associated with more than 150 publications printed between 1669 and 1690. The most widely held in modern collections, according to WorldCat (the network of library content and services at <https://www.worldcat.org>), are two versions of the satiric ballad about him, 'L—gley C—s his lamentation in New-gate who lies there in danger of his ears for printing and publishing sedition and treason, for this five years last past: a song' (1684), which pertains to his imprisonment for the selling 'The night-walker of Bloomsbury: being the result of several late consultations between a vintner, Judge Tallow-Chandler, a brace of fishmongers, and a printer' (1683). This two-page, single-sheet dialogue features a fake ghost of William

Russell (1639–83), politician and conspirator in the Rye House Plot to kill the king. For this 'seditious libel', which attributed Russell's perfidy to Gilbert Burnet, Bishop of Salisbury and Russell's close confidante, Curtis was 'tried, found guilty, and fined heavily'.[36] Other works in which Curtis is identified as the bookseller include *Stafford's memoires* (1680); a work about Robert Foulkes, minister and murderer who was executed in 1679; Henry Care's *History of the damnable popish plot* (1680 and 1681) and other works fanning the flames of the Popish Plot; and works about the Rye House Plot. Between December 1680 and October 1682, Curtis and his wife Jane also published a single-sheet, two-page, bi-weekly news-sheet called the *True Protestant Mercury*, and for this they were fined for sedition.[37] These publications and his brushes with the rougher side of the law mean Curtis tends to be remembered as a 'Whig' bookseller or publisher, aligned with one side of the competitive and corrupt political sphere in late seventeenth-century England. But Curtis is also bookseller of other, less easily categorised or politicised works. These include news pamphlets such as 'Great newes from the Barbadoes, or, A True and faithful account of the grand conspiracy of the Negroes against the English and the happy discovery of the same' (1676); *England's Remarques* (1676), a survey of counties, including agricultural conditions, parishes, nobility and so on; a table for calculating compound interest ('A president for purchasers, sellers and mortgagers' (1678)); the polemical pamphlet 'The Golden Fleece: OR, OLD ENGLAND Restor'd to its old honest VOCATION' (1679), which calls for the establishment of workhouses in which the poor would labour at making wool cloth; *A Choice collection of wonderful miracles, ghosts, and visions* (1681); *A synopsis of heraldry* by Payne Fisher (1682); a book about growing lemon and orange trees in the Low Countries (1683); and ballads and popular dramatic works.

Curtis's record suggests that he was ambitious to secure a share of the burgeoning market in topical, occasional and periodical print. Like other works he published, the elegies that have his name on them advertise the capacity of the press and the eye-catching designs available for broadside works such as elegies. This group of elegies displays many of the most popular features of the latest printed works on a single sheet suitable for posting for all to see.

Taking 'An Elegie Upon the Truly Worthy, and ever-to-be-remembered Loyal Gentleman, Captain WILL. BEDLOW . . .', as an example (Figure 7.6), we see the decorative headpiece is, if not exactly decorous, thematically apt and visually bold; the variety of type in the titles alone (five different sizes of upper- and lower-case letters and four of upper-case, and two sizes of italics) is notable (despite the typographical error in the title); the columns are even and well defined by rules; the proportions of the layout are pleasing; and the setting of the poetry, including the dropped capital at the opening, the well measured lines, the braces gripping triplets, and the neatly staged 'EPITAPH', is finely done. In particular, that is, these elegies advertise Curtis's competence as a publisher of popular, occasional poetry. Alan B. Farmer and Zachary Lesser's analysis of the market for print between 1559 and 1602 shows us that poetry was a significant part of that market (12.9 per cent): 'In early modern England', write Farmer and Lesser, 'verse was culturally central, used to address a wide range of topics, and it was equally central to print culture . . . early modern publishers must have understood the popularity of verse with their customers'.[38] While we have no comparable analysis for the later seventeenth century, the evidence suggests that we might discover similar figures supporting poetry's popularity for both readers and writers, and therefore for publisher-booksellers. Of the poetic genres prevalent at the time, funeral elegies were remarkably popular, as is evident in the numbers that survive (not only in broadside examples, on which I concentrate here, but in multi-page pamphlets and longer, multi-author collections), and the number and range of authors who wrote them. As Dennis Kay writes, the funeral elegy was a kind of starter genre for the would-be poet: it was 'accessible to writers of all ages and abilities, and was for many of them evidently a kind of laboratory in which they learnt about composition'.[39] According to Kay, seventeenth-century writers could learn more than composition from writing elegies:

> If writing elegies was one of the ways poets learnt to write in the vernacular, it was also a way they learnt the discipline of fitting what they wrote to highly particular occasions. As a consequence, it became a means of learning about decorum, of investigating, exploring, representing, analysing, anatomizing social relationships on the occasion of the subject's death.[40]

One end of the range of talents on display in funeral elegies is evident in the examples referred to in this chapter; the other end is indicated by works by poets such as John Milton, Andrew Marvell and John Dryden. As a key genre for writers and readers of poetry, the broadside funeral elegy offered an outstanding opportunity for a bookseller who commissioned printed works (what we call a publisher) to showcase the complexity, craft and excellence of their work in the presentation and reproduction of examples from an important genre within an increasingly important category of print (poetry). In the competitive field of late seventeenth-century print, Langley Curtis and his peers vied for market share in part through displaying the quality of the printed works they sponsored and sold, especially in broadside form.[41] The broadside elegies that feature this particular headpiece were designed both for readers who enjoyed the elegiac form and for writers who imagined their work in print. As such, they are one of the most prominent of visual forms of seventeenth-century literary culture.

Conclusion

Roger Chartier writes that 'a history of reading must identify the specific mechanisms that distinguish the various communities of readers and traditions of reading'.[42] My argument is that the visual is one of the 'specific mechanisms' by which we can infer groupings of readers within the market of print in early modern England. Elegies for Robert Devereux were designed to appeal to those readers with an ear for the heroic and an eye for news and who bonded with others on the basis of their desire for peaceful and moderate government in the midst of the English Civil Wars. Elegies for dissenting ministers were intended to pique the interest of the nonconforming community to which the ministers belonged and to whom the printed poems provided a shared site for mourning and communion. Elegies about public figures decorated with the skull-and-crossbones headpiece used by Langley Curtis and others in the late seventeenth century were printed for the notice of readers interested in the popular genre and their celebrity subjects, and writers surveying the publishing world for examples of marketable genres; they advertised their quality to both readers and writers. These broadside poems, then, provide concrete examples of what Maureen Bell describes as 'the many choices made' by early modern publisher-booksellers, which reveal 'an often complex negotiation of the text's meaning within the economic, social and cultural contexts and conventions current at its moment of production'.[43] The history of reading, that is, is always also a history of the materials and technologies of reproduction and the mechanisms by which works were disseminated, and of the practices of writing, in all its complexity.

Notes

1. Robert Darnton, 'What Is the History of Books?', *Daedalus*, 111:3 (1982), p. 67.
2. Maureen Bell, 'Mise-En-Page, Illustration, Expressive Form', in John Barnard and D. F. McKenzie (eds), *The Cambridge History of the Book in Britain* (Cambridge: Cambridge University Press, 2002), vol. IV, p. 632.
3. Lorna Clymer, 'The Funeral Elegy in Early Modern Britain: A Brief History', in Karen Weisman (ed.), *The Oxford Handbook of the Elegy* (Oxford: Oxford University Press, 2010), pp. 170–86 (p. 176).
4. Anon., 'An ELOGY Upon that never to be Forgotten Matron, Old Maddam Gwinn . . .' (1679).
5. Anon., 'AN ELEGIE UPON . . . Lord Brooke' (printed by Robert Austin, and Andrew Coe, 1643).
6. William Annand, 'A FUNERAL ELEGIE, Upon the Death of GEORGE SONDS . . .' (London: Printed by John Crowch, 1655).
7. Tw. Th., 'An Elegiack Memoriall of the Right Honourable Generall DEANE . . .' (London: Printed by M. S. for Tho. Jenner, 1653).
8. Anon., 'A Funerall Monument: or the manner of the Herse of the most renowned *Robert Devereux*, Earl of *Essex* and *Ewe* . . .' (London: Printed for J. Hancock in Popes-head Alley, 1646)
9. Josiah Ricraft, 'A Funerall Elegy upon the most Honored upon Earth, and now glorious in Heaven, His Excellency *Robert Devereux* Earl of *Essex* and *Ewe* . . .' (London: to be sold by John Hancock, 1646), and Thomas Philipot, 'AN ELEGIE OFFER'D UP TO THE Memory of His Excellencie ROBERT Earle of *Essex* and *Ewe* . . .' (London: Printed for William Ley at his shop, 1646) (Figure 7.1).
10. Dozens of engraved portraits of Essex survive in the collection of the National Portrait Gallery, London, dated from his lifetime through to the nineteenth century.
11. Anon., 'A Funerall Monument'.
12. Anon., 'An Elegie upon the death of the right Honourable & most renowned, ROBERT DEVEREUX . . .' (London: Printed by R. Austin, 1646).
13. Anon., 'A Funerall Monument'.
14. Sharon Achinstein, *Literature and Dissent in Milton's England* (Cambridge: Cambridge University Press, 2003), p. 32.
15. Ibid., p. 28.
16. Ibid.
17. For this project I searched Early English Books Online for works with 'elegy' and its variants in the title printed between 1630 and 1700 that are described bibliographically as having one page. There are 132 examples in the resulting collection. In no sense is this collection either representative or exhaustive, given that the survival rate of such works is low and their preservation deeply inconsistent. Nonetheless, of the 132 in

the collection, twenty can be confirmed to have subjects identified as nonconforming churchmen who died between 1663 (Henry Jesse) and 1699 (William Bates).

18. Anon., 'A PILLAR ERECTED To the Memory of that Holy, Hum*ble, and Faithful Servant of Iesus Christ, Mr. Henry Iesse . . .*' (London: 1663).
19. Robert Wild, 'ON THE Death of Mr Calamy, Not known to the Author of a long time after' (London: 1667).
20. Anon., 'An Elegiack Acrostick upon The Reverend, Learned, and much to be lamented Mr. Joseph Caryl . . .' (London: Printed for Benj. Hurlock, 1672).
21. Anon., 'AN ELEGY On the Death of the Reverend and Pious Mr. Thomas Wadsworth . . .' (London: 1676).
22. Anon., 'An ELEGY Upon the death of that Faithful Servant of the LORD . . . Mr. John Wells,' (London: printed for B. H., 1676).
23. Anon., 'AN ELEGY On the Learned and Zealous Minister of the Gospel, Mr. Christopher Fowler . . .' (London: 1677).
24. Richard Ames, 'AN ELEGY On the Death of that Learned, Pious, and Laborious Minister of Jesus Christ Mr. Richard Baxter . . .' (London: Printed for Richard Baldwin, 1691).
25. Clymer also points out that these deictics might well be quite literal: 'The connection to the deceased may have been quite tangible, even liturgical: printed elegies were often pinned to the hearse or tomb, and were read over the coffin during the burial ceremony'. Clymer, 'The Funeral Elegy', p. 175.
26. Achinstein, *Literature and Dissent*, p. 28.
27. Adele Davidson, '"A More Singular Mirror": Herbert, Acrostics, and the Biblical Psalms', *George Herbert Journal*, 38:1–2 (2014–15), p. 15.
28. Anon., 'A MEMORIAL on the Death of that faithful Servant of Jesus Christ, Nathanael Strange . . .' (London: 1666).
29. Davidson, '"A More Singular Mirror"', p. 15.
30. Anon., 'A MITE from Three MOURNERS: In MEMORIAL of THOMAS GLASS . . .' (London: 1666).
31. Lisa Jardine and Anthony Grafton's essay '"Studied for Action:" How Gabriel Harvey Read His Livy', *Past and Present*, 129 (1990), pp. 30–78, initiated recent studies in early modern marginalia. Other signal works include: William H. Sherman, *Used Books: Marking Readers in Renaissance England* (Philadelphia: University of Pennsylvania Press, 2008); Heidi Brayman Hackel, *Reading Material in Early Modern England: Print, Gender, and Literacy* (Cambridge: Cambridge University Press, 2005); and Jason Scott-Warren, 'Reading Graffiti in the Early Modern Book', *Huntington Library Quarterly*, 73:3 (2010), pp. 363–81. *Early Modern English Marginalia*, edited by the author of this chapter, is presently in press (London: Routledge, 2019), and includes essays by established and emergent scholars on the topic.

32. Achinstein, *Literature and Dissent*, p. 2.
33. J. D. Davies, 'Butler, Thomas, sixth earl of Ossory (1634–1680)', in H. C. G. Matthew and Brian Harrison (eds), *Oxford Dictionary of National Biography* (Oxford: Oxford University Press, 2004).
34. Anon., 'AN ELEGY to Commemorate . . . John Micklevvaite, Kt . . .' (London: Printed for William Miller, 1682).
35. For example, Richard Ford ('LONDON'S SIGHS For her Worthy Patriot . . .' (1678)), William Whitmore ('An ELEGIE On that Incomparable Example of Hospitality, Charity, and Generosity . . .' (1678)), William Bedloe (AN ELEGIE Upon the Truly Worthy, and ever-to-be-remembred Loyal Gentleman . . .' (1680)), Prince Rupert ('AN ELEGY ON That Illustrious and High-Born PRINCE RUPERT . . .' (1682)), the Earl of Salisbury ('AN ELEGY IN Commemoration of the Right Honourable James Earl of Salisbury . . .' (1683)) and Edmund Saunders ('AN ELEGY IN Commemoration of S^R Edmund Saunders . . .' (1683).
36. Newton Key, 'Reporting the Rye House Plot: Treason Trial Accounts, Proceedings, and "Prints" Before the State Trials', in Brian Cowan and Scott Sowerby (eds), *Rethinking the State Trials: The Politics of Justice in Later Stuart England* (London: Boydell and Brewer, forthcoming), ms excerpt shared by correspondence and therefore n.p. provided.
37. Ibid.
38. Alan B. Farmer and Zachary Lesser, 'What Is Print Popularity? A Map of the Elizabethan Book Trade', in Andy Kesson and Emma Smith (eds), *The Elizabethan Top Ten* (Farnham: Ashgate Publishing, 2013), p. 36. Farmer and Lesser claim that 'Poesy and the Arts' comprised about one-fifth of the market share of print sales between 1559 and 1602 (pp. 30–1). This share was not static; for instance, it dramatically increased to nearly 30 per cent in the last decade of the Elizabethan era (p. 32).
39. Dennis Kay, *Melodious Tears: The English Funeral Elegy from Spenser to Milton* (Oxford: Clarendon Press, 1990), p. 6.
40. Ibid.
41. Paul Hammond and Maureen Bell identify two publisher-printers, Henry Herringman and Jacob Tonson, as 'themselves almost a late seventeenth-century canon' of literary works, especially poetry, including works by dozens of poets, a list of whom 'virtually defines contemporary literature', illustrating the ways in which a reputation as printer and publisher could be built on the collection of rights to works by well known and up-and-coming poets. See Paul Hammond and Maureen Bell, 'The Restoration Poetic and Dramatic Canon', in Barnard and McKenzie (eds), *The Cambridge History of the Book in Britain*, vol. IV, p. 391.
42. Roger Chartier, 'Communities of Readers', in *The Order of Books: Readers, Authors, and Libraries in Europe*, trans. Lydia G. Cochrane (Stanford: Stanford University Press, 1994), p. 4.
43. Bell, 'Mise-En-Page', p. 635.

Chapter 8

Ottomans Reading Persian Classics: Readers and Reading in the Ottoman Empire, 1500–1700

Murat Umut Inan

On 7 September 1559, the Ottoman Naqshbandi Sufi poet and scholar Muslihüddin Sürûri (1491–1561) completed his commentary on the *Divan* (poetry collection) of Hafiz of Shiraz (died c. 1390) in Istanbul, the Ottoman imperial capital, where poems of the Persian bard were widely read and pondered. Before embarking on this commentary project, Sürûri had elucidated and interpreted the *Divan* for a circle of readers who regularly attended his classes and lectures. Captivated by the mystical meanings and messages in Hafiz's poetry, members of the circle came to Sürûri with many questions, which he unfailingly and patiently answered. As the following words from his preface to the commentary reveal, Sürûri finally decided to compile his lecture notes as well as his responses to individual enquiries in a book that would serve as a companion to reading Hafiz's poetry and thus would answer the so many questions occupying the minds of Hafiz's Ottoman readers:

> Shams al-Din Muhammad al-Hafiz al-Shirazi – May God bless his inner-most secret – belongs to the class of mystics, in which he is given the honorific titles of 'the Tongue of the Hidden' and 'the Expounder of Secrets'. All the allegories and metaphors in his poetry serve to convey mysteries of the mystical path. . . . From time to time, my friends and companions, who are men of spiritual understanding, came to me and asked questions about the esoteric aspects of Hafiz's poetry. I investigated these enquiries to the best of my knowledge and answered each of them verbally. Afterwards, I was asked to write down all these answers and compile them into a book. Hereupon, I spent some time compiling them into a Turkish commentary [on Hafiz's *Divan*], where I elucidate metaphorical and mystical meanings [in Hafiz's poems] so that those [readers] who lack [mystical] knowledge and understanding can develop mystical awareness and achieve spiritual maturity.[1]

Sürurî's preface offers a glimpse into the world of a group of readers in sixteenth-century Istanbul. Firstly, we learn that the readers gathered around Sürurî were particularly eager to study and discuss the poems of a Persian poet who was famed for his mystical erudition. Accordingly, they read Hafiz for mystical insight and wisdom. Secondly, these readers did not read the *Divan* cursorily; rather, they focused on, and were intrigued by, some parts of it and consulted an experienced reader like Sürurî for the interpretation of certain verses. Thirdly, they read the text in a classroom setting and were guided by a teacher-scholar who translated, analysed and interpreted Hafiz's poems for them. Last but not least, the same readers also looked for a commentary or guidebook that would provide access to the language and meaning of Hafiz's text. In other words, the Persian *Divan* was read or studied often with the help of a Turkish commentary tailored for the needs of Hafiz's Ottoman readers. Seen in this light, Sürurî's words provide us with preliminary, if not adequate, answers to some basic yet largely unexplored questions about readers and reading in the Ottoman world: Who were Ottoman readers? What did they read for poetry or literature, for example, and why? How did they read a text like Hafiz's *Divan*?

Elaborating on these questions, this chapter explores communities of readership and practices of reading in the Ottoman Empire, an empire in which a diverse body of readers from different backgrounds and ethnicities interacted with a wide range of texts written in various languages, including, primarily, Arabic, Persian and Turkish. The empire had a vibrant oral culture, and texts were often orally delivered to audiences on various occasions and in different settings. In particular, folktales, stories of heroism, pieces of poetry and passages from epic and mystical narratives, such as Firdavsi's (935–1020) *Shahnama* (Book of Kings) and Rumi's (1207–73) *Masnavi*, were traditionally read or recited for audiences by professional reader-reciters, whether at an imperial banquet, a Sufi assembly or a coffeehouse gathering. As texts were transmitted and received orally, reading often meant oral reading or listening to a text read aloud, which constituted one of the major strands of reading in the Ottoman world.[2]

This chapter focuses not on oral or performative aspects of reading, but rather on individual or collective reading as practised by Ottoman (i.e. Turkish-speaking) readers with varying levels of Persian literacy. The time span of the chapter covers the sixteenth and seventeenth centuries. It was during these two centuries that Ottoman readers became increasingly interested in Persian literary and mystical texts, while Ottoman scholars produced a variety of philological works to meet this readerly demand, such as commentaries, translations and vocabularies.[3] In particular, the following Persian texts appealed to the common taste and were avidly sought in the Ottoman world: the *Pandnama* (*Book of Advice*) by Farid al-Din Attar (died 1221), the *Masnavi* (literally, poem in rhymed couplets) by Jalal al-Din Rumi (1207–73), the *Bustan* (*Orchard*) and *Gulistan* (*Rose Garden*) by Sadi of Shiraz (died 1292) and Hafiz's *Divan*, copies of which filled the shelves of Ottoman libraries, whether private, foundation-sponsored or royal, and were commonly found in the booksellers' stalls.[4] Long before they entered the Ottoman world of reading, these five texts had already achieved canonical status in the wider Islamic world as standard texts circulating across literary and mystical cultures. Not surprisingly, the same texts continued to enjoy popularity and significance among Ottoman readers and were considered by Ottoman literati and scholars as 'classic' works, in the sense that they were often classified, along with other seminal texts on various topics, under such special categories as *kütüb-i mutebere*, *kütüb-i muteberat* (both meaning 'books held in high esteem') and *kütüb-i mütedavile* ('books in common circulation').[5] In what follows, first I discuss the ways in which these five texts were perceived in Ottoman reading culture while reflecting on why they became immensely popular among readers. Then I take up the question of who read these texts, by mapping out different types and circles of readership. In the third section, I discuss how and in what settings Ottoman readers engaged with the same texts. Throughout the chapter, I draw on Ottoman commentaries on, and translations of, the Persian titles cited above to delineate and discuss readers' identities, tastes and motivations. For my discussion of the reception of these titles in literary circles, I particularly make use of Ottoman biographies of poets, which shed light on habits of reading and study among readers and writers of poetry.

Five Persian bestsellers

A mystical work consisting of some 800 couplets on morality, Attar's *Pandnama* (date of composition unknown) was undoubtedly one of the most read texts in the Ottoman world.[6] As a concise advice manual written in a didactic style by one of the most revered Sufis, *Pandnama* attracted a broad spectrum of readers, from members of the court to laypeople. As Şemullah Şemi (died c. 1602) put it in the preface to his 1578 translation, Attar's *Pandnama* was not only a 'pleasant book' to read but also a 'book brimming with wisdom and happiness', implying that its wide reception among readers was hardly coincidental.[7] Perhaps not surprisingly, *Pandnama* owed much of its popularity and significance to the reputation of its author. In the eyes of readers and scholars alike, Attar was far from being an ordinary mystic: he was, to quote Edirneli Nazmi (died after 1559), another translator of Attar, a 'distinguished Sufi' whose words in *Pandnama* 'should always be read and kept in mind'.[8] On the other hand, Attar's text was not an easy read: it was, to use the words of Abdi Pasha (died 1692), a 'difficult book' that required readers to have a good command of the Persian language. This must be one of the reasons that led Abdi Pasha to write a grammatical commentary on *Pandnama* for those interested in reading or studying the text in the original language.[9]

Rumi and his *Masnavi* were perceived along similar lines. A voluminous collection of morally inspiring stories and parables, composed in some 26,000 couplets, *Masnavi* (completed shortly before 1273) was viewed as an indispensable read, not only for Sufis but also for those interested in advice literature, while also being hailed as a linguistically and semantically challenging text that required commentary, as is evidenced by the large number of interpretations and translations produced from the sixteenth century onwards.[10] Likewise, Rumi loomed large in the spiritual lives of the Ottomans as a figure who embodied moral enlightenment. But there was more to Rumi and his text than lasting legacy and alluring content: most commentators and readers of Rumi, and particularly those who were affiliated with the Mavlavi Sufi order, attached a religious significance to his *Masnavi*, which they saw not simply as a book of moral teachings but rather as a sacred text that almost ranked with the Qur'an (Islam's holy book) and the Hadith (the sayings of the Prophet Muhammad), the two major sources of Islam: 'there is no book as delightful as the Exalted Qur'an, the Noble Hadith, and the Noble *Masnavi*', wrote Şemi in the preface to his six-volume mystical commentary, which he completed in Istanbul between 1587 and 1595 and which was the first complete commentary on *Masnavi* prepared for the Turkish readers of Rumi. The sacredness of Rumi's text was rooted in the common belief that it was a source of divine knowledge, or, to quote Şemi again, 'a sacred book overflowing with divine secrets, signs, wisdom and information'.[11] Ismail Rusuhi (died c. 1631), to cite another example, joined Şemi in ascribing quasi-scriptural status to *Masnavi* in his seven-volume commentary, on which he worked from 1621 to 1628. A Sufi scholar who regularly taught and lectured on Rumi's text first in Ankara, a city in central Anatolia, and later in Istanbul, Rusuhi argued that *Masnavi* was 'a book that contains the mystery of all creation', before he concluded that 'our *Masnavi* is like the Qur'an'.[12] Clearly, Şemi's and Rusuhi's words reflect their fascination with *Masnavi* as individual readers, especially given that both scholars, who had close ties with the Mavlavi order, devoted several years of their lives to reading, teaching and writing about Rumi's text. But when we consider the wide circulation and influence of their commentaries among Rumi's readers, it seems that Şemi's and Rusuhi's portrayals of *Masnavi* contributed to its interpretation as a quasi-religious text in Ottoman reading culture. An illuminating example appears in Evliya Çelebi's (died after 1683) famous *Seyahatname* (*Book of Travels*), in which the Ottoman traveller repeatedly refers to *Masnavi* as 'the essence of the Qur'an' when sharing his observations and anecdotes about the religious and cultural locales where Rumi's text was regularly read and discussed.[13]

Though not treated with the same degree of religious significance as Rumi's *Masnavi*, the works of Sadi and Hafiz were no different in terms of the way in which Ottoman readers approached and understood them. Sadi's *Bustan* (dated 1257), a work in verse arranged in ten chapters ranging from justice and beneficence to love and humility, and *Gulistan* (dated 1258), an eight-chapter collection of moralistic stories that blend prose and verse, delighted readers across the empire with their riveting style and touches of wisdom.[14] Celebrated as inspirational texts not solely by Sufi readers but also by those who concerned themselves with morals and manners, *Bustan* and *Gulistan* were also in high demand in early schooling: the two works served, along with *Pandnama*, as textbooks widely used for the moral edification of pupils. One of these pupils was a boy named Mehmed, the future court poet Hayali Bey (died 1556). As the Ottoman biographer Aşık Çelebi (died 1572) informs us, Hayali was instructed in Sadi's texts as part of his boyhood education, in what Çelebi calls *edeb* ('manners' or 'etiquette').[15]

Compiled shortly after his death around 1390, Hafiz's *Divan*, which features, among others, some 500 ghazals (love poems), was an equally attractive text that passed from hand to hand at gatherings of friends and notably at Sufi gatherings.[16] Spiritually inclined readers remained immersed in the *Divan* for hours, mining Hafiz's poetry for esoteric clues and insights mostly under the tutelage of a senior reader well versed in Sufi literature, as was the case with Süruri and his circle of readers. Those interested in fortune telling kept the *Divan* near them to extract from Hafiz's text knowledge of divine will. As we learn from Hüseyin el-Kefevi's (died 1603) *Razname* (*Book of Secrets*), a late sixteenth-century collection of stories about bibliomancy, the *Divan* was commonly regarded as a divination text, along with the Qur'an and *Masnavi*.[17] Some passages in *Seyahatname* also shed light on the frequent use of the *Divan* for divination. During his stay in Peçuy, a city in Ottoman Hungary, Evliya Çelebi observed, for example, that men of the city who knew Persian well and were regular readers of *Bustan*, *Gulistan* and *Divan* frequently took recourse to Hafiz's text before making critical decisions such as launching a military campaign.[18] As the examples from *Razname* and *Seyahatname* suggest, the presumed prophetic significance of the *Divan* was closely related to Hafiz's established reputation as, to quote Sürûrî, 'the Tongue of the Hidden' and 'the Expounder of Secrets', which obviously made readers more attuned to the poet's choice of words and phrases as well as to his allegorical references.

Ottoman readers' engagement with *Bustan*, *Gulistan* and *Divan* were not limited to moral, mystical or esoteric concerns: these three texts were also read and studied as exemplars of Persian language and literature. *Bustan* and *Gulistan* came to be seen as texts that exemplified Sadi's masterly use of Persian. Esad Mehmed (1570–1625), for example, who rendered *Gulistan* into elegant Ottoman Turkish, was especially impressed with Sadi's language, which he touted as dexterous and textured with 'vividly delicate words' and 'charmingly subtle meanings'.[19] Learners and teachers of Persian, too, were similarly drawn to *Bustan* and *Gulistan*, which they found lexically and grammatically rich and pedagogically suitable for learning Persian: often under the instruction of a tutor steeped in Persian, those enthusiastic about learning the language studied Sadi's texts to enhance their command of grammar and vocabulary. A prayer leader named Mahmud (died c. 1575), who was not only an ardent reader of Persian literature but also a talented poet known by the name of Helaki, was one of those well known tutors who regularly used *Bustan* and *Gulistan* to teach Persian.[20] The *Divan*, on the other hand, was applauded by those literary-minded readers who were infatuated with the beauty of Hafiz's ghazals, which were seen as the epitome of Persian love poetry.[21] Some of these readers, particularly those fledgling poets who took the Persian bard as their role model, carefully studied the formal and thematic aspects of his ghazals. A young sixteenth-century poet named Nisari (dates unknown) was definitely one of these passionate readers of Hafiz. Before he began practising writing Persian lyrics, Nisari turned to no other poet but Hafiz, as Mustafa Ali (1541–1600) highlighted when giving the poet's short biography in his universal history entitled *Künhü'l-Ahbar* (*Essence of History*). The beginning poet read the *Divan* from cover to cover, scrutinising the composition of every single ghazal. It was thanks to his close readings of the *Divan* that Nisari honed his poetic craft and produced a collection of Persian love poems modelled on Hafiz's ghazals.[22]

Five reader profiles

Ottoman readers of the five Persian classics cannot be strictly defined or demarcated along lines of ethnicity, social class, profession or educational background. But still, relying on commentarial and biographical works that throw light on occasions and motivations for reading across the Ottoman social landscape, one can distinguish five major categories or groups of readers, which were far from being mutually exclusive.

The first group included those scholars who were professionally engaged with a series of canonical texts, including the classics of Persian. Ottoman commentators and translators, for instance, provide good examples of such readers. Specialised in textual analysis and interpretation, these professional readers made a lifelong commitment to reading, glossing and translating literary, mystical and religious texts. Süruri and Şemi, for example, established themselves in sixteenth-century Istanbul as professional readers who made their living by teaching, lecturing and writing about the Persian classics, and, as such, shaped the way Ottoman readership interpreted these texts. Another professional reader who was renowned for his dedication to reading and analysing Persian canonical texts was the Ottoman scholar Ahmed Sudi (died c. 1600), whose education and career as a philologist reflect how he transformed into a scholarly reader and became a source of inspiration for beginning readers of Persian. After receiving his early schooling in his hometown Sarajevo and his philological training in Istanbul, Sudi travelled across the empire to sharpen his reading and interpretive skills in cities that served as centres of intellectual ferment and were home to famous scholars. During his stays in Amid (a city in south-eastern Turkey, known today as Diyarbakır), Damascus and Baghdad, the itinerant philologist engaged in close readings of *Gulistan* and *Divan* under the advisorship of esteemed philologists and poets of the time. This provided him with a unique reading experience, on which he later drew in his commentaries on Sadi and Hafiz. Finally back in Istanbul in the 1570s, Sudi joined the Ibrahim Pasha palace school, where he tutored a select group of boys, who were levied for imperial service, in Persian language and literature.²³ Among Sudi's students was a boy from the Balkan city of Mostar, named Derviş, who later came to be known as the bureaucrat Derviş Pasha (died 1603). Following his graduation from the palace school, Derviş was accepted to the court of Murad III (reigned 1574–95), where he attracted the sultan's attention with his poetic talent and impressive command of Persian, and quickly became one of his companion poets. In the introduction to his translation of a Persian work, which he dedicated to the sultan, Derviş touched on his intensive education in the palace school and gratefully acknowledged the formative influence of his 'mentor' Sudi on his becoming a cultivated reader:

> For many years I resided in that palace,
> where I read and wrote day and night
> Like the crescent, I progressed day by day
> My mentor was always helpful to me
> May he be rewarded in both worlds!
> He embellished me with knowledge
> May God be pleased with him in both worlds!²⁴

Those who sought to take their basic reading skills in Persian to a higher level formed another group of readers, who can be categorised as beginning readers. Often referred to as *mübtediler* ('beginning students') or *tullab* ('students'), Ottoman students of Persian like Derviş were included in that category.²⁵ As part of their formal training in Persian literacy, these student readers were introduced to the classics by their instructors, who were often those scholarly readers well acquainted with Persian belles-lettres. Under the supervision and help of these instructors, pupils read the classics word by word and line by line, paying particular attention to their lexical and grammatical structure. Sir Paul Rycaut (1628–1700), who served as secretary to the British ambassador in Istanbul in the 1660s, noted that *Pandnama*, *Gulistan*, *Bustan* and *Divan* were among the 'books' students at the Topkapı palace school 'read commonly in the Persian language'.²⁶ While pupils educated at palace schools for service in the Ottoman court and bureaucracy formed an important body of the student readership, those who underwent Sufi training from an early age constituted an equally significant majority. The schoolboys residing in the Mavlavi convent in sixteenth-century Muğla, a city in south-west Turkey, for example, read the *Masnavi* with a Sufi master named Ibrahim Şahidi (1470–1550), who compiled for them a Persian–Turkish vocabulary book which included words mostly selected from Rumi's text. Composed in verse for easy memorisation, the book was primarily targeted at budding readers of Rumi, whom Şahidi called *mübtedi*s ('beginning students') and *etfal* ('kids') in delineating his intended audience in the first pages of his lexicographical work.[27] It would be misleading, however, to think that the category of beginning readers consisted entirely of schoolboys: novice adult readers of Persian who aspired to read or study the classics along with a knowledgeable reader or a didactic commentary also belonged to that category. Ahmed Sudi, for example, consistently referred to such readers as *Farsi taallümüne ragıb olanlar* ('those eager to learn Persian'), *talib-i tahsil-i Farsi olan* ('those interested in studying Persian') or simply as *talibler* ('interested readers'), suggesting there existed a novice readership that went beyond school circles.[28]

Spiritually oriented readers with particular interests in Sufism represented a significant part of the Ottoman reading public. Designated in mystical commentaries as *ihvan* ('brethren') and *yaran* ('companions'), these readers were often members of Sufi orders, pursuing mystical knowledge and understanding under the guidance of a Sufi mentor.[29] Sufi readers approached the classics with diverse but intersecting expectations: some pored over these texts to derive moral lessons or to attain spiritual enlightenment, others to discover the hidden mystical meanings or to better understand the subtleties of the mystical journey leading to union with the Divine, and still others to arouse an ecstatic mystical experience on ritualistic occasions. As pointed out at the beginning of the chapter, in the Istanbul of the 1550s, a group of Naqshbandi Sufis led by Süruri routinely came together to probe the underlying mystical content in Hafiz's poems. Earlier, Süruri had led a Sufi reading group focusing on Rumi's text, as his 1537 commentary that uncovers the mystical texture of *Masnavi* suggests. Given that Süruri wrote his *Masnavi* commentary not in Turkish but in Persian, it seems that this reading group consisted of those who were either native speakers of Persian or Turkish-speaking readers who had a good knowledge of the language, or a mixture of both.[30] Between 1537 and 1548, Süruri delivered public lectures on *Masnavi* at a local mosque in Istanbul 'every day in the afternoon', as noted by Aşık Çelebi. Following the lectures, some of the audience would accompany Süruri on his way to his house nearby, where he would answer specific questions raised from reading *Masnavi* as well as general queries on a variety of subjects.[31] A Mavlavi Sufi poet named Şuri Çelebi (died 1582), on the other hand, was an absorbed reader of *Masnavi*, a text which touched Şuri deeply, evoking in him strong feelings that often culminated in spiritual intoxication. As a travelling dervish, Şuri visited various Mavlavi convents across the empire, from Edirne in Thrace to Damascus. As Aşık Çelebi vividly notes, Şuri would ecstatically read *Masnavi* and dance while chanting Rumi's verses at gatherings of whirling dervishes.[32]

The elite readership of the classics included sultans, members of the dynasty, courtiers and highest-ranking officials who were well read in Persian. Melek Ahmed Pasha (died 1662), one of the grand viziers of Mehmed IV (reigned 1648–87), for example, habitually read *Pandnama*, which he even memorised in its entirety.[33] Though not as passionate as the Pasha, Zeyrek Agha (dates unknown), a boon companion of Murad III (reigned 1574–95) and one of the dwarf eunuchs at his court, particularly cherished Attar's book of advice, as implied in Şemi's preface to his *Saadetname (Book of Happiness)*, a *Pandnama* translation he presented to Zeyrek Agha.[34] Süleyman the Magnificent (1494–1566), on the other hand, was a keen reader of Hafiz's *Divan*, which he saw as one of the model texts that were instrumental in his becoming a lyric poet.[35] Süleyman's sons, too, were attracted to the *Divan*: in particular, the princes Selim, who succeeded his father as Selim II (reigned 1566–74), and Bayezid (1526–62) were both poet-readers who inherited their father's interest in reading Persian poets and above all Hafiz.[36] Sadi's *Bustan* was another of Selim's favourite books. Selim would read *Bustan* with the poet Abdi (dates unknown), a member of the literary circle at his princely court in Manisa. Upon Selim's request, Abdi also prepared a translation of *Bustan* in 1556 to help the prince with reading Sadi's intricately woven text.[37] Bayezid's favourite was *Pandnama*, which he regularly flipped through during his years of princely training in Kütahya. Bayezid urged Emre (dates unknown), one of the poet-translators in his retinue, to translate Attar's text into Turkish so that it could reach a wider audience, whom the prince referred to as *kavm-i Rum* ('the people of Rum', meaning Turkish readers in Ottoman Anatolia and Rumelia). In the preface to his 1557 translation, Emre quoted Bayezid's request:

> Holding it in his hands, he said:
> 'Dress this beautiful book in a Turkish garment!
> Let this Persian beloved in Turkish robe
> sway among the people of Rum forever!'[38]

As Bayezid's words suggest, Ottoman sultans and princes were also passionate about cultivating a culture of reading that extended beyond the court. They often encouraged wider reading and study of the classics by providing continued patronage for scholars working on translations and commentaries that would make these texts accessible to the general reading public. This, in turn, played a significant role in the dissemination of these texts within and beyond elite circles.[39] One of these scholars was the famous madrasah professor Muhammed Zaifi (died shortly after 1557). When Zaifi presented his *Pandnama* translation to Süleyman on 10 April 1543, the sultan welcomed his work and rewarded him generously.[40] As a devoted reader of *Masnavi*, Murad III, a prolific Sufi poet himself, consistently supported Ottoman mystical scholarship. It was Murad III who inspired Şemi in February 1587 to embark on a complete Turkish commentary on the six-volume *Masnavi*. As Şemi completed each volume of his commentary, he was invited to the court to introduce his work to the sultan, who was charmed by Şemi's translations and interpretations, which opened a wider window into Rumi's mystical world. It was thanks to Murad III's sponsoring of Şemi's commentary that *Masnavi* gained a wider Turkish readership, inasmuch as more and more readers approached Rumi's text through Şemi's commentary, which became such a 'world-famous' commentary that its copies and pages were found in 'every place' and in 'every study room'.[41]

Finally, those who were professionally involved with literature were the most attentive readers of the classics, including not only the novice poets who pursued literary careers but also those established writers who were driven to create literary masterpieces that for centuries would elicit as much readerly interest as those of the Persian masters.[42] These bilingual author-readers read the classics as much for pleasure as for literary material and inspiration and, as such, turned to them time and time again. As readers preoccupied with the art of literary writing, many Ottoman poets buried themselves in Sadi and Hafiz in particular, both delighting and instructing themselves by navigating through their language, style and imagery. As mentioned above, Hafiz's poems fascinated Nisari as an apprentice poet, who visited and revisited the *Divan* as he laboriously composed poems in imitation of Hafiz.

Mihri Hatun (died after 1512) was perhaps the most famous woman poet-reader of the early sixteenth century. Born in Amasya, an Ottoman city with a lively literary culture, Mihri received her early literary training from her poet father and quickly established herself as a member of the literati associated with the court of prince Ahmed (died 1513), son of Bayezid II (reigned 1481–1512), who was the governor of Amasya from 1481 to 1512. Mihri enjoyed unbroken support from the prince's court, where she also developed a deeper interest in Persian arts and literature as the prince managed to attract artists and literati from Iran. Mihri's poems in her *Divan* give us glimpses into her solid reading background in the classics of Persian as well as Arabic poetry, which served as a springboard for her poetic production and creativity.⁴³

The historian and littérateur Mustafa Ali (1541–1600) was a lifelong reader of Hafiz. Many of Ali's Turkish poems, compiled in four volumes dated from 1567 to 1602, bear traces of Hafiz's influence.⁴⁴ 'I read the *Divan* of Hafiz the Master closely', wrote Ali in one of his poems, proudly acknowledging that he was an engaged reader of the Persian *Divan*.⁴⁵ The prefaces Ali wrote for the two books he thought of as his Persian masterpieces, namely *Mecmaü'l-Bahreyn* (*The Confluence of the Two Seas*, dated 1591–2), a volume of fifty-three ghazals imitating Hafiz, and *Rebiü'l-Manzum* (*The Spring of Poetry*, dated 1594–5), a collection of poems paralleling the verses of eminent Persian poets, notably Umar Khayyam (1048–1131), are particularly revealing of his experiences as an avid reader of Hafiz. In the preface of the former book, Ali wrote: 'One day, at the beginning of the hijri year 1000 [October–November 1591 CE], I craved to read Hafiz's *Divan* on the spur of the moment. It gave me great pleasure.' It was one of those 'times of loneliness and unhappiness', Ali added, when he delved into Hafiz's poetic world, which aroused in him a desire to compose Persian poems as aesthetically pleasing as those of Hafiz.⁴⁶ As the preface of the latter book suggests, Ali's readings of the *Divan* continued unabated after he completed *Mecmaü'l-Bahreyn*. In this preface Ali mentions that during the year 1002 (1593–4 CE), he devoted his time exclusively to reading Hafiz's *Divan* and writing his universal history, *Künhü'l-Ahbar*. Ali explains that he picked Hafiz because of his desire 'to acquaint himself with the subtleties of poetry'.⁴⁷

Like Mustafa Ali, the poet, historian and theologian Kemal Pashazade (1469–1534) was an avid and dedicated reader of Persian poetry. In particular, Pashazade's intention to write a Persian magnum opus similar to *Gulistan* led him to an intensive reading of Sadi. He perused the book chapter by chapter, taking notes about its linguistic, stylistic and compositional features. The end product of Pashazade's hours of reading of Sadi was an ornately crafted Persian work that was tightly patterned on *Gulistan*. Pashazade completed his book the year before his death and entitled it *Nigaristan* (*Garden of Images*), a title echoing that of Sadi's book.⁴⁸

Diverse modes of reading

How did the Ottomans read the classics? In terms of the way reading was practised, Ottoman readers interacted with these texts both individually and in groups. Professional readers, in particular, were more inclined to read the classics in private. During the 1530s, Sürûri continuously read *Masnavi* in seclusion, silently and intensively, focusing his whole attention on Rumi's allegories and symbolic expressions. Sürûri's tenacious readings yielded a six-volume commentary, which he wrote in Persian and completed in 1537. Comparably, Mustafa Ali's reading of the *Divan* was an individual, intensive reading accompanied by lengthy reflections and note-taking on technical and conceptual aspects of Hafiz's poetry, which consequently paved the way for his *Mecmaü'l-Bahreyn*. Individually focused readings of the classics were not exclusive to commentators and poets. Advanced readers of Persian, too, read with concentration, though not necessarily at the same level as that of professional readers. The bibliophile Carullah Efendi's (1659–1738) case provides a good example. A *qadi* (Islamic judge) who owned a private library that ran to some 3,500 volumes, Carullah Efendi was an inquisitive reader who often filled the margins of his books with notes and quotations.[49] Quite expectedly, among his Persian books were *Masnavi*, *Pandnama* and Hafiz's *Divan*, which he read along with Sürûri's and Sudi's commentaries, which he purchased in 1700 and 1736, respectively. A concise biography of Hafiz is recorded in one of the early pages of his copy of *Divan*. Carullah Efendi quotes this biography from a Persian work he had read, namely the *Nafahat al-Uns* (*Breezes of Intimacy*) by the famous Persian Sufi poet and biographer Abd al-Rahman Jami (died 1492). Carullah Efendi also records in the margin of the same page a Persian couplet that thematically resonates with that of Hafiz, though he does not mention the source of his quotation. The copious readerly marginalia found in Carullah Efendi's Persian book collection not only show the breadth of his reading but also testifies to his concentrated readings of a range of volumes, including the *Divan*.[50]

More often than not, beginning readers and students of Persian read in groups and under the supervision of a professional reader who would first read the texts aloud to them. When read collectively, the classics were studied section by section over a period of time. Following the reading aloud of a passage, for example, the group would read the same passage first aloud and then silently. The teacher-reader would then explain the grammar of the passage before finally translating and interpreting it. This was the way, for example, members of the reading group headed by the Persianist and poet Helaki studied *Bustan* and *Gulistan*. Participants of the Rumi circle run by Ismail Rusuhi followed a similar path of reading. As a reciter and interpreter of *Masnavi*, Rusuhi read a section of the text for his audience and expounded Rumi's mystical teachings first, before having them read the same section aloud as a group. Rumi's readers then re-read the given section verse by verse, together with Rusuhi, who often interrupted the reading to explain pronunciation, grammar and meaning.

A common practice that accompanied collective readings of the classics was memorisation, which helped beginners, especially those with literary aspirations, not only to better grasp the grammatical flow of these texts but also to familiarise themselves with the stylistic language of the Persian masters. Novice readers were expected to practise reading the passage of the day at home and come to the next session having committed it to memory and ready to recite it. The texts frequently selected for memorisation were *Bustan* and *Gulistan*. During his formative years, a student of poetry named Isa, who later became an accomplished poet, writing under the penname Necati (died 1509), read *Gulistan*, along with fellow trainee poets, to memorise it page by page, as he hints in one of his verses.[51] Isa and the reading circle of which he was a part were far from being an exception: memorisation as a form of reading was ubiquitous in venues of literary learning. In his brief but vivid depiction of Istanbul during the reign of Selim II (1566–74), the poet Ulvi (died 1587), for instance, highlights that *Bustan* and *Gulistan* held sway over the city's literary scene, inasmuch as the two books were ubiquitously read and memorised by readers and students new to poetry.[52]

In terms of the medium through which Ottoman readers explored the classics, one can identify three modes of reading. Obviously, readers who had a good grasp of Persian read these texts in the original language, while those unlettered in Persian depended on Turkish translations. Readers, whether students or laypersons, who sought to achieve some mastery of Persian, on the other hand, often looked for a full-fledged commentary that provided a grammatical analysis, prose translation and a literal or mystical interpretation of the original text. The production and circulation of a large corpus of commentaries lead us to think that a significant portion of Ottoman readers read the classics through the eyes of commentators. European travellers' accounts of Ottoman bookshops and libraries reveal a similar picture. The diary of Antoine Galland (1646–1715), who stayed in Istanbul in 1672–3, for instance, indicates that *Bustan*, *Gulistan* and *Divan* were read with Sudi's commentaries, which were in vogue among readers at the time.[53] Reading in translation was no less common. Readers, for example, who were curious to learn about the moral principles outlined in *Pandnama* but were unacquainted with the Persian language relied on translations of Attar's text. Edirneli Nazmi's rendering of *Pandnama* was aimed at such readers. In his preface to the translation, which he completed in Aleppo on 6 May 1559, Nazmi drew attention to the needs of readers of translations from Persian:

> Since this book is in Persian,
> those illiterate in Persian cannot understand it,
> and only those who know Persian can comprehend it.
> ...
> I wish those who hear about this book
> to understand it well, and to read and receive its lessons.
> I believe the book's lessons are essential,
> which is why I translated it in its entirety.
> ...
> Those who have no knowledge of the Persian language
> will, I hope, benefit from reading this [translation of] *Pandnama*.[54]

Mehmed Rahmi's (died 1568) *Bustan* translation addressed a similar readership. Rahmi regarded Sürûrî's Persian commentary on *Bustan* as a text written for a limited readership, and decided to prepare a Turkish translation that would cater to readers 'who were not familiar with the Persian language', as he made clear in the preface of his translation.[55] The prefaces by Nazmi and Rahmi both suggest that readers of translations engaged with the classics in a simple verse or prose translation. Although this was the case for the majority, readers familiar with poetry, and especially with poetic metre and rhyme, read Persian masters in polished verse translation. Esad Mehmed's ornate translation of *Gulistan* was primarily intended for Turkish poets who had yet to master reading and writing skills in Persian.[56] A seventeenth-century verse translation of Hafiz's *Divan* by the poet-translator Feridi (dates unknown) was similarly produced for readers of poetry who wanted to experience the language and rhythm of Hafiz's poems while reading the Persian bard in Turkish.[57]

In terms of the focus of readers, one can distinguish four forms of reading. Grammatical reading was one. Students of Persian primarily read the classics to improve their grammar and vocabulary. Accordingly, under the instruction of a teacher, who was often a scholar specialised in commentarial writing, they studied the grammatical structure of the texts, focusing their attention on their morphological, phonological and syntactical aspects. Derviş and his fellow pupils at the Ibrahim Pasha palace school, for example, read the classics grammatically as Ahmed Sudi kept a close eye on them. Philological reading was a more advanced level of reading, practised rather by professional readers. Sudi's commentaries, for instance, are informed by his deep philological reading of Sadi and Hafiz. As his copious references to scholarly sources suggest, Sudi consulted dictionaries, commentaries and grammars as he went through the classics philologically.[58] Mystical reading, on the other hand, was a common form of reading among Sufi readers, who concentrated their attention more on mystical concepts, allegories and messages, and relatively less on grammar and vocabulary. Mystical reading thus involved an unearthing of the underlying meaning or wisdom in a given text. In his preface to the opening volume of his commentary on *Masnavi*, Süruri uses the words *mütalaa* ('reading' or 'studying') and *mülahaza* ('reflection') to capture his immersive, mystical exploration of Rumi's text.[59] Literary reading was most visible in circles of poetry, where the classics were read not simply for literary pleasure but also as models of literary emulation. Nisari's diligent reading of Hafiz's poems can be seen as an example of reading with attention to literary details such as rhyme, prosody and figures of speech. Likewise, *Mecmaü'l-Bahreyn* can be interpreted as an outgrowth of Mustafa Ali's literary reading of the *Divan*, a form of reading which he referred to by the verb *tetebbu itmek* ('to read closely').

Concluding remarks

The ways in which the five Persian bestsellers were perceived and engaged with in the Ottoman Empire present us with a thriving reading culture shared by a diverse community of readers, marked by multiple forms of reading, and underpinned by a variety of preoccupations and aspirations. The five classics stirred interest from Turkish readers spread not only across a vast geography, from the Balkans to the Arab lands, but also across a wide social landscape, from the royal court to Sufi lodges.

Whether read for pleasure or for a purpose, such as grammatical, mystical or literary training, the works of Attar, Rumi, Sadi and Hafiz equally enjoyed popularity and prestige in the Ottoman reading world, especially during the 1500s and 1600s. It would, therefore, be misleading to conclude that the five texts were categorically distinct from one another. In terms of readers' expectations and habits of reading, however, these texts can range on a continuum from the mystical to the grammatical-literary. At one end of the continuum are *Masnavi* and *Pandnama*, which were often read mystically and to which an overwhelming majority of readers attributed esoteric significance. Towards the other end of the continuum, we find *Bustan* and *Gulistan*, which were generally employed for learning and teaching Persian while treated as exemplars of Persian literary writing. Hafiz's poetry, on the other hand, can be located somewhere in the middle of the continuum: the *Divan* was read as much as an esoteric text providing the key to divine wisdom as a literary text that enjoyed a paramount status, attracting readers with a penchant for literary or spiritual matters, or both.

Of the five reader groups, it was the scholar-readers who left their imprint on Ottoman readership, especially when we take into account both the number of eager audiences who crowded their classes and public lectures, and the reception of their commentaries and translations by a diverse array of readers, whether young or adult, student or lay, elite or mystical. The philological work produced by scholar-readers thus helped expand the classics' readership and popularity. The elite readers played an equally significant role in this regard by offering patronage to scholar-readers. In particular, as close and seasoned readers of the classics, the sultans and princes encouraged the wider circulation of these texts and, to this end, sponsored the production of commentarial works, which gave impetus to the efflorescence of a wider interest in and reception of Persian language and literary-mystical culture in the Ottoman world.

As texts deeply entrenched in and shaped by a vibrant culture of reading, learning and writing, philological and biographical sources prove to be particularly helpful in charting and exploring the Ottoman history of readers and reading, a history that otherwise offers scant material on the identities and motivations of readers or on forms and settings of reading. A close reading of these sources, and particularly of their prefaces, unearths a wealth of material that would otherwise remain invisible, while giving us a perspective from which to explore the interconnected ways in which reading was understood and practised. Seen in this light, the material drawn from commentarial and biographical works can help nuance our understanding of the multifaceted nature of what constituted reading in an early modern culture like that of the Ottomans.

Notes

1. Muslihüddin Sürurî, *Şerh-i Hafız* (MS Ayasofya 4056, Süleymaniye Manuscript Library, Istanbul), folio 1b. Unless noted otherwise, all translations from Ottoman Turkish and Persian are mine.

2. On books, readers and reading in the Ottoman world, see, among others, Johann Strauss, 'Who Read What in the Ottoman Empire (19th–20th Centuries)?', *Middle Eastern Literatures*, 6:1 (2003), pp. 39–76; Christoph K. Neumann, 'Üç Tarz-ı Mütalaa: Yeniçağ Osmanlı Dünyası'nda Kitap Yazmak ve Okumak', *Tarih ve Toplum: Yeni Yaklaşımlar*, 1 (2005), pp. 51–76; Zehra Öztürk, 'Osmanlı Döneminde Kıraat Meclislerinde Okunan Halk Kitapları', *Türkiye Araştırmaları Literatür Dergisi*, 5:9 (2007), pp. 401–45; Tülün Değirmenci, 'Bir Kitabı Kaç Kişi Okur? Osmanlı'da Okurlar ve Okuma Biçimleri Üzerine Bazı Gözlemler', *Tarih ve Toplum: Yeni Yaklaşımlar*, 13 (2011), pp. 7–43; Joseph R. Hacker, 'Authors, Readers and Printers of Sixteenth-Century Hebrew Books in the Ottoman Empire', in Peggy K. Pearlstein (ed.), *Perspectives on the Hebraic Book* (Washington, DC: Library of Congress, 2012), pp. 17–63; Henning Sievert, 'Eavesdropping on the Pasha's Salon: Usual and Unusual Readings of an Eighteenth-Century Ottoman Bureaucrat', *Osmanlı Araştırmaları/ Journal of Ottoman Studies*, 41 (2013), pp. 159–95; Emine Fetvacı, *Picturing History at the Ottoman Court* (Bloomington: Indiana University Press, 2013), pp. 25–58; Tülün Değirmenci, 'Osmanlı İstanbul'unda Hamzaname Geleneğine Göre Kamusal Okuma', in Coşkun Yılmaz (ed.), *Antik Çağ'dan XXI. Yüzyıla Büyük İstanbul Tarihi* (Istanbul: ISAM, 2015), vol. VII, pp. 634–49; Berat Açıl (ed.,) *Osmanlı Kitap Kültürü: Carullah Efendi Kütüphanesi ve Derkenar Notları* (Ankara: Nobel, 2015); Meredith Moss Quinn, 'Books and Their Readers in Seventeenth-Century Istanbul', PhD dissertation (Harvard University, 2016); İsmail E. Erünsal, *Osmanlı Kültür Tarihinin Bilinmeyenleri: Şahıslardan Eserlere, Kurumlardan Kimliklere*, 2nd edition (Istanbul: Timaş, 2019), pp. 69–94.
3. For commentaries and translations, see Sadık Yazar, 'Anadolu Sahası Klasik Türk Edebiyatında Tercüme ve Şerh Geleneği', PhD dissertation (Istanbul University, 2011). For vocabularies, see Yusuf Öz, *Tarih Boyunca Farsça-Türkçe Sözlükler* (Ankara: Türk Dil Kurumu, 2010).
4. See İsmail E. Erünsal, *Ottoman Libraries: A Survey of the History, Development and Organization of Ottoman Foundation Libraries* (Cambridge, MA: Department of Near Eastern Languages and Literatures at Harvard University, 2008); İsmail E. Erünsal, *Osmanlılarda Kütüphaneler ve Kütüphanecilik* (Istanbul: Timaş, 2015); Sooyong Kim, 'An Ottoman Order of Persian Verse', in Gülru Necipoğlu, Cemal Kafadar and Cornell H. Fleischer (eds), *Treasures of Knowledge: An Inventory of the Ottoman Palace Library (1502/3–1503/4)* (Leiden: Brill, 2019), vol. I, pp. 635–56. For Ottoman booksellers, see Antoine Galland, *Journal d'Antoine Galland pendant son séjour à Constantinople (1672–1673)*, 2 vols, ed. Charles Schefer (Paris: Ernest Leroux, 1881); İsmail E. Erünsal, *Osmanlılarda Sahaflık ve Sahaflar* (Istanbul: Timaş, 2013).
5. For these categories, see Abdüllatif Latifi, *Tezkiretü'ş-Şuara ve Tabsıratü'n-*

Nuzama, ed. Rıdvan Canım (Ankara: Atatürk Kültür Merkezi Başkanlığı, 2000), pp. 368, 530, 535.

6. On Attar and his works, see Leonard Lewisohn and Christopher Shackle (eds), *Attar and the Persian Sufi Tradition: The Art of Spiritual Flight* (London: I. B. Tauris, 2006).
7. Şemullah Şemi, *Saadetname* (MS Kadızade Mehmed 400, Süleymaniye Manuscript Library, Istanbul), folios 2b–3b.
8. Edirneli Nazmi, *Pend-name-i Nazmi (Tercüme-i Pend-name-i Attar)*, ed. Kudret Altun (Kayseri: Laçin, 2004), pp. 68, 72.
9. For Abdi Pasha's commentary, see *Müfid* (MS Turk e.82, Bodleian Library, University of Oxford).
10. For translations of and commentaries on *Masnavi*, see İsmail Güleç, *Türk Edebiyatında Mesnevi Tercüme ve Şerhleri* (Istanbul: Pan Yayıncılık, 2008). On Rumi and his poetry, see Franklin D. Lewis, *Rumi, Past and Present, East and West: The Life, Teachings and Poetry of Jalal al-Din Rumi* (London: Oneworld Publications, 2000).
11. Abdülkadir Dağlar, 'Şem'i Şem'ullah: Şerh-i Mesnevi, I. Cilt (İnceleme-Tenkitli Metin-Sözlük)', PhD dissertation (Erciyes University, 2009), pp. 86, 136.
12. Ahmet Tanyıldız, 'İsmail Rusuhi-yi Ankaravi: Şerh-i Mesnevi, Mecmuatü'l-Letayif ve Matmuratü'l-Maarif, I. Cilt (İnceleme-Metin-Sözlük)', PhD dissertation (Erciyes University, 2010), pp. 78, 81.
13. Evliya Çelebi, *Günümüz Türkçesiyle Evliya Çelebi Seyahatnamesi: 1–6. Kitaplar*, ed. Seyit Ali Kahraman and Yücel Dağlı (Istanbul: Yapı Kredi Yayınları, 2013), p. 6/138; and Evliya Çelebi, *Günümüz Türkçesiyle Evliya Çelebi Seyahatnamesi: 7–10. Kitaplar*, ed. Seyit Ali Kahraman and Yücel Dağlı (Istanbul: Yapı Kredi Yayınları, 2013), p. 9/93. For Çelebi's remarks on the popularity of Rusuhi's *Masnavi* commentary, see Çelebi, *Günümüz Türkçesiyle Evliya Çelebi Seyahatnamesi: 1–6. Kitaplar*, p. 1/248.
14. On Sadi and his works, see Homa Katouzian, *Saʿdi: The Poet of Life, Love and Compassion* (London: Oneworld Publications, 2006).
15. Aşık Çelebi, *Meşairü'ş-Şuara*, ed. Filiz Kılıç (Ankara: Kültür ve Turizm Bakanlığı, 2018), p. 651.
16. On Hafiz and his poetry, see Leonard Lewisohn (ed.), *Hafiz and the Religion of Love in Classical Persian Poetry* (London: I. B. Tauris, 2010).
17. For more on el-Kefevi's book, see Kefeli Hüseyin, *Razname (Süleymaniye, Hekimoğlu Ali Paşa No. 539): Çeviriyazı ve Tıpkıbasımı*, ed. İ. Hakkı Aksoyak (Cambridge, MA: Department of Near Eastern Languages and Literatures at Harvard University, 2004).
18. Çelebi, *Günümüz Türkçesiyle Evliya Çelebi Seyahatnamesi: 1–6. Kitaplar*, p. 6/139.
19. See Mehmet Özdemir, 'Türk Edebiyatında Gülistan Tercümeleri ve 17. Yüzyıl Yazarlarından Hocazade Esad Mehmed Efendi'nin Gül-i Handan (Terceme-i Gülistan)'ı', PhD dissertation (Gazi University, 2011), p. 173.
20. Kınalızade Hasan Çelebi, *Tezkiretü'ş-Şuara*, ed. Aysun Sungurhan-

Eyduran (Ankara: Kültür ve Turizm Bakanlığı, 2009), vol. II, p. 432. For the learning of Persian in the Ottoman world, see Murat Umut Inan, 'Imperial Ambitions, Mystical Aspirations: Persian Learning in the Ottoman World', in Nile Green (ed.), *The Persianate World: The Frontiers of a Eurasian Lingua Franca* (Oakland: University of California Press, 2019), pp. 75–92.

21. For example, in the introduction to his biographical dictionary of poets, the Ottoman poet and literary critic Latifi (died 1582) refers to Hafiz as a wordsmith particularly gifted in love poetry. See Latifi, *Tezkiretü'ş-Şuara ve Tabsıratü'n-Nuzama*, p. 83.
22. For Nisari's biography, see Mustafa İsen, *Künhü'l-Ahbar'ın Tezkire Kısmı* (Ankara: Atatürk Kültür Merkezi Yayınları, 1994), p. 277.
23. On the life and works of Sudi, see Murat Umut Inan, 'Crossing Interpretive Boundaries in Sixteenth-Century Istanbul: Ahmed Sudi on the *Divan* of Hafiz of Shiraz', *Philological Encounters*, 3:3 (2018), pp. 275–309.
24. Derviş Paşa, *Murad-name*, ed. Beyhan Kesik (Giresun: Kiraz Ofis Baskı Merkezi, 2009), p. 83. The Persian text Derviş Pasha translated is entitled *Sakhanama (Book of Generosity)*, which is a work in verse by the Persian poet Banai (dates unknown). In translating this work for the sultan, Derviş Pasha retitled it *Murad-name (Book of Murad)*.
25. For the term *mübtediler*, see Sudi, *Kitab-ı Şerh-i Hafız* (MS Koğuşlar 933, Topkapı Palace Library, Istanbul), folio 2b; and Hulusi, *Vesiletü'l-Meram* (MS İzmir 418, Süleymaniye Manuscript Library, Istanbul), folios 2a–b. For *tullab*, see Lamii Çelebi, *Şerh-i Dibace-i Gülistan* (MS Hacı Selim Ağa 956, Hacı Selim Ağa Manuscript Library, Istanbul), folio 3a.
26. Paul Rycaut, *The Present State of the Ottoman Empire*, 3rd edition (London: John Starkey and Henry Brome, 1670), p. 31.
27. For Şahidi's vocabulary, see Atabey Kılıç, 'Türkçe-Farsça Manzum Sözlüklerden Tuhfe-i Şahidi (Metin)', *Turkish Studies*, 2:4 (2007), pp. 516–48.
28. For Sudi's readerly categories, see Sudi, *Şerh-i Bustan* (MS 5494, Beyazıt State Library, Istanbul), folio 1b; Sudi, *Şerh-i Gülistan* (MS Hamidiye 1158, Süleymaniye Manuscript Library, Istanbul), folio 2a; Sudi, *Kitab-ı Şerh-i Hafız*, folio 2b.
29. For the terms *ihvan* and *yaran*, see, for instance, Hulusi, *Vesiletü'l-Meram*, folio 2a and Şemi, *Saadetname*, folio 2a.
30. For Süruri's commentary, see Süruri, *Şerh-i Mesnevi* (MSS Konya Mevlana Müzesi 2043–2048, Konya Manuscript Library, Konya).
31. Çelebi, *Meşairü'ş-Şuara*, p. 417.
32. Ibid., p. 609.
33. Çelebi, *Günümüz Türkçesiyle Evliya Çelebi Seyahatnamesi: 1–6. Kitaplar*, p. 6/97.
34. Şemi, *Saadetname*, folios 2a–3a.
35. On Süleyman's interest in Hafiz's poetry, see Murat Umut Inan, 'Rethinking the Ottoman Imitation of Persian Poetry', *Iranian Studies*, 50:5 (2017), pp. 671–89.

36. For Selim's poetry collection, see *Selîmî (II. Selîm) Divânçesi*, ed. Beyhan Kesik (Ankara: Vizyon Yayınevi, 2012). For Bayezid's, see *Şahi Divanı*, ed. Filiz Kılıç (Ankara: Kültür ve Turizm Bakanlığı, 2018).
37. For Abdi and his translation, see Hakan Sevindik, 'Yeni Bir Hamse Şairi: Abdi ve Manzum Bostan Tercümesi', *Selçuk Üniversitesi Edebiyat Fakültesi Dergisi*, 35 (2016), pp. 105–30.
38. Emre, *Terceme-i Pend-nâme-i Attar*, ed. Azmi Bilgin (Istanbul: Enderun Kitabevi, 1998), p. 34.
39. For Ottoman literary patronage, see Murat Umut Inan 'Imperial Patronage of Literature in the Ottoman World, 1400–1600', in Hani Khafipour (ed.), *The Empires of the Near East and India: Source Studies of the Safavid, Ottoman, and Mughal Literate Communities* (New York: Columbia University Press, 2019), pp. 493–504.
40. For Zaifi's translation, see Pir Mehmed b. Evrenos b. Nureddin Zaifi, *Kitab-ı Bostan-ı Nasayih*, ed. Ümit Tokatlı (Kayseri: Erciyes Üniversitesi Yayınları, 1996).
41. Esrar Dede, *Tezkire-i Şuara-yı Mevleviyye*, ed. İlhan Genç (Ankara: Kültür ve Turizm Bakanlığı, 2018), p. 159.
42. For the Ottoman literary world, see Selim S. Kuru, 'The Literature of Rum: The Making of a Literary Tradition (1450–1600)', in Suraiya N. Faroqhi and Kate Fleet (eds), *The Cambridge History of Turkey* (Cambridge: Cambridge University Press, 2013), vol. II, pp. 548–92.
43. For Mihri's *Divan*, see *Mihri Hatun Divanı*, ed. Mehmet Arslan (Ankara: Kültür ve Turizm Bakanlığı, 2018). On Mihri and her poetry, see Didem Havlioğlu, *Mihrî Hatun: Performance, Gender-Bending, and Subversion in Ottoman Intellectual History* (Syracuse: Syracuse University Press, 2017).
44. For Mustafa Ali's four-volume poetry collection, see Gelibolulu Mustafa Ali, *Divanlar: I. Divan, II. Varidatü'l-Enika, III. Layıhatü'l-Hakika, IV. Divan*, ed. İ. Hakkı Aksoyak (Ankara: Kültür ve Turizm Bakanlığı, 2018).
45. Ibid., p. 329.
46. Mehmet Atalay and Orhan Başaran, 'Gelibolulu Ali'nin Mecmau'l-Bahreyn Adlı Eseri – I', *Doğu Araştırmaları*, 6 (2010), p. 79.
47. Mehmet Atalay and Orhan Başaran, 'Gelibolulu Ali'nin Rebiu'l-Manzum Adlı Eseri – I', *Doğu Araştırmaları*, 9 (2012), p. 68.
48. For *Nigaristan*, see Mustafa Çiçekler, 'Kemal Paşa-zade ve Nigaristan'ı', PhD dissertation (Istanbul University, 1994).
49. On Carullah Efendi and his book collection, see Muhammed Usame Onuş, 'Bir Osmanlı Alimi Veliyyüddin Carullah Efendi'nin Terceme-i Hali', in Açıl (ed.), *Osmanlı Kitap Kültürü*, pp. 17–43.
50. For Carullah Efendi's Persian books and their marginalia, see Berat Açıl, 'Edebiyatın İlmi veya İlmin Edebiyatı: Carullah Efendi'nin Edebiyat Koleksiyonunu Kenardan Okumak', in Açıl (ed.), *Osmanlı Kitap Kültürü*, pp. 339–70.

51. *Necati Beg Divanı*, ed. Ali Nihat Tarlan (Ankara: Akçağ Yayınları, 1992), p. 166.
52. Tahir Üzgör, *Türkçe Divan Dibaceleri* (Ankara: Kültür Bakanlığı Yayınları, 1990), p. 368.
53. Quinn, 'Books and Their Readers in Seventeenth-Century Istanbul', pp. 64–5.
54. Nazmi, *Pend-name-i Nazmi*, pp. 68–72.
55. Mehmed Rahmi, *Tuhfe-i Dustan, Şerh-i Bustan* (MS A 6178, National Library, Ankara), folio 2b.
56. See Özdemir, 'Türk Edebiyatında Gülistan Tercümeleri', p. 173.
57. For Feridi's translation, see Emrullah Yakut, 'Feridi'nin Manzum Hafız Divanı Tercümesi (İnceleme-Metin)', PhD dissertation (Istanbul University, 2015).
58. For Sudi's references, see Inan, 'Crossing Interpretive Boundaries', pp. 283–4.
59. For these two terms, see Süruri, *Şerh-i Mesnevi* (MS Konya Mevlana Müzesi 2043), folio 1b.

Chapter 9

Books, Readers and Reading Experiences in the Viceroyalties of New Spain and Peru in the Sixteenth to Eighteenth Centuries

Pedro M. Guibovich Pérez

The theme of this chapter is books and readers in the viceroyalties of New Spain (or Mexico) and Peru during the sixteenth, seventeenth and eighteenth centuries. It takes into consideration reading experiences, as well as their social and political repercussions in the colonial context. My chapter takes as its point of departure the reflections of literary critic Angel Rama, and in particular his *La ciudad letrada*. In every viceregal capital there was a 'lettered city' which, according to Rama, formed a protective ring by maintaining the seat of power and executing its orders. Clerics, administrators, educators, professionals, writers and a variety of intellectual servants constituted the lettered city. Not only did they serve the seat of power, but they also held some power themselves. The urban character of this elite group, their role as 'intermediaries managing the instruments of social communication and the fact that the creation of an ideology of power destined for the public developed through them' maintained their power. But their supremacy was also based, according to Rama, in the fact that its members were 'the only practitioners of writing in a space lacking in writing'.[1] Rama's lettered city was a conglomerate composed of Spanish immigrants and their descendants – the criollos – in which the other ethnic groups – Indians, mestizos, mulattos, and Africans – did not participate.[2] Recent studies of colonial society have added nuance to the Uruguayan writer's ideas, demonstrating that literacy included diverse sectors of the indigenous and African-descendant population. Although readers were a minority in the colonial context, they were protagonists in the history of Mexico and Peru, and have left a valuable documentary trail.

In order to study the consumption of books and the ways in which inhabitants of colonial Spanish America used these practices, first one must understand how the reading public emerged. On this topic I will discuss the teaching of reading and writing in urban and rural contexts. The emergence of a reading public was essential for the development of a market in books, supplied primarily from Europe, as local presses were limited in terms of both topics and quantity of production. While the most significant readers were those whose professions required reading (clerics, lawyers, doctors, merchants), there were also women, slaves and indigenous people who read; and literacy therefore allowed the non-elite, non-European/criollo population to negotiate and challenge the systems of power. A history of the reading public and its reading practices enriches our understanding of the intellectual life of the colonial period, challenges understandings inherited from nineteenth-century historiography, which tended to judge that period as backward and reactionary, turns the book into a historical protagonist, and values the social and political dimensions of reading.

From an early stage of the European colonisation of the Americas, books arrived in New Spain and Peru, mostly printed but also, albeit to a lesser extent, manuscripts. Some of them arrived legally, within the shipments of goods from the merchants who trafficked with products on both sides of the Atlantic, but they also arrived within travellers' luggage or inside the boxes of the crew members. There was no shortage of books forbidden by the Crown and the Church; like stowaways, they surreptitiously crossed the Atlantic. Some permitted and others forbidden, books played an essential role in the process of transmission of new knowledge from the Old World to the American lands; and if books arrived, it was because there was a demand for them. Therefore, this chapter begins by explaining the emergence of the reading public in the colonial milieu.

The formation of a reading public

Numerous European immigrants, mainly Spaniards, arrived in Hispanic American lands attracted by the possibilities of enriching their wealth, ascending socially or establishing a new Christendom. The group was truly heterogeneous; and equally heterogeneous were their interests. Among them were those who by their own profession had a mastery of reading and writing, mainly ecclesiastics, Crown officers, physicians and lawyers. Many of them settled, and their descendants aspired to benefit from the privileges of their ancestors or to create ways to reach a better future.

As has been pointed out by Dorothy Tank de Estrada, the ability to read was of importance in the society of New Spain, mainly because reading helped with learning the catechism and with the moral formation of Christians. For many criollos in New Spain, basic instruction consisted of the rudiments of reading and Christian doctrine. It was common to learn first how to read, and then move on to writing and arithmetic. For that reason, more people learnt to read than to write in New Spain.[3] Instruction was a social priority. Therefore, the criollos, the Indians and other groups saw education as a means of social promotion and upward mobility. The same occurred in Peru.

In the viceroyalties of New Spain and Peru, religious orders – Dominican, Mercedarian, Franciscan, Augustinian and Jesuit – established convents, colleges and primary schools for the education of criollos and Indians. I will discuss the latter more extensively later in the chapter. In cities and other settlements, there were primary schools in the charge of a teacher, either a layperson or a cleric, where children learnt the rudiments of reading, writing and arithmetic, as shown by the numerous notarial contracts subscribed between teachers and the parents, tutors, or preceptors of the pupils.[4] Also important were the schools (*colegios mayores*) run by religious orders for the intellectual formation of their members. Among the latter, the Jesuit colleges of San Pedro and San Pablo, in Mexico City, and of San Pablo, in Lima, stood out for the teaching of Latin.

The mastery of reading, writing and Latin opened doors to enter a religious order, Spanish imperial administration, and universities. Despite their enormous social and political gravity, the universities have generally occupied a rather secondary place in studies of colonial intellectual culture. They were attended not only to obtain an academic degree or qualification, considered essential for a career in the civil or ecclesiastical administrations, but above all for weaving social relations, which were vital for social progress once the classrooms were left behind. Those who received instruction in private schools, convents, *colegios mayores* and universities constituted a minority, but one with great social and political power.

Alongside them, a group of indigenous peoples were no strangers to reading and writing either, and also consumed both printed texts and manuscripts. For this native population, both in New Spain and in Peru, learning the Christian doctrine came first in terms of importance, followed by literacy. Both became essential for the clergy and the imperial administration. In all the convents of New Spain, writes Pilar Gonzalbo, instruction was organised in such a way that it reinforced social differences. Young children were classified in two categories according to their family origin. The *macehualtin*, whose parents were workers on community lands or at the service of the Spaniards, learnt the foundations of Christian doctrine and were soon available to take up productive tasks. By contrast, the *pipiltin*, members of the elite, were destined to be authorities of their respective communities, for which reason more instruction was considered: the catechism, and then reading and writing in their own language, the liturgical song, and the memorisation of Latin phrases necessary to enable them to act as auxiliaries in liturgical ceremonies. There was no systematic policy of teaching Spanish, but there were those who learnt it in the continuous interaction in convents, on the street or in some schools. As Gonzalbo points out, educated children acted as catechists and as denouncers of the practitioners of the cults considered idolatrous.[5]

In the extensive Peruvian viceroyalty, after the conquest of the Incas, one of the objectives of the Spaniards was to develop a literate group of natives, basically to act as intermediaries, who would be able to teach the Spanish language and the Christian doctrine to the other indigenous people, as well as to assist members of the Catholic clergy in their struggle against the survival of traditional religious beliefs and practices. In 1545, the first archbishop of Lima, Jerónimo de Loayza, instructed the clergy of his diocese to gather the children of the local nobility and train them as lay catechists. Initially this task was carried out by the friars, who taught children to read and write in Castilian, the catechism, as well as sacred music, and the liturgy (so that children could attend mass and other liturgical celebrations). Additionally, as a condition of their right to manage the indigenous labour force, some Spanish *encomenderos*[6] established schools of religious instruction and trained the children of the elite to teach the other Andean inhabitants.[7]

In 1572, Viceroy Francisco de Toledo issued measures to strengthen Archbishop Loayza's project of creating a literate Andean class. Following the advice of jurist Juan de Matienzo, the viceroy reiterated some dispositions related to the foundation of *doctrinas* (or rural parishes), reminded the clergy of their obligation to enforce doctrinal instruction in the Spanish language, and ordered the establishment of schools for the indigenous youth, especially for the children of the caciques ('chiefs'), in all native settlements. The priests had to hire the most competent among the Ladino Indians of their parishes to teach children up to the age of fourteen how to read, write and speak in Spanish.[8] In addition, the Third Council of Lima, held between 1582 and 1583, ordered the teaching of reading and writing in Spanish to all indigenous children.⁹ John Charles notes that the Indians' competence in the language and the adoption of other marks of *ladinidad*, such as Spanish practices and dress, were long-term goals of the Council.¹⁰

Deep into the seventeenth century, a royal charter, signed in 1691 and addressed to the Bishop of Cuzco, ordered every city, village, settlement and *pueblo de indios* to establish a school to teach Indians the Spanish language, with the caveat that in large towns there must be two schools, one for boys and one for girls. It was stipulated that in order to force Indians to learn the Spanish language and to send their children to school, any Indian who did not know the language could not obtain a 'republican trade' (*oficio de república*). Learning the language was essential for correct evangelisation 'because by knowing the Castilian language, they will be instructed radically and fundamentally in the mysteries of our holy Catholic faith'.¹¹

The policy of teaching Indians to read and write in the Spanish language persisted into the eighteenth century. Then, there were bishops who were decidedly involved in the establishment of schools of first letters for children. A singular case is that of Baltasar Jaime Martínez de Compañón, who opened numerous schools during his government of the diocese of Trujillo between 1779 and 1788. But while he succeeded in establishing schools for criollo children, the same did not happen with his projects for the Indians. Nevertheless, the plan as it was designed is a very interesting example of the educational project that stimulated the Catholic Enlightenment.

Teaching Spanish literacy alongside Christian doctrine had some practical advantages. The students repeated aloud the catechists' readings of the prayers contained in the catechism and transcribed the words written in them before moving on to other types of texts. Indigenous children received daily catechism, while adults had it on Wednesdays, Fridays, Sundays and holidays, after mass. The 'Doctrine' consisted of the reading and recitation of the basic catechism (the articles of faith, the Ten Commandments, the seven sacraments, the theological and cardinal virtues, and the seven deadly sins) as well as the main prayers (the Lord's Prayer, the Hail Mary, the Creed and the Salve Regina). The lectures could deal with subjects as diverse as the belief in a single god, the eternity of the soul or the meaning of the sacraments.¹²

In New Spain and in Peru, literacy in cities and other settlements, even rural ones, created a reading public who consumed books, but who were also capable of having a voice of their own when demanding greater justice or defending their rights, as will be seen later.

Development of the book trade

In New Spain and Peru, the clergy were the main consumers of books. This explains why many religious books were imported from the main publishing centres in Europe. But in addition, and in spite of prohibitions and the adverse comments of moralists, books of very diverse subject matter, among them chivalric romances, crossed the Atlantic from an early stage of colonisation. Booksellers from the major editorial centres of the Old World discovered the enormous earning potential of the American market. Inevitably, the printers of Seville, as well as those in other Spanish cities, were involved in the American trade. According to Irving Leonard, in the seventeenth century, unscrupulous Sevillian printers made fortunes by exporting large quantities of unauthorised books to the colonies, particularly theatrical plays in three acts – which enjoyed the special favour of the public – and editions of mediocre works falsely attributed to well known writers. During the first half of the sixteenth century, the influence of printers from Seville had led the typographic art to an unprecedented degree of perfection. The most famous publishing firm was the Cromberger House, which for years enjoyed exclusive rights for the operation of a printing press in Mexico City and the supply of books to New Spain.[13]

The export of books from Seville to New Spain, asserts Clive Griffin, promised to be a good business, but some Sevillian booksellers and printers protested and declared that if the representatives of the Crown revoked the monopoly granted to Jacobo Cromberger on the export of books, they would sell them at prices lower than those allowed to Cromberger. Griffin argues that it is not clear whether Cromberger made a lot of money with that monopoly or whether there was a significant demand for books before 1553, when the university began operating in Mexico City. The same author notes that he did not find any document in the Sevillian archives that supports the shipment of books to New Spain by Cromberger between 1537 and 1546. However, Griffin observes a remarkable activity of the Sevillian press of Cromberger every year shortly before the departure of the Atlantic fleets bound for New Spain. This, apparently, would indicate that editions destined to the Indies were printed.[14]

The first evidence of the existence of a book trade in the Peruvian viceroyalty dates back to the mid-sixteenth century. It details a remittance made by Alonso Cabezas, a citizen of Lima, probably from Seville, on 1 November 1549, to his partner Pero Ortiz, who resided in Nombre de Dios, for seventy-nine volumes to be sent on board the *Magdalena*. Most of the shipped works were of a religious nature and next to these there was the *Chronicle of King Don Rodrigo* and nine chivalric romances, without specifying the titles.¹⁵

The existence of a sector of the population consuming books explains the establishment in the viceroyalty of Peru of the first commercial company exclusively dedicated to the book trade: the Sarria-Méndez. On 26 March 1605, Juan de Sarria, an active bookseller from Alcalá de Henares, led to Seville several pack animals carrying sixty-one packages of goods addressed to Miguel Méndez, his partner in Lima. Sarria sent them on the *Nuestra Señora del Socorro*, a ship destined for Portobelo. In Portobelo, one of the sons of Juan de Sarria and his namesake monitored the transportation of that cargo from Seville to Panama by road, and from there to El Callao by sea. While crossing the isthmus, several of the packages got wet and Sarria had to repack the books in Panama. Ninety-one books were lost, among which was the only copy of *Don Quixote*. Most of the lost books were religious writings, with the exception of several copies of *La belleza de Angelica* by Barahona de Soto, the *Viaje entretenido* by Rojas Villaldrando, some works of Cicero and *romanceros*. A number of unclear circumstances delayed the book shipment from the isthmus to Lima. Sarria either did not find a way to send the boxes or decided to wait a while for prices to rise. The cargo did not in fact reach Lima until mid-1606.¹⁶

Firms such as Sarria-Méndez and similar catered to a number of large and small retailers, some of them itinerant, who dealt with various kinds of goods, including books. For example, on 24 January 1605, the aforementioned Miguel Méndez signed in Lima a contract with Cristóbal Pérez, a native of Seville. Méndez contributed 1,470 pesos in goods, whereas Pérez gave his 'person, application, and care' (*persona, applicación y cuydado*). Books were included, along with fabrics, horns, flutes, pictures and crucifixes. Pérez had to pay regular sales bills to trade only within the district of the Audiencia of Lima. The contractual arrangement lasted until 1611, and it consisted of Pérez touring the valleys of Chile and Peru.

The interest in obtaining earnings and in ensuring the sale of books led some booksellers to publish catalogues of books in American lands. Such was the case of Tomás López de Haro, printer, editor and book merchant, who in 1682 and 1683 published catalogues of books to be sold in Veracruz, Puebla and Mexico City. In each of these cities, a network of agents was responsible for book distribution in the viceroyalty of New Spain.¹⁷

In his study on the book trade between Spain and America during the first half of the seventeenth century, Pedro Rueda shows that 54.3

per cent of the shipments were destined for Central America, the Caribbean and New Spain, while 45.6 per cent went to Panama, from where they would be sent to the Andean area.[18] Between 1750 and 1820, about one and a half million printed items were exported from Spain to New Spain. Editions printed in Spain dominated the local market, where religious-themed books maintained a slight predominance over those on civil or secular themes, although the number of novels and comedies was nevertheless considerable. In parallel to the increase in trade, libraries in New Spain multiplied.[19]

Several circumstances played in favour of Mexico becoming the main book market in Spanish America. Firstly, from the Old World it was easier to access the Mexican port of Veracruz than the Peruvian port of El Callao, which ships from Europe reached either by crossing the Isthmus of Panama or by circumnavigating the Strait of Magellan. A second factor was the greater urban development of New Spain and, consequently, of its educational institutions. But it is also important to bear in mind that the economic development of the region, particularly in the second half of the eighteenth century, was partly due to mining.

Whether sold by large or small traders, the great majority of books were printed in Europe. But what about local production? It could not be expected to have a large presence in the colonial market, due to the small number of printers in New Spain and Peru. The very limited number of printing presses, bureaucratic red tape, high costs of paper, poor quality of ink and scarcity of moveable type imposed severe restrictions on book production in colonial workshops. Moreover, the colonial printers, like many printers today, kept producing not only books but also flyers, forms and other kinds of shorter texts.

Types of books

The work of printers and book merchants ceased to be of interest to scholars during most of the nineteenth century because throughout Latin America a negative reading of the colonial past prevailed: the Black Legend. According to this reading, Spain kept its American colonies in a situation of cultural backwardness, far from the knowledge of European science and literature. Furthermore, according to this narrative, the books that were read were mainly religious or those allowed by the Church, the Crown and the Inquisition.

In fact, the types of books that were read dealt with very diverse matters, some allowed and others prohibited. It was obvious that, as a Catholic monarchy, Spain would ensure the non-dissemination of political and religious ideas contrary to the interests of the Church and the state; the same happened in non-Catholic countries. Control over what the public read was part of the culture of the Old Regime societies. But valuable information has survived about the interception of literature considered forbidden in the ports of New Spain.

Despite the prohibitions by the Church, the state and the Inquisition, forbidden books crossed to American lands generally hidden in passengers' baggage, which was not usually inspected. During the second half of the eighteenth century, as trade between Spain and America intensified, larger quantities of books arrived on American soil. Moreover, the self-interest of the new ruling dynasty, the Bourbons, encouraged the reading and translation of authors of the European Enlightenment, which increased the curiosity of Americans about new forms of political organisation and about the natural sciences.

Colonial libraries

Books from European and local printers enriched institutional and private libraries in New Spain and Peru. In the convents and monasteries, founded with the double purpose of serving as residence and teaching centres for the friars, there were extensive collections of books. Thus, for example, in the Augustinian college of San Pablo, in Mexico City, Fray Alonso de la Veracruz created, in 1575, a library that came to possess not only a large number of books, but also instruments and maps. The chronicler of the order, Fray Juan de Grijalva, offers a brief description of its history and content:

> our father master [Fray Alonso de la Veracruz] put in the college an outstanding library, which he had brought the year before from Spain, obtained (as he says himself) from diverse places and universities where there were books from all disciplines, of all known arts and languages. The first instalment was sixty crates of books, to which this great man continued to add all those that came to his notice and were not yet in the library. He adorned the library with maps, celestial and terrestrial globes, astrolabes, clocks, cross-staffs, planispheres, and all those instruments that serve the liberal arts, so that [the library] became the most illustrious thing, and of greatest value, in the kingdom.[20]

Other seminary colleges and some universities in Spanish America also managed to gather extensive collections of books.

In principle, the libraries of convents had to serve the friars in their studies, and the need to keep them updated led religious communities to invest in the purchase of the latest publications. In the seventeenth century, the library of the convent of La Merced, in Mexico City, was famous for the quantity and quality of its literary and scientific works.[21] No less famous was the Biblioteca Palafoxiana (or Palafox Seminary), established by Bishop Juan de Palafox y Mendoza, who in 1646 donated his collection of 4,000 volumes to the college/seminary of San Juan and San Pedro in that same city, which was later enriched with other acquisitions (Figure 9.1).[22]

In the main cities of New Spain and Peru, the Jesuits established numerous colleges for their members. Apart from serving as a residence, lessons in Latin, philosophy and theology were also delivered in them. The libraries were nourished by books in various forms, including donations and purchases in the local and European markets. The procurators of the Indies, established in Cadiz, were in charge of providing the latest bibliographical novelties to the libraries of the Jesuit colleges. In the middle of the eighteenth century, the

Figure 9.1 General view of the library of the Palafox Seminary in Puebla, Mexico, by José de Nava (1771). Courtesy of the John Carter Brown Library at Brown University

library of the College of San Pablo in Lima looked imposing, with its shelves full of books, large windows that illuminated the reading room and the portraits of the most notable writers of the order hanging from the walls. It is understandable that the prestige of the order led some men of letters to donate their books as a way to preserve what had cost them so much to gather. Although a description of the library of the college of San Pedro and San Pablo has not survived, we can imagine it particularly rich in its printed and manuscript collections. The famous intellectual Carlos de Sigüenza y Góngora donated to this library his rich collection of 'original books or maps of the ancient Mexican Indians'.[23]

Access to the libraries of religious institutions was usually limited to their members, although this was eventually extended to their lay friends. Only in the mid-eighteenth century did the proposal to establish public libraries emerge in America. But, contrary to our modern idea, the public library, as understood by the enlightened, was not a service oriented to the community, but one organised for the benefit of groups of scholars, and in particular the scholarly elite. Such was the idea that José Eusebio de Llano Zapata from Lima had in mind when he proposed to Cayetano Marcellano de Ayamonte, Archbishop of Charcas, his support for the establishment of a public library in Lima 'that was open during its hours for the free use of men of letters who would like to consult it'.[24] It is clear that the writer from Lima wanted to end the monopoly and limited access imposed by the libraries of convents. In his opinion, the library ought to be a space dedicated to the consultation of books, as well as a place 'where all the originals that can be found about the events in our history will be kept, compiled and archived'. He reckoned one of the greatest benefits of a public library should be the instruction of those 'who, for lack of means to buy books, bewail in our countries an involuntary backwardness, which is as sensible as the talent that adorns them and the spirit that animates them are great'.[25]

The transmission of knowledge had to be elitist, since this guaranteed the predominance of privileged groups within the social body. Although the creation of a public library in Lima did not materialise, in Mexico City, the Turriana, named after its founders, two clerical brothers named Torres, opened its doors in 1804. It was a library aimed at a cultured public. Hence, one of the provisions of the constitution established that the librarian should take special care not to give books with maps and engravings to anyone except 'the people who can make good use of them, in order to prevent many idlers from coming just to enjoy themselves at the Library'.[26]

Private libraries constituted a group no less important in the list of colonial bibliographical collections. For example, the cleric from Lima Fernando de Avendaño enjoyed fame among his contemporaries not only as judge and ecclesiastical visitor of the Archdiocese of Lima, but also because he was considered a man of letters (*letrado*). In a seventeenth-century manuscript, Fray Rodrigo de Cárdenas says that de Avendaño 'led a good and modest life' and that he was:

> a man dedicated to his trades and studies and, as such, keen on collecting a copious library and hunting for rare books. When we could not find a book we needed, we looked for him at his library and he would lend it to us.[27]

The prelates of both viceroyalties possessed extensive collections of books. It was not unusual that, together with their entourage of secretaries and relatives, the bishops destined for America carried their books as part of their luggage. Once in their diocese, such collections were installed in special rooms and were increased with new acquisitions. Later, after the death of the bishop, the books went to swell the collections of colleges and seminars. Lawyers and physicians also had extensive libraries.

For the secular or ecclesiastical man of letters, the library constituted a work tool which, in general, occupied a room in the house: the studio. According to Charles de la Roncière, the 'studio' or office was annexed to the bedroom in Tuscan houses of the fifteenth century.[28] In Italy, as in Peru, it was a private, intimate space, to which it was possible to retire in order to meditate, read and work away from importunate gazes and voices. Figure 9.2 shows an example.

According to the testimony of a contemporary, Doctor Antonio de Árpide y Ulloa, rector of the University of San Marcos, could 'always be found in his studio, occupied with his books and papers not only in matters related to his profession as a prosecutor, but also with others that he studied out of curiosity, because he had been very great at gathering books and reading them, and at conferring and disputing over points of law'.[29] The books serve not only for studying but also as a means of evasion. According to the Jesuit Diego Calleja, the 'pastime' of the Mexican nun Juana Inés de la Cruz was her library, 'where she entered to console with four thousand friends, which were how many books she composed it of almost without cost, because no one printed [a book] without donating it [to her library] . . .'.[30]

The owners paid special attention to the decoration of their studios, with paintings and elaborate furniture. The room that contained the library of Manuel de Mollinedo y Angulo, Bishop of Cuzco, included

Figure 9.2 Portrait of Agustin Sarmiento in his study in Lima (1669). Courtesy of the John Carter Brown Library at Brown University

paintings by the most famous artists of the Spanish court (Juan Carreño de Miranda and Claudio Coello).[31] The decoration created an atmosphere conducive to study, while praising its owner. It is a very idiosyncratic expression of his aesthetic tastes and interests, as well as of the consideration he had for books.

Reading experiences

Although the circulation and possession of books by members of colonial society can be researched via a variety of archival sources (letters, inquisitorial records, notarial registers, etc.), the study of their reading is harder. This challenge is owing to two factors. In the first place, there has been no great interest among students of colonial culture in documenting reading practices; more confounding, reading practices frequently have been interpreted as synonymous with the possession of books. In the second place, evidence of reading tends to be ephemeral, leaving no trace upon the book in question. So, as Mary Hammond has observed, investigating the history of reading requires detective work.[32] In spite of these limitations, I will present a few examples illustrating reading experiences in the colonial context.

As mentioned, many books came to Spanish America with immigrants from Europe. Travellers would bring a diverse selection of books to entertain themselves during the long and onerous crossing of the Atlantic. In order to avoid the diffusion of illegal emigrants and books that contained ideas contrary to the Catholic faith, the Spanish Crown charged the Inquisition with the inspection of ships that arrived at American ports. The norms indicated that officials of the Inquisition were to interview the captain and the ship's officials regarding the events of the trip, the passengers and the goods on board. In 1575, Juan Palomares de Vargas, captain of the *Nuestra Señora de Begonia*, upon arriving at the port of Veracruz, was interviewed by the Inquisition's commissioner regarding the books that the crew brought for their 'recreation or pastime'. The captain declared that he possessed the *Cancionerio*, by Fernán Pérez de Guzmán – a book of poetry that 'he read from time to time' – and 'another on the *Entrada* of the King in Sevilla'; and that he had no further books beyond those. According to his statement, the captain was the only person aboard who was reading, quite probably during his moments of leisure, which must not have been very long, given his responsibilities on the ship. Moreover, he knew that certain books were prohibited by the Inquisition, because he declared that the crew carried no copies of 'books of hours'.[33]

Once the books were unloaded from ships, they travelled different paths. Not a few books on religious themes went to members of the clergy for their instruction. Listening to their being read aloud during mealtimes was widespread in men's and women's religious institutions. This was a means of seeking the reinforcement of the listeners' piety and morality. Thus, in the convent of the nuns of Santa Teresa in the city of Puebla, in the dining room (refectory) there was 'a room, as capable and decent as it was religious and devout, with enough brightness for clarity [. . .] among which can be seen a niche with a small shelf of books that they read while eating [. . .] and in front of the windows is the pulpit where they read, before proceeding to the great door that opens to the cloister'.[34] Because reading constituted an important form of instruction, it had to be done with great care. In the founding documents of the convent of San Jerónimo of Puebla it was established that the woman charged with the reading had to undertake it 'neither too hurried nor too slow; neither in too loud a voice nor so softly that she can't be understood; but with gravity and weight, like a person who is teaching others'.[35] On the other hand, the Jesuit Francisco Xavier Salduendo writes that the reading aloud of the biography of Antonio Cordero, a Jew who converted to Christianity, in the dining room of the college of San Pablo of Lima, provided the assembled community with 'plates delicious to the understanding, for being well-written and adorned with history' and 'effective reinforcements of the will'.[36]

It was also common practice for confessors of nuns and lay pious women (*beatas*) to recommend readings as models for their religious life. In Lima, the Jesuit Juan Pérez Menacho often charged the *beata* Jerónima de San Francisco with the reading of the work Santa Teresa of Ávila. In her autobiography, the *beata* wrote: 'I later sought out the book, and once I began reading I couldn't stop, for the great comfort and joy I felt from that great teacher instructed by the Holy Spirit'. In the work of Santa Teresa she found

> the mercies that God had made for me, as seen in a paragon. Reading gave me a thousand pleasures, and I rejoiced to see the grand mercies that I had received from the hand of God without deserving them, without his impeding them, that only through His kindness had He favoured this ungrateful one: that I might be inspired by such devotion to this saint, to her book and to her image, whom I have always had with me, and will have until I die.[37]

The same devotion to reading and the cultivation of intellect was felt by the afore-mentioned Sister Juana Inés de la Cruz, who in her convent in Mexico City said she wanted to avoid 'any obligatory occupation that might encumber the liberty of my study', as well as any 'murmurs of the community that might disturb the hushed silence of my books'.[38]

Reading Catholic books could also nurture the piety of the laity, Portuguese converts from Judaism among them. Attracted by the possibility of living in peace, various Portuguese *conversos* emigrated to the viceroyalties of New Spain and Peru to dedicate themselves to commerce, agriculture or mining. Given that the Inquisition had prohibited Jewish texts, *conversos* nourished their religiosity with Catholic religious literature, in particular that which dealt with the history of the people of Israel or contained passages from the Old Testament. Such is the case of *El Espejo de Consolación* by the Franciscan Juan de Dueñas, a work published in six volumes between 1546 and 1570, which was a compilation of numerous histories extracted principally from the Old Testament. In them it is explained how, in the heart of adversities, pious men amended their lives, and in this way found God and interior peace. In 1603 Antonio Mendes was denounced before the Inquisition of Mexico by Manuel Gil for

> having brought into the room where he lived [with Gil] a copy of the *Espejo de Consolación* which contains many Old Testament stories. One night he read it with great feeling. He wanted to keep it in [Gil's] bookcase, but [Gil] would not let him because he thought it was one of the prohibited books. Mendes replied that that one book was worth more than all the others that [Gil] had.[39]

Books of hours were also read by *conversos* because they contained texts from the Old Testament. Álvaro de Rodríguez had translated the Seven Penitential Psalms from a book of hours, to memorise them and pray with them 'for understanding them as good to save his sinning soul'. Upon being questioned by the Inquisitors of Lima in 1639 if he often prayed with translated psalms, he said that years before, being with some Jews, he had found an incomplete book of hours in the vernacular and from them had copied the psalm 'Lord, do not rebuke me' (Psalm 38) and that afterward he had got rid of the book and the psalm.[40]

Books made their way even to the most remote parts of the Peruvian Viceroyalty. At the beginning of the 1770s, Alonso Carrió de la Vandera, in his capacity as commissioner for improving the mail system between Montevideo and Lima, arrived in Tucumán. He found accommodation at the home of a 'gentleman' who 'expressed himself in an unusual manner and asked strange questions'. But what captured Carrió's attention the most was that the said character owned 'four very worn-out books almost falling out of their bindings'. These were: Fernán Méndez Pinto's *Historia Oriental de las Peregrinaciones*; Baltasar de Vitoria's *Teatro de los dioses de la gentilidad*; Ginés Pérez de Hita's *Historia de los bandos de Zegríes y Abencerrajes o Guerras civiles de Granada*; and *Historia de Carlomagno y de los doce Pares de Francia*.⁴¹ After leafing through the books, which he had read as a young man, the commissioner praised the 'library' and asked the gentleman if he had read other texts. The gentleman replied that 'he knew these books by heart and went over them every day so as not to forget their content, because one should read only a handful of books of the highest quality'. It seemed to Carrió an extravagant notion.⁴² This is to be expected, as Carrió de la Vandera was very familiar with the literature of his time and was therefore surprised by such a small collection of books, which he sarcastically referred to as a 'library', and by such an unusual manner of reading the works of the sixteenth and seventeenth centuries.

Also during the second half of the eighteenth century, in the context of greater commercial exchange with Europe, numerous works of the Enlightenment arrived, principally by French, German and English authors. In Lima, in the early 1780s, Santiago Urquizu, an official of the mint house, had been able to amass an enormous library. 'My fondness for books and my father's frankness in gratifying me in that fondness means that I never miss an occasion to acquire the best that I find', he wrote. Urquizu was part of a small circle of readers who shared books and ideas. The reading of the works of Voltaire and Holbach turned out to be particularly seductive. Of Voltaire, Urquizu wrote that 'despite the contempt that this author deserves [. . .] I enjoyed myself [. . .] and it made me laugh several times, which kept me reading'. The work of Holbach appealed to him for how it challenged the existence of God and because it attributed 'the marvel that we exist to us ourselves, and that which surrounds us to the action and combination of bodies among themselves'. In a conversation between Urquizu and the Dominican friar Mariano Arbites, both concluded that 'religion was a chimera, full of contradictions, invented by men solely in order to attract and subject and trick the ignorant'. Upon reaching this point, Urquizu felt that he had gone too far, felt remorse and denounced himself before the Inquisition.⁴³

French literature also circulated in Mexico and, as in Lima, was read and discussed. In 1795 a reader denounced to the Mexican Inquisition a work entitled *Lettres de Julie à Eulalie ou Tableau du libertinage de Paris*, because he thought it 'noxious'. He wrote to explain his reason for reading it: 'This book is written in a captivating style and for that very reason its reading is all the more noxious. I have read it, by God Our Lord, for no other reason than to denounce it to this Holy Tribunal.' Without fear he declaimed the effects of its reading: 'The obscenities that are narrated within it have produced no other effect than to fill me with horror'. And he ended confessing: 'All in all, his eloquence so confounded me that I found it difficult to put down, to attend to my needed work'.[44] Among readers, the literature of the Enlightenment generated mixed feelings of attraction and repulsion.

Lettered Indians

Books circulated from one hand to another, from one shelf to another, from the city to the countryside, and vice versa. Although the many Indian readers did not leave us testimonies of their reading experiences, we can affirm that some of them were not aliens to printed texts. There were Indians, generally of the elite, who owned collections of books, but there were others who managed to consult the libraries of parish priests and circulated books among themselves, which alarmed the Spanish authorities in the Peruvian viceroyalty. The clergyman Bartolomé Álvarez, enthusiastic defender of the extirpation of native religions, reported in his 1588 memorial to Philip II having witnessed Indians in the Andean highlands who acquired the *Siete partidas* by Alfonso X the Wise, and the *Práctica civil y criminal e instrucción de escribanos* by Gabriel de Monterroso, purchases that, according to the zealous ecclesiastic, were proof of the Indians' intention to initiate lawsuits or 'to do evil'.[45]

Viceroy Toledo also stated his reservations about the introduction of printed texts: 'It is not convenient that profane books and [books] of bad example are brought to these realms because they will be received by the Indians, since many of them already know how to read'.[46] The Third Council of Lima explicitly banned 'all books pertaining to profane matters or telling or teaching lascivious and immodest things, not only in consideration of their damage to the Faith, but also to decency, as is to be expected from reading such books, and therefore those found to possess them shall be severely punished by the bishops'.[47]

The mestizo chronicler Guamán Poma denounced the obstacles that the friars and *encomenderos* put in place to keep Indians from learning how to read and write, due to their interest in maintaining control over them, continuing with the abuses of Spanish settlers, disobeying the provisions of the Crown and, above all, for fear that they could initiate legal actions.[48] Despite the obstacles put forth by some members of colonial society, literacy progressed and allowed Indians to access the printed literature of the colonisers. As has been shown in some investigations, this access provided them with the resources to make their claims for better justice, to litigate before civil and ecclesiastical courts, to denounce the authorities and to compose political opinions (*pareceres*).[49]

Don Cristóbal Castillo was principal *curaca* of the Indian *reducción*[50] of Cotahuasi, in the Condesuyos Province, when in 1616 he decided to address letters in Quechua to different members of the *ayllu* Mungui (i.e. the clan) to convince them to recognise his authority and abide by his orders: pay the full fee, appoint captains for the *mita* labour system, execute various services and, in particular, give up on becoming an annex of Pampamarca. In his correspondence, he set out the obedience of his subjects as a Christian requirement, using vocabulary, expressions and propositions directly or indirectly taken from the Quechua texts published by the Third Provincial Council of Lima between 1584 and 1585.[51] These and other Council texts circulated profusely in the Archdiocese of Lima, because priests were required to consult them to govern their parishes properly.[52]

In 1650, Don Pedro Taparaco, Don Cristóbal Capcha, Don Alonso Julia Chaupis, Don Francisco Malqui, Don Tomás Guamán Capcha and Don Antonio Capcha, principal *curacas* and other native authorities of the rural parish of San Pedro de Paccho, denounced their priest, Diego de la Palma, for contravening the ecclesiastical rules against demanding offerings, charging for the administration of the sacraments, and other faults. What is interesting about this case is that they based their claims on the synodal dispositions promulgated by the Catholic Church at the beginning of that century.[53]

An emblematic case of an indigenous person who had the power to access European print culture was that of Felipe Guamán Poma de Ayala. Rolena Adorno has argued that, besides offering a testimony of his personal experience, Guamán Poma's *Nueva Coronica* is an important source through which to study the intellectual climate in the late sixteenth and early seventeenth centuries, when the relations between the native inhabitants and the European society were subject to debate. The chronicler's own strategic argument, as Adorno points out, demonstrates that he was familiar with the positions in favour of the Indians advocated by Bartolomé de Las Casas and Domingo de Santo Tomás. In his work, Guamán Poma also refers to literary works related to the last three decades of the sixteenth century, published both in America and in Europe. It is evident that the Andean writer was fully aware of the nascent American literary culture. Moreover, among the first twelve books published in South America, which appeared in the last fifteen years of the sixteenth century, Guamán Poma read a large number of those dedicated to religious and theological matters.[54]

A contemporary of the Peruvian chronicler was the writer Fernando de Alva Ixtlilxochitl, author of an important historical work about the reign of Texcoco, in the central valley of Mexico. As John Frederick Schwaller has pointed out, by writing a narrative history in a European style, Alva sought to incorporate the history of the New World into the history of the (Christian) world brought by the Spaniards. To achieve this, he interwove European chronologies with the events that took place in pre-Hispanic Mexico.[55] Dealing with the period in which the Chichimeca nobles lived in Tulancingo before leaving for Tula, Alva wrote: 'in the year of the Incarnation of Christ, Our Lord, [in] the 13th acatl and our [year CE] 542, when Virgil was the Supreme Roman Pontiff and during the second year of his pontificate, and on the twelfth year of Justinian's Empire, and in Spain on the twelfth year of Theudis' government'.[56] Undoubtedly, he was, like Guamán Poma, familiar with book literature from the Old World.

The books in the hands of the Indians served, among other purposes, to build legal and historical discourses, but also to nourish religious piety. Following the directives of Trent, the First (1555) and Third (1585) Provincial Councils of Mexico forbade the circulation and possession of manuscript copies of devotional texts. Despite this, some peasant communities produced manuscript copies of liturgical and devotional texts. An anonymous manuscript in the Nahuatl language, kept in the National Library of France, contains sermons for most of the Sundays of the year, a translation of a treatise on good government and a short monologue on the correct worship of Christian images.[57] It is not easy to determine the purpose for which the compilation was composed, but it was very probably devotional.

It is important to remember that a manuscript text is always an open text, that is, exposed to intervention through additions or corrections by other hands; and, consequently, subject to a distortion of the doctrinal message. This explains the ecclesiastical prohibition of manuscripts in any native language. In any case, the study of the circulation of literature in manuscript form is still a little-explored field of research, in particular for the Peruvian case.

Conclusion

La ciudad letrada by Ángel Rama was an important milestone in Latin American literary production, as it led to rethinking the role of literate elites and writing in the period of Spanish rule in New Spain and Peru. Several of the theses of Rama's book were subject to revision, mainly by scholars of colonial history and literature. There is no doubt that men of letters played an essential role in maintaining the colonial order and that this was possible thanks to their literacy and their access to books. But along with the criollos, there were other groups of inhabitants, mostly indigenous people and to a lesser extent women, for whom reading and writing were essential tools. The readers and the books that they consulted were very diverse, as were their forms of appropriation. Instead of talking about the lettered city, then, it might be useful – and more accurate – to talk about the republic of letters in the colonial context.

Notes

1. Angel Rama, La ciudad letrada (Hannover: Ediciones del Norte, 1985), p. 25.
2. Ibid., pp. 32–3.
3. Dorothy Tank de Estrada, 'La enseñanza de la lectura y la escritura en la Nueva España, 1700–1821', in Historia de la lectura (Mexico City: El Colegio de México, 2010), p. 49.
4. Archivo Regional del Cuzco. Protocolo del escribano Pedro de Cáceres, No. 34, folios 192r–v, 205r–v.
5. Pilar Gonzalbo, 'La lectura de evangelización en la Nueva España', in Historia de la lectura en México (Mexico City: El Colegio de México, 1990), p. 37.
6. Encomendero means the possessor of an encomienda, that is, a Spaniard to whom a group or groups of Indians have been entrusted. The encomendero usually demanded labour and tribute from the Indians in exchange for payment, protection and religious instruction. See Kenneth Mills and William Taylor, Colonial Spanish America: A Documentary History (Wilmington: Scholarly Resources, 1998), p. 349.
7. John Charles, Allies at Odds: The Andean Church and Its Indigenous Agents, 1583–1671 (Albuquerque: University of New Mexico Press, 2010), pp. 18–19.
8. Ibid., p. 20.
9. Enrique Bartra (ed.), III Concilio Provincial de Lima 1582–1583 (Lima: Facultad Pontificia y Civil de Teología de Lima, 1982), p. 80.
10. Charles, Allies at Odds, p. 20.
11. Emilio Lisson Chaves, La Iglesia de España en el Perú (Sevilla: Editorial Católica, 1943–1956), vol. V, pp. 479–80.
12. Charles, Allies at Odds, p. 21.
13. Irving Leonard, Los libros del conquistador (Mexico City: Fondo de Cultura Económica, 1979), p. 104.

14. Clive Griffin, 'La primera imprenta en México y sus oficiales', in Idalia García and Pedro Rueda (eds), Leer en tiempos de la colonia. Imprenta, bibliotecas y lectores en la Nueva España (Mexico City: Universidad Nacional Autónoma de México, 2010), pp. 8–9.
15. Leonard, Los libros del conquistador, p. 111.
16. Ibid., p. 276.
17. Pedro Rueda, 'Los catálogos de Tomás López de Haro: las redes atlánticas del negocio europeo del libro en Nueva España, 1682–1683', in Pedro Rueda and Lluis Agustí (eds), La publicidad del libro en el mundo hispánico (Siglos XVII–XX) (Barcelona: Calambur, 2016), pp. 44–5.
18. Pedro Rueda, Negocio e intercambio cultural. El comercio de libros con América en la carrera de Indias (Siglo XVII) (Seville: Diputación de Sevilla, Universidad de Sevilla and Escuela de Estudios Hispano-Americanos, 2005), pp. 54–5.
19. Cristina Gómez Álvarez, Navegar con libros. El comercio de libros entre España y Nueva España (1750–1820) (Madrid: Trama Editorial, 2011), pp. 129–35.
20. Fray Juan de Grijalva quoted in Elías Trabulse, 'Los libros científicos en la Nueva España, 1550–1630', in Alicia Hernández Chávez and Manuel Miño Grijalva (eds), Cincuenta años de Historia de México (Mexico City: El Colegio de México, 1991), p. 17.
21. Ibid., pp. 20–1.
22. Pedro Ángel Palou Pérez, 'Breve noticia de la Biblioteca Palafoxiana', Artes de México, 68 (2004), pp. 50–1.
23. Idalia García, 'Imprenta y librerías jesuitas en la Nueva España', in Pedro Rueda and Idalia García (eds), El libro en circulación en la América colonial (Mexico City: Ediciones Quivira, 2014), p. 224.
24. See José Eusebio Llano Zapata, Memorias histórico, físico, crítico apologéticas de la América Meridional (Lima: Instituto Francés de Estudios Andinos, Pontificia Universidad Católica del Perú and Universidad Nacional Mayor de San Marcos, 2005), pp. 594–5.
25. Ibid., p. 598.
26. See Silvia Salgado, 'La biblioteca y la librería coral de la catedral de México', in Rueda and García (eds), El libro en circulación en la América colonial, p. 200.
27. Archivo Histórico Nacional, Madrid, Inquisición, libro 1043.
28. Charles de la Roncière, 'La vida privada de los nobles toscanos en el umbral del Renacimiento', in Philippe Ariès and Georges Duby (eds), Historia de la vida privada. Poder privado y poder público en la Europa Feudal (Madrid: Taurus, 1990), p. 221.
29. Luis Antonio Eguiguren, Diccionario histórico y cronológico de la real y pontificia universidad de San Marcos y sus colegios (Lima: Torres Aguirre, 1940), vol. I, p. 289.
30. José Luis Martínez, El libro en Hispanoamérica. Origen y desarrollo (Madrid: Fundación G. Sánchez-Ruipérez, 1986), p. 65.

31. Pedro Guibovich Pérez, 'Los espacios de los libros', Lexis, 27:2 (2003), p. 184.
32. Mary Hammond, 'Book History in the Reading Experience', in Leslie Howsam (ed.), The Cambridge Companion to the History of the Book (Cambridge: Cambridge University Press, 2015), p. 240.
33. Francisco Fernández del Castillo, Libros y libreros en el siglo XVI (Mexico City: Fondo de Cultura Económica, 1982), p. 370. Books of hours were prohibited because they contained prayers that were considered superstitious.
34. Rosalva Loreto López, 'Leer, contar, cantar y escribir. Un acercamiento a las prácticas de lectura conventual. Puebla de los Ángeles, México, siglos XVII–XVIII', Estudios de historia novohispana, 23 (2000), p. 78.
35. Ibid., p. 80.
36. Pedro Guibovich Pérez, 'Autores, censores y producción de libros en el virreinato peruano', in Rueda and García (eds), El libro en circulación en la América colonial, p. 101.
37. Nancy Van Deusen, 'El cuerpo como libro viviente, Lima 1600–1640', Histórica, 31:1 (July 2007), p. 33.
38. Gallegos Rocafull, El pensamiento mexicano en los siglos XVI y XVII (Mexico City: Universidad Nacional Autónoma de México, 1974), p. 344.
39. David M. Gitlitz, Secrecy and Deceit: The Religion of the Crypto-Jews (Philadelphia: Jewish Publication Society, 1996), p. 430.
40. Pedro Guibovich Pérez, 'Los libros de los doctrineros en el virreinato del Perú, siglos XV–XVII', in Wulf Oesterreicher and Roland Schmidt-Reise (eds), Esplendores y miserias de la evangelización de América. Antecedentes europeos y alteridad indígena (Berlin: De Gruyter, 2010), p. 79.
41. The last book mentioned might be Nicolao de Piamonte, Historia del emperador Carlomagno y de los doce pares de Francia.
42. 'Concolocorvo' (Alonso Carrió de la Vandera), El lazarillo de ciegos caminantes (Barcelona: Editorial Labor, 1973), p. 118.
43. Pedro Guibovich Pérez, Lecturas prohibidas. La censura en el Perú tardío colonial (Lima: Pontificia Universidad Católica del Perú, 2013), pp. 110–11.
44. Pablo González Casanova, La literatura perseguida en la crisis de la colonia (Mexico City: SEP, 1986), p. 132.
45. Carlos Garatea, Tras una lengua de papel. El español en el Perú (Lima: Pontificia Universidad Católica del Perú, 2010), p. 127.
46. Charles, Allies at Odds, pp. 30–1.
47. Bartra, III Concilio Provincial, p. 103.
48. Garatea, Tras una lengua de papel, pp. 141–2.
49. Woodrow Borah, El Juzgado general de indios en la Nueva España (Mexico City: Fondo de Cultura Económica, 1985); Caroline Cunill, Los defensores de indios de Yucatán y el acceso de los mayas a la justicia real (Mérida: Universidad Nacional Autónoma de México, 2012); and

José Carlos de la Puente Luna and Renzo Honores, 'Guardianes de la real justicia: alcaldes de indios, costumbre y justicia local en Huarochirí colonial', Histórica, 40:2 (December 2016), pp. 11–47.

50. A reducción was a town that had resulted from the forced resettlement of groups of Indians in colonial times. See Mills and Taylor, Colonial Spanish America, p. 351.
51. César Itier, 'Las cartas quechuas de Cotahuasi: el pensamiento político de un cacique del siglo XVII', in Bernard Lavalle (ed.), Máscaras, tretas y rodeos del discurso colonial en los Andes (Lima: Instituto Francés de Estudios Andinos and Instituto Riva-Agüero, 2005), pp. 44–5.
52. Guibovich Pérez, 'Los libros de los doctrineros en el virreinato del Perú'.
53. Archivo Arzobispal de Lima. Visitas, leg. 14, exp. 13.
54. Rolena Adorno, 'Las otras fuentes de Guamán Poma: sus lecturas castellanas', Histórica, 2:2 (December 1978), p. 138.
55. John Frederick Schwaller, 'The Brothers Fernando de Alva Ixtlixochitl and Bartolomé de Alva: Two Native Intellectuals of Seventeenth-Century Mexico', in Gabriela Ramos and Yanna Yannakakis (eds), Indigenous Intellectuals: Knowledge, Power, and Political Culture in Mexico and the Andes (Durham, NC: Duke University Press, 2014), p. 47.
56. Ibid., p. 58.
57. David Tavárez Bermúdez, Las guerras invisibles. Devociones indígenas, disciplina y disidencia en el México colonial (Mexico City: El Colegio de Michoacán, CIESAS, Universidad Autónoma Metropolitana and Universidad Autónoma Benito Juárez de Oaxaca, 2012), p. 237.

Chapter 10

'Read it o're and o're': *Eikon Basilike* and Sacramental Reading in the Seventeenth Century

Kyle Sebastian Vitale

Much has been written about the success of the *Eikon Basilike*, published in 1649 by Royalist supporters after the English Parliament's execution of King Charles I. Parliamentarians proscribed traditional sacramental ceremony, forbidding the Book of Common Prayer's burial rite and denying the usual laudatory gravestone epitaphs.[1] Anticipating this enervation, Royalist printers dispersed the octavo *Eikon*, containing twenty-eight chapters of Charles's apologetics, confessions, and prayers alongside a saintly frontispiece, to ensure that Charles would be defined in posterity and theology as a holy martyr. Scholarly consensus speaks to the staggering effect of this effort as the book became an instant bestseller, textually delivering Charles back to his people.[2] Critics emphasise the book's powers as a devotional support, model of behaviour and even celebrity lodestone during a time of loss and persecution.[3] Elizabeth Skerpan-Wheeler calls the *Eikon* 'a model of devotion and right conduct', while Laura Knoppers observes that the *Eikon* 'embodied and inspired the virtues of piety and devotion'.[4]

The *Eikon Basilike* was welcomed with open arms by supporters of the king, who relished the prospect of knowing Charles again as text and image.[5] Yet the *Eikon*'s success is at once overstated and understated by modern critics, in ways that blur rather than clarify seventeenth-century reading habits. It is overstated in that the Royalist response to the *Eikon* was less consistent than supposed. Critics look to the book's contents as proof of its readership, citing how readers could easily adopt the book's general Psalmic prayers and tone to identify and empathise with Charles in his Davidic exile.[6] Yet in their printed elegies and lamentations, Royalists often reject or ignore the *Eikon*. One Royalist states outright, 'We want an *Emblem* for him', as if the *Eikon* simply did not exist.[7] Other critics situate Royalist lament within their devotion to the Book of Common Prayer, outlawed by Parliament in 1645. As Judith Maltby writes, the Book of Common Prayer 'structured and shaped the year', giving a sense of order to worship and life.[8] The prayer book, more than the Bible, helped the Royalist amalgam of Arminian and proto-Catholic Protestants ritualise their experiences of death, confession and hope. Denying Charles his burial rites denied his supporters a kind of sacramental closure. One Royalist writes that 'black-mouth'd Miscreants engrave / No Epitaph, but Tyrant, on thy Grave'.[9] The elegance and density of the *Eikon*'s symbolism falls short here against the denial to Charles of the most basic linguistic pittance – words on a grave. Another Royalist laments that, with the death of Charles, 'All rhetoric's dumb'.[10] Even assuming hyperbolic language is in use here, the degree and specificity of these and other laments suggest a strategy that rejects and ignores the *Eikon* as a way to express grief and bereavement.

By contrast, its success is also understated, in that the *Eikon*'s many kinds of editions suggest a wider, more diverse readership than has often been supposed. The *Eikon* is by no means a consistent book: its editions span a range from standard, often poor copies to versions with inked-in frontispieces, elevating it into a kind of book of hours. For most standard editions, the *Eikon* served devotional purposes; as Ramie Targoff elucidates, this meant language and image in particular rhythms, cadences and cycles that could give communities of believers a common script, while rehearsing and emboldening the matrix of beliefs individuals held within that community.[11] Yet for a smaller set of editions, the book's use pushed past devotion into sacrament. The line here is thin, but runs along the degree and manner to which users or readers expect materiality to convey or inspire the presence of God, and the effects of such presence on the user/reader. As Jim Daems and Holly Faith Nelson observe in the introduction to their edition of the *Eikon*, '[For readers f]aced . . . with kingly absence, *Eikon Basilike* served as an incarnational text, for it provided a revered, material textual body for Charles I'.[12] Like the actions of baptism or the Supper, which offer healing grace and divine presence in various shades, depending on one's degree of non-conformity, so the *Eikon* could extend Charles's healing presence through more intentional devices. David Gay writes of the book's frontispiece that 'the King's person is extraordinary as it allows for the perception of the sacred by others. The portrait of the King, in turn, occasions the perception of the "sacred" in the book.'[13] Although this observation is affirmed and appreciated by various rubricated and ornamented editions, criticism tends to rely heavily on a language of devotion that can limit the power of sacramental moments like these in the book's printing history.

These overstated and understated claims often manifest as universal acceptance by Royalists and bitter rejection by non-conformists like John Milton. This chapter seeks to complicate and enlarge those claims as a way of rendering the complexity of seventeenth-century sacramental reading habits. At once, the *Eikon Basilike* was a glorious political success and a devotional guide, an ornament of deeper spiritual significance and an object to be performatively rejected. We should keep in mind that, as Adrian Streete reminds us, seventeenth-century political-religious rhetoric is often an 'adaptable and multifarious language', capable of extremes and contradictions that defy modern notions of rationality.[14] The same may be said of the *Eikon Basilike*'s reception.

This chapter looks briefly into the theological contexts surrounding seventeenth-century worship and reading practices, as a way to illustrate the multifariousness of the *Eikon*'s cultural moment. It then looks into two editions of the *Eikon* housed at the Folger Shakespeare Library – a vicesimo-quarto with rubricated language and additional illustrations, and an edition featuring a coloured frontispiece.[15] These editions signal reading possibilities beyond prayer book devotion. Writing of presence in text, Ryan Netzley suggests that a kind of sacramental reading in the seventeenth century looks less to linguistic content than to the ways a text underscores the absent presence of divinity.[16] Readers are beckoned to an affective, not just intellectual, response to that Eucharistic presence. As Gay observes, the frontispiece offers something similar, and special editions of the *Eikon* further enable that reading process.[17] With the *Eikon*'s material capacities considered, the chapter then turns to Royalist elegies for clues to readership. In doing so, it will argue that Royalists respond to Charles' presence and absence unevenly, performing their reading struggles and sacramental aches after the regicide. To date, criticism largely separates the *Eikon*'s printing history from the history of Royalist spiritual lament. Certainly there can be no assurance that Royalists widely read the Folger's specific editions, and this chapter does not make that argument. Yet Royalists were seeking, in their responses to the regicide, what Kenneth Fincham and Nicholas Tyacke call the 'imagery and ritualism' of their former lives.[18] By enlarging our conception of the *Eikon*'s material potential alongside more variegated responses to the book at large, this chapter provides a complex snapshot of seventeenth-century spiritual readers bereft of the rituals that defined their lives.

This chapter also makes the *Eikon*'s reception messier for an ontological reason: religious belief, like any other element of identity, is simultaneously informed by tradition and formed in personality. Because spiritual belief arises first as a universal human impulse, and then as a thing ordered and patterned by language, creed and treatise, the same should be understood about spiritual interactions with any given text. Book history tends to take religious belief as a quantifiable measure of cultural (dis)order, analysable in theological debate and printing history. This chapter analyses both; but it then takes the blank spaces in Royalist elegies as performed reminders of the human hearts at play in any reading experience, particularly the spiritual ones, and particularly as we continue to write our histories of the book.

Reading as devotion and sacrament

The *Eikon Basilike* was born into a culture with, as Nandra Perry describes it, 'an epistemology centered on the imitability of the Word's signifying power'.[19] Charles inherited from Elizabeth I and James I a Church that emphasised the spiritual power of the heard sermon and corporate reading of the Book of Common Prayer. In the Word, read and heard, the faithful met God's saving grace. Describing this epistemology in its Reformation roots, James Kearney observes that 'the incarnation of the logos means that all language – fragments of text, scraps of parchment – has been glorified. Writing itself is sacred.'[20] Incidents like the cutting and pasting of Gospel text at Little Gidding in the 1630s suggest the visceral ways in which the word of God was revered in the period.[21] Under Charles, this theology took on further material expression. In his *Articles . . . in the first trienniall visitation*, Archbishop William Laud first requires that churches have 'the whole Bible of the largest volume, and the Book of Common Prayer, both fairly and substantially bound'.[22] The presence of the prayer book alongside scripture, and the impact of their material presence, are equally important for the health of a church.

In focusing on the appearance of holy texts in church, Laud identifies one detail in a much larger movement within the Caroline Church. Under growing Arminian influence, Charles's Church sought to re-enliven ornamentation and material accoutrement in worship – shifting what Lori Anne Ferrel marks as *adiaphora*, or non-essential elements of worship, into more essential roles that still remain separate from the sacrality of baptism and the Eucharist.[23] In a speech to the Star Chamber in 1637, Laud argues that the Calvinism of Elizabeth and

James, and its inheritance in more extreme non-conformist focus on 'words', cannot sustain a Church without a concomitant due reverence towards Christ's body and its material accoutrement.[24] Accordingly, the Caroline Church reintroduced high ceremonialism and what Fincham and Tyacke call a 'sacrament-centered piety', which reinvigorated the role of material objects in worship.[25] This quasi-theology emphasised 'sacramental power', or the role of material signs in the conveying of God's grace. This policy meant not only elevating the value of baptism and the Eucharist, but also reintroducing altar rails, candles and other material effects to enrich worship.[26]

The Arminian push was, at root, an argument for a mode of reading. While carefully avoiding any statements about sacrament that affirmed Roman Catholic theology, it asked worshippers to gaze upon and have their minds led by material spiritual accoutrement in addition to scriptural words. The unique relationship between things and ideas so evident in sacrament – the reflection of forgiveness in the washing with water in baptism, and the immanent, conjoined presence of worshipper and divinity in the Supper – became a larger interpretive framework in worship. Darren Oldridge explains that Arminianism's English incarnation in Laudianism sought to enliven the 'sanctity of material objects', though he is careful to point out that reverence and worship were made '*towards* or *before*' but not '*to*' such objects; nonetheless, these objects assisted worshipers to commune with the divine.[27] In this way, Laud could enforce the quality of the material texts across England, ensuring the beautification of their form as itself a help to worship. Without formally dismissing the textual modes of corporate worship that Targoff has elucidated, Charles's Church pressed a theology of materialism that upheld Protestant theological articles forged under Elizabeth I while seeking to redefine their modes of practice.[28]

Recent criticism has suggested that this material, interpretive push qualifies as a mode of sacramental exercise, if not restoring more of the sacraments themselves. Writers like Kimberly Johnson and Ryan Netzley enumerate a mode of sacramental reading that moves beyond the rehearsals and community-building of devotion to engage individuals intimately in the presence of divinity through text. As practised in late sixteenth- and early seventeenth-century England, devotion served both common and private functions that reiterated liturgical gestures and bolstered spiritual growth. Targoff writes that devotional books were full of 'liturgical forms that could be retrieved "elsewhere," in moments of devotional need'.[29] Similarly, Richard Hooker, whose *Of the Laws of Ecclesiastical Polity* remains a seminal work of English theology, writes that devotion bolsters a robust faith to foster 'piety' and 'zeal', supporting and rehearsing faith in practice.[30] This definition hearkens back to traditional readings of the *Eikon*, a book intended to promote zeal for Charles in his death. Yet the line between devotional and sacramental practice was increasingly thin in the seventeenth century. Netzley argues that 'devotional' verse increasingly became a weightier exercise, making the space between reader and text immanently incarnational; this more demanding mode of reading elucidated the presence of Christ as suggested in the written word, turning the rehearsals of devotion into actual transformative experiences with God.[31] This echoes Hooker's words on sacrament, which works deeper than devotion to 'make us pertakers of Christ'.[32] Sacramental reading, then, imbibing Arminian thinking, implies a more fundamental interaction with the body – a whole engagement with the materiality of reading. It looks to the whole text – including its spatial arrangements, ornamentation and textual enhancements – to make contact with a presence in the text. This mode of reading enhances the traditional reading practices imagined with the *Eikon*. As Arnold Hunt writes, sacrament is a 'communal and ritual' act that 'confirm[s] and strengthen[s] the assurance of one's salvation' on a more fundamental level.[33] Like devotion, it can draw a community together and embolden it; as a step beyond devotion, it draws the reader's mind and body to engage with fundamentals of salvation, like the sacraments themselves.

Charles often fostered this mode of reading by inserting himself into the cultural texts of his nation. Unlike his father James I, who commanded the direction of court masques from his seated throne, Charles and Henrietta Maria participated in them, bringing metaphors of kingly power to life by bestowing his presence into court art. Court masques, in practice and in print, were no longer addressed to the monarch, but were themselves records of sacral gesture and grace in action.[34] Charles's presence supplied what Richard McCoy describes as 'an animating and redemptive real presence', a presence that heightened the import of spiritual metaphors throughout a given masque.[35] In succeeding his father, Charles also played out a textual performance that inherited and fulfilled the words written to him in *Basilikon Doron*, his father's famously literary letter. As Kevin Sharpe writes, 'in remarkable engravings which belong to the last years of Jacobean and the first of Caroline rule, Charles is figured with the King James Bible and James's *Works*, or as the royal word become flesh'.[36] Reading or viewing was no longer simply about entertainment or edification: it offered an opportunity to interact with monarchy and divinity. Put in terms of sacramental reading, Netzley writes: 'the sacrament insists that God is right here at hand, a gift for the taking, and then challenges communicants, devotees, and readers to respond appropriately to this presence'.[37] In Caroline England, reading as sacrament meant seeking out divine presence in its royal, redemptive and textual forms.

Much of this is not news for *Eikon* studies – indeed, at Charles's death Royalists faced a kind of sacramental-aesthetic vacuum, one that more sacramental modes of reading could sooth and admonish. Royalists held in mind, consciously and unconsciously, this expansive context of real presence in words, decorative value and sacramental reading as they read the *Eikon*. New for *Eikon* studies must be fresh integrations of sacramental reading practices with a willingness to parse out specific editions of the *Eikon* and Royalist elegiac tropes. A refreshed paradigm can illuminate new details in our understanding of this incredible book's life.

Eikon Basilike

Devotional texts of the period were often printed in octavo and vicesimo-quarto so that readers could carry them and use them privately; the bulk of *Eikon* editions available in England were also printed as octavo, small enough for Royalists to enjoy surreptitiously.[38] The book's standard form proved consistent: a black and white allegorical frontispiece of Charles kneeling, grasping a crown of thorns and stamping down an earthly crown while eyeing a heavenly one; an accompanying 'Explanation of the Emblem'; the original twenty-eight chapters with their concluding prayers in italics, entitled 'Meditation'; supplementary details, usually the 'King's Prayers' and various correspondences; and a sonnet epitaph on Charles's death written by James Howell. The contents promoted a prayerful attitude: before reaching the table of contents, readers were to meditate on the frontispiece, which echoed Christ in Gethsemane. Towards the end of the book, Howell's sonnet urged readers to read and reread the text and to rely on it as a source of spiritual nourishment in the midst of despair.

The vast majority of *Eikon* editions proved to be cheap, devotional versions of this content, often rushed to satisfy supplier demands. Francis Madan records multiple correspondences and orders signalling the droves of volumes printed 'to satisfy an urgent and widespread demand for the King's book at a more popular price'.[39] Often this popular price devalued the book's presence. These standard, rushed editions sometimes used decaying typeface, resulting in poor title pages, mispagination and typographical errors.[40] Madan records a degree of inflation and lost value resulting from this overabundance: Richard Holdsworth of Cambridge writes that 'The King's bookes are so excessive deare, that I believe you would not have soe many of them at their prices'.[41] These versions 'dully printed in dull paper' clearly satisfied a mass readership, so much so that poor quality seems not to have deterred demand.[42] As critical consensus rightly shows, the book fed a massive, gut-level need for some kind of devotional guide in the midst of an unheard of crisis in England.

Against these versions, Holdsworth contrasts 'one of the best', referring to a version with red lettering.[43] For Holdsworth, and arguably readers like him, there are more carefully wrought versions of this standard text to imagine and cherish. In Laud's words, versions could be found that were 'fairly and substantially bound'.[44] Certainly, an element of collectorship is present here, as interested parties with money seek elevated versions of popular objects. Yet the speciality of these editions proves theologically specific: rather than gold-gilt pages or manuscript presentation copies, specific elements of these editions are emphasised in ways that promote sacramental reading practices. They use material cues to limn Charles's body, asking readers both to read Charles's words and to interact with his body physically. Like the Bible's narrative of Christ incarnate, the *Eikon*'s incarnation of Charles illustrates his sacramental presence, lending phrases, moments and material not just for devotional succour, but more deeply to open his blood, words and teaching for transformation or communal, ritual reading.

One such example, Folger number 266-313.1q, is peculiar in size, colour and ordering. A vicesimo-quarto (24mo, roughly 11 cm tall) printed by John Williams in 1649, the book fits in the palm of the hand, is bound too tightly to open fully and is printed small enough to require dedicated focus. Further emphasising this focus, Williams moves Howell's sonnet from the end of the book to directly after the frontispiece, a rare ordering suggesting that the book be read through the lens of this particular poem. Howell describes Charles as 'thou earthly God; celestial Man', then suggests, 'he that would know thee right, then let him look / Upon Thy rare incomparable Book, / And read it o're and o're; which if he do, / Hee'l find thee *King*, and *Priest*, and *Prophet* too.' The sonnet urges readers to make the book a ritual, or a habitual material practice that connects them to a 'King' and 'Priest'. The act of materially rereading helps readers discover the body of Charles anew, translating him into a variety of sacred offices.

And the miniscule size promoted secretive communities as much as individual reading. We can recall Hunt's observations that sacrament, unlike devotion, is a communal practice, and Maltby has explored how Royalists valued the communal act of meeting together to read their prayer books.⁴⁵ Editions like this vicesimo-quarto would have allowed Royalists to carry the book on their body. As Lois Potter emphasises, the *Eikon* 'is a totally private – "secret" – work . . . it reveals while seeming to conceal'.⁴⁶ Where Royalists met for communal prayer book services, they could now, in a physical and mental community, secretively carry their *Eikon* and meet Charles ritually in his sacred offices after death.

The book's rubricated title page and ornate chapter miniatures (see Plate 5 and Figure 10.1) further emphasise the possibilities of sacramental reading for this text. In this particular title page, the C and R

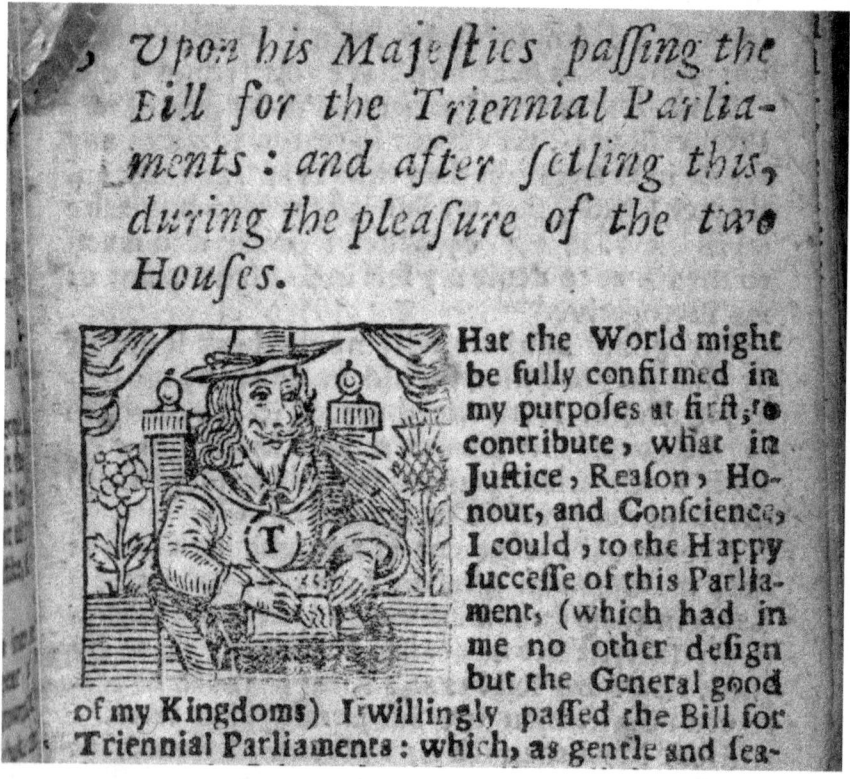

Figure 10.1 Charles I and John Gauden, *Eikon Basilike* (London: John Williams, 1649), B1 recto. Call #: 266- 313.1q. Reproduced by permission of the Folger Shakespeare Library under a Creative Commons Attribution-ShareAlike 4.0 International License

dominating the top of the page are reddened, as are the crucial words 'Pourtracture', 'Majestie', 'Solitudes', 'Sufferings' and 'Prayers'. By emphasising the themes of the frontispiece and sonnet, the reddening endows these themes with physical presence, drawing the paratextual matter into the life of the book's central contents. As readers turn the page, the book assists them to keep the ideas of Charles's sacerdotal roles in mind, building and strengthening his presence in the text. Readers literally transmute the 'idea' of Charles from an image or memory in their mind as they open the text, to a visual representation of the man in the frontispiece, to a textual encoding of that image as 'king' and 'priest' in the sonnet, and then to the words that populate the book itself. Ornate chapter openings continue this theme: several chapters feature a miniature Charles with the initial letter emblazoned on his chest, as if he embodies the letter itself. Just as he did in the court masques, Charles embodies the words that comprise the order of worship in each chapter. The act of turning a page translates Charles from king to priest and incarnated word, performing the words of the sonnet. Yet only in the totality of these material features, from the repositioned sonnet to the chapter headings, can the reader fully participate in this sacramental reading, where participation in a material process makes sacerdotal presence tangible and accessible.

While these physical features are theoretically possible in any edition of the *Eikon*, their presence in a miniature is especially impactful. Brigitte Buettner has written extensively on the relationship of objects to worshippers, and comments that 'Miniatures celebrated the art object . . . and visually sacralized the relationship between them and the viewer'.[47] As a self-aware, miniature version of itself, this edition of the *Eikon* similarly celebrates its own status as an 'incomparable Book' and visually codes the sacred work it accomplishes for the benefit of readers. In doing so, it participates in sacramental aesthetics; as Sarah Beckwith describes it, a sacramental object in Reformation England 'caused what [it] signified'.[48] In its miniaturisation, this edition self-references its specialness as 'the book of Charles': the internal physical features then help readers to bring Charles alive. Readers do not simply pray the prayers of Charles: they habitually reread and reincarnate his textual flesh.

A second Folger holding, E311, is more standard than the vicesimo-quarto, but its peculiar frontispiece also signals possibilities for sacramental reading (see Plate 6). The edition is an octavo and features the usual order of content. Unique to this edition and only three or four others like it, however, is the coloured frontispiece. The Folger's notes describe the frontispiece as 'inked in colour' and

Madan notes that it was actually an advance copy integral to the later 1651 *Works*.⁴⁹ The colour scheme vividly inks Charles's robe in red, the various crowns, building interior and rays of light in gold, and the tablecloth and exterior landscape in green. Beyond colour, its layout is also of interest. Set with wide white margins across two facing pages, the image works more like an inset than a fold-in illustration, giving the impression of an excerpt from a medieval book of hours. The image does not fold out to be viewed alongside the 'Explanation of the Emblem'; peculiarly, it occupies its own space, inviting readers to immerse themselves in it like a book of hours before considering interpretive support. Like the vicesimo-quarto, this edition again sacralises the act of viewing and reading, investing readers in a viewing that is itself sacramental, drawing readers into divine presence.

The frontispiece is traditionally read as a reference to the passion of Christ, where the Eucharist and dynamics of spiritual presence are instituted. As Christ communicated with the Father in the Garden regarding his sacrifice, so, as one critic notes, Charles sits at a 'convergence of verbal messages' that signify 'the expression of the divine will in the appearance of light'.⁵⁰ However, where English books of hours were enamoured of the Virgin Mary, so this colourised frontispiece also calls up scenes of the annunciation. Annunciation scenes typically show Mary interrupted while reading the Old Testament, as the text of the law becomes the logos of grace within her. Text is realised in flesh as, traditionally, a light or line of sight moves from the angel to Mary. The *Eikon* frontispiece suggests a resonant reversal: the royal logos incarnated into text. While Charles kneels, his reading interrupted, two lines ascend and descend from his head. One line's Latin phrase indicates Charles's failing public image through the 1630s. From this troubled fleshy existence, readers are to follow the line of sight across the book's gutter to the image of Charles, where he becomes a triumphant text. Where Mary reads the Old Testament, Charles reads 'Christi Tracto', again likening his media translation to Christ's. In Christ, the letter is fulfilled in life; Charles carries life again into the letter by relocating his presence in the text. As with the vicesimo-quarto, it is only in the physical alteration, and ornamentation of the book, that the reader's eyes are called to linger, to ponder and to interpret. What they find is an invitation to sacramental reading, to meeting Charles's presence.

The vicesimo-quarto and illuminated frontispiece reveal that the *Eikon Basilike*, at base a mass-produced devotional book, could express its deeper sacramental potential physically. Describing this spread of possibilities, Andrew Lacey writes that 'Charles and his book were texts, teaching to everyone the arts of holy living and holy dying'.[51] Much of that education becomes more or less powerful in relation to printing history. By emphasising Charles's textual incarnation and giving readers the power to trace and enact that incarnation, the book could enable more sacramental negotiations with readers that made Charles present.

Yet it is telling that these editions make explicit moves to catch reader attention in the opening pages. Sacramental material by no means assures a sacramental response from readers, and these texts work to instruct readers how to read. As Roger Chartier notes, tension thrives between a book's physical and textual features and its actual reception.[52] After the regicide, Royalists, one of the book's key audiences, suffered deep personal and sacramental losses. While it is attractive (and traditional) to plug the *Eikon*'s rich content into this loss and assume the best, Royalist lamentation proves more complex. We have no evidence that anyone but single owners read the Folger's editions; but bearing in mind that readers bring needs and hopes to their books, we can use their elegies to further limn a picture of sacramental reading following the regicide.

Struggling Royalists and sacramental reading

Royalist elegies are stuffed with sacramental imagery, but that fact does not equate to a consistent flocking towards the *Eikon*. Maltby reminds us that 'Prayer Book Protestants attempted to make sense of their suffering Church in time-honoured ways: as identification with the sufferings of Christ, or as divine judgement for sin'.[53] In their bookish meetings, Royalists soaked up the martyrological images of Charles in the *Eikon*, but also incorporated an underbelly of judgement and failure. They practised traditional tropes of mourning by likening Charles to Christ, a fuzzy mathematics that makes out the *Eikon* as not unlike scripture. Yet they also struggled to substitute the real Charles with an image of him; they agonised over the sacred status of this book; and they wondered how reading could possibly restore their loss. Lacey is thus accurate, but perhaps too general, when he claims that 'royalist apologists presented both the book and the author as textbooks for the reader's instruction'.[54] As this chapter's introduction emphasised, some elegies intentionally act as if the *Eikon* does not exist: 'We want an *Emblem* for him'.[55] Even where the *Eikon* succeeds, Royalists seem confused. At the same time, in their uneven acceptance and rejection, Royalists see the *Eikon* as an expert summation of their grievances and as a place to grieve productively. Scholars are often quick to write off the 'ruck of elegies' drawn together in two collections, *Vaticinium Votivum* and *Monumentum Regale*, as 'trite disclaimer[s] about the inability of rhetoric to meet the occasion'; yet a closer look sees Royalists using the *Eikon* in order to think systematically and cogently through their sacramental loss.[56]

On one level, Royalist elegies seem to read the *Eikon* sacramentally, as its Folger incarnations invite. 'An Elegie' from the *Monumentum* states that '*His glorious own Record* gave this presage / Which next to hallowed writ, and sacred page, / Shall busie pious wonders, and abide / To Christian pilgrimage the second *guid*'.[57] Though seemingly a devotional guide, the *Eikon* is elevated to scriptural status 'next to hallowed writ', garnering wonder and respect while guiding its readers. The reference to Christian pilgrimage, a practice typically drowning in saints' relics, extends physical value to the book's presence, beyond its words. An 'Epitaph' echoes the same themes, claiming that 'Within this sacred VAULT doth lie / The Quintessence of MAJESTIE; / Which being Set, more Glorious shines, / The best of KINGS, best of Divines . . .'.[58] 'An Elegie' looks to the *Eikon* as a kind of Eucharist, an object holding the 'quintessence' of a king. Only when this vault is 'set', a reference to its printing, does it shine. Divine presence here requires material signage, elucidating clear sacramental reading practices made more evident in the *Eikon*'s special editions.

The same elegy then turns to Charles's 'Pourtracture', where he is drawn 'to th' Life'; if readers seek a better representation, 'Angels must Limn it out'. In deliberate challenge to the facts, the elegy insists on Charles's livelihood through the book. The book comes to represent the truth of scripture itself: the poem 'Caroli' declares 'When the *Mahumetan* or *Pope* shall look / On his Soul's best *Interpreter*, his *Book*, / His *Book*, his Life, his Death, will henceforth be / The *Church of England*'s best *Apologie*'.[59] In the repetition of 'his book' the poet marks a through-line from the *Eikon* to the lifeblood of the Church itself, modelling Christ's similar presence in the Word of God.

These poems reveal efforts to apply sacramental interpretation to the *Eikon*. Royalists acknowledge the parallels to Christ in the *Eikon* and Charles's own writing, and expand the metaphor as far as possible. One elegist writes, 'This *Scene* was like the *Passion-Tragedie*, / His *Saviour's Person* not could Act but Hee'. He repeatedly refers to Charles as the silent or 'Pascal' lamb and the scaffold before the Banqueting Hall as Calvary, with darkness supposedly descending on the noon of the regicide.[60] In calling up the Passion, the elegist likely intends the Last Supper as well, where Christ puts his presence into the bread – as Charles does into his book. Like the original Passion, the regicide's moments and scenes become sacramentally significant. One elegy claims that Charles 'Die'd here to re-*Baptize* it [England] in His Blood'.[61] Another writer worries that unclean criminals 'Gaze on the Beams', referring to the frontispiece, as though unworthily partaking in the traditional gazing upon the Eucharist. In the presence of such holiness, these criminals 'must / Confess 'tis *they* were guiltie, but *Hee* just!'[62] Throughout the *Eikon*, elegists see the power to enact penance, baptism and presence, much like Howell's sonnet speaking of Charles as a priest. One Royalist even envisions Charles administering his own sacrament, 'having past this flood / In Robes of scarlet di'd in His own Blood'.[63] Royalists clamber to infuse the *Eikon* in sacramental tones they fear will be entirely lost in the new Parliamentarian government.

Yet in as many places throughout the Royalist elegies, connections and references that should be easily made to the *Eikon* are notably absent. One elegy included in the *Vaticinium* to Lord Arthur Capel describes 'the King, who like one general Soul, / Did through each nerv and agile muscle rowl; / And like some publick Conduit did dispence / To everie Vein, both Sap and Influence', without making the logical jump to the proliferating *Eikon*.[64] Charles offers life and transformation in a metaphor that fails to easily imply the mass publication, spread and typography of the book. Another elegist writes, 'Trembled ye not, ye furies, for to see / When yee convened, such reverence in his face?'[65] The word 'reverence' appears everywhere in Arminian exhortations to value material spiritual accoutrement, but that gaze in this elegy is never directed towards the frontispiece, a reverential and increasingly ubiquitous face indeed as editions proliferated throughout England. Rather than look to the *Eikon*, the topos of despair leads these elegies into an identity and spiritual crisis that rejects the *Eikon*, quite out of keeping with the narrative of quietly satisfied devotion we typically accept.

Francis Gregory epitomises a repeated request to be shown how, if at all, to lament Charles's passing. Gregory asks, 'instruct us to that just respect / With which thy Hallowed Ashes must be deckt'.[66] Another writes, 'And can I, / Who want *my self*, write *Him* an Elegie?'[67] Where scholarly consensus insists that the *Eikon* served as a model for readers amid confusion and doubt, these elegists bemoan the absence of any model and can record only their confusion. Royalists repeatedly lament that they can no longer read or write of Charles, precisely the needs the *Eikon* supposedly fills. Writing, a traditional mode of courtly reverence and one Gregory's own lamentation requires, seems to fail:

> Hands cannot write for Trembling; let our *Eie* / Supplie the Quill, and shed an *Elegie*. . . . Words are not here significant. . . . Thy *Book* is our best Language; what to this / Shall e're be added, is Thy *Meiosis*: / Thy *Name's* a *Text* too hard for us: no men / Can write of it, without *Thy Parts* and *Pen*.[68]

In the elegy's conceit, writing and reading become impossible without the progenitor of both, whose death stops print while beckoning tears. The *Eikon* is a 'best Language', but that hardly seems to help. 'Thy *Name's* a *Text* too hard for us' seems to bar any considerations of Charles. Charles cannot be read by his own subjects, never mind by later citizens. The plea of Howell's sonnet to 'read it o're and o're', to engage the *Eikon* as a book of sacraments, becomes impossible.

In this mode of response, the *Eikon* becomes an object upon which to perform grief. Apophasis proves a powerful way for Royalists to express their sacramental frustrations. The rhetorical move works similarly in the resignation of 'Thy *Book* is our best Language', which denigrates the Royalist's own elegy. Any more writing beyond this 'book' is 'meiosis', which the *Oxford English Dictionary* (OED) cites either as a reductive figure of speech or litotes.[69] The elegist draws attention to the similar but substandard goals of his elegy against the *Eikon*, giving his elegy some, though lesser, sacramental power: 'Thy name is thy best Epitaph. / To carve thy Statue were amiss: Thy Book thy best *Colossus* is.'[70] This odd habit of systematically applauding, ignoring and lukewarmly naming the *Eikon* expresses the Royalists' and the *Eikon*'s very spiritual condition: empowered to speak by loss, but bereft of the central signifier (Charles) that gives their textual sacramentalism meaning.

A number of elegies reach rhetorical extremes that verge on the apocalyptic. Supporters of the Crown and its metonymy for divine authority, Royalists are bereft of their signified, perceive their constructed cathedral of liturgical, textual worship crumbling, and proclaim the dissolution of words and, eventually, the Word itself. The same breath that reverences Charles's story utters 'No more of *Annals*; let great Rome grow mute / In quoting *Catiline*, or recording *Brute*'; after all, how can annals persist when England's 'fatal *Glorie* / Is Summ'd, Cast up, and Cancell'd in this *Storie*'?[71] 'A Deepe Groane Fetch'd at the Funerall of that Incomparable and Glorious Monarch, Charles the First' complains that the regicide 'hath undone the Annals, and engross'd / All th' *Heroes* Glory which the Earth e're lost'.[72] All annals that cannot speak of it are deemed 'faithless and apocryphal', specifically without sacred valence.[73] This destruction of annals, and of the 'story' of England itself, points even deeper. One elegist goes so far as to declare 'All rhetoric's dumb', while another describes elegies themselves as 'a borrowed Periwig / Of Metaphors' used 'To ransack far-fetch't Phrases from the Skies'.[74] If, as Kearney argues, the Reformation makes all writing sacred, then the regicide makes all writing worthless. The *Eikon* itself can be nothing more than 'that ghastly Text' which trots a re-animated corpse across London.[75]

This uneven response to the *Eikon* affirms while complicating the traditional scholarly consensus of the book's success. The book proved immensely useful to Royalists coming out of the regicide, yes; but that use was often for the purposes of performed rejection or blindness, rather than universal acclaim or attentiveness to a pious model. Put simply, sometimes ignoring the solution for a while just feels better. When reading the *Eikon*'s printing history alongside Royalist lament, it becomes clear that the cultural moment was flexible enough for Royalists to stage all forms of spiritual response to the regicide while maintaining their loyalty to the idea of the Crown. In many ways, the book's contents even predict these responses. Francis Gregory asks to be instructed how to reverence Charles's remains; Howell's sonnet answers him by exhorting him to read over and over again. Other elegies worry over the image of Charles and the lack of reverence given his presence; the coloured frontispiece begs for special consideration. Royalists have what they need in the *Eikon Basilike*, a feat of political-spiritual strategy unmatched in the Western printed canon. When they are ready for devotion or sacramental reading, the book can respond; until then, it supplies an object upon which Royalists can nobly express their deepest wounds and blindest confusions.

Royalist elegies drape the *Eikon* not in easy confessional creeds, but in the real anguish of souls making sense of a damaged sacramental system. The *Eikon*'s variable content and sacramental registers were capable of hosting a vast range of human emotional and spiritual forces. In its printing history, and in the sight of grieving Royalists, the *Eikon* becomes a source for sacramental interpretation that can reconcile present tragedy with spiritual hope. In the *Eikon Basilike* the history of reading reaches one of its high peaks, a text fully encapsulating the desires, losses and potential of a whole population.

Towards religious complexity

Scholarly consensus of the *Eikon Basilike*'s success proves both overstated and understated: it too often simplifies the nuances in Royalist responses to the book, while missing the actual material factors that differentiate political, devotional and sacramental realities throughout the book's printing history. The *Eikon* is a Gordian knot of cultural reference, and with our eyes increasingly opened to the complexities of early modern spirituality and printing practices, perhaps the history of the *Eikon* moving forward can be told only in the details. Deeper studies into the *Eikon*'s variability, particularly content order and reader marks with an eye towards spiritual contexts, are certainly warranted. The textual moment of this book powerfully evinces the ways that human emotion inflects spiritual belief, as played out in acts of reading. It is seductive to assume that English citizens were traumatised by the regicide and found solace in this book's devotions and prayers. After such a shocking event, how could the *Eikon* fail? Yet a closer look at printing history through descriptive bibliography and reception theory reveals far more complex spiritual intentions at work.

We cannot know how a Royalist would have actually responded to the Folger's holdings. Yet the chaotic response of Royalist elegies marks the richness of their spirituality, the disorganisation with which the regicide burdened the Church, and the gap between Royalists' lived, spiritual messiness and our clean, confessional historiographies. Excitingly, that messiness and confusion is written into the material realities of the text. The *Eikon* productively challenges stubborn wishes in modern scholarship that religion remain tidily within formal bounds of sacred texts, buildings and people. The reality of religious belief, then and now, is realised in the cultural moment of the *Eikon*, and not in the façades of fairly bound books. This is not to say that religious belief is always in crisis or in denial. It is to say that Christian belief is a practice in dialogue with emotion and circumstance, finding its ultimate rock in the assurances of faith and presence offered to it by the divine.

Literary criticism continues to delve into the knot of spirituality at the nexus of material and reception history, clarifying inconsistencies in our knowledge while discovering and making new ones. *Eikon* studies, carrying the weight of England's greatest sacred text after the King James Bible and the Book of Common Prayer, faces a crucial moment to begin a new phase that deepens the narrative of its book with more democratic, and archive-informed, studies. The King's Book affords opportunities to witness a sacramental book in action, expanding our insights into readers' experiences with the sacred in the act of reading a book.

Notes

Many thanks to colleagues who read versions of this chapter and shared rich insights and conversation, especially Kristen Poole, Julian Yates, Alice Dailey, Lori Anne-Ferrell, Lois Potter, Mary Hammond, and Jonathan Rose.

The figure and plates which relate to this chapter are reproduced by permission of the Folger Shakespeare Library under a Creative Commons Attribution-ShareAlike 4.0 International License.

1. Nicole Jacobs, 'Robbing His Captive Shepherdess: Princess Elizabeth, John Milton, and the Memory of Charles I in the "Eikon Basilike" and "Eikonoklastes"', *Criticism*, 54:2 (2012), pp. 227–55; Jennifer Woodward, *The Theatre of Death: The Ritual Management of Royal Funerals in Renaissance England, 1570–1625* (Rochester: Boydell, 1997), pp. 116, 199; Olivia Bland, *The Royal Way of Death* (London: Constable, 1986), pp. 51–6.
2. Robert Wilcher, '*Eikon Basilike*: The Printing, Composition, Strategy, and Impact of the King's Book', in Laura Lunger Knoppers (ed.), *The Oxford Handbook of Literature and the English Revolution* (New York: Oxford University Press, 2013), pp. 289–308; Alice Dailey, 'Beyond Typology: King Charles and the Martyrdom of Conscience', in *The English Martyr from Reformation to Revolution* (Indiana: University of Notre Dame Press, 2012); Francis Madan, *New Bibliography of the Eikon Basilike of King Charles the First, With a Note on the Authorship* (Oxford: Oxford University Press, 1950).
3. Elizabeth Skerpan-Wheeler, 'The First "Royal": Charles I as Celebrity', *PMLA*, 126:4 (2011), pp. 912–34.
4. Elizabeth Skerpan-Wheeler, 'Eikon Basilike and the Rhetoric of Self-Representation', in Thomas Corns (ed.), *The Royal Image: Representations of Charles I* (New York: Cambridge University Press, 1999), p. 164; Laura Lunger Knoppers, *Politicizing Domesticity from Henrietta Maria to Milton's Eve* (New York: Cambridge University Press, 2011), p. 86.
5. Joad Raymond, 'Popular Representations of Charles I', in Corns (ed.), *The Royal Image*, p. 65.
6. Dailey, *The English Martyr*, pp. 216–17.
7. *Monumentum Regale or a tomb, erected for that incomparable and glorious monarch, Charles the First, King of Great Britane, France and Ireland* (London, 1649), p. 24.
8. Judith Maltby, 'Suffering and Surviving: The Civil Wars, the Commonwealth and the Formation of "Anglicanism"', in Christopher Durston and Judith Maltby (eds), *Religion in Revolutionary England* (Manchester: Manchester University Press, 2006), pp. 158–80.
9. *Monumentum*, p. 38.

10. *Vaticinium Votivum or, Palæmon's Prophetick Prayer* (London, 1649), p. 45.
11. Ramie Targoff, *Common Prayer: The Language of Public Devotion in Early Modern England* (Chicago: University of Chicago Press, 2001).
12. *Eikon Basilike*, with selections from *Eikonoklastes*, ed. Jim Daems and Holly Faith Nelson (Orchard Par: Broadview, 2006), p. 16.
13. David Gay, 'Prayer and the Sacred Image: Milton, Jeremy Taylor, and the *Eikon Basilike*', *Milton Quarterly*, 46:1 (2012), pp. 1–14.
14. Adrian Streete, *Apocalypse and Anti-Catholicism in Seventeenth-Century English Drama* (Cambridge: Cambridge University Press, 2017), p. 2.
15. *Eikon Basilike* (London, 1649), Folger Shakespeare Library, 266–313.1q; and *Eikon Basilike* (London, 1649), Folger Shakespeare Library, E311.
16. Ryan Netzley, 'Introduction', in *Reading, Desire, and the Eucharist in Early Modern Religious Poetry* (Toronto: University of Toronto Press, 2011).
17. Gay, 'Prayer and the Sacred Image'.
18. Kenneth Fincham and Nicholas Tyacke, *Altars Restored: The Changing Face of English Religious Worship, 1547– c. 1700* (New York: Oxford University Press, 2007), p. 253.
19. Nandra Perry, *Imitatio Christi: The Poetics of Piety in Early Modern England* (Notre Dame: University of Notre Dame Press, 2014), p. 160.
20. James Kearney, *The Incarnate Text: Imagining the Book in Reformation England* (Philadelphia: University of Pennsylvania Press, 2009), p. 15.
21. Michael Gaudio, *The Bible and the Printed Image in Early Modern England: Little Gidding and the Pursuit of Scriptural Harmony* (New York: Routledge, 2017).
22. Church of England, *Articles to be inquired of in the first trienniall visitation of the most reverend father William* (London, 1637).
23. Lori Anne Ferrell, 'Introduction', in *Government by Polemic: James I, the King's Preachers, and the Rhetoric of Conformity, 1603–1625* (Stanford: Stanford University Press, 1998).
24. William Laud, *A speech delivered in the Starr-chamber* (London, 1637).
25. Fincham and Tyacke, *Altars Restored*, p. 284.
26. Darren Oldridge, *Religion and Society in Early Stuart England* (Brookefield: Ashgate, 1998), p. 8.
27. Ibid., pp. 240, 151.
28. Maltby 'Suffering and Surviving', p. 162; Targoff, *Common Prayer*.
29. Targoff, *Common Prayer*, p. 46.
30. Richard Hooker, *The Lawes of Ecclesiastical Polity* (London: 1597), book V, pp. 73, 196.
31. Ryan Netzley, 'Reading Indistinction: Desire, Indistinguishability, and Metonymic Reading in Richard Crashaw's Religious Lyrics', in *Reading, Desire, and the Eucharist*.
32. Hooker, *The Lawes*, p. 106.

33. Arnold Hunt, 'The Lord's Supper in Early Modern England', *Past and Present*, 161:1 (1998), pp. 39–83.
34. Kyle Vitale, 'Grace of Life: Marriage, Campion's Lord Hay's Masque, and Sacraments of Conjunction', *Religion and Literature*, 48:2 (2016), pp. 21–48.
35. Richard McCoy, *Alterations of State: Sacred Kingship in the English Reformation* (New York: Columbia University Press), p. 15.
36. Kevin Sharpe, *Image Wars: Promoting Kings and Commonwealths in England, 1603–1660* (New Haven: Yale University Press, 2010), p. 140.
37. Neztley, 'Introduction', p. 4.
38. Madan, *New Bibliography*.
39. Ibid., p. 16.
40. Ibid., p. 18.
41. Ibid., p. 16.
42. Ibid.
43. Ibid.
44. Church of England, *Articles to be inquired*.
45. Judith Maltby, *Prayer Book and People in Elizabethan and Early Stuart England* (Cambridge: Cambridge University Press, 1998).
46. Lois Potter, *Secret Rites and Secret Writing: Royalist Literature, 1641–60* (Cambridge: Cambridge University Press, 1989), p. 170.
47. Brigitte Buettner, 'Profane Illuminations, Secular Illusions: Manuscripts in Late Medieval Courtly Society', *Art Bulletin*, 74:1 (1992), p. 78.
48. Sarah Beckwith, *Shakespeare and the Grammar of Forgiveness* (Ithaca: Cornell University Press, 2011), p. 29.
49. Madan, *New Bibliography*, p. 74.
50. Gay, 'Prayer and the Sacred Image', p. 2.
51. Andrew Lacey, 'Texts to be Read: Charles I and the *Eikon Basilike*', *Prose Studies*, 29:1 (2007), p. 5.
52. Roger Chartier, 'Labourers and Voyagers: From the Text to the Reader', in David Finkelstein and Alistair McCleery (eds), *The Book History Reader* (New York: Routledge, 2006), pp. 47–59.
53. Maltby, 'Suffering and Surviving', p. 170.
54. Lacey, 'Texts to be Read', p. 7.
55. *Monumentum*, p. 24.
56. Robert Wilcher, *The Writing of Royalism, 1628–60* (Cambridge: Cambridge University Press, 2001), pp. 306, 296.
57. *Monumentum*, p. 19.
58. A.B., *Epitaph* (London, 1649).
59. *Monumentum*, p. 23.
60. *Vaticinium*, p. 70.
61. Ibid., p. 49.
62. Ibid., p. 37.
63. Ibid., p. 39.
64. Ibid., p. 56.

65. F.H., 'Elogie' (London, 1649), p. 2.
66. Francis Gregory, 'An Elegy upon the death of King Charls' (London, 1649) (Wing/E465).
67. *Monumentum*, p. 21.
68. Gregory, 'An Elegy'.
69. *OED*, 'Meiosis', def. 1a. See 1b for litotes, which the *OED* cites as rare.
70. Gregory, 'An Elegy'.
71. *Vaticinium*, pp. 36, 50.
72. *Monumentum*, p. 35.
73. *Vaticinium*, p. 46.
74. Ibid., p. 45.
75. *Monumentum*, p. 34.

Chapter 11

Plurilingual Poetry and the Hinterland of Intertextuality: Europeanising Reading Culture in the Early Modern Iberian World

Maya Feile Tomes

> ... y en las alas fue del viento
> lastimando tu dulce voz postrera
> las orillas del Ganges, la ribera
> del Rey del Occidente,
> flechero Parahuay, que de veneno
> la aljaba armado, de impiedad el seno,
> tu fin sintió doliente.[1]

Luis de Góngora (1614), *Canción* XIV, vv. 7–13

The story of European presence in the Americas is also the story of European(ising) reading culture there – part of the wider history, with its own by now more than quincentennial tradition, of reading and writing across the Iberian world and of the global history of reading as a whole. This same story also of course spells more than 500 years of history of the colonisation, and in many cases complete obliteration, of other forms of literacy – including a variety of visual, spatial and material-cultural literacies (if 'literacy' is not itself too Eurocentric a term) – that had existed in the Americas prior to this. So too does it mark the imposition of the Roman alphabetic writing system on Amerindian languages – including Nahuatl in Mexico, Tupí in Brazil and Guaraní in Paraguay, to name but three – which thereafter became 'legible' (by whom? *for* whom?) in that form. The spread of European paradigms and practices of reading across the globe thus interacts in fundamental ways with the colonisation of knowledge itself[2] – to say nothing of that most infamous form of reading from early Hispano-American colonial history that was the ritual of the *Requerimiento*, the notorious Spanish legalistic document through the declamation of which (in a language local listeners could not possibly understand) Iberian incomers sought to take possession of the lands they encountered: reading-out-loud as speech act, and of the most appropriative and imperialistic order. There have even been attempts to understand the conquest of the continent in relation to contemporary cultures of reading within the Iberian Peninsula, the idea here being that the diet of chivalric adventure romances on which the conquistadors-to-be were reared was instrumental in determining their subsequent attitude to and behaviour in the Americas.[3] In other words, the conquest of America has been written into the history of reading itself.

Around any story of European reading in the Americas, then, thrums the shadow of loss: of tales not told, some no longer tellable. This pall – and the colonial implications thereof – must be borne in mind throughout all treatments of the subject, this one included. What follows is the tale of some more 'literary' dimensions of the imported European reading culture in the themselves imported European literary languages: in the Iberian case, Spanish and/or Portuguese and – given the nature of intellectual culture in Renaissance Europe at the time – also Latin. That Latin – by which we mean not only the language of the Romans whose writings loomed so large for early modern Europeans but also the form ('neo-Latin') still in active use at the time – features in this group should not surprise: as the idiom of the Catholic Church, of humanist culture and of numerous specialised professional fields, it too made the journey across the Atlantic and was for a time as 'alive' in America as anywhere else.[4] Indeed, some of the first words read aloud from a printed page on the American mainland were likely in Latin;[5] and the first piece of poetry to come off an Ibero-American press certainly was.[6] The extent to which Italian-language material circulated within the Iberian world is also coming to be increasingly recognised.[7] Iberian imperial reading culture, then, was fundamentally plurilingual. Together, this group of languages – which we might call the 'international literary', or indeed 'international readerly', languages of the early Iberian world – were spread across ever larger swathes of the globe by the mechanisms of imperial expansion, from the Iberian Peninsula to the Americas to the Philippines. Reading within the Iberian Pacific – an area currently garnering great interest among scholars of global early modern bibliographic and material-cultural networks – could be the subject of another chapter in itself, to say the least; here, we focus on the Iberian Atlantic, especially Hispano-America. Although in time European literary culture(s) would spread across the whole American continent, this happened in the Iberian Americas sooner than it did anywhere else.[8]

Much attention has been devoted in recent years to how America came to assert itself during the sixteenth and seventeenth centuries as a new locus of enunciation, or 'writerly' space.[9] America-based and American-born authors produced works from the earliest sixteenth century onwards, either for circulation in the area or else dispatched to Europe for publication (whence, in turn, they were often re-imported): in just one early example of what was to prove this much repeated pattern, for instance, Jesuit missionary José de Anchieta's Latin-language poem *De Gestis Mendi de Saa* – the first-ever full-length (European-style) epic to be produced in the Americas – was composed in Brazil and published in Portugal (Coimbra, 1563). But it was during this same period that America emerged also as a *readerly* space. Reading material was imported from the earliest days of the colony, institutions of learning to instruct pupils in the corresponding cultures of literacy were soon set up[10] and printing presses were established with notable alacrity, starting with that in Mexico City in 1538: just a few decades after European arrival on the continent, and a whole century before the first printing press in North America.[11] As a result, works by Virgil, Sallust, Josephus and Erasmus (among many others) were being studied in Mexico by the 1520s;[12] Ovid was being translated in Lima by the turn of that same century, while Italian Renaissance epics by the likes of Ariosto enjoyed newfound Peruvian popularity;[13] and luminary of seventeenth-century Spanish Peninsular poetry Luis de Góngora (1561–1627) was read across the Americas – and beyond – from his own lifetime onwards.[14]

In the words from *Canción* XIV that form our epigraph, Góngora himself imagines the voice of his poem's subject radiating from its European point of articulation out across the world to India and to America, where it is picked up by the inhabitants of Paraguay. In the cultural metaphor in which 'singing' and 'speaking' denote poetic composition, 'perceiving' or 'hearing' must betoken receiving: for our purposes, 'reading'. What might once have been taken as classic tropes of overweening ambition and surreally extended spatial imagination, moreover, can no longer be dismissed as poetic hyperbole alone: in the ever larger and more connected Iberian imperial world, Góngora could indeed write in the expectation of a transatlantic, even a global, reading public – which is precisely what he got. Among so many other things, then, *Canción* XIV thematises the invention of America as a reading space.

At the same time, even as America emerged as a fully fledged readerly (and writerly) space, there arose in Europe a reactionary movement that sought to deny its existence: early modern intellectuals of a particular persuasion doubted and even outright denied that Ibero-America was a properly 'literate' locus – the remarks of Spanish ecclesiast-bibliographer Manuel Martí and of Dutch polemicist Cornelius de Pauw are most regularly cited, though there are numerous others[15] – while Ibero-American literati strove tirelessly to demonstrate the contrary, both through direct engagement with the matter and by flooding the European market with their works.[16] (Indeed, the need to engage a pan-European readership is one of the ways in which the persistence of Latin as one of the literary languages of the Americas has often been explained.) The negative view, however, has proved remarkably enduring, continuing to colour approaches to the field even to this day:[17] Ibero-American literary culture remains widely un(der-)represented in the broad sweep of cultural-historical narratives still standardly constructed by Anglo-American scholars today, even though – paradoxically – it is in the Iberian, not the Anglophone, Americas that Europeanised traditions of reading are arguably the richest and certainly the longest. To tell the story of reading in the Iberian Americas, then, is to redress widespread misconceptions, themselves inherited from the early modern period, about the nature of literary culture in the wider Iberian world. What at first sight might appear a Eurocentric story, then, is in fact a corrective to an enduring anti-Ibero-American polemic.

What follows is inevitably only a slice of the rich and variegated history of European(ised) reading culture in the early Americas. The territory under consideration is vast and the early modern or 'colonial' period centuries long: here, we focus on the eighteenth, offering two case studies. Both relate to Jesuits, which is also to say to men, and ones pillowed by the structures of religious life at that. We thus run straight up against categories of both gender and social environment. As a counterweight, our focus will not be on religious readings – there is a superabundance of evidence for that type of readerly activity in the early Americas already – but rather on their consumption of more secular types of material, especially imaginative literature and poetry.

Detecting 'readness'

The enabling condition for European-language reading in non-European parts of the world is, clearly, the availability (or production) of relevant reading material. In the earliest days this will have been limited to that which incomers had about their person – Columbus himself travelled with all manner of manuals and manuscripts – or brought in limited quantities for particular purposes: from the Bibles and breviaries carried by private individuals for small-scale religious activity to the personal library of 238 volumes which Columbus's own son Hernando (1488–1539) brought with him to the Caribbean for a two-month sojourn in Santo Domingo in 1509.[18] Before long, however, printed material was being imported to the Americas systematically and substantially – at least 10,000 volumes to Mexico City alone between 1576 and 1585,[19] plus untold further quantities of contraband – and would continue to arrive throughout all the years of the colony, particularly to the major centres of Europeanised learning in Mexico, Peru and the region of the River Plate. It is sobering to imagine each and every one of these volumes being packed onto vessels in Spanish ports and ploughing their way across the Atlantic, there to be unloaded and lugged onwards – often transferred straight overland to the Pacific coast to be shipped on down to places like Peru – to the myriad destinations across the continent where they ended up, and where many can still be found in libraries and private collections today. Others, having been thus transferred overland to the western seaboard, were then dispatched on a second enormous transoceanic voyage – following the renowned route between Acapulco and Manila – to the island territories of the Iberian Pacific. Such import information is illuminating in that it can be taken, at least to a certain degree, as evidence not only of imposition but of active demand for material and, in turn, of genuine readerly appetite, especially in cases of large or repeat orders: booksellers across the American continent were, for instance, placing regular requests for copies of *La Araucana* – Spanish conquistador Alonso de Ercilla's renowned Castilian epic poem on the conquest of Chile, completed and printed in instalments in Spain in 1569–89 – from the sixteenth century itself onwards, where it proved as popular as in the Iberian Peninsula itself;[20] indeed, one might say that it was the first Iberian world bestseller. We are dealing, in other words, with the invention of the American reading public; in economic terms, with the emergence of the American reading market. This was when one first had to start hoping that one's publisher had good distribution on both sides of the Atlantic.

Catalogues, order slips and ship logs only take us so far, however. To say that books arrived in the Americas is not necessarily the same as saying that they were actually read there – and indeed, in some cases, it is perfectly clear that they were not:[21] factors such as collectability, the cultural prestige of the object and the religious aura of the text all drove the market for import as well. The handledness of an object is one good indicator of its use, of course – though the *most* handled items do not survive at all. How else, then, to go about diagnosing 'readness'? It is this that we consider in what follows.

For our purposes, one major mode of discerning what material was consumed in colonial Ibero-America in the day to day is to look to the schools. In an institutional sense, the history of European(ised) reading in the Americas is indivisible from the history of the educational systems established there, which in turn is indissociable from the activities of pedagogically minded European missionaries: initially the Franciscans, whose actions were key in the early Mexican context, and above all the Jesuits, pedagogic Order par excellence.[22] Members of the Society of Jesus (Jesuits), whose own foundation story is rooted in a quasi-apocryphal tale about diets of reading,[23] began arriving in the Americas from the mid-sixteenth century onwards, coming to be present in such force that they were almost single-handedly directing the continent's educational establishment by the time of their expulsion from Spanish America two centuries later, in 1767. The Jesuits are famed for their much-touted *modus procedendi* ('way of proceeding') and their highly developed curricula, as codified in the *Ratio Studiorum* ('System of Studies') of 1599: a multi-year programme of education prescribing the courses to which students were subject and the literature to which they were to be exposed.[24] As such, the *Ratio Studiorum* and associated teaching aids offer an invaluable window onto generations of Ibero-American schoolboys' daily diet of classroom reading – a programme of study predicated, in addition to intensive religious and philosophical instruction, on a thorough grounding in the Greco-Roman texts of European antiquity, especially its Latinate side. This in turn stimulated the market for both import and in situ printings: to return to the Mexican case, dozens of editions of classroom texts, grammars and manuals for poetic composition came off the press there every year.[25] Crucially, the Jesuit *modus procedendi* also extended to reading habits themselves: a set of practices that included line-by-line analysis of texts and grammatical annotation and elucidation, along with religious and literary exegesis. It was also a form of reading accompanied – encumbered? – by a colossal commentary tradition. We thus know not only what was being read but also *how*: a type of '*modus legendi*'. In these and other ways, then, it is no exaggeration to say that the Jesuits shaped the colonial continent's reading habits, turning out so many of the individuals who would go on to be active in colonial society and whose needs and interests drove the market for the transatlantic trade as well as local printings of new books – of which they themselves were often the authors. The demands of the Jesuit classroom thus constitute one version of the history of reading in the Americas, at least among a certain milieu and gender: the history of mandatory (male) Ibero-American classroom reading. Although in fact to call this diet 'Ibero-American' per se is misleading: the remarkable and today often forgotten reality is that, thanks to the strictures of the *Ratio Studiorum* (and the Jesuits' diligence in its instantiation), the daily diet of reading in the classrooms of the Iberian Americas was for decades and centuries practically identical to that in equivalent Colleges across the world, from Europe to Latin America, Goa to Macau to Manila – imported and imparted wherever Jesuit presence made itself felt.

But the Jesuit classroom too can take us only so far: it may account for a lot, but it does not account for the sum totality of reading. It does not even account for the totality of the Jesuits' own reading: not only Virgil's perennially prescribed *Aeneid* but also, for instance, Ercilla's bestselling *Araucana* is known to have enjoyed great popularity within the global Iberian Jesuit community.[26] Contrary to what one might conclude from the *Ratio Studiorum* alone, then, cultures of reading among Ibero-American Jesuits were neither wholly Latinate nor solely ancient. We too must therefore find ways of moving beyond the Jesuit classroom and into the domain of the 'extracurricular'.[27] Our first attempt to do so comes courtesy of an eighteenth-century Mexican Jesuit named Francisco Javier Alegre, author of a fascinating yet little-known work of literary history in which he surveys a vast array of texts spanning the full spectrum of languages, periods and genres. Crucially, moreover, he actively claims to have read them all.[28] (He also claims to have composed his own work from memory!) Though not un-catalogic in its quantities, the epistemological stakes – or at least pretensions – of Alegre's text are fundamentally different from those of any catalogue or lexicon, of which compilers may not always have seen, let alone read, all that they list: here, by contrast, is an explicit claim-to-reading.

Our second case study also stars an eighteenth-century Jesuit. Here, however, we take a different tack, seeking to determine what was read not at the level of explicit statement but rather from the evidence of patterns of literary response, taking signs of literary engagement as proof of prior reading. This is already true at the 'macro' level, that is, at the level of entire literary movements: the best index of Góngora's 'readness' in the Americas, after all, is not so much the bald import statistics as the waves of *gongorismo* and indeed *antigongorismo* which seized the Ibero-American literary scene just as they had the European, resulting in a veritable efflorescence of American Gongorine texts.[29] And it can also be pursued at the 'micro', which is to say, at the level of intertext: individual echoes or allusions to other works which, when identifiable with at least a reasonable degree of surety, allow us to draw inferences about the items lurking in the author's reading experience. Behind every intertextual allusion, a whole hinterland of reading lies. This is a subtler but, if performed with due caution, arguably also a surer guide to any individual author's personal reading history: taking signs of intertextual engagement as a window onto the diet imbibed and filtered through the mind of the reader into their words as a writer. It is also a more democratic lens, detecting readings of all stripes, from the complete cover-to-cover or classroom varieties to works skim read, fragments half-remembered, nuggets gleaned in anthologies, and so forth: in other words, all the sorts of readings which do not tend to make it into the 'official bibliography', but may be presences nonetheless. It arguably even offers something of a re-valorisation of the scholarly 'cult' of intertextuality itself: often maligned as an overly academic or at any rate now over-tired line of inquiry,[30] for our purposes it represents a powerful diagnostic tool. If reconstructing diets of reading is the aim, intertextuality offers an invaluable lens through which to glimpse what lies beyond, lurking in the hinterland of an individual author's reading – and individual histories of reading amount to the history of reading itself.

Francisco Javier Alegre: a life of reading

Francisco Javier (or Xavier) Alegre was born in 1729 in the Mexican port town of Veracruz.[31] He lived and pursued studies as part of the Jesuit educational establishment in a variety of locations around Mexico; he also spent seven years in Havana, Cuba. His whole education – indeed, his entire existence until the age of nearly forty – was thus conducted in Central America and the Caribbean. In the wake of the Jesuit expulsion of 1767, he came to find himself in Italy, where he lived in the Romagnan capital of Bologna until his death in 1788. Versed in a host of languages both ancient and modern, he produced works spanning a variety of fields and genres, from theological treatises to original epic poetry, as well as numerous translations, including of the *Iliad* and the pseudo-Homeric *Batrachomyomachia*. His literary activities have led him to be recognised as one of the foremost Ibero-American classicists of his day and even hailed as the (unsung) father of comparative literature and literary criticism *avant la lettre*.[32]

Even more prolific than Alegre's writings, however, were his readings. Indeed, from the testimony of his contemporary biographer, fellow exiled Mexican Jesuit Manuel Fabri (1737–1805), one gets the impression of a life quite devoted to the cause. Fabri insists throughout the biography on Alegre's insatiable readerly appetite – there are references to bookwormish activity on practically every page – as also on his above-average aptitudes for it: his consumption is voracious, his memory capacious.[33] Particular periods are said to have been given over to particular things, such as the time he read only the lives of the saints, or the time he ploughed through material in Italian until he had mastered the language; anecdotes see him going into bookshops in Mexico (or, later, libraries in Italy) and being able to discourse knowledgeably on every item on the shelves. In younger years he is said to have frequently read to the point of ill health, necessitating despatch to kindlier climes such as those of Cuba; and it is his fanatical reading that gets him in the end too, at the age of fifty-eight: 'as a result of all his hard work and his indefatigable commitment to reading and writing ['indefessa . . . legendi ac scribendi contentione'] from which he never knew a moment's rest, his debilitated constitution finally got the better of him'.[34] Reading is thus even in the diagnostics of his death.

Extraordinary erudition and tireless devotion to the literary cause are of course well-worn tropes of the scholarly life, especially in the quasi-hagiographical genre of Jesuit biography to which Fabri's life of Alegre belongs. An initial impulse may therefore be to take all this with a sizeable pinch of salt. One work in particular, however, attests to the really quite striking compass of Alegre's readings. This is the *Arte poética*, a Spanish-language work in three cantos, composed sometime in the mid-1770s during his early years of Italian exile.[35] In the *Arte poética*, which is itself in verse (in 'silva' form), Alegre sets out to offer a programme of poetic theory in the manner of ancient Roman author Horace's genre-defining *Ars poetica* and the tradition to which it gave rise. Indeed, Alegre's *Arte poética* is itself an adaptation of an earlier work in this same vein: seventeenth-century French author Nicolas Boileau-Despréaux's *L'Art poétique* (1674), in which Boileau formulated a poetics for the contemporary French literary scene. Alegre has not merely translated Boileau's work into Spanish, however: he has also replaced all its Gallic literary references with appropriate Hispanic – specifically, Peninsular Spanish – ones. To the 'main' body of the text Alegre then appends copious annotations expanding on ideas touched upon in the poem proper: it is here that the real substance of the work lies.

Alegre's *Arte poética* was never published in its own day and is still less well known today. For those do who know it, however, it is this – together with the *Antonio suo* (1776),[36] a shorter Latin-language prose piece focusing on epic poetry – that has led him to be hailed as a pioneer of comparative literature. In it he offers a veritable 'survey course' in European poetry and poetic theory. Greco-Roman authors (the subject of Canto I) are naturally well represented – and not only the usual suspects but also the likes of Pacuvius, Apuleius and Oppian and right down into the niches of Nemesianus and Nonnus. The bulk of the *Arte poética*, however, is given over to discussion of the literature not of European antiquity but of European (early) modernity, in both its vernacular and its neo-Latin dimensions. Alegre proceeds from smaller-scale poetic forms discussed in Canto II – the eclogue, elegy, ode, sonnet, epigram, madrigal and satire – to the 'meatier' genres in Canto III – tragedy, comedy and, of course, epic. The basic pattern is to offer versified *aperçus* on the relevant genre and its foremost exponents in the poem proper, before folding out into extensive discussion in the notes. The number of authors surveyed by this means is quite staggering: at least 263, many with several works each.[37] The figures swiftly multiply. Moreover, while Peninsular Spanish literature is the advertised subject, Italian works scarcely lag behind, and in fact – in quantitative terms if not discursive focus – French authors are the most highly represented of all. Portuguese and English writers also feature, as do a handful of Hispano-Americans.

Of Peninsular Spaniards themselves, the towering figures of Garcilaso de la Vega, Calderón de la Barca, Lope de Vega and Miguel de Cervantes are all given due attention, as are both Góngora and Ercilla – the latter usually alongside his Lusophone counterpart Luís de Camões, author of Portuguese global epic *Os Lusíadas* (1572). These are all flanked, however, by scores of lesser known works – from the obscure to the anonymous – from which Alegre cites liberally. The Italian and French cases likewise range from Tasso and Ariosto, Molière and Voltaire to all manner of others. If his claim to have composed the *Arte poética* by heart is serious, not *sprezzatura*, it is a feat of memory indeed! From the British Isles, meanwhile, a svelte quintet is drawn, from Milton – with whom Alegre has many doctrinal bones to pick, albeit in the process revealing just how closely he has read him[38] – to Welsh epigrammatist John Owen. Milton is also singled out (for censure) in the 1776 *Antonio suo*, albeit acknowledged as the 'most famous of the English poets' ('Miltoni celeberrimi . . . Anglorum vatis').[39] It is well known that Milton read *Os Lusíadas* in England in the seventeenth century:[40] the *Arte poética* now raises the tantalising possibility that by the eighteenth *Paradise Lost* was itself being read by the likes of Alegre in the Gulf of Mexico.[41]

And this of course is the point. The *Arte poética* offers not just a window onto Alegre's personal diet of reading but onto a diet of reading conducted overwhelmingly in the Iberian Americas.[42] Though not produced until his years of Italian exile, there is no way Alegre could have imbibed and assimilated all this material during the few short years that had elapsed since the expulsion: on the contrary, his command of the field clearly points to familiarity acquired over the course of many years of consumption. He is indeed reported by Fabri as having remarked that, while later life is for serious theological contemplation, youth is for belles-lettres – and certainly it would seem that a substantial proportion of his own younger days in Central America and the Caribbean were spent in that pursuit.[43] Furthermore, he himself states in the prologue to the *Arte poética* that he first began work on it in Mexico, but was forced to start again from scratch after the manuscript went missing amid the turmoil of the expulsion[44] – and, whatever one makes of this claim (common among eighteenth-century ex-Jesuits), it is clear that his acquaintance with the material under discussion long predates his time in Italy. This means that, some further percentage of items encountered for the first time upon arrival in Europe notwithstanding, the vast majority of authors discussed in the *Arte poética* must have been available for reading in the eighteenth-century Iberian Americas. Moreover, a not insignificant proportion of the works discussed dates from the mid-eighteenth century itself, suggesting a reasonably swift and systematic process of transfer of material from Europe across the Atlantic. Passing comments at times even offer insight into the speed with which some of this more contemporary material arrived, such as when Alegre refers to having read Spanish Peninsular poet Eugenio Gerado Lobo's early eighteenth-century *Selva de las Musas* in Mexico 'as a boy'.[45] He also knew Luis Antonio Oviedo de Herrera's epic on Saint Rose of Lima, composed in the eponymous Peruvian capital in the early eighteenth century and sent for publication in Spain (Madrid, 1711), whence copies boomeranged back across the Atlantic.[46]

While some scholars have emphasised the at times years of delay with which European works arrived in the Americas,[47] then, one might equally choose to stress the alacrity and (relative) reliability with which it occurred. Similarly, unlike those who would paint a downbeat picture of the stifling effect of the Spanish Inquisition on literary material imported to the Americas[48] – officially restricted to a selection of doctrinally approved works from Spain only – one can point instead to the rich and multilingual range of material to which Alegre clearly had access in mid-eighteenth-century Mexico and Cuba.

Alegre's little-known *Arte poética* is under-utilised in many ways. For our purposes, it is most especially under-exploited as a source of evidence for the range of European reading material available in eighteenth-century Ibero-America. It also raises the issue of *Ratio Studiorum* versus reality: here is a man who spent the first half of his life in a series of Jesuit educational environments, yet Greco-Roman classics and theological tomes were by no means the only things consumed; on the contrary, his official diet was supplemented by wide 'extracurricular' reading, including (from the perspective of the Jesuits, of the Inquisition, or both) all sorts of ideologically 'suspect' material: from the Roman erotic poet Tibullus, who makes him blush, to Góngora, who makes him blanche, to Milton, who makes him bristle.[49] As such, Alegre's *Arte poética* could be said to constitute a kind of complement or companion piece to the *Ratio Studiorum*: a literary barometer for the type of 'extracurricular' material in which individuals of his ilk might reasonably be expected to be versed.

Of course, as this last sentence hints, Alegre's work is of value in this regard only insofar as it can be shown to be in any way typical of the reading habits of those in the eighteenth-century Jesuit Iberian world more broadly. Thankfully, there is every sign that it is: a high degree of overlap has, for instance, already been found between works discussed by Alegre and those known to Guatemalan-born fellow Jesuit Rafael Landívar (1731–93), easily the best-known Latin-using writer to have emerged from eighteenth-century Iberian America.[50] In the final section, we now further test Alegre's 'representativity' through examination of a text by another Iberian Jesuit: Catalan-born missionary to Paraguay, José Manuel Peramás. Here we also switch to our second procedure, approaching the diagnosis of Peramás's literary diet not at the level of overt reference but rather of that which is not officially advertised yet intertextually detectable nonetheless. In other words, we proceed actively against the grain of what Peramás explicitly claims to have read, seeking instead to discover what lurks between and beyond the lines – in his hinterland of reading.

José Manuel Peramás: reflexes of reading

José Manuel Peramás (1732–93), *confrère* and almost exact contemporary of Alegre, plotted his own wide-ranging course around the Iberian Atlantic world: born near Barcelona and educated in various locations around Spain, he travelled in early adulthood to the then Province of Paraguay, where he spent twelve years – in areas falling within today's Argentinian territory – as a missionary to the Guaraní, before embarking on a parallel voyage of expulsion (back) to Europe and into Italian exile, where he ended up down the road from Bologna-based Alegre in the small Romagnan town of Faenza.[51] Reading was a major feature of Peramás's life experience too, both in America – he was for many years a teacher at the prestigious Jesuit university in Córdoba del Tucumán – and during and after the expulsion: he is said to have sustained himself during the long voyage of exile from Buenos Aires to Italy (1767–8) with a self-devised programme of prayer, writing and of course reading (*lectio*), and *lectio* remained one of his most cherished daily activities until the last.[52] Indeed, the function – escapist, consolatory or otherwise – of reading and writing in the exilic experience of the Iberian and Ibero-American Jesuits is an emergent new area of investigation in itself.[53]

Of his own writings, Peramás is best known for the *De Administratione Guaranica Comparata ad Rempublicam Platonis Commentarius* of 1793, a Latin politico-philosophical treatise in which he compares the Jesuit missionary settlements among the Guaraní to the ideal state imagined by Plato. As well as the oeuvre of the latter, the work betrays clear familiarity with, among others, Thomas More, Ludovico Muratori and even the above-mentioned Canarian-born Brazilian missionary, José de Anchieta. Here, however, we will consider not the *De Administratione* but a far less well-known Peramasian work, *De Invento Novo Orbe Inductoque Illuc Christi Sacrificio* ('On the Discovery of the New World and the Introduction of the Christian Sacrament to It'):[54] a three-canto epic, also in Latin, offering a fictionalised account of the voyages of Columbus with a decidedly Jesuit spin, published in Peramás's exilic Italian hometown of Faenza in 1777. Like the *Arte poética*, then, it too was composed in Italy, also in the mid-1770s. It too, however, clearly represents the distillation of many more years' worth of reading than those theretofore spent in Italy, pointing to extensive literary activity performed at unpinpointable moments across Peramás's international past.

Peramás prefaces the *De Invento Novo Orbe* (*DINO* hereafter) with a short introduction in which he lists the authors of whom he professes to have made active use during the composition of the work. These include Lucretius,[55] Horace and Virgil among classical poets, and Girolamo Fracastoro, Jacopo Sannazaro, Jacques Vanière and Tommaso Ceva among the early moderns. Of the latter, two are Jesuits and three Italian; all are Latin-using. This, then, is his 'official bibliography': the works on which Peramás explicitly claims to have drawn – and of which there is indeed clear evidence of engagement in the epic. Yet through the lens of intertextuality we can glimpse something more: works not listed in the bibliography, but of which there nonetheless seem to be signs of engagement. Crucially for our purposes, the most obviously detectable texts in this category – unlike the ones in the 'bibliography', with its Latin-only criterion of selection – are works in the Spanish vernacular. We have already learnt from Alegre that it is safe to assume that an individual the likes of Peramás would have been steeped in his own contemporary literary culture as well as in the biblical and classical; and, sure enough, those vernacular authors whom we appear to able to detect with the greatest degree of confidence are precisely the major Iberian players one would expect: canonical literary figures including Góngora, Ercilla and Garcilaso de la Vega. The official bibliography is one thing, therefore; the prism of intertextuality opens up a vista onto a whole other dimension of the author's diet of reading, and a translingual one at that: texts transferred across the language boundary from the Castilian in which they were written – and in which Peramás will have read them – to the Latin verse form in which he reconstitutes them.

We will consider just two examples. The first is drawn from the *DINO*'s opening canto, when Peramás is describing the habitat of the Guaraní:

> Guaranium prope litus, ubi sublime cacumen
> arboris alatae numquam tetigere sagittae,
> torquendis gens illa licet non tarda pharetris.
> (*DINO* 1.118–20)

> Nearby is the shore of the Guaraní, where no winged arrows have ever touched the lofty tree canopy, even though the people there are scarcely slow to wield their quivers.

The most obvious intertext in play is a portion of the Second Georgic (*Geo.* 2.122–5) of Virgil – one of the 'officially referenced' authors – in which the natural environment and consummate bowmanship of the inhabitants of India are evoked in terms nearly identical to Peramás's Guaraní here; indeed, the wider section of the *DINO* to which these lines (*DINO* 1.100–20) belong represents a sustained re-working of *Geo.* 2.109–35 – a section sometimes known as the 'The Marvels of the East' – here reappropriated (and cardinally reorientated) with reference to the western hemisphere. Alongside this more 'official' intertext, however, something else appears to be shimmering through the lines: a glimmer of the very Gongoran verses featured in our epigraph above. Góngora's references to the 'flechero Para[g]uay' ('Paraguayan archer') – standardly glossed by editors as 'Guaraní'[56] – and to the river which Góngora calls the 'Rey del Occidente' (the River Paraguay itself) resonate strongly with Peramás's own evocation of the Guaraní, with their prowess as archers and their riverbank haunts. If this is so then *DINO* 1.118–20 is really a passage with double determination, reworking not only Virgil on India but Góngora on the Guaraní – both texts with which Iberian Jesuit missionary-to-Paraguay Peramás will have had every reason to be familiar.

Our second flash 'from the beyond' is drawn from the third and final canto of the *DINO*, from a sequence of extended poetic geography. The inclusion of this type of literary-geographical episode is itself indicative of his familiarity with the *topos* of the terrestrial survey: a major set-piece sequence in the classical and early modern European epic traditions, with which Peramás thus further demonstrates his acquaintance. Among so many other things, one is struck by his evocation of the Isthmus of Panama:

> Illic vario discrimine litus
> quodque supra vagus oceanus, quodque alluit infra.[57]
> Latior Arctoo tellus quae subjacet axi,
> latior Austrinum quae fert et frigus et auras.
> In medio Panamae fauces vastissima regna
> partibus exaequant binis, Boreamque nivalem
> Pacifico prohibent fluctus confundere ponto.
> (*DINO* 3.435–41)

There is the shore at which the sprawling ocean laps on the upper side and the coastline against which it washes from below, kept apart by a ragged margin. On the one side is the enormous stretch of land that lies beneath the northern pole, on the other the equally vast portion that endures the cold and the wind of the South. In the middle, the Straits of Panama divide the enormous territory into two equal parts, preventing the snowy North Wind from churning up the waters of the Pacific.

Compare the description of the same Panamanian isthmus from the poetic geography in Canto 27 of Ercilla's *Araucana*:

> vees al sur la poblada y montuosa
> tierra, que en punta prolongarse viene,
> que los dos anchos mares por los lados
> la van adelgazando los costados.

> A Panamá y al Nombre de Dios mira,
> que sus estrechos términos defienden
> a dos contrarios mares, que con ira
> romper la tierra y anegar pretenden.
> (*Arauc.* 27.41e–h, 42a–d)

> To the South [of Mexico] you see the dense and mountainous landscape tapering to a point, with the two immense stretches of sea whittling away its edges on either side. Behold Panama City [on the Pacific coast] and Nombre de Dios [on the Atlantic seaboard], their narrow (or strait-like) limits warding off two opposing oceans bearing furiously down upon the land in an attempt to shatter and submerge it.

The similarities between Ercilla and Peramás appear unmistakeable – and, as we have said, *La Araucana* is known to have been widely read and enjoyed across the Iberian imperial world, including by Jesuits. Or, then again, perhaps it is not – or not only – Ercilla who is to be detected here: perhaps it is rather fellow Hispanic poet Bernardo de Balbuena or Italian Jesuit Niccolò Giannettasio or Góngora himself again (this time not the Góngora of the *Canciones* but of the *Soledades*) or Croatian-born Bernardo Zamagna or any of the other writers from the wider Italo-Iberian world – both Latin- and Spanish-using – whose works feature poetic portrayals of Panama rendered with varying degrees of closeness to Peramás's one here.[58] Perhaps it is even the seemingly unlikely figure of Vincentius Placcius, a seventeenth-century German Protestant whose evocation of Panama in his own Columbus epic, *Atlantis Retecta* (1659/68), is easily closest to Peramás's of all,[59] suggesting – a priori improbable though engagement with Protestant Placcius might appear – that Peramás had absorbed that work, too. None of these texts features in Peramás's 'official bibliography' – yet some or all of them clearly hover in the ranks of texts that throng his hinterland of reading, as accessed through the prism of intertextuality. Moreover, though none is listed by Peramás, all – bar Placcius – are among those discussed by Alegre. For a lettered eighteenth-century Iberian Jesuit, these were clearly knowable – readable, *read* – authors.

Fittingly, the *DINO* – which, unlike the *Arte poética*, did see the light of publication in its own day – is itself a text which soon found its way to far-flung corners of the globe, including both Palma de Mallorca and California by the nineteenth century. With the exception of a lightly annotated copy today held in Italy in the library at Forlì, however, concrete evidence of actual reading of the epic is harder to come by. It most certainly was read, however, by at least one figure in Mexico – homeland of *confrère* Alegre – who came upon it in the early nineteenth or even late eighteenth century.[60] This reader, who would go on to become rector of Mexico City's university, claimed to have been reared on a diet of Jesuit works[61] – Peramás's poem among them.[62] Thousands of miles and yet just a few short decades from its point of publication, the *DINO* thus found its way into the hands of at least one receptive reader on the other side of the Atlantic – and, given what we now know about reading culture in the hyperconnected early modern Iberian world, this should not surprise.

Conclusion: lessons from Jesuits

Alegre and Peramás are instructive on two fronts: the particular and, more importantly, the general. On the one hand, their texts offer windows onto individual diets of reading: the literary consumption of two historical persons who lived and worked across the wide Ibero-American world, racking up an impressive range of locations between them – from Mexico and Cuba to Spain and Paraguay, and, ultimately, Italy. But we can also speak in terms of generality, or rather generalisability: these individuals' diets of reading – wide-ranging, multilingual reading of material both classical and contemporary, curricular and extracurricular – are by no means atypical, at least among readers of a certain gender and time and belonging to certain communities. Alegre and Peramás may hail from different corners of the globe, yet their status as Iberians and as Jesuits (and the interaction between these two categories of identity) will have given them a high degree of parity, or parallelism, of experience and ensured that they will have been exposed to a significant degree to a similar range of literature – as will countless other Iberian and Ibero-American figures like them. The *Ratio Studiorum* offers one window onto the substance of this diet, Alegre's *Arte poética* another; the intertextual tissue of a text like Peramás's showcases the results in action. What emerges is a picture of readings of all stripes in a variety of European languages, not just the classics of Greco-Roman literature or the Church-approved canon. This was not a world in which material was regularly unavailable, militantly monolingual or meaningfully hamstrung by the strictures of the Inquisition.

We have observed of both Alegre and Peramás that it is often difficult to establish with certainty at what point in their international careers the reading of any given work will have taken place. It is also immaterial: the point, precisely, is that acquaintance with these texts could, by virtue of the interconnected Iberian context in which they operated, have been acquired in any one of the locations through which they passed. The parabolas which they and others like them charted across the discontinuous spaces of the Iberian imperial sphere, engaging in literary activity all the while, attest to the enormity and intensity of the diffusion of European reading culture in the global Iberian context. Its traces and consequences remain inscribed across the page of the world today.

Notes

1. '... and on the wings of the wind / the dulcet tones of your last utterance flew, / wounding the shores of the Ganges / and the bank of the King of the West; / the Paraguayan archer – steeped in poison / his quiver, in heresy his heart – / perceived your demise with anguish'. All translations from Spanish and Latin are my own.
2. See Walter Mignolo, *The Darker Side of the Renaissance: Literacy, Territoriality, and Colonization* (Ann Arbor: Michigan, 2003).
3. Irving Leonard, *Books of the Brave: Being an Account of Books and of Men in the Spanish Conquest and Settlement of the Sixteenth-Century New World* (Cambridge, MA: Harvard University Press, 1949) is seminal; for nuancing, see Rolena Adorno, *The Polemics of Possession in Spanish American Narrative* (New Haven: Yale University Press, 2007), pp. 214–19.
4. See recently Andrew Laird, 'Latin America', in Philip Ford et al. (eds), *Brill's Encylopaedia of the Neo-Latin World* (Leiden: Brill, 2014), pp. 821–32; Andrew Laird, 'Colonial Spanish America and Brazil', in Sarah Knight and Stefan Tilg (eds), *The Oxford Handbook of Neo-Latin* (Oxford: Oxford University Press, 2015), pp. 525–40.
5. Ignacio Osorio Romero, 'Latín y neolatín en México', in Ignacio Osorio Romero et al. (eds), *La tradición clásica en México* (Mexico City: UNAM, 1991), pp. 7, 76; Andrew Laird, *The Epic of America: An Introduction to Rafael Landívar and the* Rusticatio Mexicana (London: Duckworth, 2006), p. 9.
6. Cristóbal Cabrera's *Dicolon Icastichon* (Mexico City, 1540): see Osorio Romero, 'Latín y neolatín', pp. 13–15; Andrew Laird, 'Classical Letters and Millenarian Madness in Post-Conquest Mexico: The *Ecstasis* of Fray Cristóbal Cabrera (1548)', *International Journal of the Classical Tradition*, 24:1 (2017), pp. 78–108 (p. 80).
7. For example, Rodrigo Cacho, 'Iberian Myths and American History in Balbuena's *El Bernardo*', in Javier Muñoz-Basols et al. (eds), *The Routledge Companion to Iberian Studies* (London: Routledge, 2017),

pp. 238–48; Joanne van der Woude, 'La Primera Parte del Parnaso Antártico: Print and the Politics of Translation in Early Peruvian Poetry', in Matthew Duquès, Maya Feile Tomes and Adam Goldwyn (eds), *Brill's Companion to Classics in the Early Americas* (Brill, forthcoming).
8. See further Feile Tomes, 'Introduction', in Duquès et al. (eds), *Brill's Companion*.
9. Rodrigo Cacho, 'Balbuena's *Grandeza Mexicana* and the American Georgic', *Colonial Latin American Review*, 24:2 (2015), pp. 190–214; Rodrigo Cacho and Imogen Choi (eds), *The Rise of Spanish American Poetry, 1500–1700: Literary and Cultural Transmission in the New World* (Oxford: Legenda, 2019).
10. Ignacio Osorio Romero, *Colegios y profesores jesuitas que enseñaron latín en Nueva España, 1572–1767* (Mexico City: UNAM, 1979); Andrew Laird, 'Nahua Latinists: Classical Learning and Indigenous Legacies in Sixteenth-Century Mexico', in Duquès et al. (eds), *Brill's Companion*.
11. The next was that of Lima, in 1584. The first press in North America was that founded at Harvard in 1638.
12. Laird, 'Nahua Latinists'.
13. See most recently van der Woude, 'La Primera Parte del Parnaso Antártico'.
14. On Gongorism in Mexico, see Rolena Adorno, *Colonial Latin American Literature: A Very Short Introduction* (Oxford: Oxford University Press, 2011), pp. 77–109; Martha Lilia Tenorio, *El gongorismo en Nueva España: ensayo de restitución* (Mexico City: Colegio de México, 2013); Luis Castellví Laukamp, *Hispanic Baroque Ekphrasis: Góngora, Camargo, Sor Juana* (Legenda, forthcoming). The ongoing 'Góngora global' project, led by Mercedes Blanco (Université Paris–Sorbonne) and collaborators, points to major centres of activity also in Peru, Brazil and even the Philippines.
15. See David Brading, *Mexican Phoenix. Our Lady of Guadalupe: Image and Tradition Across Five Centuries* (Cambridge: Cambridge University Press, 2001), pp. 131–9, 154–5; Andrew Laird, 'Patriotism and the Rise of Latin in Eighteenth-Century New Spain: Disputes of the New World and the Jesuit Construction of a Mexican Legacy', *Renæssanceforum*, 8 (2012), pp. 231–62 (pp. 244–51).
16. See Arnold L. Kerson, 'Diego José Abad, *Dissertatio Ludicro-Seria*', *Humanistica Lovaniensia*, 40 (1991), pp. 357–422; Laird, 'Patriotism and the Rise of Latin'; Felipe Reyes Palacios and José Quiñones Melgoza (eds), *Nicolas Boileau-Despréaux, Francisco Javier Alegre: Arte Poética. Edición bilingüe* (Mexico City: UNAM, 2014), pp. 10–12.
17. See Jorge Cañizares-Esguerra, *How to Write the History of the New World: Histories, Epistemologies, and Identities in the Eighteenth-Century Atlantic World* (Stanford: Stanford University Press, 2001), pp. 1–10; Laird, *The Epic of America*, pp. 3–8.
18. Edward Wilson-Lee, *The Catalogue of Shipwrecked Books: Young*

Columbus and the Quest for a Universal Library (London: William Collins, 2018), pp. 120–4.

19. Osorio Romero, 'Latin y neolatín', p. 12. Numbers may have been higher still: see van der Woude, '*La Primera Parte del Parnaso Antártico*', on the 'minimum of 8500 books' moved between Seville and Mexico in 1594–1600 by a single pair of book-trading brothers. Recently, see also Natalia Maillard Álvarez, 'Early Circulation of Classical Books in New Spain and Peru', in Andrew Laird and Nicola Miller (eds), *Antiquities and Classical Traditions in Latin America* (Chichester: Wiley/SLAS, 2018), pp. 26–40; in general, see Leonard, *Books of the Brave*.
20. Miguel Martínez, *Front Lines: Soldiers' Writing in the Early Modern Hispanic World* (Philadelphia: University of Pennsylvania Press, 2016), pp. 32, 148, 153–9.
21. Helen Hazen, 'The Cloistered Books of Peru', *American Scholar*, 6 March 2017, available at <https://theamericanscholar.org/the-cloistered-books-of-peru/> (accessed 26 September 2019).
22. On the Franciscans, see Laird, 'Nahua Latinists'; on the Jesuits, Osorio Romero, *Colegios y profesores*.
23. Robert Goodwin, *Spain: The Centre of the World, 1519–1682* (London: Bloomsbury, 2015), p. 47.
24. Yasmin Haskell, 'Practicing What They Preach? Vergil and the Jesuits', in Joseph Farrell and Michael Putnam (eds), *A Companion to Vergil's Aeneid and Its Tradition* (Malden: Wiley-Blackwell, 2010), pp. 203–16.
25. Ignacio Osorio Romero, *Floresta de gramática, poética y retórica en Nueva España (1521–1767)* (Mexico City: UNAM, 1980); Osorio Romero, 'Latin y neolatín'.
26. José de Acosta, *Historia natural y moral de las Indias* (Seville: Juan de León, 1590), pp. 146–9; Walter Hanisch Espíndola, *Juan Ignacio Molina: sabio de su tiempo* (Caracas: Universidad Católica Andrés Bello, 1974), p. 13.
27. Cf. Haskell, 'Practicing What They Preach?', pp. 207–10.
28. Alegre in his prologue (no pagination) to the *Arte poética* – henceforth *AP*, cited by canto and note number.
29. See note 14 above.
30. See recently Gian Biagio Conte, *Stealing the Club from Hercules: On Imitation in Latin Poetry* (Berlin: De Gruyter, 2017).
31. Manuel Fabri, 'De Auctoris Vita Commentarius', in Francisco Xavier Alegre, *Institutionum Theologicarum* (Venice: Antonio Zatta, 1789), vol. I, pp. vii–xxxi. The biography is reproduced in Spanish translation in Joaquín García Icazbalceta (ed.), *Opúsculos inéditos latinos y castellanos del P. Francisco Xavier Alegre* (Mexico City: Díaz de León, 1889) and in Bernabé Navarro (ed.), *Vidas de mexicanos ilustres del siglo XVIII – Juan Luis Maneiro y Manuel Fabri* (Mexico City: UNAM, 1956). See also Julio Pimentel Álvarez, *Francisco Javier Alegre y Diego José Abad: humanistas gemelos* (Mexico City: UNAM, 1990).

32. Allan F. Deck, *Francisco Javier Alegre: A Study in Mexican Literary Criticism* (Rome/Tucson: Jesuit Historical Institute/Kino House, 1976), p. 32; Arnold L. Kerson, 'Francisco Javier Alegre's Translation of Boileau's *Art poétique*', *Modern Language Quarterly*, 41:2 (1981), pp. 153–65 (pp. 153–5); Jeffrey H. Kaimowitz, 'Translation of the Apologetical Essay Appended to the *Alexandriad* of Francisco Javier Alegre', *Dieciocho*, 13:1–2 (1990), pp. 135–48 (p. 135); Ernest J. Burrus, 'Alegre Capetillo, Francisco Javier', in Charles E. O'Neill and Joaquín María Domínguez (eds), *Diccionario Histórico de la Compañía de Jesús* (Rome/Madrid: Institutum Historicum, S.I./Universidad Pontificia Comillas, 2001), pp. 43–4 (p. 44); Reyes Palacios and Quiñones Melgoza, *Arte Poética*, pp. 12, 33–4, 164.
33. Fabri, 'De Auctoris Vita', p. xxx.
34. Ibid., p. xxvi.
35. Editions are García Icazbelceta (ed.), *Opúsculos inéditos*, and Reyes Palacios and Quiñones Melgoza (eds), *Arte poética*.
36. The *Antonio suo* is available in Latin with Spanish translation in Pimentel Álvarez, *Humanistas gemelos*, pp. 1–10; in English, in Kaimowitz, 'Translation of the Apologetical Essay'.
37. See García Icazbalceta, *Opúsculos inéditos*, pp. 206–27; reprinted in Reyes Palacios and Quiñones Melgoza, *Arte poética*, pp. 245–73.
38. *AP*, III n.83.
39. Pimentel Álvarez, *Humanistas gemelos*, p. 2.
40. Cecil Maurice Bowra, *From Virgil to Milton* (New York: St Martin's Press, 1967), p. 195; see also Richard Helgerson, *A Sonnet from Carthage: Garcilaso de la Vega and the New Poetry of Sixteenth-Century Europe* (Philadelphia: Pennsylvania University Press, 2007), p. 17.
41. Fabri, 'De Auctoris Vita, p. xvii also reports that it was while in Havana that Alegre first learnt English.
42. Cf. Reyes Palacios and Quiñones Melgoza, *Arte poética*, p. 9; Kerson, 'Francisco Javier Alegre', p. 154.
43. Fabri, 'De Auctoris Vita', p. xxv; see also pp. xxi–xxii.
44. *AP*, Prologue.
45. *AP*, I n.19.
46. There was even a Mexican edition of 1729.
47. Guillermo Serés, 'Presentación', in Laura Fernández et al. (eds), *Clásicos para un Nuevo Mundo. Estudios sobre la tradición clásica en la América de los siglos XVI y XVII* (Bellaterra: Universitat Autònoma de Barcelona, 2016), pp. 7–8; Reyes Palacios, *Arte poética*, p. 164 n.13.
48. Serés, 'Presentación', p. 7; contrast Cañizares-Esguerra, *How to Write the History*, p. 10. See also Maillard Álvarez, 'Early Circulation of Classical Books', pp. 26–8.
49. *AP*, II n.5; *AP*, I n.7 (though cf. *AP* II, n.26); *AP* III, n.83. See further note 55 below.
50. Laird, *The Epic of America*, pp. 27–9, p. 82 n.100.

51. Peramás's biography is the anonymous 'Josephi Peramasii Vitae Sinopsis', in José Manuel Peramás, *De Vita et Moribus Tredecim Virorum Paraguaycorum* (Faenza: Archi, 1793), pp. xvii–xxvii. For Spanish translation, see Guillermo Furlong, *José Manuel Peramás y su Diario del Destierro (1768)* (Buenos Aires: Librería del Plata, 1952).
52. Anon., 'Josephi Peramasii Vitae Sinopsis', pp. xxiii–xxiv.
53. See Yasmin Haskell, 'Suppressed Emotions: The Heroic *Tristia* of Portuguese (Ex-)Jesuit, Emanuel de Azevedo', *Journal of Jesuit Studies*, 3:1 (2016), pp. 42–60; Antonio Astorgano Abajo (ed.), *Lorenzo Hervás y Panduro: Biblioteca jesuítico-española (1759–1799)* (Madrid: Libris, 2007).
54. See Maya Feile Tomes, 'News of a Hitherto Unknown Neo-Latin Columbus Epic, Part I. José Manuel Peramás's *De Invento Novo Orbe Inductoque Illuc Christi Sacrificio* (1777)', *International Journal of the Classical Tradition*, 22:1 (2015), pp. 1–28; 'Part II', *International Journal of the Classical Tradition*, 22:2 (2015), pp. 223–57; 'Further Points on Peramás', *International Journal of the Classical Tradition*, 22:3 (2015), pp. 383–9. On the geographical episode, see 'The Angel and Ameri(c)a: Performing the "New World" in José Manuel Peramás's *De Invento Novo Orbe* (1777)', in Yasmin Haskell and Raphaële Garrod (eds), *Changing Hearts: Performing Jesuit Emotions Between Europe, Asia and the Americas* (Leiden: Brill, 2018), pp. 121–46. An edition of Peramás's epic is in preparation.
55. Lucretius was himself officially off the menu for Jesuits, for ideological reasons – though in reality was widely read nonetheless: see further Yasmin Haskell, 'Sleeping with the Enemy: Tommaso Ceva's Use and Abuse of Lucretius in the *Philosophia Novo-Antiqua* (Milan 1704)', in Juanita Feros Ruys (ed.), *What Nature Does Not Teach: Didactic Literature in the Medieval and Early-Modern Periods* (Brepols: Turnhout, 2008), pp. 497–520; Mariantonietta Paladini, *Lucrezio e l'epicureismo tra Riforma e Controriforma* (Naples: Liguori, 2011), pp. 177–90.
56. Gerardo Diego (ed.), *Antología poética en honor de Góngora: desde Lope de Vega a Rubén Darío* (Madrid: Revista de Occidente, 1927), p. 49; Bernardo Alemany y Selfa, *Vocabulario de las obras de don Luis de Góngora y Argote* (Madrid: Revista de Archivos, Bibliotecas y Museos, 1930), p. 727.
57. Cf. Virgil, *Georgics*, 2.158.
58. Balbuena, *Bernardo* 18.105a–b; Giannettasio, *Nautica* 18.976–82; Góngora, *Soledades* 1.424–29; Zamagna, *Navis aëria* 2.643–4; among others.
59. Compare *DINO* 3.435–43 with Placcius, *Atlantis Retecta* 1079–86.
60. Feile Tomes, 'Part II', pp. 229–34.
61. Agustín Pomposo Fernández de San Salvador, *Los jesuitas quitados y restituidos al mundo* (Mexico City: Mariano Ontiveros, 1816), p. 16.
62. Ibid., p. 19.

Chapter 12

Printed Private Library Catalogues as a Source for the History of Reading in Seventeenth- and Eighteenth-Century Europe

Helwi Blom, Rindert Jagersma and Juliette Reboul

To paraphrase a common saying: 'Show me your bookcase and I will tell you who you are'. The situation is a little more complex for the researcher interested in historical readers and the contents of private libraries from the past. If some historical collections survived in their original form for a few generations, old and inherited libraries were often dismantled, collections broken up, and books deemed worth preserving scattered across many new libraries. Yet there are several ways to discover what historical libraries contained and, by studying them, to understand who their owners were. Various sources can allow us to explore the interests of historical readers and former reading cultures: traces of provenance, ego-documents, probate inventories and catalogues all contain information on books, collections and their owners.[1] This chapter discusses printed catalogues of private libraries as historical sources. Our leading question will be: to what extent and in what capacity can printed catalogues of private libraries contribute to the history of reading and, in particular, the history of seventeenth- and eighteenth-century European readers?

The first ground-breaking scholarly use of printed private library catalogues dates from 1910, when Daniel Mornet published his article 'Les enseignements des bibliothèques privées (1750–1780)'.[2] His quest to reassess the influence of Enlightenment writers traditionally accepted as the forefathers of modernity led him to consider the utility of a corpus of 500 Parisian printed catalogues kept in Toulouse.[3] In 1917, following Mornet, Dutch researcher Sophie A. Krijn looked at 100 Dutch catalogues compiled between 1700 and 1750 in order to analyse the spread of French books in the Dutch Republic.[4] Around the same time, Harold Mattingly and Ian Burnett drew up a list of all the book sale catalogues kept in the British Museum, including many for private libraries.[5] Although interest in private libraries led to sporadic publications in the decades following Mornet's article, only a handful of researchers made extensive use of printed catalogues of private libraries to study the history of ideas.[6] The more general question of the contents and uses of different kinds of book lists and catalogues as historical sources and bibliographical aids was developed from the 1950s onwards through numerous publications. The most influential among the early ones were those of Archer Taylor in the United States, Graham Pollard and Albert Ehrman in England, and the team of François Furet in France.[7] When much work was undertaken on probate inventories in the broader context of social history and the history of mentalities in the 1960s and 1970s, the books in those inventories became the subject of an increasing number of separate studies.[8] Some researchers explicitly stated that the information contained in probate inventories constituted a better base for the analysis of historical book ownership and reading cultures than printed catalogues, because the latter would have been drawn up only for larger collections considered to hold a substantial value. Dominique Varry, for example, reduced the utility of sale catalogues of private libraries to the study of bibliophilia.[9]

Yet thanks to a renewed interest by historians in reception studies and book cultures in the 1980s, studies of printed catalogues of private libraries as well as book sale catalogues gained wider traction. Besides new contributions to methodological discussion on the use of book lists as a (book) historical and bibliographical source, a wide range of conferences and publications on seventeenth- and eighteenth-century private libraries and their (printed) catalogues have seen the light in recent decades.[10] In general, these studies and digital projects are regionally or nationally oriented, but their authors have chosen diverse angles of research in which quantitative or qualitative aspects play roles of varying importance. Some of them focus on book ownership and prosopographical research.[11] Others are primarily interested in the role sale catalogues played in the book trade.[12] The subject of classification and the ways in which printed catalogues were used in the long eighteenth century regularly resurfaces.[13] Also at the heart of several articles and projects is the synchronical and/or diachronical study of the presence of certain authors, and types of texts and books.[14] Over the last few years, numerous projects concerned with the virtual reconstruction of libraries have been initiated. While most of them focus on medieval monastic libraries and handwritten inventories, some pay attention to early modern collections and envisage using different types of sources to reconstruct private collections and make their contents virtually accessible.[15] The tradition of establishing inventories of published catalogues of private libraries continued after the 1910s; however, studies on the material really took off from the 1970s onwards, driven by librarians and researchers alike.[16] The advent of digital humanities has opened new possibilities for large-scale research based on printed catalogues of private libraries. Our own project, MEDIATE (Measuring Enlightenment: Disseminating Ideas, Authors and Texts in Europe), aims to bring to light new perspectives on readers and reading cultures in eighteenth-century Europe, and especially on the circulation of books associated with the Enlightenment, using purpose-built digital tools.[17]

Although the research of the last decades has shown the usefulness of private library catalogues in reception studies and for the history of reading, the caveats formulated by Dominique Varry have not lost their relevance, because they are inherent to the source. Printed catalogues of private libraries are part of a larger body of texts whose main purpose is to list books. This corpus includes all sorts of lists: catalogues designed by or for individual library owners, probate inventories, inventories of trade stock, satirical catalogues, catalogues of public libraries, indices of forbidden books and bibliographical repertories. Lists of books come in different shapes and sizes, with notable distinctions regarding their form, purpose, content and use.[18] As far as the form is concerned, one could for example distinguish between handwritten, printed and digital lists of books. One could also look at the bibliographical format, whether the list appeared as a separate publication or whether it was inserted in another book. Some lists were compiled for commercial reasons, including lists of newly published books, auction catalogues and catalogues of circulating libraries. Others might have served legal purposes (probate inventories) or domestic ones, such as catalogues compiled for the personal use of book owners. Some were published to honour the life achievements or memory of the possessor of the books listed, or were intended to publicise the collection. We can also categorise these catalogues by their content, the nature of the collections, the way they are organised, or the presence of paratextual elements. The pluriform properties of the genre lead to many questions. Do the books compiled together describe existing/real collections or do they refer to some imagined ensemble, such as catalogues of ideal libraries and satirical catalogues? Do the catalogues describe an entire collection, a selection from it, or perhaps several collections put together? Do they list any other material besides books? Indeed, paintings, prints, curiosities and even sometimes a complete set of household belongings may be recorded alongside the content of libraries. Finally, book catalogues were used in multiple ways, not only as a means to manage the contents of personal or public libraries, but also as bibliographical reference works, guides on the formation of the ideal private library or (more practically still) as an early version of the *Bookman's Price Index*.[19]

There have been several attempts to categorise printed catalogues of private libraries and to create typologies of book lists, but the results have been at times confusing and conflicting. For example, Bert van Selm's project 'Book Sales Catalogues of the Dutch Republic' is vague about the reasons behind its choices. Some of the categories might overlap, like 'auction catalogue private library', 'catalogue private library', 'manuscript private library' and 'memorial catalogue'. Similarly, the terms 'ventes publiques' and 'catalogues de vente' are used by Bléchet and in the database 'Esprit des livres' to describe a corpus that includes catalogues that were not intended to have a commercial purpose.[20] With regard to French catalogues, Nicole Masson has demonstrated that, depending on the approach and factors taken into account (that is, analytical bibliography, presentation, classification, sales conditions, and others), different typologies of these 'catalogues de vente' can be elaborated.[21] In fact, comparing data from different regions is a delicate if not impossible task. For instance, if we take a look at the available data for France, the Dutch Republic and the British Isles (Figure 12.1), we find that the methodologies used by the main studies in the field and the type of catalogues included or excluded from their union lists differ substantially for each national context. This complicates any attempt to comprehend the development of private library cataloguing at a European level.

A typology referring to commercial purposes should in any case differentiate between auctions and fixed-price sales (*ventes à l'amiable*), as well as between retail sale (*vente au détail*) and bulk sale (*vente en block*). While this differentiation has been attempted by Alan Munby and Lenore Coral with categories such as 'auctions' and 'lower fixed prices', their list does not differentiate between private and booksellers' collections. It is the highly permeable character of the book list itself that complicates attempts at a definition and categorisation of the material: the nature of private library catalogues is such that they tend to serve different purposes and mutate from one type to another. For instance, one might print a catalogue privately for one's personal use, aim at the same time to promote the collection and perhaps hope that someone will be interested in buying it. Also, a handwritten domestic catalogue or probate inventory can at some point be turned

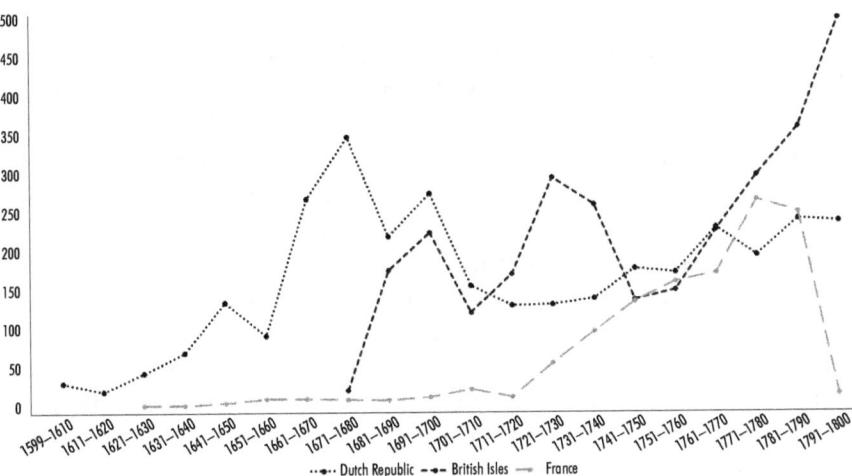

Figure 12.1 Numbers of surviving editions of catalogues published between 1599 and 1800, as recorded by Gruys for the Dutch Republic, by Bléchet and then Marion for France, and by Munby and Coral for the British Isles

Sources: J. A. (Hans) Gruys, 'Rijklof Michael van Goens. Het mysterie van de 24.200 verdwenen catalogi', in Ton van Uchelen and Hannie van Goinga (eds), *Van pen tot laser: 31 opstellen over boek en schrift* (Amsterdam: De Buitenkant, 1996), pp. 150–6; Françoise Bléchet, *Les ventes publiques de livres en France, 1630–1750: répertoire des catalogues conservés à la Bibliothèque Nationale* (Oxford: Voltaire Foundation, 1991); Michel Marion, *Collections et collectionneurs de livres au XVIIIe siècle* (Paris: H. Champion, 1999); Alan N. L Munby and Lenore Coral (eds), *British Book Sale Catalogues 1676–1800: A Union List* (London: Mansell, 1977)

into a printed sale catalogue, and the latter can later serve as a bibliographical manual. In fact, sale catalogues of private libraries often appear as items in printed sale catalogues, thus indicating a change in purpose. For instance, lots 1137 to 1165 of the library of English clergyman Michael Lort, sold in 1791, contain no less than fifty-five catalogues, forty-six of which refer to private libraries.[22] Finally, the term 'private' itself hides the reality of the widespread public use of private libraries, which their owners frequently opened to relatives, friends and other casual visitors.[23] This was the case not just for elite libraries but also for genteel and bourgeois private libraries.

Previous research has pointed out that difficulties in using catalogues do not solely lie in defining a typology of catalogues: there are further pitfalls in trying to analyse and interpret their contents, in particular a potential confusion between book ownership and reading culture. Early critics of Mornet's study of catalogues pointed out that a book owned is not necessarily a book read.[24] Several studies of seventeenth- and eighteenth-century libraries containing thousands of books relate book ownership to consumerism, following observations by early modern European moralists and philosophers. Long before Jean de La Bruyère famously mocked a book owner showing off his leather-bound collection, blissfully unaware of the books' contents,[25] Jean Lepautre had already produced an engraving illustrating the embodiment of this type of 'mad' booklover.[26] Published in 1693, the *Menagiana* contain a juicy anecdote about a French *surintendant des finances* who allegedly asked Gilles Ménage to purchase a complete library on his behalf: he worried that people would discover upon his death that he didn't own one.[27] While some collectors owned books they had never read or even opened, others read books that they didn't own. They borrowed books from friends and circulating and subscription libraries, and listened to them being read aloud. Besides, books in libraries were not all necessarily purchased by the owners themselves: some were gifts, others were inherited. This troubles the question of whether a library (catalogue) reflects the reading interests of the owner.

Printed catalogues of private libraries were not designed to give an inventory of all titles actually read by the owner, but nor do they always list all the books possessed by an individual. It is important to acknowledge that printed catalogues represent an image of the library frozen in time. Often they were compiled at a turning point in the life of a collection: the death of an owner, a (forced) sale due to bankruptcy, a departure, a loss of interest. Sometimes they were used as a way to clean up or restart a collection. Even manuscript domestic catalogues, offering better perspectives on the dynamics of book collecting and the management of libraries by individual owners, are limited in their capacity to testify to the totality of the books that were part of owners' (previous and subsequent) collections. Books that were actually present in the library of an individual might not appear in a published catalogue for numerous reasons. They might have been given away or kept aside for other purposes. A comparative study of inventories and printed catalogues of the same collection certainly shows that there can be important discrepancies between the ways books are listed in the two sources.[28] Another reason for this kind of discrepancy is the fact that booksellers, at least in the seventeenth and eighteenth centuries, would sometimes add part of their stocks to what was presented as a private collection, despite legal restrictions on the practice.[29] This is perhaps why Ann Middleton had a page inserted in the sale catalogue of her husband's library (1750–1) stating: 'I take this opportunity to assure the Public, that this *Catalogue* contains the genuine Library of Dr. Middleton, without any Alteration, and is sold for my Advantage'.[30] Because of censorship laws in eighteenth-century

France, booksellers issued official catalogues that omitted forbidden books present in the collection for sale, but at the same time found ways to advertise and sell these clandestine publications. In some copies of eighteenth-century French catalogues we find handwritten lists of items that were part of a *'vente secrette'* that took place in the fringe of the official sale.[31] One should also keep in mind that wealthy owners could divide their book collection between different residential properties. The catalogue produced after the passing of Sir William Burrell in 1796 states that only his 'town-library' (811 lots) was up for sale.[32] In 1791, following an illness, Burrell had moved permanently to his country estate of Deepdene in Sussex, where he owned a second library. While some sale catalogues inform the buyer that the collection they describe is a complete library or only part of it, such assurances are often difficult to verify. The commercial character of sale catalogues also led booksellers to ignore cheap print and old volumes. Instead of listing these works in the catalogues, they thought it sufficient to inform the public that, at the beginning of each session, they would sell a number of unidentified books. This practice was so common in France that in 1792 the editor of the catalogue announcing the sale of the library of Laideguive de Becheville explicitly warned interested buyers that each session would start immediately with the sale of the lot numbers indicated in the printed order of sale.[33]

Another important pitfall relates to the way titles were recorded in catalogues. Certainly catalogues are in general more detailed than inventories. Yet despite the larger number of details given in catalogues, the description of an item does not always allow the researcher to know which work is presented, let alone the particulars of its edition.[34] Titles can be shortened, authors' names omitted, and it can be difficult to know which title or edition was owned in the absence of a year or place of publication. Then there are the obvious mistakes made by the compiler or the printer. These issues often come together. It is possible that mistakes of this kind happened during the compiling of the inventory of books, as compilers often worked in pairs, with one transcribing the titles read out by the other. Catalogues can also be vague about the titles and the number of books contained in certain lots. Expressions like 'packet' and *'volumes dépareillés'* were commonly used to refer to collections of smaller books, ephemera and books deemed less interesting.[35] The note in the inventory of the library of Cardinal de Richelieu saying that a description of the contents of a bundle of mixed titles 'eust excédé le prix de leur valleur' ('would have exceeded their value'), probably reflected a principle that guided the work of many compilers.[36]

One of the main objections made to using catalogues as a source to study the history of reading is the fact that printed catalogues represent only the collections of a learned readership among the social and financial elites of a particular period. The question of the representativeness of any corpus of printed catalogues of private libraries is a complex one, because it is closely related to questions of survival rates. A study by Hans Gruys shows that the survival rates of catalogues printed in the eighteenth-century Dutch Republic oscillates between 6 and 21 per cent, depending on the city.[37] In the Dutch Republic it was compulsory to publish a catalogue for every book sale. Hence, these figures are based on the discrepancy between the number of book sales given in local registries of book auctions and that of surviving catalogues. We cannot extrapolate from Gruys's study to other European contexts any assumptions concerning the survival rates of catalogues, however. Survival rates depend on several factors. Voluminous catalogues as well as those of prestigious libraries and famous individuals stood better chances of being preserved. Catalogues of larger libraries, especially professional libraries and encyclopaedic ones, were sometimes preserved to be used as reference works.[38] Chance often plays an important part in the preservation of individual copies: the Herzog August Bibliothek (Wolfenbüttel, Germany) put together by famous collectors Julius (1528–89) and August II (1579–1666), Dukes of Brunswick-Lüneburg, still contains a large collection of catalogues sent over by several European book agents in charge of buying books for each collector. After the end of a sale, used catalogues could sometimes be archived by collectors and librarians and hence preserved.

There is also a clear discrepancy between the number of catalogues ascribed to male and female owners. As David Allan states:

> At the same time the nature of heritable property ordinarily descending under primogeniture also meant that documentary records tended by default to ascribe ownership to men even where female family members might in practice have been the most frequent users, even the original acquirers, of certain books.[39]

The case of the Bodleian copy of the catalogue of the library of Charles-Nicolas Huguet de Sémonville (died 1729) is quite extraordinary in this respect: unlike other known copies of this catalogue published in Paris in 1732, it also includes a supplement listing those of Huguet's widowed daughter, Charlotte-Madeleine, who died three years after her father.[40]

Printed catalogues of private libraries further present the problem of anonymity, as the name of the library owner is not always (fully) stated on the catalogue. Initials, personal details and handwritten annotations (as far as these can be trusted) can nevertheless give indications of his or her identity. This can be problematic for the history of reading, as it seems that some of these catalogues were purposefully attributed to private collectors when in fact they were composed of bookseller's stocks.

Linking books listed to specific owners can also be difficult in catalogues advertising more than one library. In France and the Dutch Republic, catalogue compilers usually divided collections according to ownership. In the British Isles, however, the contents of multiple libraries were often rearranged in one list. London bookseller James Buckland mixed several libraries when he compiled a sale catalogue of the libraries of Dissenting ministers John Killinghal and Edward Bentley along with those of 'several other eminent persons deceased'.[41] None of the descriptions of the 1,089 lots indicates who the actual owner of each item was.

Despite all these shortcomings, pitfalls, problems and exceptions, printed catalogues of private libraries remain a unique and rich source for the study of the history of books and readers, thanks to several interrelated factors:

1. *Numbers*. Thousands of catalogues of private libraries were printed in France, the Dutch Republic and the British Isles in the long eighteenth century. Although no surviving copies have (yet) been identified for a large proportion of them, the corpus of catalogues at our disposal is extremely rich. It is biased towards large catalogues and prestigious collections, but we can find records of smaller and more humble collections, especially from the mid-eighteenth century onwards, when the population of book owners became increasingly heterogeneous.[42]

2. *Accessibility*. Unlike most manuscript catalogues and probate inventories, printed catalogues were generally produced in multiple copies, increasing their chances of being preserved.[43] Thanks to the recognisable template of their titles and because they are books, printed catalogues of private libraries are easier to track down in catalogues of public collections than manuscript lists of books hidden within probate inventories, the latter not often being itemised in notarial archives. Further, many printed library catalogues from the seventeenth century onwards are now available online in specialised repositories like BSCO and the Philosophical

Libraries project and in databases such as Google Books, EEBO, ECCO or Gallica.

3. *Density of the information provided.* Taking into account the other factors, private library catalogues provide a quick and unique overview of what individual collections probably looked like at a certain point in time. Admittedly, ego-documents give an insight into which books were actually read and convey a better idea of reading experiences and practices. But these sources are rare and generally focus on few specific titles. Meanwhile, catalogues of stocks and new publications of booksellers do not provide information on buyers.

4. *Bibliographical detail.* Library catalogues generally give more detailed descriptions of the editions that were owned than probate inventories and ego-documents. Besides specifications regarding the format, number of volumes, place and date of publications of some books, private library catalogues often indicate special characteristics of individual copies, noting their physical appearance, such as the type of binding or the type of paper, and recording whether pages or volumes are missing.

5. *An insight into the second-hand book trade.* Sale catalogues of private libraries give us an insight into the recirculation of books. They offer information about the provenance of certain copies, especially those that were annotated or owned by famous persons, and thus enable us to follow the footsteps of particular books.[44] Further, the practice of naming the retailers of the catalogue illuminates (trans)national networks of booksellers and other book agents.

6. *Annotated prices.* The first thing scrawled prices can reveal is whether a specific book of the collection was actually bought or not. The handwritten prices in the margins of a copy of the catalogue of the collection of Balthazar Boreel (1673–1744) given to his widow as proof of the auction results clearly show that not all the books were sold.[45] The study of the variation of prices for similar editions and titles over a long period of time and in different countries could also help estimate the fluctuating demand for certain works and editions. There is, however, considerable difficulty in interpreting any price.[46] The fact that some catalogues display two sets of manuscript prices, on the left and right margins of the text, only adds to this problem. When the catalogue itself does not provide further information, one can only speculate what both sets represent. Moreover, comparison of several copies of the same catalogue can bring to light inexplicable differences between the prices recorded.[47]

7. *Named purchasers*. Margins of commercial catalogues sometimes display handwritten names or scribbled initials. These could refer to the people who bought the lots advertised or to the commissioners representing them.[48] If the names of those identified as individual buyers reappear several times during a sale or in different catalogues, the catalogues can help us to get an idea of specific reading interests.
8. *Further studies*. Catalogues contain (mostly anonymous) comments that provide valuable bits of information for the study of the history of the book and reception studies. These annotations can pertain to the state or rarity of a certain copy, the quality of a particular edition, the description of the item or the withdrawal of an item from the sale. The unknown owner of numerous eighteenth-century catalogues published in Lille apparently used them as a checklist, crossing out titles he already possessed himself (or didn't want?) and indicating those he could find elsewhere, for example in the collection of his brother Joseph.[49] Lastly, bored readers and children seem to have left existential questions and 'artistic' doodles in catalogues.

To conclude, catalogues of private libraries are a rich source in spite of their pitfalls. With the right methods, they can be used successfully to study questions such as the developing composition of readerships, bestselling literature and the existence of shared reading interests. In this context, we want to point out that the history of reading does not necessarily have to be limited to the actual act of reading. Indeed, researchers like Philippe Martin and Pierre Bayard have noted various and differing levels in the 'appropriation' of books.[50] The starting point of our own research has been a long-debated question: what did people read in the eighteenth century, or, more accurately, what did people actually read in a period that we now call the Age of Enlightenment? Earlier uses of catalogues were limited in scope due to practical difficulties mostly related to a time-consuming manual approach. The ongoing digitisation of historical library catalogues and the democratisation of digital tools allow for large-scale studies of catalogues. With its purpose-built digital database, a data-driven project like MEDIATE has the potential to confirm or challenge traditional narratives of the reception of books, readership composition and readers' tastes in Europe.[51] Full transcriptions of catalogues of private libraries will allow us to map the presence of books and authors in thousands of eighteenth-century homes across Europe.[52] This bottom-up approach first will allow us to identify works that were commercially successful at the time but have since been almost forgotten. Second, prosopographical studies of groups of owners defined by location, gender, profession, religious denomination, political and other affiliations might bring to light unexpected shared affinities for certain authors, books and genres. Meanwhile, each discrepancy and deviation might indicate a personal reading interest. Finally, bringing together and analysing data from several regions will provide us with a solid base for the study of transregional phenomena in the history of reading.

Notes

This project has received funding from the European Research Council (ERC) under the European Union's Horizon 2020 research and innovation program under grant agreement No. 682022. We would like to thank Alicia Montoya, Joanna Rozendaal, Anna de Wilde and Evelien Chayes for their comments on earlier versions of this chapter.

1. For a typology of relevant sources, see István Monok, *Könyvkatalógusok és könyvjegyzékek Magyarországon, 1526–1720, Forrástipológia, forráskritika, forráskiadás* (Szeged: Scriptum, 1993), pp. 93–5 (summary in German).
2. Daniel Mornet, 'Les enseignements des bibliothèques privées (1750–1780)', *Revue d'histoire littéraire de la France*, 17 (1910), pp. 449–96. Our chapter does not aim to give an exhaustive list of all publications related to printed catalogues of libraries used as a book historical source. However, it offers an overview of the work undertaken in the field of early modern private libraries that complements István Monok's 'Les bibliothèques privées et la lecture à l'époque moderne: un apercu des orientations de la recherche en Europe, 1958–2008', in Dominique Varry (ed.), *50 ans d'histoire du livre: 1958–2008* (Lyon: Enssib, 2014), pp. 140–56.
3. Mornet, 'Les enseignements', pp. 492–6.
4. Sophie A. Krijn, 'Franse lektuur in Nederland in het begin van de 18e eeuw', *De Nieuwe Taalgids*, 11 (1917), pp. 161–78.
5. Harold Mattingly and Ian A. K. Burnett, *List of Catalogues of English Book Sales, 1676–1900, now in the British Museum* (London: British Museum, Department of Printed books, 1915). See also Martinho da Fonseca, *Lista de alguns catálogos de bibliothecas públicas e particulares de livreiros e alfarrabistas* (Lisbon: Libanio da Silva, 1913).
6. For example: George L. McKay, *American Book Auction Catalogues, 1713–1934* (New York: New York Public Library, 1937); Antonio Rodríguez Moñino, *Catálogos de libreros españoles, 1661–1798: intento bibliográfico* (Madrid: Tip. de los Sucesores de J. Sánchez Ocaña,

1942); *Catálogos de libreros españoles, 1661–1840: intento bibliográfico* (Madrid: Langa, 1945); and Walter Gobbers, *Jean-Jacques Rousseau in Holland. Een onderzoek naar de invloed van de mens en het werk (ca. 1760–ca. 1810)* (Ghent: Koninklijke Vlaamse Academie voor Taal- en Letterkunde, 1963).

7. Archer Taylor, *Book Catalogues: Their Varieties and Uses* (Chicago: Newberry Library, 1957); Graham Pollard and Albert Ehrman, *The Distribution of Books by Catalogue from the Invention of Printing to A.D. 1800: Based on Material in the Broxbourne Library* (Cambridge: Printed for presentation to members of the Roxburghe Club, 1965); François Furet (ed.), *Livre et société dans la France du XVIIIe siècle* (Paris: Mouton, 1965). See also Émile Dacier, 'Des livres précieux sans en avoir l'air: les anciens catalogues de vente', *Bulletin du bibliophile*, 3 (1952), pp. 117–42; Sears Jayne, *Library Catalogues of the English Renaissance* (Berkeley/Los Angeles: University of California Press, 1956).

8. For example: Michel Marion, *Les Bibliothèques privées à Paris au milieu du XVIIIe siècle* (Paris: BnF, 1978); Jean Quéniart, *Culture et société urbaines dans la France de l'Ouest au XVIIIe siècle* (Paris: Klincksieck, 1978); Elisabeth S. Leedham-Green, *Books in Cambridge Inventories: Book-Lists from Vice-Chancellor's Court Probate Inventories in the Tudor and Stuart Periods* (Cambridge: Cambridge University Press, 1986); Robert J. Fehrenbach and Elisabeth S. Leedham-Green (eds), *Private Libraries in Renaissance England: A Collection and Catalogue of Tudor and Early Stuart Book-Lists* (Binghamton: Medieval & Renaissance Texts & Studies, 1992–2004, and online <https://plre.folger.edu>, accessed 15 August 2019); Henrik Grönroos and Ann-Charlotte Nyman, *Boken i Finland. Bokbeståndet hos borgerskap, hantverkare och lägre sociala grupper i Finlands städer enligt städernas bouppteckningar 1656–1809* (Helsinki: Svenska litteratursällskapet i Finland, 1996); Karin M. P. Strengers-Olde Kalter, 'Boeken in Bossche boedels. De belangstelling voor lectuur in de achttiende eeuw', *Noordbrabants Historisch Jaarboek*, 14 (1998), pp. 143–79; José de Kruif, *Liefhebbers en gewoontelezers: leescultuur in Den Haag in de achttiende eeuw* (Zutphen: Walburg Pers, 1999); Ruud Lambour, 'Het boekenbezit van Amsterdamse doopsgezinden uit de Gouden Eeuw', *Doopsgezinde Bijdragen Nieuwe Reeks*, 40 (2014), pp. 135–60; Federica Dallasta, *Eredità di carta. Biblioteche private e circolazione libraria nella Parma farnesiana (1545–1731)* (Milan: Franco Angeli, 2010); Gina Dahl, *Book Collections of Clerics in Norway, 1650–1750* (Leiden: Brill, 2010); and Mari Tarvas (ed.), *Bibliothekskataloge der Tallinner Literaten des 18. Jahrhunderts. Quellenedition aufgrund überlieferter Nachlassverzeichnisse, herausgegeben, kommentiert und mit einer Einführung und einem Index versehen* (Würzburg: Königshausen und Neumann, 2014). See also Günter Berger, 'Inventare als Quelle der Sozialgeschichte des Lesens', *Romantische Zeitschrift für Literaturgeschichte*, 5 (1981), pp. 368–80.

9. Dominique Varry, 'Aperçu sur les bibliothèques privées de l'Eure confisquées sous la Révolution', *Annales de Normandie*, 45:3 (1995), pp. 327–8.
10. For works dealing primarily with questions regarding methodology and the source material itself, see, among others: Reinhard Wittmann (ed.), *Bücherkataloge als buchgeschichtliche Quellen in der frühen Neuzeit* (Wiesbaden: O. Harrassowitz, 1984); Sears Jayne, *Library Catalogues of the English Renaissance*, 2nd edition (Godalming: St Paul's Bibliographies, 1983); Archer Taylor, *Book Catalogues: Their Varieties and Uses*, 2nd edition, revised by Wm. P. Barlow Jr (Winchester: St Edmundsbury Press, 1986); Yann Sordet, 'Une approche des "catalogues domestiques" de bibliothèques privées (XVIIe–XVIIIe siècle), instruments et miroirs de collections particulières', *Bulletin du bibliophile*, 1 (1997), pp. 92–123; Malcolm Walsby, 'Book Lists and Their Meaning', in Malcolm Walsby and Natasha Constantinidou (eds), *Documenting the Early Modern Book World: Inventories and Catalogues in Manuscript and Print* (Leiden: Brill, 2013), pp. 1–24; Frédéric Barbier, Thierry Dubois and Yann Sordet (eds), *De l'argile au nuage: une archéologie des catalogues (2e millénaire av. J-C – 21e siècle). Catalogue de l'exposition* (Paris: Bibliothèque Mazarine/Bibliothèque de Genève, Éditions des Cendres, 2015); Anja Dular, 'Problematika raziskovanja zgodovine zasebnih knjižnic – zanke in uganke [Problems Arising When Researching the History of Private Libraries – Traps and Puzzles]', *Knjižnica*, 59:3 (2015), pp. 17–32; Flavia Bruni and Andrew Pettegree (eds), *Lost Books: Reconstructing the Print World of Pre-Industrial Europe* (Leiden: Brill, 2016); Hartmut Beyer, Katrin Schmidt, Jörn Münkner and Timo Steyer, 'Bibliotheken im Buch: Die Erschließung von privaten Büchersammlungen der Frühneuzeit über Auktionskataloge', in Hannah Busch, Franz Fischer and Patrick Sahle (eds), *Kodikologie und Paläographie im digitalen Zeitalter* (Norderstedt: Books on Demand, 2017), vol. IV, pp. 43–70. With regard to conferences, the 'Invitational Conference on Book Catalogues: Their Collecting, Preservation, Cataloguing and Use', held at the Grolier Club in New York City in January 1995 (see 'Book Catalogues, Today and Tomorrow: Reports and Presentations from the 1995 BSA Conference', *Papers of the Bibliographical Society of America (PBSA)*, 89:4 (1995)), was the first of many gatherings of academics and librarians around the subject of printed catalogues and book sales. See for example: Annie Charon and Élisabeth Parinet (eds), *Les ventes de livres et leurs catalogues: XVIIe–XXe siècle. Actes des journées organisées par l'Ecole nationale des chartes (Paris, 15 janvier 1998) et par l'ENSSIB (Villeurbanne, 22 janvier 1998)* (Paris: École nationale des chartes, 2000); Robin Myers, Michael Harris and Giles Mandelbrote (eds), *Under the Hammer: Book Auctions since the Seventeenth Century* (New Castle, DE: Oak Knoll Press; and London: British Library, 2001); 'Book Catalogues, Tomorrow and Beyond: Proceedings of the 2008 Conference Sponsored by the Grolier Club and the Bibliographical Society',

Papers of the Bibliographical Society of America (PBSA), 102:4 (2008), pp. 541–80; and the conference 'Selling and Collecting: Printed Book Sale Catalogues and Private Libraries in Early Modern Europe', University of Cagliari, 20–21 September 2017.

11. For example: Michel Marion, *Collections et collectionneurs de livres au XVIIIe siècle* (Paris: H. Champion, 1999); Annie Charon, *Esprit des livres* (Paris: École nationale des chartes, 2015) – édition électronique at <https://elec.enc.sorbonne.fr/cataloguevente> (accessed 15 August 2019); the Philosophical Libraries project (Pisa) at <http://picus.unica.it> (accessed 15 August 2019); David Pearson's project on English book owners in the seventeenth century at http://www.bibsoc.org.uk/content/english-book-owners-seventeenth-century (accessed 15 August 2019); David Pearson, 'The English Private Library in the 17th Century', *Library*, 14:4 (2012), pp. 379–99; and the Early Modern Scholars' Libraries Project (Wolfenbüttel) at <http://www.hab.de/de/home/wissenschaft/forschungsprofil-und-projekte/fruehneuzeitliche-gelehrtenbibliotheken.html> (accessed 15 August 2019). There has also been a flood of micro-studies using published catalogues to investigate early modern book collections owned by individuals or specific groups (women, scholars, writers, medical doctors, clergymen, members of different religious denominations, aristocrats). For two early national overviews see: Wolfgang Adam, 'Privatbibliotheken im 17. und 18. Jahrhundert. Forschungsbericht 1975–1988', *Internationales Archiv für Sozialgeschichte der Deutschen Literatur*, 15:1 (1990), pp. 123–73; and Henk W. de Kooker and Bert van Selm, *Boekcultuur in de Lage Landen, 1500–1800: bibliografie van publikaties over particulier boekenbezit in Noord- en Zuid-Nederland, verschenen voor 1991* (Utrecht: HES, 1983).

12. This is for instance the case for: Hans Dieter Gebauer, *Bücherauktionen in Deutschland im 17. Jahrhundert* (Bonn: Bouvier, 1981); Bert van Selm, *Een menighte treffelijcke boecken: Nederlandse boekhandelscatalogi in het begin van de zeventiende eeuw* (Utrecht: HES, 1987); Myers, Harris and Mandelbrote (eds), *Under the Hammer*; Lis Byberg, *Brukte bøker til bymann og bonde: bokauksjoner i den norske litterære offentlighet 1750–1815* (Oslo: Det Humanistiske Fakultet, Universitetet i Oslo, 2007); Pedro Rueda Ramírez, 'Libros venales. Los catálogos de los libreros andaluces (siglos XVII–XVIII)', *Estudios Humanísticos. Historia*, 11 (2012), pp. 195–222; Iwona Imánska, *Per medium auctionis: aukcje książek w Rzeczypospolitej (XVII-XVIII w.)* [*Per medium auctionis; Book Auctions in the Polish Commonwealth (17th–18th Centuries)*] (Toruń: Wydawnictwo Naukowe UMK, 2013); and Pedro Rueda Ramírez and Lluís Agustí (eds), *La publicidad del libro en el mundo hispánico (siglos XVII–XX): Catálogos de venta de libreros y editors* (Barcelona: Calambur, 2016). See also Cynthia Wall, 'The English Auction: Narrative of Dismantlings', *Eighteenth-Century Studies*, 31:1 (1997), pp. 1–25.

13. For example, in: Friedhelm Beckmann, *Französische Privatbibliotheken:*

Untersuchungen zu Literatursystematik und Buchbesitz im 18. Jahrhundert (Frankfurt am Main: Buchhändler Vereinigung, 1988); Valérie Neveu, 'L'inscription de la classification bibliographique dans le champ des sciences (fin XVIIe–début XVIIIe s.)', November 2010, Angers, France, at <https://halshs.archives-ouvertes.fr/halshs-00599276> (accessed 15 August 2019); Emmanuelle Chapron, 'Circulation et usages des catalogues de bibliothèques dans l'Europe du XVIIIe siècle', in Frédéric Barbier and Andrea De Pasquale (eds), *Un'istituzione dei Lumi: la biblioteca. Teoria, gestione e pratiche biblioteconomiche nell'Europa dei Lumi* (Parma: Museo Bodoniano, 2013), pp. 29–49; Emmanuelle Chapron, 'Monde savant et ventes de bibliothèques en France méridionale dans la seconde moitié du XVIIIe siècle', *Annales du Midi*, 283 (2013), pp. 409–29.

14. See, for example: Anne François, 'Les collections privées de livres et d'instruments de musique au travers des catalogues de vente bruxellois, durant les règnes de Marie-Thérèse et Joseph II d'Autriche (1740–1790)', *Études sur le 18e siècle*, 19 (1992), pp. 79–82; Helwi Blom, 'La présence de romans de chevalerie dans les bibliothèques privées des XVIIe et XVIIIe siècles', in Thierry Delcourt and Élisabth Parinet (eds), *La Bibliothèque bleue et les littératures de colportage* (Paris: École des Chartes/La maison du boulanger, 2000), pp. 51–67; Alicia C. Montoya, 'French and English Women Writers in Dutch Library Catalogues, 1700–1800: Some Methodological Considerations and Preliminary Results', in Suzan van Dijk, Petra Broomans, Janet F. van der Meulen and Pim van Oostrum (eds), *'I Have Heard About You'. Foreign Women's Writing Crossing the Dutch Border: From Sappho to Selma Lagerlöf* (Hilversum: Verloren, 2004), pp. 182–216; Paul J. Smith, 'La présence de la littérature française renaissante dans les catalogues des ventes aux enchères en Hollande au XVIIe siècle. Bilan et perspectives', *Renaissance and Reformation/Renaissance et Reforme*, 34:3 (2011), pp. 185–202; Charon, *Esprit des livres* (manuscripts); the Philosophical Libraries project (philosophical works).

15. For example, the Bibliothèque Mazarine en ligne at <http://www.bibliotheque-mazarine.fr/fr/evenements/projets/bibliotheque-de-mazarin-en-ligne>; Montesquieu. Bibliothèque & éditions at <http://montesquieu.huma-num.fr/bibliotheque/introduction>; and the project Bibliothèques Privées à l'Âge Moderne (BIPrAM) at <https://cahier.hypotheses.org/bipram> (all accessed 15 August 2019).

16. See Antonio Rodríguez Moñino, *Historia de los catálogos de librería españoles (1661–1840): estudio bibliográfico* (Madrid: Artes Gráficas Soler, 1966); Christian Péligry, *Les catalogues de bibliothèques du XVIIe, XVIIIe et XIXe siècles, jusqu'en 1815: contribution à l'inventaire du Fonds ancien de la Bibliothèque Municipale de Toulouse* (Toulouse: Bibliothèque municipale de Toulouse, 1974); Elizabeth Webby, 'A Checklist of Early Australian Booksellers' and Auctioneers' Catalogues

and Advertisements: 1800–1849' (in three parts), *Bulletin of the Bibliographical Society of Australia and New Zealand*, 3 (1978), pp. 123–48; 4:1 (1979), pp. 31–66; 4:2 (1979), pp. 95–150; Alan N. L. Munby and Lenore Coral (eds), *British Book Sale Catalogues 1676–1800: A Union List* (London: Mansell, 1977); Jeanne Blogie, *Répertoire des catalogues de ventes de livres imprimés* (Brussels: Fl. Tulkens, 1982–2003); Frans Vandenhole, *Inventaris van veilingcatalogi 1615–1914 met topografische, alfabetische en inhoudsindexen* (Ghent: Rijksuniversiteit te Gent, 1987); Maria G. Ceccarelli, *Vocis et animarum pinacothecae. Cataloghi di biblioteche private dei secoli XVII–XVIII nei fondi dell'Angelica* (Roma: Istituto poligrafico e Zecca dello Stato, 1990); Françoise Bléchet, *Les ventes publiques de livres en France, 1630–1750: répertoire des catalogues conservés à la Bibliothèque Nationale* (Oxford: Voltaire Foundation, 1991); Gerhard Loh, *Verzeichnis der Kataloge von Buchauktionen und Privatbibliotheken aus dem deutschsprachigen Raum* (Leipzig: Universitätsbibliothek Leipzig, 1995–); Gerhard Loh, *Die europäischen Privatbibliotheken und Buchauktionen. Ein Verzeichnis ihrer Kataloge* (Leipzig: Universitätsbibliothek Leipzig, 1996–); J. A. (Hans) Gruys and Henk W. de Kooker (eds), *Book Sales Catalogues of the Dutch Republic, 1599–1800: Guide* (Leiden: IDC Publishers, 1997). See also the database 'Book Sales Catalogues Online' at <http://primarysources.brillonline.com/browse/book-sales-catalogues-online> (accessed 15 August 2019); Pierre Delsaerdt and Dries Vanysacker, 'Repertorium van Antwerpse boekenveilingen 1750–1800', *De Gulden Passer*, 75 (1997), pp. 5–119; the database of early modern sale catalogues conserved in Lyon and Grenoble hosted on the website of the Institut d'Histoire du Livre at <http://ihl.enssib.fr/bases-de-donnees/catalogue-de-vente-de-livres-anciens> (accessed 15 August 2019); Michael North, *Printed Catalogues of French Book Auctions and Sales by Private Treaty, 1643–1830, in the Library of the Grolier Club* (New York: Grolier Club, 2004); Harald Ilsøe, *Biblioteker til salg. Om danske bogauktioner og kataloger 1661–1811* (Copenhagen: Museum Tusculanums Forlag, København, 2007); Stefania Bergamo and Marco Callegari (eds), *Libri in vendita. Cataloghi librari nelle biblioteche padovane (1647–1850)* (Milan: Franco Angeli, 2009); Robin C. Alston, *Inventory of Sale Catalogues of Named and Attributed Owners of Books Sold by Retail or Auction 1676–1800: An Inventory of Sales in the British Isles, America, the United States, Canada, India* (Yeadon: privately printed for the author, 2010); Charon, *Esprit des livres*. Some of the studies of book owners and the nature of the collections also contain extensive bibliographical lists of catalogues. This is the case for: Mornet, 'Les enseignements'; Gebauer, *Bücherauktionen in Deutschland*; Beckmann, *Französische Privatbibliotheken*; Marion, *Collections et collectionneurs*. Printing auction catalogues of private libraries was mostly a Western European phenomenon, hence the scarcity of bibliographical lists of such publications for Eastern Europe.

A large corpus of handwritten book lists and catalogues from the region covered by the ancient Kingdom of Hungary has, however, been made available by the team of István Monok, at <http://real-eod.mtak.hu/view/series/Adatt=E1r_XVI-XVIII=2E_sz=E1zadi_szellemi_mozgalmaink_t=F6rt=E9net=E9hez.html> (accessed 15 August 2019).

17. Alicia Montoya, 'Middlebrow, Religion, and The European Enlightenment: A New Bibliometric Project, MEDIATE (1665–1820)', *French History and Civilization*, 7 (2017), pp. 66–79, at <http://h-france.net/rude/vol7/montoya7> (accessed 15 August 2019).

18. In this chapter we use the word 'catalogue' in its broad sense as 'descriptive list'. On terminological issues regarding lists of books, see: Marie-Renée Cazabon, 'Catalogue', in Pascal Fouché, Daniel Péchoin and Philippe Schuwer (eds), *Dictionnaire encyclopédique du livre* (Paris: Éditions du Cercle de la Librairie, 2002), vol. I, pp. 469–79; and Concepción Rodríguez Parada, 'Los catálogos e inventarios en la historia del libro y de las bibliotecas', *BiD: textos universitaris de biblioteconomia i documentación*, 18 (2007), at <http://www.ub.edu/bid/18rodri4.htm> (accessed 15 August 2019). See also Yann Sordet, 'Pour une histoire des catalogues de livres: matérialité, formes, usages', in Barbier, Dubois and Sordet (eds), *De l'argile au nuage*, pp. 15–46.

19. For an eloquent illustration, see the case of Pierre Adamoli studied by Yann Sordet, *L'Amour des livres au siècle des lumières. Pierre Adamoli et ses collections* (Paris: École des chartes, 2001).

20. Bléchet, *Les ventes publiques de livres en France*; Charon, *Esprit des livres*.

21. Nicole Masson, 'Typologie des catalogues de vente', in Charon and Parinet (eds), *Les ventes de livres*, pp. 119–27.

22. *A Catalogue of the Entire and Valuable Library of the Late Rev. Michael Lort* (London: Leigh and Sotheby, 1791).

23. See, for example: Abigail Williams, *The Social Life of Books: Reading Together in the Eighteenth-Century Home* (New Haven: Yale University Press, 2017).

24. Alphonse Dupront, 'Livre et culture dans la société française du XVIIIe siècle. Réflexion sur une enquête', in Furet (ed.), *Livre et société dans la France du XVIIIe siècle*, pp. 185–238.

25. Jean de La Bruyère, *Les Caractères* [. . .], ed. Louis Van Delft (Paris: Imprimerie nationale, 1998), ch. 13,' De la Mode', part 2, p. 416.

26. Jean Lepautre, *La Folie du siècle* (Paris: Jollain, 1664), plate III, reproduced in Jean-Marc Chatelain, *La bibliothèque de l'honnête homme: livres, lectures et collection en France à l'âge classique* (Paris: BnF, 2003). The quatrain under the image says: 'C'est bien le plus grand fou qui soit dans la nature/Que celui qui se plaist aux livres bien dorez,/Bien couvers, bien reliez, bien nets, bien époudrez/Et ne les voit jamais que par la couverture'. The word 'bibliomania' (in the French form 'bibliomanie'), in the sense of excessive love of books, oriented especially towards qualities other than their contents, such as special bindings or rarity,

probably dates back to the seventeenth century. It appears in a letter written by Guy Patin in 1652 (dated 20 December), in which he refers to his 'caprieuse bibliomanie'. See *Correspondance française de Guy Patin*, ed. Loïc Capron (Paris: Bibliothèque interuniversitaire de santé, 2015). For a definition of the word see also Eliana Raytcheva, 'Bibliomane', in Fouché, Péchoin and Schuwer (eds), *Dictionnaire encyclopédique du livre*, vol. 1, pp. 279–80.

27. *Menagiana* (Paris: Florentin et Pierre Delaulne, 1693), p. 257.
28. Otto Lankhorst, 'Dutch Book Auctions in the Seventeenth and Eighteenth Centuries', in Myers, Harris and Mandelbrote (eds), *Under the Hammer*, pp. 65–88.
29. Hannie van Goinga, *Alom te bekomen: veranderingen in de boekdistributie in de Republiek 1720–1800* (Amsterdam: De Buitenkant, 1999), pp. 185–9.
30. *A Catalogue of the Entire Library of the Reverend Conyers Middleton, D.D.* [. . .] (London: Samuel Baker, 1750–1).
31. For example: North, *Printed Catalogues of French Book Auctions*, nos 92, 97 and 99. See also the copy of the *Catalogue des livres, tableaux, estampes et desseins de feu M. Gersaint, dont la vente se fera en détail lundi 25 mai 1750* [. . .] *en sa maison Pont Notre-Dame* in the National Library of Florence at <https://books.google.nl/books?id=ZEBfKFioKB4C&> (accessed 15 August 2019). It contains a handwritten list of seventy-two books with the remark: 'Ces livres défendus n'étaient pas compris dans le catalogue de Mr. Gersaint et la vente en fut faite en cachette dans le souterrain de la maison' ('These forbidden books were not listed in Mr. Gersaint's catalogue and the sale was done secretly in the basement of the house').
32. *A Catalogue of the Town-library of the Late Sir William Burrell* [. . .] (London, 1786).
33. *Catalogue des livres de la bibliothèque de feu M.L.B.D.* [. . .] (Paris: Méquignon, 1792), p. 60.
34. An item sold in 1706 and simply titled as 'New Inventions' could refer to dozens of books printed before it was sold. See *A Curious Collection of Choice Books, being the Library of Thomas Kirke* (Leeds, 1706).
35. It is impossible to identify, for example, items listed as 'five books on British History' and 'Ten ditto on Foreign History' in *Catalogue of the Valuable Library . . . of the Late Holland Watson, Esq.* (Liverpool: Branch & Son, 1829), p. 8.
36. Jean Flouret, 'La bibliothèque de Richelieu', *Revue française d'histoire du livre*, 24 (1979), 615.
37. Gruys, 'Rijklof Michael van Goens', pp. 150–6.
38. Dominique Varry, 'Grandes collections et bibliothèques des élites', in Claude Joly (ed.), *Histoire des bibliothèques françaises* (Paris: Electre, 2008), vol. II, pp. 295–323 (p. 302).
39. David Allan, 'Book-Collecting and Literature in Eighteenth-Century

Britain', in *The Yearbook of English of English Studies*, 45 (2015), pp. 74–92 (p. 76).
40. 'Supplement au catalogue des livres de M. Huguet de Semonville, contenant Ceux de feuë Madame la Marquise de Costentin, sa Fille', in *Catalogus librorum ill. viri d. Caroli-Nicolai Huguet de Semonville, senatus parisiensis decani* (Paris: Gabriel Martin et Louis Guérin, 1732), pp. 141–56, also available at <https://books.google.nl/books?id=4jJbAAAAQAAJ&> (accessed 15 August 2019).
41. *A Catalogue of the Libraries of . . . Mr. J. Killinghal, of Southwark; Mr. E. Bentley, of Coggeshall; and Several Other Eminent Persons Deceased* (London: James Buckland, 1741).
42. Among the owners of book collections advertised in catalogues printed in France during the second half of the eighteenth century we find numerous merchants, pharmacists, artists, a peddler and a painter.
43. The scarce information we have on print runs of published catalogues indicates that they could vary considerably.
44. On the subject of medieval works and works owned by famous collectors, see: Roger Middleton, 'Chrétien de Troyes at Auction: Nicolas-Joseph Foucault and Other Eighteenth-Century Collectors', in Peter Damian-Grint (ed.), *Medievalism and 'manière gothique' in Enlightenment France* (Oxford: Voltaire Foundation, 2006), pp. 261–83. In one particular case, a handwritten note on the title page of the catalogue seems to allow us to follow the journey of what appears to be a complete library from one owner to another. It claims that the books in the library of Laetitia Wiggett, sold in 1790, were those of William Anderson, 'who died a young man, and left them to Mr. Wiggett' in 1767. If Mrs Wiggett, a Norwich resident, was indeed a patron of the local arts according to lists of subscribers printed in some volumes of poetry, all the books listed in this particular catalogue pre-date the death of Anderson, bar four dated 1768, 1771 and 1773. The content of the library hence makes the claim plausible. *A Catalogue of All the Entire and Well-chosen Library of the Late Mrs. Letitia Wiggett* (Norwich: Edward Crane, 1790).
45. *Catalogus Exquisitissimorum Librorum. Juridicorum, Historicorum, & Miscellaneorum [. . .] Heer Balthazar Boreel* (Amsterdam: Salomon Schouten, [1745]) (Amsterdam, City Archives, Bibliotheek F 526).
46. On the tricky subject of interpreting early modern book prices, see for example: J. E. Elliott, 'The Cost of Reading in Eighteenth-Century Britain: Auction Sale Catalogues and the Cheap Literature Hypothesis', *English Literary History*, 77:2 (2010), pp. 353–84; Francesco Ammannati and Angela Nuovo, 'Investigating Book Prices in Early Modern Europe: Questions and Sources', *Italian Journal of Library, Archives and Information Science (JLIS.it)*, 8:3 (2017), pp. 1–25.
47. For example: the *Bibliotheca Cantiana* (Leiden: Johannes Verbeek & Hermanus Verbeek, [1724]). Copies in: London, British Library: SC 434 and Manchester, Chetham's Library, Cc.7.51(3).

48. Marika Keblusek, 'Gekocht in Den Haag. Hertog August van Wolfenbüttel en de Haagse Elzeviers', in Berry Dongelmans, Paul Hoftijzer and Otto Lankhorst (eds), *Boekverkopers van Europa: het 17de-eeuwse Nederlandse uitgevershuis Elzevier* (Zutphen: Walburg Pers, 2000), pp. 211–24.
49. See the *Catalogue des livres curieux, qui se vendront dans la salle de l'Hôtel de Ville le 4 de Septembre 1713. delaissez par le Trépas de Mr. de Larre, vivant Pasteur de Verlenghem* (Lille, 1713), pp. 17, 21, 32, 34 (Lille, Méd. Jean Lévy, L8–564).
50. Philippe Martin, *Une religion des livres: 1640–1850* (Paris: Éditions du Cerf, 2003), pp. 523–64; Pierre Bayard, *Comment parler des livres que l'on n'a pas lus* (Paris: Les Éditions de Minuit, 2007).
51. For a project description, see <http://www.mediate18.nl> (accessed 15 August 2019).
52. In the early stages of our project, our research material tends to confirm signs of an ongoing democratisation of book ownership. Based on our corpus, people named on the title pages of seventeenth-century catalogues were mostly well known scholars, rich lawyers and high-ranking clergymen. This changes in the eighteenth century, when we find book owners from increasingly varied backgrounds. See De Kruif, *Liefhebbers en gewoontelezers*. See also Rolf Engelsing, 'Die Perioden der Lesergeschichte in der Neuzeit', in *Zur Sozialgeschichte deutscher Mittel- und Unterschichten* (Gottingen: Vandenhoeck und Ruprecht, 1973), pp. 112–54.

Chapter 13

Reading, Visual Literacy and the Illustrated Literary Text in Eighteenth-Century Britain

Sandro Jung

While histories of eighteenth-century reading traditionally focus on the literacy of manuscript or typographic text, these histories frequently assign a peripheral role to illustrations – despite the fact that the inclusion of illustrations in editions of literary texts entailed a conscious decision on the part of the publishers that added to the production cost of the work. Because books are affordable to some and not to others, the higher price of illustrated books affected access to these publications. This additional cost was warranted on the basis that illustrations could contribute to the brand identity of a book, especially when the volume was conceived as part of a series; but the embellishing function of the illustrations also helped booksellers to differentiate their volumes from others that were not distinguished by illustrations. Beyond serving the marketability of books, the role of illustrations was an interpretive, literacy-enhancing one: the non-typographical nature of the printed images necessitated a reflective engagement on the part of the reader, which relied on special skills to comprehend graphic representations that had their origins in the material culture and the relationships of readers' daily experience.

This chapter focuses on this literacy-enhancing function of book illustrations by offering accounts of eighteenth-century illustrated works for different audiences. It examines strategies used by illustrators to cater to different degrees of visual literacy, considers the importance of context for the reading of images and reflects on how both affect the reading experience. Building on Robert Hume's research into the cost of book consumption, including the correlation between book cost and buying power,[1] the chapter considers illustrated works produced for readers ranging across the economic spectrum of the book-buying public, from those untrained in symbolic forms of visual culture to those possessing complex literacy. Introducing case studies of three texts that were repeatedly illustrated throughout the eighteenth century – James Thomson's *The Seasons* (a series of four poems, each devoted to a different season and published between 1726 and 1730), Samuel Richardson's *Pamela* (1740) (an epistolary novel) and Salomon Gessner's *The Death of Abel* (1760) (the translation of the German biblical poem published in 1758) – it will examine the ways illustrations of these works catered to different consumer groups and shaped both the typographic and the visual literacy of their users. The term 'illustration' here means a printed image in a book and entertaining an interpretive relationship with the text visualised, which needs to be recovered by the reader.

A comparison of different modes of representation realised in and on different media using different technologies sheds light on the correlation between technology and readability. Visual literacy allows readers to bridge the mimetic distance between real-life objects and figures, on the one hand, and their being translated into the conventions of graphic design, on the other. It requires a suspension of disbelief, taking for granted that the figures and things imprinted on the planar surface of the page serve as placeholders for their three-dimensional real-life equivalents. In making sense of the printed image, readers recognise that compilations of different actions and objects need to be interrelated and be read as part of temporal and spatial frameworks that convey simultaneity or sequentiality. The often schematically created life-likeness of figures and objects in illustrations needs to be grounded in readers' own experience of the subjects depicted. In short, the experience of real persons and things needs to be reanimated and transferred to graphic representations.

Visual literacy entails a learning process in which printed illustrations are recognised as components of a larger world of images. Beyond this, it facilitates an understanding of illustrations as media engendering religious and other ideological messages and endowed with an affective and symbolic power. In this respect, an image of a mother with child, for example, can be just that, whereas it can also signify the codified mother of Christ with her son. Visual literacy not only is thus grounded in the textual realm of children's alphabet books, which instruct their users in the supposed congruence of image and text, but also is shaped by readers' exposure to images outside the book, in the shape of shop signs, public monuments and other material culture bearing visual embellishment. The more images a viewer encounters and recalls, the more complex associations among images become. Thus visual literacy operates mnemonically by recovering meanings, by identifying their suitability in their application to an image viewed, and by assembling these meanings into new meanings.

Research on book illustrations has too often been subject to what Jonathan Rose has termed 'receptive fallacy'.[2] The majority of modern critical readers engaged in the study of text–image relations seek to locate particularised relationships between text and book illustration. Too frequently they assume that, in an illustrated edition, an exclusive closed-circuit relationship existed between text and image. They frequently take for granted that the image was specifically produced to accompany the printed text, and that the image distinguished itself from others and was unique, thereby associating a particular reading experience with the illustrated edition. Such reading for uniqueness is justified if the focus is on a single edition that is understood in isolation from other editions. It falls short of recognising and acknowledging the historical realities of the opportunistic and responsive use of images, where each image is generated in the knowledge of and with reference to earlier ones. Equally, it does not help us understand how pervasive interpretive book illustrations were in the shaping of visual literacy through the probing of illustrations in search of their meaning(s).

In the eighteenth century, literary book illustrations were characterised by a mobility and versatility which, through the mechanisms of reprinting and recycling in adapted form, made possible their appearance in different editions of the same work issued by different publishers. More than that, their mobility was not limited to the medium of the literary edition, but it extended to other print forms, such as periodicals and anthologies, in which illustrations functioned differently from the text–image relationship of an edition of a single author. This mobility also, on occasion, operated transnationally, in that printed images conceived and published in Britain were reused and appropriated, for example, in America. The same illustrations were, at times, used to adorn editions of different texts.

The limitations of illustration studies are highlighted when, rather than seeking to recover historical reading experience and practices of image use, its exponents categorically presuppose the complex meaning of an image which an ideal reader ostensibly constructed. We assume that an illustration has a single meaning, when in fact the same images in different contexts generate different meanings. The reprinting of illustrations, as well as the technologies used to reproduce them (the copper-engraved illustration as opposed to the woodcut, for instance), thus can alter the functions and meanings assigned to these illustrations.

One example will suffice to illustrate that different uses of the same designs will create unique meanings. In the course of the year

1792, the London painter Thomas Stothard designed a series of twenty-four vignettes (each measuring 4.2 cm × 2.5 cm) for the 1793 edition of Thomas Baker's annual *The Royal Engagement Pocket Atlas*.[3] These miniature illustrations, engraved by William Angus, visualised scenes from Thomson's *The Seasons* and carried poetic quotations as captions. The vignettes were at the head of the memorandum pages of the *Atlas* and familiarised the attentive reader with a serial narrative supported by snippets of poetry which readers may or may not have recalled from prior readings of the poem or similar visual renderings they had encountered elsewhere. The tonal fineness of the copper-engraved vignettes underpinned their status as part of a culture of conspicuous consumption, and the memorandum book, which retailed at prices of between 3s. 6d. and 10s.6d., depending on the binding, catered to those with sufficient income and leisure to require this kind of ego-document. The memorandum portion of the publication provided space to record appointments and allow the organisation of one's time. However, the focus on the daily activities of life was qualified by the presence of the vignettes and the invitation to pause and reflect on their meaning, especially in relation to the poetry captions. Whereas the *Pocket Atlas* was significantly cheaper than the edition of *The Seasons* (12s.6d.) which John Stockdale published in London in 1794 and which included fourteen full-page plates by Stothard, it nevertheless mediated a pictorial narrative of the poem to a privileged readership.[4] Stothard's two sets of illustrations differ fundamentally from one another due to their different designs and size, the plates for Stockdale's edition measuring 7.2 cm × 12 cm, but also due to the particular text–image frameworks they are embedded in. In subject, too, the two sets of illustrations differ, for Stothard adopts the romantic-sentimental as the predominant mode for his plates for Stockdale. Death and tragedy are absent from his designs.

Thomson's work had readers among all classes, subject to their ability to purchase belles-lettres. An eighteenth-century reader may have been familiar with an extensive archive of illustrations of Thomson's work that both adorned books and were issued and sold separately. Reprinted several times, Joseph Wenman's 1785 pocket edition, which retailed at a price of 9d., reached a large number of readers and introduced them to the signature episode of Celadon and Amelia, which was illustrated numerous times throughout the eighteenth and nineteenth centuries. The volume boasted a frontispiece which mediated Thomson's poem via the sensual depiction of the dead Amelia with bare bosom on display (Figure 13.1). Apart from the lower quality of the engraving, Wenman's frontispiece – in contrast

Figure 13.1 Frontispiece, *The Seasons* (London: Joseph Wenman, 1785). Reproduced from a copy in the author's collection

to Stothard's designs for Stockdale's edition – focused readerly attention through the sensational death of Amelia after being struck by lightning. Wenman's was among the cheapest illustrated editions of *The Seasons* in the century. Whereas Wenman offered a full-page rendering of Amelia's eroticised body, Stothard's illustrations in the *Pocket Atlas* avoided the erotic. Few readers would have purchased the *Pocket Atlas* specifically for its vignette series, but the appeal of Wenman's frontispiece may have induced purchasers to choose his edition from among those competing.

Stothard's illustrations for the *Pocket Atlas* relied on readers' progressive tracing of their subjects. They required a kind of attention and ability to decode his engraved miniature paintings that were significantly more demanding than the apprehension of the meaning of Wenman's frontispiece. Those who had purchased earlier numbers of the *Pocket Atlas* were aware of the publication boasting visual series of different literary texts, whereas those for whom the 1793 series was their first experience of the title would have been introduced to an unusual format of literary illustration that was significantly smaller than the copper-engraved illustrations generally commissioned for editions of literary texts. The latter group might have included those who, across the Atlantic, purchased and used the inaugural number of *The American Repository of Useful Information* for 1795. This was the only number of the annual to lift illustrations from Baker's *Pocket Atlas*, reprinting the designs for Thomson's poem but in a significantly less sophisticated manner than offered by the London engraver, William Angus.

Less than a year after their appearance in the *Pocket Atlas*, three of Stothard's vignettes were reprinted in 1793, not however in a periodical. They featured as part of the frontispiece of Robert Morison's quarto edition of *The Seasons*. From London, the images had thus travelled to Scotland, where Morison published his subscription edition in his native Perth. In the frontispiece, the three octagonal vignettes are reshaped into ovals resembling medallions or gems so as to fit into the pedestal design of the illustration. The serial character of the original images is eliminated, and they are introduced into a composite illustration. An elite edition, boasting eight full-page plates based on specially commissioned paintings by London artists Richard Corbould and Charles Catton, at a price of £1.5s., the Morison edition would have been out of the reach of many. Compared with the large plates, the three vignettes in the frontispiece would have attracted little attention and would have been primarily decorative.

Four of Stothard's vignettes appear again in an 1804 edition of *The Seasons* that was published by the London-based booksellers J. Brambles, A. Meggitt, and J. Waters. This edition, in duodecimo, was significantly cheaper than Morison's, each number of which sold for 5s.3d.[5] Stothard's vignettes here are no longer realised in copper engravings, which made them so attractive in the *Pocket Atlas*. Rather, they are simplified woodcuts and appear as headpieces at the start of each of the seasons. These illustrations are complemented by a set of four full-page illustrations designed by John Burnet and engraved by Robert Scott, both Scottish artisans. Since the woodcuts appeared, uncaptioned, at the start of each individual season, on pages that also contained text, readers would have encountered these illustrations in a way that did not establish a clear reference to the specific text illustrated – as Stothard had done via the poetry caption in the *Pocket Atlas*. Instead, the woodcuts served as synoptic gateways through which the text could be read. Their descriptive focus – depicting activities characteristic of each season – mediated experience with which the readers of the edition would be familiar.

The four copper-engraved plates – which likely were part of a more expensive variant of the edition, a cheaper one featuring only the woodcuts – introduced social scenes of happiness and sentiment, as well as family contentment. Only one full-page plate, that for 'Spring', introduces the shepherd leaving his cottage for work. The poetry captions with which the full-page engravings are supplied do not effectively gloss that which is being presented, and at times generate tension between the textual and visual narratives presented. The 'Autumn' plate, which renders a dancing scene, in fact requires the specific poetry caption in order to understand that the male dancer on the left represents a 'toil-strung youth'. By contrast, the simpler design of the woodcut headpieces based on Stothard's *Pocket Atlas* illustrations enables a straightforward attribution of meaning to what is being represented. The woodcut, in its ability to convey subjects simply, also became a medium that could be used not only to illustrate the text for which it was originally conceived, but also to visualise editions of cognate works which could be produced more cheaply if new designs did not need to be purchased. In this manner, woodcuts originally embellishing editions of *The Seasons* repeatedly featured in editions of Robert Bloomfield's *Farmer's Boy*.[6]

These illustrations usually lacked text-related specificity and instead used a modal representational repertoire that denominated images as pastoral, georgic, tragic or sentimental. These basic modes were known to readers of all classes through biblical and other religious images that readers would have encountered in ballads, chapbooks and school books. Examining the transfer of an image from one medium to another sheds light on the process of adapting the same image for different readerships. Whereas an artisan translated the copper-engraved design of Stothard into the medium of the woodcut, he retained the central focus on the subject, without introducing – with the exception of trees – any background paraphernalia. The added trees naturalised the images and anchored them in a reality that readers knew. They furthermore functioned as a framing device. By contrast, unnecessary detail, such as the many figures depicted in Stothard's ice-skating scene (Figure 13.2), are eliminated, resulting in a clear focus on the two individuals enjoying themselves on the ice

Reading, Visual Literacy and the Illustrated Literary Text   277

Figure 13.2 Vignette for January, *Royal Engagement Pocket Atlas for 1793*. Reproduced from a copy in the author's collection

Figure 13.3 Woodcut vignette, *The Seasons* (London: J. Brambles, A. Meggit, and J. Waters; Gainsborough: H. Mozley, 1804). Reproduced from a copy in the author's collection

(Figure 13.3). Similarly, Stothard's fairly complex, crowded composition of one of the June vignettes rendering a harvest scene is simplified in its woodcut adaptation, the engraver omitting one of the harvesters. The choice of the vignette designs for the 1804 edition ensured that the illustrations remained as general in their representation of the season as possible. This aim of introducing images that did not evoke specific association with the often anthologised and visualised interpolated episodes such as those of the Perishing Man in the snow (in 'Winter'), which was included in Stothard's 1797 series for the *Pocket Atlas*, thus underpinned the choice of the designs for the headpieces.

The reuse of (parts of) Stothard's vignette series for the *Pocket Atlas* by three publications reveals the versatility of book illustrations in general and of the vignette form in particular. Both English and American readers encountered the vignettes in pocket diaries and sought to make sense of them by relating their subjects to their prior reading experience (if any) of *The Seasons* or other images. Whereas the vignettes were centre stage in the pocket diaries, they were integrated, in the frontispiece to the Morison edition, into an image structure that supported a portrait of the poet, Thomson. They would thus have been secondary. In the 1804 pocket edition of *The Seasons*, they regained prominence at the start of each of the individual seasons, although readers would have lacked the interpretive cues of the pocket diary to offer specific interpretations of the subjects depicted.

The price of print commodities regulated their availability among different reading groups, and also affected the level of complexity of visual media contained in editions of literary works. The production cost of both the text and any illustrations accompanying the text had to allow a unit price that was sufficiently affordable to ensure the selling of all or most of the print run. One way to reduce the production cost of an illustrated book was to simplify the illustration. This simplification, first and foremost, related to the design itself, which could be executed more speedily in a woodcut than in a more compositionally and tonally complex copper engraving. While readers unable to purchase expensive subscription editions such as Robert Morison's may have possessed a degree of visual literacy that would have enabled them to make sense of the high-cultural moments of leisure and sentiment visualised by Catton and Corbould, books with less costly illustrations usually included simpler illustrations which did not require sophisticated interpretive skills. In this respect, book illustrations are highly context dependent, their meaning affected by the ways in which they are technologically realised and related to the text they visualise. They carry meanings that are constructed within the codex but rely on the conventions of extratextual visual culture for readers to apprehend links between the world depicted in the book and the real world.

The cost of an illustration thus determines its detail and complexity, as well as the quality of the engraving and its printing. It affects the readability of illustrations. Those with less disposable income were less able to purchase books that boasted many illustrations, and if they did purchase illustrated works these would likely have been down-market editions in which the images were straightforwardly representational, as opposed to the more metaphorical and symbolical renderings in up-market books.

The particular representational manner adopted frequently reflected the level of visual literacy expected in the target audience. At a basic level, it gave shape to what was being depicted: figures and objects, as well as actions. Beyond the superficial identification of persons and things, relationships were established by means of sequential (temporal) and associative readings, which demanded an understanding of how the two-dimensional book illustration created the illusion of action through a static snapshot of an activity. This associative way of reading an illustration conceived the image as characterised by dynamism and process rather than as a frozen capturing of a state of existence.

In a work like *The Seasons*, readers encountered numerous challenges. The most obvious would have been the Miltonic poetic diction that Thomson devised. This paraphrastic language did not prevent labouring-class readers such as John Clare from avidly consuming the poem. At the same time, it induced a number of publishers to commission paratextual material that helped readers to make sense of the text. Illustrations were the most striking of these paratexts, in that they translated aspects of the work into accessible representational modes. Early nineteenth-century editions increasingly moved away from the high-cultural allegorical modes that had characterised the illustrated editions up to the 1790s. Instead, a more realistic impulse, as well as another that sentimentalised, was introduced at the beginning of the next century. The frontispiece to J. Mackenzie & Co.'s 1804 London edition reflects this change. It depicts the personified seasons in the shape of children and serves as an example of how different degrees of visual literacy could operate on the illustration and make sense of it. These children no longer are the stylised putti of earlier illustrations of the text, which bore little realistic reference to the experience of young readers, nor were they the allegorical figures found in the tableau engravings of the original 1730 quarto edition. They did

Figure 13.4 Frontispiece, *The Seasons* (London: J. Mackenzie & Co., 1804). Reproduced from a copy in the author's collection

not engage in those activities centrally engaged with in Thomson's work. Rather, their activities are those that in a general way connect leisure with the season in which the action takes place (Figure 13.4). So a boy in the top right-hand corner is filling his hat with water from a spring, while (in the background) hay rigs are visible. The image conveys an association between the thirsty boy in the foreground and the harvesting activity in the background. To those skilled in the decoding of metaphorical illustrations, the boy is readable as a placeholder for adults engaged in the harvest, while he serves as an extension of an experience they may not know but can relate to. Thus the image mediates the seasonal activity of harvesting indirectly through the boy's thirst, the implication being that this thirst will have been triggered by exertion. If a representation of the harvest is intended, then it is as stylised as the depiction of a girl making a floral garland, the scene framed by a sheep on her left. To a child reader, the sheep may appear supplemental, without carrying any specific meaning other than a reference to animal life. Those reading the image metaphorically may associate the girl with the sheep, concluding that she is a young shepherdess. A second boy, in the lower left-hand corner of the frontispiece, is gathering grapes from vines. This is the most direct rendering of an agricultural activity emblematic not only of the season of autumn but also of the choice of subject for the illustration of that season as well. The fact the edition contained both a memoir of Thomson and 'a Complete Index & Glossary', as the title page informs readers, indicates that its publisher was catering to those, like children and young readers, who may have required these two paratextual aids to understand Thomson's production.

The frontispiece illustration, at a basic level, rendered a visual narrative through the children depicted. Equally, to readers steeped in the reading of metaphorical images, the boys and girls may have been seen as allegorical figures. Published seventy-four years after the first illustrated edition of *The Seasons*, Mackenzie's frontispiece was the first to introduce the realist mode, using four children to exemplify the different seasons. By that time the work was used at schools and, at a price of 2s., an edition like Mackenzie's was sufficiently cheap to cater to young readers.

Whereas *The Seasons* was issued in a number of illustrated formats, ranging from miniature editions to Peltro William Tomkins's 1798 folio, other bestselling texts – such as the popular productions of the Swiss poet, engraver and bookseller Salomon Gessner – were predominantly published in small-format pocket editions. Compared with versions of Thomson's work, editions of *The Death of Abel* contained fewer illustrations, although in the 1790s illustrations based on high-cultural renderings of the work and using fashionable artistic styles increasingly accompanied new editions. The designers of these later illustrations self-consciously deployed representational conventions that allowed them to tell complex stories. Their images are characterised by detail, and they do not, as do the illustrations accompanying pocket editions, focus on the moment of murder, the muscular Cain killing his brother.

The earliest frontispiece accompanying Mary Collyer's English translation reduced Gessner's story to the moment the fratricide takes place. Although a prototype of visual interpretation that would be reused throughout the century, this simply executed illustration had a high-cultural origin as a unique artwork by Titian, who painted it in 1542–4. Titian's painting, which was an exclusive medium, and on display at the Church of S. Maria della Salute in Venice, would not have been known to most readers encountering the frontispiece on opening the book. Familiarity with the specific image and the identification of its origin were not central to the functioning of the illustration, however. It was the centralising of an act of murder which would have been meaningful. Steeped in religious practice, readers

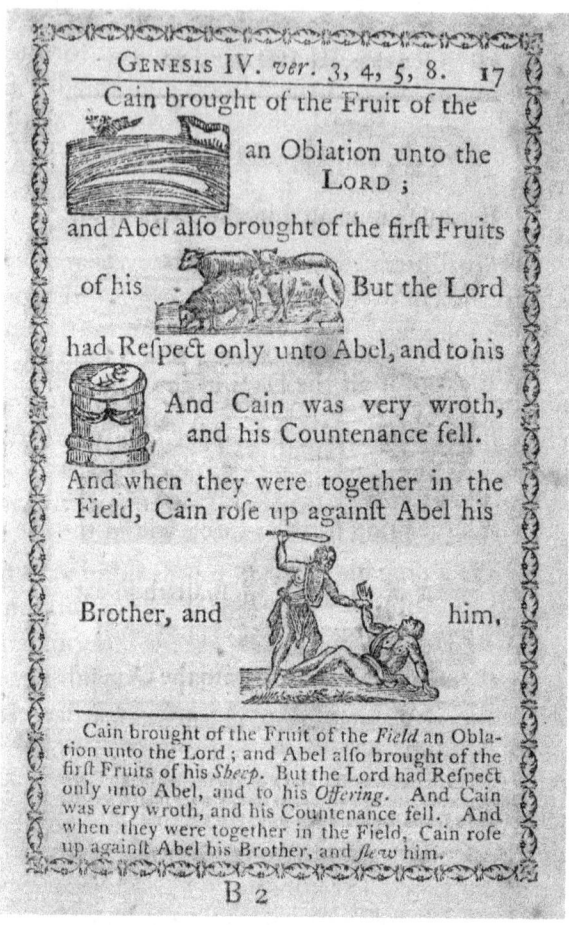

Figure 13.5 *The Curious Hieroglyphic Bible* (Worcester, MA: Isaiah Thomas, 1788), p. 17. Courtesy, American Antiquarian Society

may have seen other visualisations of the fratricide in popular print culture (including illustrated Bibles and chapbooks), in churches and in friezes on building façades. In fact, *The Curious Hieroglyphic Bible* that Isaiah Thomas published in Worcester, Massachusetts, in 1788 drew on an established tradition of visualising the fratricide, not only representing it in the form of a rebus woodcut but glossing this woodcut at the bottom of the page as the slaying of Abel (Figure 13.5).[7] The textual gloss thus reinforces, fixes and directs the meaning of the illustration.

The copper-engraved adaptation of the Titian image served as a fixed dead metaphor which unmistakably conveyed the killing of Abel by Cain. The altars in the background underscore its biblical origin. Unlike illustrations for editions of *The Seasons*, which relied on their intratextual connection with the text visualised, the iconic, widely recognised image of Cain killing his younger brother functioned beyond the text it accompanied. It was therefore both intratextual and transtextual, meaningful even to those who did not encounter the frontispiece in the edition but who purchased the print separately.

The reworked Titian image was not reused in subsequent editions, which featured similar images equally centralising the murder. At first, these illustrations featured as full-page frontispieces, as in the 2s. 1767 edition, where the scene resembles a framed painting in a church. Subsequently, the rendering of Abel's murder was realised in the smaller format of the title-page vignette (Figure 13.6). While this vignette was a cost-effective alternative to a full-page frontispiece and embellished a number of editions as the only illustration included, it was also combined, on occasion, with series of other full-page illustrations. In one case, T. Osborn and J. Mozley's 1783 edition, it was even adapted as a tailpiece and executed as a woodcut (Figure 13.7). The woodcut reduced the background paraphernalia that the adaptation of the Titian image still included and positioned Cain in the upper right-hand corner, club in hand. He is about to destroy his brother, whose arms implore mercy. Abel is encompassed by the overly dark left-hand area of the image, which is made up of plant growth, into which his existence appears to be absorbed. Positioned directly under the phrase 'The End', which concludes the typographic text of *The Death of Abel*, the vignette may have functioned as a morality-enforcing reminder of the need to govern passion.

While the vignette continued to be reprinted, an illustration that demanded greater familiarity with the text was introduced into a number of editions. It featured both Adam and Eve mourning over the body of their son, with Cain seen in the background. The narrative the image conveys is more complex than that of the murder scene. It was essential that readers identified Adam and Eve as the parents of the dead Abel, despite the fact that they appear far too young.

Whereas the illustration based on the Titian painting was relatively straightforward to read as a visual casting of the biblical fratricide, on occasion other editions using this image or reworkings of it boasted explanatory captions such as 'Abel Slain by his wicked Brother Cain' and 'At the same Instant, with Arm strengthened with Rage, Cain swings a massy Club, and smote the Head of his Brother'.[8] Aggression and violence were thus emblematised in an action that was accessible to readers. The caption may have served as a safeguard,

Figure 13.6 Title page, *The Death of Abel* (London: H. Collyer, 1799 reprinting of the 1765 illustration). Reproduced from a copy in the author's collection

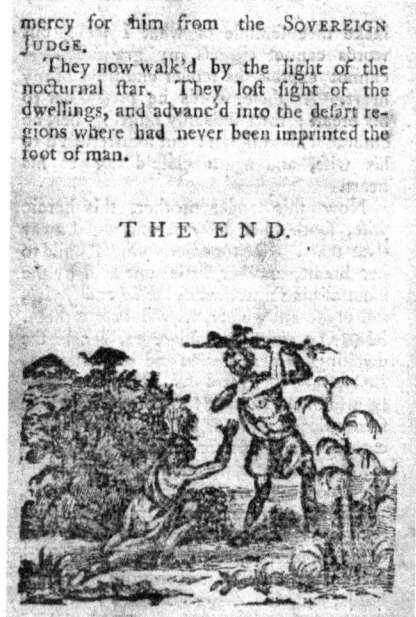

Figure 13.7 Woodcut vignette, *The Death of Abel* (London: T. Osborn and J. Mozley, 1783). Reproduced from a copy in the author's collection

ensuring that what was being depicted was properly understood. By contrast, the scene of mourning in which the devastated Eve is about to faint on beholding Abel required further explanatory information. For J. Collyer's 1768 edition, the image was captioned 'Adam & Eve beholding the dead Body of Abel and hearing the Curses of Cain'. The frontispiece interrelated two actions, the viewing of the dead Abel by his parents and their hearing their eldest son pronouncing curses. Centralised by the caption, Adam and Eve are identified both as parents and mourners.

This illustration was widely reprinted with a number of minor variations,[9] not only in London editions but also in the provinces, including Bolton and Newcastle, where it was respectively used in B. Jackson's 1786 and M. Brown's 1787 editions. Compared with the original version of the illustration on which Brown's frontispiece was based, the later image, because of its different caption, offers readers an alternative interpretation (Figure 13.8). Titled 'Death of Abel',

Figure 13.8 Frontispiece, *The Death of Abel* (Newcastle: M. Brown, 1790 reprinting of the 1787 illustration). Reproduced from a copy in the author's collection

the frontispiece directly identifies the victim of Cain's rage, whereas a textual caption, 'He is dead! I kill'd him!', centralises the murderer. Unlike his parents, whose gestures are supposed to communicate their shock and horror, Cain's perspective enables the reader to grasp the extent of his guilty action as well as his torment, an experience of Cain's horror at his own action that the image itself would not have conveyed if not amplified by the caption. The caption thus adds precision and directs the meaning of the plate, counteracting any kind of ambiguous meaning the reader may have construed. Ambiguity of sorts is still present, however, for the reader needs to make sense of the pair standing over the dead Abel. The designer of the plate may have expected those viewing the image to identify Adam and the fainting Eve, although it would also have been possible to identify the woman as Thirza, Abel's wife in Gessner's rendering of the story.

The fact that, out of the forty illustrated editions of Gessner's classic published in eighteenth-century Britain, the majority reused variants of one of the two illustrations described above demonstrates not only the cost-effective adoption of images for reprinting but also the effectiveness of these images. They were far more accessible to readers of all classes than the sophisticated illustrations designed by Thomas Stothard and Henry James Richter for the 1797 and 1795 editions issued respectively by T. Heptinstall and Vernor & Hood. The widespread reprinting of these illustrations familiarised a large number of readers with these images and the ways in which they presented a biblical subject and its moral message to abstain from violence.

The cost-effective reprinting of illustrations reflects a practice that in the eighteenth century made a store of images available to a much larger number of readers than could be affected through more complex and costly illustrations, which few could afford.[10] Because of their strong presence in reading communities, reprinted images affect reading in ways that visual apparatuses meant for the elite do not. Richter's set of four illustrations, which advertisements termed 'Four admired Engravings',[11] tellingly did not include the killing of Abel. Instead, the artist selected sentimental scenes characterising the benevolence of the characters, thereby putting forward a visual reading that is at odds with Titian's. The frontispiece depicts Cain kneeling in front of his father, asking his forgiveness, and its subject is glossed by a three-line quotation from Book 1. It depicts a moment that precedes the killing of Abel.

The format of the illustrated page is unusual: two-thirds of the page is occupied by the image, whereas the remainder of the page carries the credit line referencing Richter as both designer and engraver, the text

Figure 13.9 Frontispiece, *The Death of Abel* (London: Vernor & Hood, 1801 reprinting of the 1795 illustration). Reproduced from a copy in the author's collection

quotation underneath and, at the bottom of the page, the credit line to Vernor & Hood as publishers (Figure 13.9). A reader encountering these illustrations would have recognised the markers of symbolic capital that confirmed the status of the illustrations, which were also issued as part of an upmarket edition 'on a very fine Vellum Paper, with first Impressions of the Plate[s]', priced at 5s.6d.[12] They sold as fashionable print objects by a well known artist, and in the three editions the publishers issued before 1801 they catered to collectors.

The markers of symbolic capital on the original pages featuring Richter's illustrations were omitted when Edinburgh bookseller James Robertson had them reprinted in his 1806 edition. Richter was no longer credited as designer, nor were the long quotations used:

Robertson replaced them with one-line captions. Users of the editions published by Vernor & Hood and Robertson would thus have had a different reading experience. In the former, readers encountered the text punctuated by Richter's engravings. The edition's paratext presented Gessner's work as a modern classic but also designated the illustrations as tasteful objects published by one of the market leaders in the specialist field of illustrated literature. This contextualisation of the illustration was omitted in Robertson's edition, which included less expertly executed, reversed copies of Richter's engravings and provided minimalist textual cues to guide readerly interpretation of the images. Opting for a single-line caption was certainly cost-effective but also reduced the complexity of the text–image relationship that readers had to negotiate. An alternative to Robertson's single-line caption from *The Death of Abel* was the provision of a page reference: the frontispiece to the 1770 London edition 'printed and sold by the booksellers',[13] which depicted yet another version of Cain killing his brother, was captioned 'See Book IV Page 103', instructing the reader to locate the relevant passage and relate it to the image. This kind of cross-referencing necessitated that readers leaf through the volume, whereas Robertson's caption allowed the more convenient consultation of text and image on the same page.

Robertson selected his illustrations on the basis that they were recently published and fashionable. Their reprinting reflected less the popularity of Vernor & Hood's edition, which retailed at the steep price of 4s., than the availability of attractive illustrations that did not require resizing or much alteration.[14] Robertson sought to produce a quality edition that was unrivalled in Scotland and aligned itself with London trends in illustrations.

When Samuel Richardson published his 1742 edition of *Pamela*, he sought to capitalise on the reputation of his epistolary novel by offering an unprecedented apparatus of engraved illustrations for a work of fiction.[15] He recruited Hubert-François Gravelot and Francis Hayman to furnish a series of twenty-nine designs which – apart from telling the story of the servant maid, Pamela – embedded the actions of the heroine, Mr. B. and the other characters within the material culture of the upper classes, while importing the French rococo style to the design of figures and interiors. These illustrations were novelties, as well as complex semiotic systems communicating Richardson's ideals of dignity, grace and sentiment,[16] their originators taking for granted that readers were able not only to unravel the power dynamics governing relationships among different characters but that they were also able to interpret the meanings of gesture and facial expression. They were thus rooted in an artistic repertoire of performance which would have been codified by decorum and societal convention. However, these expensively engraved illustrations had little reach beyond the few purchasers who could spend £1.4s. on the four-volume set.

Far more important for spreading knowledge of the work among different classes of readers were redactions that abridged the text and, as in the case of Francis Newbery's 1s. edition of *Pamela* (1769), supplied readers with a simple visual narrative.[17] Newbery issued abridgments of *Clarissa*, *Joseph Andrews* and *Tom Jones*, capitalising on their established reputation, as well as on textual knowledge that circulated in popular (oral) culture. In the case of the 'media event' of *Pamela*, popular knowledge of the text was fed not only by the editions themselves but also by such spectacular material culture spin-offs as waxworks of the scenes in the novel. The frontispiece to Newbery's volume, which was designed and engraved by John Lodge, adopts the representational function of the portrait and focuses on the heroine by presenting her as simply dressed, probably a servant, who, in her relation to the built environment in the background, is linked to the country and to (agricultural) labour (Figure 13.10). This

Figure 13.10 Frontispiece, *The History of Pamela; or, Virtue Rewarded* (London: Francis Newbery, 1775 reprint). Reproduced from a copy in the author's collection

identification is general, lacking specific characteristics emphasising Pamela's personal attractiveness. It does not require knowledge of the cultural habits inscribed in the illustrations by Gravelot and Hayman. At face value, then, Newbery's Pamela represents a female figure who metonymically stands for female role models such as mothers, governesses or even the Virgin Mary. To the consumers of Newbery's abridgement, which was aimed at both children and readers of limited buying power, the female's dress would appear simple, while the same dress, to a fashionable reader, may have been identified as a specially designed country dress for the upper classes.[18] Social station and the immersion in cultural practices thus affected perception and readability, especially in works that were mediated only by a single illustration, the frontispiece. Newbery's frontispiece offered a version of Pamela that focused on the character rather than engaging with her actions. Yet the abridgement relied on the episodic and punctuated the narrative with five illustrations, in addition to the frontispiece, which visualised well known scenes from the work.

Given the quality of the engravings and the absence of captions, the readability of one of the remaining illustrations in the volume is assured only by the reader interrelating the text and the image as part of the reading process. As in the 1741 pirated edition of *Pamela*, published by C. Whitefield, which included a plate that visualised Pamela's despair at not being able to escape from the garden of the Lincolnshire estate where Mr. B. holds her captive, the Newbery edition boasts an image that visualises the moment of Pamela throwing her dress into the pond in order to make her persecutors believe she has drowned. It was this moment also which Richardson had originally intended to use as a frontispiece for a two-volume edition, which did not materialise.[19] His friend Aaron Hill had characterised the scene as possessing 'something too intensely reflective of the passions, at the pond, that would make . . . significant calls for expression and attitude'.[20] The Newbery image did not capture the protagonist's state of mind in her facial expression, since the unsophisticated execution of the engraving did not allow such nuance. At the same time, without knowledge of the text, it is not easy to identify the material floating on the surface of the water as a woman's dress. This is information that can be gleaned only from the text itself, especially when American reprints of the Newbery abridgement translated the illustration from the original copper-engraved design into a woodcut[21] and relevant detail aiding the interpretation was lost. Newbery and those adapting these frequently reprinted illustrations did not help readers to elucidate the meaning of the image. Rather, this illustration was understood to be consumed as part of an integral reading of the image alongside the text it embodied, which clarified what in the image was not clear.

The wood engraver Thomas Bewick illustrated a redaction of Richardson's novel for the 1s. chapbook that Thomas Saint published 'with fine Cuts' in Newcastle in 1787.[22] The York printers Wilson, Spence, & Mawman reused the wood engravings in the edition they issued in 1799. Bewick approached the episode of the protagonist contemplating suicide by positioning Pamela near the water, an object floating on the water nearby. In contrast to Saint, the later publishers made sure to add an explanatory caption, 'Pamela, after her escape into the Garden, intending to drown herself', which does not reveal that the floating object is, in fact, the protagonist's dress. Rather, it focuses on the sitting heroine contemplating suicide, which idea is, however, quickly rejected by Pamela in favour of a scheme to make those in search of her assume that she has escaped from them forever by drowning (Figure 13.11). This frontispiece vignette is reused later in the same volume, thus assigning a centrality to Pamela's psyche and her thoughts about suicide that the Newbery frontispiece did not.

Like the frontispieces to the majority of editions of *The Death of Abel*, Bewick's cautioned against committing a mortal sin, though its 'effect on the juvenile readers . . . must have been disheartening'.[23]

Figure 13.11 Frontispiece vignette, *The History of Pamela; or, Virtue Rewarded* (York: Wilson, Spence, & Mawman, 1799). Reproduced from a copy in the author's collection

Figure 13.12 Frontispiece, *The History of Pamela; or, Virtue Rewarded* (London: printed for the booksellers, and for J. Kendrew, York, c. 1820). Reproduced from a copy in the author's collection

Yet this moral reminder iconically realised in the frontispiece did not survive into the nineteenth century. When York bookseller James Kendrew undertook his own chapbook version of *Pamela* in the 1820s, this focus on religion was given up in favour of the episode in which Pamela conceals a letter for Parson Williams under the sunflower in the garden (Figure 13.12). The fact that this frontispiece was selected and supplied with only a short gloss underneath it ('The alarm of Pamela at the apprehension of being discovered in taking the Letter intended for M^r. Williams w.^{h} she had concealed under the tiles.') indicated that popular knowledge of the episode had familiarised readers over a period of more than fifty years with a scene from *Pamela* that was used as an iconic characterisation of the work as a whole. Compared with the earlier frontispieces commissioned by Newbery and Saint, Kendrew's was both of a higher execution standard and catered to readers able to read the expression of anxiety on the kneeling Pamela's face, as well as Mrs Jewkes's searching look. The sunflower, which is the third agent in the scene of the novel, is depicted close to Pamela, although it is not mentioned in the text underneath, which is not lifted from Richardson's work.

In the case of *The Death of Abel*, readers frequently encountered the central moment of fratricide in the largest number of illustrations accompanying editions of the work. These illustrations were part of an archive of a visual culture existing outside the framework of the edition with which readers were familiar. They were thus iconic variations of a subject that readers young and old had learnt about from their infancy. Characterised by little compositional complexity, illustrations of the killing of Abel did not necessitate glosses; if captions were added, they reinforced particular dramatic elements of the scene depicted or offered the perspective of one of the parties introduced. Illustrations of the biblical fratricide were thus read on two levels: readers recognised the scene from Genesis, yet additional features germane to Gessner's text and not mentioned in the Bible were also identified. This is not to say that every reader would have been able to differentiate between components that derived from the Bible only and those added by Gessner.

The fact that the earliest illustrated English edition of *The Death of Abel* boasted a version of a high-cultural painting highlights the pervasiveness of recycling practices of images available for reproduction. Since the meaning of images depended on their context of presentation, the reuse of an illustration as a general image promoting an ethos of instruction, as in the frontispiece to Isaiah Thomas's *The Sugar Plumb* (1787), affected its meaning (Figure 13.13). The illustration was appropriated as the frontispiece to the Boston bookseller Samuel Hall's 1793 chapbook edition of *Pamela* and this endowed the image with a new meaning. Not recognising the appropriation of Thomas's frontispiece, which was copied from Francis Newbery's edition of *The Sugar Plumb* (1775), imposed a fixity of meaning onto the image that, in the reality of late eighteenth-century American print culture, it did not possess.[24] While the readers of Thomas's edition were encouraged to see the female figure in the woodcut as the source of the 'entertaining and instructive collection of stories', as the title characterises the contents of *The Sugar Plumb*, in Hall's edition readers are invited to identify the figure as the mother-instructor Pamela. The readability of the image thus was conditioned by the context of the title page, which necessitated that readers endow the woman with a concrete identity.

Readers' visual literacy negotiated the subjects and representational conventions of the illustrations they encountered when reading

Figure 13.13 Frontispiece, *The Sugar Plumb* (Worcester: Isaiah Thomas, 1787). Courtesy, American Antiquarian Society

a book. Depending on the particular text–image relationship in which the illustrations were embedded, their meanings varied, especially if the same images were given different functions and placement in the printed volume, as in the case of the multifarious uses of Stothard's vignettes. Since few literary texts were issued in such a large number of editions and at so many different prices as *The Seasons*, Thomson's work reveals how cost considerations affected the production of illustrative apparatuses. The cheaper editions routinely did not introduce the latest artistic fashions or non-realistic modes of representation. By contrast, those meant for a more literate and affluent readership frequently deployed allegory, metaphor and symbolism to convey the ideational complexity of the work. Editions of *The Seasons* reveal a clear correlation between the cost of the illustration and the kind of visual literacy the booksellers targeted with their volumes. They catered to differently educated classes of readers, and in turn shaped the readerly ability to decode printed images and understand them as a meaningful part of the paratextual apparatus of an edition.

Notes

1. See Robert Hume, 'The Value of Money in Eighteenth-Century England: Incomes, Prices, Buying Power – and Some Problems in Cultural Economics', *Huntington Library Quarterly*, 77:4 (2014), pp. 373–416.
2. Jonathan Rose, 'Rereading the English Common Reader: A Preface to a History of Audiences', *Journal of the History of Ideas*, 52:1 (1992), p. 49.
3. On *The Royal Engagement Pocket Atlas*, see Sandro Jung, 'Thomas Stothard's Illustrations for *The Royal Engagement Pocket Atlas*, 1779–1826', *The Library*, 12:1 (2011), pp. 3–22; and Sandro Jung, 'Reading the Romantic Vignette: Stothard Illustrates Bloomfield, Byron and Crabbe for the *Royal Engagement Pocket Atlas*', in Ian Haywood, Susan Matthews and Mary Shannon (eds), *Romanticism and Illustration* (Cambridge: Cambridge University Press, 2019), pp. 143–70.
4. See Sandro Jung, *James Thomson's 'The Seasons', Print Culture, and Visual Interpretation, 1730–1842* (Bethlehem: Lehigh University Press, 2015), pp. 158–62.
5. *Caledonian Mercury*, 29 January 1793.
6. See Jung, *James Thomson's 'The Seasons'*.
7. *The Curious Hieroglyphick Bible; or, Select Passages in the Old and New Testaments* (Worcester: printed by Isaiah Thomas, 1788), p. 17.
8. *The Death of Abel* (London: Dodesley, Durham, and Field, 1764); *The Death of Abel* (London: printed for S. Toplis and J. Bunney et al., 1779).
9. Only one frontispiece offers a significant variation on the parents' shocked beholding of their dead son's body. Whereas Adam and Eve, as well as the two brothers, had constituted the central characters of the scene, in W. Kemmish's 1s. 1794 London edition, they are joined by two further spectators whose identity is unclear, unless one of them is Thirza. Facing the frontispiece, the title-page vignette depicts the fratricide itself, thus inverting the temporal scheme of the biblical story by requiring the reader to look at the images from right to left to understand the origin and cause of the frontispiece scene.
10. See Sandro Jung, *The Publishing and Marketing of Illustrated Literature in Scotland, 1760–1825* (Bethlehem: Lehigh University Press, 2017).
11. *Whitehall Evening Post*, 22 October 1796.
12. *Morning Chronicle*, 28 December 1795.
13. There were several editions of the title published by 'the Booksellers' in 1770 that included different frontispieces. The edition referred to here is the one held by the Bodleian Library, University of Oxford (shelfmark: Vet. A5 f.4220).
14. His edition, as with his two-volume edition of the *Poems of Allan Ramsay* (1802), recycled existing illustrations from other publishers. See Sandro Jung, 'James Robertson's *Poems of Allan Ramsay* (1802) and the Adaptation of Other Scottish Booksellers' Book Illustrations of the Works of Ramsay', *Scottish Literary Review*, 8:1 (2018), pp. 139–58.

15. See Thomas Keymer and Peter Sabor, *'Pamela' in the Marketplace: Literary Controversy and Print Culture in Eighteenth-Century Britain and Ireland* (Cambridge: Cambridge University Press, 2009).
16. See T. C. Duncan-Eaves, 'Graphic Illustration of the Novels of Samuel Richardson, 1740–1810', *Huntington Library Quarterly*, 14 (1951), pp. 355–6.
17. See Sandro Jung, 'The Other *Pamela*: Readership and the Illustrated Chapbook Abridgment', *Journal for Eighteenth-Century Studies*, 39:4 (2016), pp. 513–31.
18. For this point, I am indebted to a conversation with Professor Michele Cohen.
19. See Robert Folkenflik, 'The Rise of the Illustrated Novel to 1832', in Alan Downie (ed.), *The Oxford Handbook to the Eighteenth-Century Novel* (Oxford: Oxford University Press, 2016), p. 316.
20. *The Works of the Late Aaron Hill*, 4 vols (London: printed for the benefit of the family, 1754), vol. IV, p. 164.
21. See, for instance, *The History of Pamela; or, Virtue Rewarded. Abridged from the Works by Samuel Richardson* (Boston: printed and sold by S. Hall, 1794).
22. *Newcastle Courant*, 8 December 1787. On a variant printing of the edition, see T. C. Duncan-Eaves, 'An Unrecorded Children's Book by Thomas Bewick', *The Library*, series 5, 4 (1951), pp. 272–3.
23. Keymer and Sabor, *'Pamela' in the Marketplace*, p. 172.
24. See Barbara E. Lacey, *From Sacred to Secular: Visual Images in Early American Publications* (Newark: University of Delaware Press, 2007), pp. 156–7.

Chapter 14

Reading Aloud, Past and Present

W. R. Owens

A great deal of research on the history of reading has focused on the process by which, during the later Middle Ages, reading was transformed from something that was usually done aloud, as a social activity, to something that was usually done silently, and alone. This transformation has been regarded (quite rightly) as a most significant cultural and social development. Nowadays, indeed, in general discourse 'reading' is to all intents and purposes identified with 'silent reading'. It is true that reading aloud remains important in how young children are introduced to reading, but – significantly – it is left behind once they become 'skilled' readers, meaning that they are able to read silently.

In this chapter I want to focus attention on the practice of reading aloud, and to open up for discussion three quite basic points. The first is that histories of reading need to take greater account of reading aloud if we are to understand properly the cultural significance and experience of reading in the past. The second is that reading aloud was not 'replaced' by silent reading, but continued alongside it for much longer than is sometimes recognised, and we need to think more about the implications of this and the reasons for it. The third is that reading aloud is not just a thing of the past, but has a distinctive and valuable role to play in present-day society.

One of the earliest descriptions of reading aloud comes in the Hebrew Bible (which forms the 'Old Testament' in the Christian Bible). The book of the prophet Nehemiah, probably composed about 400 BCE, includes a memorable account of the first public reading of the Torah, the Law of Moses.

> And all the people gathered themselves together as one man into the street that was before the water gate, and they spoke unto Ezra . . . to bring the book of the law of Moses, which the LORD had commanded to Israel. And Ezra the priest brought the law before the congregation both of men and women. . . . And he read therein . . . from the morning until midday . . . and the ears of all the people were attentive unto the book of the law.[1]

The historian Simon Schama has emphasised the significance for Jewish culture of how the act of reading is represented in this ancient text. It was, he says, 'a shared, common experience, the impact of its vocalisation not even dependent on literacy. . . . The performance assigned to Ezra was all about mouth and ear, about the living force of words.' It established for Jews the idea that reading was 'intensely participatory', not something done in 'silent solitude', but 'a demonstrative public performance meant to turn the reader from absorption to action; a reading that has necessary, immediate, human implications'.[2]

The practice of reading aloud was not confined to Judaism. Within Islam, the Qur'ān was – and still is – read aloud in its Classical Arabic language.[3] Right across the Hellenistic, Roman and early Christian world, reading was something you almost always did aloud and usually in company. There is a famous story in his *Confessions* of St Augustine's astonishment at seeing St Ambrose read silently: 'his eyes scanned the page and his heart explored the meaning, but his voice was silent and his tongue was still'. Silent reading was not in fact as uncommon as Augustine seems to imply here, and indeed later on in the *Confessions* he describes how, at the moment of his conversion, he himself read 'in silence' a passage from St Paul.[4] Nevertheless, even if plenty of people did read silently, it is generally true that, in the ancient world, to 'read' a text often meant hearing someone reading it to you, or hearing yourself reading it aloud.[5] If you were a wealthy Roman, you might even include in your household staff a specially trained *lector*, whose sole function was to read works of literature aloud to you, your family and friends.[6]

Why, though, was reading aloud such a widespread practice at this time? One answer is that these were essentially oral and aural cultures, in which writing was closely associated with voice and listening. Religious texts, works of literature and learned writings of all kinds were disseminated largely by means of the spoken word. It has also been argued that there is a technical reason why silent reading was not common. This is that texts were presented in what is known as *scriptio continua* (continuous writing), in capital letters, without any spaces between words, and using little or no punctuation. Paul Saenger, one of the main proponents of this view, claims that 'the ancient reader . . . normally had to read orally, aloud or in a muffled voice, because overt physical pronunciation aided the reader to retain phonemes of ambiguous meaning'. He argues that it was not until words began to be separated by spaces, in about the seventh century, that silent reading could become widespread. The development of silent reading was further encouraged by the increased use of punctuation and other devices to guide the eye from one part of a text to another, but according to Saenger it took until about the thirteenth century before silent reading of word-separated texts became a regular practice in literate society throughout Western Europe.[7]

Saenger sees the change from vocalised to silent reading as something of a revolution, not only because it made reading faster and enabled easier comprehension of complex ideas, but because using the eyes alone transformed reading into a wholly internal and individual practice which facilitated solitary reflection and, potentially at least, freed the reader from external attempts to control understanding and interpretation of what was being read.[8] In the words of Roger Chartier, 'this "privatization" of reading is undeniably one of the major cultural developments of the early modern era'.[9]

The establishment and spread of silent reading did not, however, wholly supplant the practice of reading aloud. Historians of reading have recognised that it continued for a very long time, but I would suggest that its extent and importance have been underestimated in many general accounts. So, for example, in his widely acclaimed *A History of Reading*, Alberto Manguel devotes only a single chapter (out of twenty) to what he calls 'Being Read To'. In that chapter he describes: oral readings from the scriptures at mealtimes in medieval Benedictine monasteries; social reading in domestic houses and at casual gatherings in the eighteenth century and beyond; and readings by workers to fellow workers in cigar-making factories in Cuba in the mid-nineteenth century.[10] Similarly, in his survey, *A History of Reading*, Steven Roger Fischer spends little time on the practice of reading aloud after the classical period, though he devotes a whole section of one chapter to 'Silent Reading'.[11] A recent three-volume collection of essays on *The History of Reading* (of which I myself was a co-editor), while not ignoring reading aloud, does not give it anything like the prominence it deserves.[12]

A number of specialist historical studies have noted the persistence of reading aloud, and some have begun to challenge the assumption that the history of reading is a record of steady and inevitable progress from oral to silent reading. According to Joyce Coleman, in the fourteenth and fifteenth centuries elite audiences in England and France who were perfectly capable of reading by themselves in private nevertheless preferred listening to books being read aloud in company, finding this 'an emotionally and intellectually engaging, multisensory, sociable, satisfying, and productive focus of human interaction'.[13] Roger Chartier likewise argues that in Renaissance Europe reading aloud was practised in urban settings by literate people who regarded it as 'an exercise in sociability' which fostered bonds of friendship and familial relationships.[14] D. R. Woolf demonstrates that works of history by authors from the late Middle Ages through to the seventeenth century and well beyond were intended to be read aloud as well as silently, even though over this period the settings in which such oral readings took place shifted from courts, great households or public spaces into the more intimate setting of the private home.[15] Andrew Cambers, in a study of 'godly reading' in the seventeenth century, argues that reading aloud, in company, publically and privately, was a central strand in Puritan piety.[16] Nor was the practice confined to Puritans: in an article on Samuel Pepys, Elspeth Jajdelska points out that instances of reading aloud or listening to others reading aloud are ubiquitous in his diary.[17] By the eighteenth century, according to Jacqueline Pearson, 'solitary recreational reading by women tended to be associated with idleness and selfishness', whereas reading aloud within the family or with female companions was generally approved of as a social activity.[18] More recently, Abigail Williams has presented a wealth of evidence from unpublished as well as published sources to challenge the idea that in the eighteenth century reading had become a silent, solitary activity, arguing instead that 'eager readers and canny printers and publishers celebrated the social and educative role of books out loud and in company' and that an ability to read out loud well was 'at the centre of polite accomplishment'.[19] In their study of reading in New England in the years before the American Civil War, Ronald J. Zboray and Mary Saracino Zboray note many examples showing how reading aloud was a way of relieving the tedium of tasks like sewing, cooking and childcare, and provided comfort to people who were blind or sight-impaired, or who were ill or dying. Their conclusion is that oral reading in homes, churches, schools and public halls took place on such a scale that 'spoken dissemination [of texts] far exceeded silent reading'.[20] Kate Flint provides further evidence of the varied social uses to which reading aloud by women was put in the nineteenth century, including reading to children, to the sick, to servants, as an accompaniment to household activities, on Sundays and at special occasions, such as Christmas.[21] In his magisterial account of *The Intellectual Life of the British Working Classes*, Jonathan Rose emphasises that 'by far the most pervasive form of mutual education [for working-class people] was, quite simply, reading aloud'.[22]

Studies like these have much to tell us about the ubiquity of reading aloud over the past 600 or 700 years, about why the practice continued alongside silent reading, and about the circumstances in which it took place. Valuable and suggestive as such studies are, though, there is much still to be uncovered and analysed about the nature and extent of reading aloud in the past. Kevin Sharpe suggests that even among scholars familiar with the practice, 'none has adequately considered its importance, or the relationship of "readers" and auditors for the processes of the absorption and comprehension of, and the reaction to, texts'.[23] Sharpe's implicit questioning of a separation between 'readers' and 'auditors' is itself worth further consideration. We need only think of the medieval mystic Margery Kempe to begin to recognise the importance of 'reading by listening'. Though she is often described as 'illiterate', it is clear that Kempe's education consisted in her remarkable ability to memorise texts read aloud to her, including 'the Bible with commentary by doctors, St Bridget's book, Hilton's book, Bonaventure's *Stimulus Amoris*, the *Incendium Amoris*, and other such books'.[24] We seem to need a concept such as 'reader as listener' for a case like Kempe, and she is by no means alone in this.[25]

In seeking to appreciate the extraordinary significance of reading aloud in the past, and its place in people's lives, a good place to begin is with the Bible, one of the most widely read books of all time. Under the impetus of the Protestant Reformation, the Bible began to be translated into the vernacular languages of Europe, and the translated text became available to many more readers by means of the new technology of printing by movable type. Guglielmo Cavallo and Roger Chartier have claimed that the importance attached to the Bible within Protestant cultures was such that it 'raised Bible reading to the level of a model for all other possible forms of reading'.[26] Reading aloud was pre-eminent: the Bible was experienced through the ear at least as often as through the eye alone. We may take as an example the case of William Maldon, an illiterate young man in the late 1520s, who was inspired to learn to read by hearing William Tyndale's translation of the New Testament being read aloud:

> Divers poor men in the town of Chelmsford... bought the New Testament of Jesus Christ and on Sundays did sit reading in the lower end of the church, and many would flock about them to hear their reading. Then came I among the said readers to hear their reading of that glad and sweet tidings of the gospel.... Then thought I, I will learn to read English, and then I will have the New Testament and read therein myself .... The Maytide following, I and my father's apprentice, Thomas Jeffary laid our money together, and bought the New Testament in English ... and so [read] it at convenient times.[27]

We can observe here how reading aloud could be a 'democratising' force, with knowledge previously in the hands of a few (the clergy) being made accessible to ordinary people, and how the experience of hearing a work like the New Testament being read aloud could act as an incentive to acquire the skill of reading for oneself.

It is important to note, however, that listening to the Bible being read aloud was by no means confined to poor or illiterate people in early modern England, but applied right across the social spectrum. In aristocratic and gentry households, it was common practice to listen to the Bible being read aloud by a domestic chaplain; lower down the social scale, the Bible might be read to the family (including servants) by a father or mother, or, sometimes, children would read to their illiterate or semi-literate parents. A diary kept by the Elizabethan Puritan gentlewoman Margaret Hoby is full of references to her reading, sometimes by herself, but more often listening to someone else. The Bible is read to her by her chaplain, Richard Rhodes, and sometimes Hoby reads it aloud to her mother or to other people.[28] Anne Clifford's diary, kept between 1616 and 1619, contains similar evidence of this kind of 'reading by listening'. She records how her husband's chaplain read the Bible with her every day (getting through about three books each month), but she also listened to readings by other people: on 18 April 1617, 'being Good Friday I spent most of the day in hearing Kate Buxton read the Bible and a book of Preparation to the Sacrament'.[29]

Reading the Bible aloud in the home was frequently prescribed by the authors of popular devotional works. *A Garden of Spirituall Flowers* (1609) set out some 'rules' for reading the Bible, covering not only individual reading, but communal reading as well, recommending the reading aloud of 'one Chapter in the Morning, another at Meales, another in the Evening before Prayer: beginning at the beginning of the Bible and continuing to the end'.[30] Lewis Bayly's best-selling *The Practice of Pietie* (1612) advises the godly householder to 'call every morning *all* thy *Familie* to some *convenient* room; and first, either reade thy selfe unto them a Chapter in the *Word* of God, or cause it to be read distinctly by some *other*', with the same practice to be carried out each evening.[31] In a sermon preached in 1684, John Tillotson, later to become Archbishop of Canterbury, declared it to be the primary 'Duty of all *Fathers* and *Masters* of *Families*' to institute 'family religion', including 'reading some Portions of the *Holy Scriptures*' every morning and evening.[32]

There is a great deal of evidence that such family readings were common. In the early seventeenth century, a London turner, Nehemiah Wallington, described how, early one Sunday morning, he assembled his family for communal reading and discussion of the Bible and other religious books: 'One did read Leviticus 26, of which I did speak what God put into my mind; then I went to catechizing, and then to read out of *The Garden of Spiritual Flowers*, very useful to our souls, and some others read out of the Psalms.'[33] Near the end of the century, Elizabeth Walker would listen to her maids reading a chapter of the Bible each morning and evening, and on Sundays would call the whole family together 'to hear them read the Scriptures'. She herself was evidently highly skilled at reading aloud. According to her husband:

> Tho' she read quick, she did it so smoothly and distinctly, and would place the Emphasis upon some word in every Sentence so intelligently, without any affected tone or vehement alteration of her Voice, that the change was scarce perceptible, (not so much as betwixt what we call *flat* and *sharp* in Musick,) and yet would strangely facilitate the understanding of the Sense to low Capacities, an infallible evidence of her clear understanding it herself.[34]

There is much evidence that oral reading of the Bible in families was also a widespread practice in New England. David D. Hall cites the cases of Joseph Buckingham, whose duty as a servant was to read the Bible aloud to the family 'every day . . . at least one chapter, and often two or three chapters', and of Samuel Goodrich, whose father read a chapter aloud to his household every day, and thus, Goodrich calculated, had 'read that holy book through . . . thirteen times, in the space of about five and twenty years'. As Hall notes, one consequence of such repeated reading aloud was that readers and their listeners came to know many passages of the Bible by heart.[35] There were other benefits. In the nineteenth century, John Ruskin, who as a boy was 'forced' by his mother to read the Bible to her over the course of a year, 'aloud, hard names and all, from Genesis to the Apocalypse', thought that he owed to this discipline 'not only a knowledge of the book . . . but much of my general power of taking pains, and the best part of my taste in literature'.[36]

This practice of daily Bible reading in the home lasted a very long time, and though often described as 'patriarchal' it was by no means the responsibility only of fathers. In the 1730s, the second wife of the novelist Samuel Richardson read aloud from the Psalms in the nursery, with her daughters 'standing in a circle', and after breakfast the younger children 'read to her in turn the Psalms, and lessons for the day'.[37] In the nineteenth century, Florence Nightingale's mother read the Bible aloud to her daughters every morning, and when Florence herself became head of her own household she would gather her servants together and read the Bible to them every day at morning prayers. The same was true of the Quaker Elizabeth Fry's mother, and of Mary Carpenter, the Unitarian social reformer, who each read the Bible aloud to their children twice a day, morning and evening.[38]

Right into the early years of the twentieth century, many children growing up across the Anglophone world heard the Bible read to them at home regularly, sometimes daily. A woman born in Australia in 1911 describes how, in her family, after dinner they would 'read round' the Bible, meaning that each person present would take turns to read a passage.[39] In the 1920s in Oxfordshire, on Sundays before breakfast, the novelist John Buchan 'would read a passage from a huge old family Bible . . . to a congregation consisting of all the children then at home . . . and such of the staff as could be spared from jobs to do with the breakfast or the nursery'.[40] My own mother, when I was growing up in Northern Ireland in the 1950s, read a chapter of the Bible to me and my sisters every morning before we went to school.

We need now to consider further what some of the effects of listening to reading may have been. It is clear from many sources that reading aloud was not just a method of conveying information to listeners, but that the listeners were active participants. As Mary Ellen Lamb has put it, in the act of listening to a single voice, the members of Elizabeth Hoby's household 'formed a community of readers'.[41] In his study of the politics of reading in the seventeenth century, Kevin Sharpe argues, further, that '*listening* to texts in no way diluted their impact on early modern auditors'.[42] We get some sense of how engaged listeners could be from an account in the *Memoirs* of Henri de Campion, a lieutenant in the Normandy Regiment between 1635 and 1642, where he describes reading aloud with three fellow officers:

> One of us would read some good book aloud, and we would examine the finest passages in order to learn to live well and to die well. . . . Many people enjoyed listening to our discussions, which, I believe, were useful to them.

Roger Chartier, who quotes this passage, emphasises its social as well as intellectual significance: 'reading aloud, combined with interpretation and discussion of what was read, fostered friendship, and these friendly study groups could attract a wider audience, which benefited by hearing the texts read aloud and discussed'.[43]

There is a lot of evidence that the kinds of intellectual engagement, enjoyment and social interaction stimulated by hearing works read aloud kept the practice alive in later historical periods. Evidence for this can be found in diaries, journals, letters, memoirs and other sources, published and unpublished. One convenient way of accessing such evidence is via the UK Reading Experience Database (RED), an online database which is freely available and fully searchable. Among the over 34,000 records are many instances of reading aloud taking place.[44] Some of the readers and listeners are famous people, particularly writers of the eighteenth and nineteenth centuries, but less well known people are also represented.

A good example of the latter is an account of London costermongers listening to reading, drawn from Henry Mayhew's famous work, *London Labour and the London Poor*, first published in 1851. Most costermongers were illiterate but, according to Mayhew, they were 'very fond of hearing anyone read aloud to them, and [would] listen very attentively'. As well as newspapers, they enjoyed popular novels, and after the reading would discuss them with great animation. They would even listen politely to religious tracts being read aloud, though, according to one of Mayhew's informants, 'sermons or tracts gives them the 'orrors'.[45] The costermongers, we might say, were 'ear-readers', not 'eye-readers'. So too was an elderly charwoman, Mrs Hogarth, who could not read herself, but would join with other lodgers in the house where she lived on the first Monday of each month to listen to the landlord reading that month's number of *Dombey and Son*. According to John Forster, who reported this to Dickens, the novel made such an impression on her that she thought it could not possibly be the work of a single author, but must have taken 'three or four men' to put together.[46] The examples of the costermongers and the charwoman suggest that it is a mistake to regard 'reading through hearing' as an intellectually passive activity.

In RED, and elsewhere, there is compelling evidence of the lasting effect that hearing books read aloud could have on the listeners. As we might expect, some of these accounts are memories of hearing books read aloud in childhood. Frances Power Cobbe, the Anglo-Irish writer, social reformer and women's suffrage campaigner, was seven years old when she first heard John Bunyan's allegory *The Pilgrim's Progress* being read aloud by her father. She loved this 'marvellous tale' so much that he gave her his own copy to keep, and she 'read it over and over continually for years, till the idea it is meant to convey, – Life a progress to Heaven – was engraved indelibly on my mind'.[47] The Welsh author and journalist Howard Spring remembered Sunday evening sessions in the kitchen, when his father would read aloud from *The Pilgrim's Progress* or *Robinson Crusoe*. 'He would read a little; then, one by one, the children would take their turns. If we mispronounced a word once, he would correct us irritably; if twice, he would clout us across the head.' In this way, Spring says, 'we became acquainted with wholesome English'. Spring was only fifteen when his father died, but his mother kept up the Sunday evening readings. 'We went through book after book by Dickens. He pleased my mother immensely.'[48] The Irish poet William Allingham spent many winter evenings in Ballyshannon sitting with his grandmother and Aunt Bess – he drawing, they doing their knitting – all listening intently to his Aunt Maryanne reading aloud a novel by Sir Walter Scott. 'At any thrilling crisis, ejaculations of interest or excitement were heard, and the end of a chapter often gave rise to comments, always on the incidents and characters, just as though they were real, never on the literary merits of the work or the abilities of the author'. Scott's novels were the 'staple' reading, but Allingham remembered also listening to readings of John Galt's *Laurie Todd* (1830) and Horace Smith's *Brambletye House* (1826), 'with the catchphrase, 'Think of that, young man!''.[49]

Some of this family reading was on a positively heroic scale. Virginia Woolf's father, Leslie Stephen, read books not only like *Tom Brown's Schooldays* and *Treasure Island* to his children, but also 'Carlyle's *French Revolution*, Jane Austen, Hawthorne, Shakespeare, and the great English poets, especially Milton'. Most remarkably, we are told that he read aloud to them all thirty-two volumes of Scott's collected novels, and 'when we had finished the last he was ready to begin the first over again'. The young Woolf was herself keen on reading aloud. In a single year, 1897, when she was fifteen, she read to her sister Vanessa the following novels: *Felix Holt*; *John Halifax, Gentleman*; *North and South*; *Wives and Daughters*; *Barchester Towers*; *The Scarlet Letter*; *Shirley*; *Villette*; *Alton Locke*; and *Adam Bede*.[50] Other children in the nineteenth century acquired the faculty of reading long novels aloud. As a boy, Stanley Baldwin spent 'long periods with an aunt who was fond of being read to', and by the time he was nine years of age he had read to her the whole of Scott's *Guy Mannering*, *Ivanhoe*, *Redgauntlet*, *Rob Roy*, *The Pirate* and *Old Mortality*.[51]

There is some evidence that being required to listen to books being read aloud could become wearisome, and even oppressive. Apparently the pleasure of spending evenings 'sitting in the dark, oil-lit drawing-room listening to Leslie [Stephen] reading aloud' waned somewhat as his children grew older.[52] The social pressure on young women to take part in communal reading of books was certainly resented by some – particularly when the books chosen to be read had to meet with the approval of others. Harriet Martineau objected to spending time on such activities when what she really wanted to do was get on with the serious study of philosophy:

> Young ladies ... were expected to sit down in the parlour to sew – during which reading aloud was permitted – or to practise their music; but so as to be fit to receive callers, without any signs of blue-stockingism which could be reported abroad. ... If ever I shut myself into my own room for an hour of solitude, I knew it was at the risk of being sent for to join the sewing-circle, or to read aloud, – I being the reader, on account of my growing deafness.[53]

Florence Nightingale also chafed at the constraints placed upon women by the demands of social life. In a manuscript written during the year before she went off to Paris to begin nursing, she lashed out, memorably, at being forced to sit around 'in company' listening to each other read aloud:

> Everybody reads aloud out of their own book or newspaper – or, every five minutes, something is said. And what is it to be 'read aloud to'? The most miserable exercise of the human intellect. Or rather, is it any exercise at all? It is like lying on one's back, with one's hands tied and having liquid poured down one's throat. Worse than that, because suffocation would immediately ensue and put a stop to this operation. But no suffocation would stop the other.[54]

The testimony of Martineau and Nightingale is an important corrective to any idea that communal reading sessions must always and inevitably have been enjoyable. Nevertheless, there is vastly more evidence that reading aloud gave much pleasure to readers and hearers alike. In an autobiography first published in 1911, George Acorn, the son of illiterate parents living in poverty in the East End of London, relates how he managed to buy for 3½d. a second-hand copy of *David Copperfield*. He read it aloud to his parents:

> And how we all loved it, and eventually, when we got to 'Little Em'ly', how we all cried together at poor old Peggotty's distress! The tears united us, deep in misery as we were ourselves.[55]

From a very different social class, the architect Charles H. Reilly described how, in the early twentieth century, his whole family would gather on Saturday evenings to listen to his father reading *The Pickwick Papers*: 'We had our favourite scenes and would beg for them time after time'.[56] Works by writers now long since forgotten could also give much pleasure. One evening in August 1825, Anne Lister read aloud to her aunt some short stories by Theodore Hook, to the evident enjoyment of them both. 'Excellent', she commented in her diary. 'Don't know when I have laughed so much or so heartily. We both laughed.'[57]

Listening to a work of literature being read aloud could bring it alive and heighten its emotional impact in ways that silent reading might fail to do. In the early nineteenth century, Harriet Martineau recalled the effect on her mother and sister of spending an evening listening to the novelist Amelia Opie reading from her forthcoming novel *Temper, or, Domestic Scenes* (1812). Opie apparently read aloud 'in a most overpowering way', so much so that her hearers came home 'with swollen eyes and tender spirits'. According to Martineau, when her mother and sister read *Temper* in print, 'they could hardly believe it was the same story'.[58] In 1837, only a few months after its first publication, Emma Wedgwood declared that *The Pickwick Papers* 'reads aloud much better than to oneself'.[59] Somewhat similarly, in February 1922, the experience of hearing Middleton Murry reading a Chekov short story was a revelation to Katherine Mansfield. When she had read the same story to herself, silently, she said, 'it seemed to me nothing. But read aloud it was a masterpiece. How was that?'[60]

It is clear, too, that the act of reading aloud could be as pleasurable for the reader as for the listeners. George Eliot, for example, adored reading aloud, particularly with her beloved partner, George Lewes. She told Harriet Beecher Stowe: 'I spend nearly three hours every day in this exercise of reading aloud, which, happily, I can carry on without fatigue of lungs. Yet it takes strength as well as time.' She was pleased to have been able to make 'the evenings cheerful for [her father] during the last five or six years of his life by reading aloud to him Scott's novels'.[61] It is well known that Dickens devoted much of the latter part of his life to giving public readings from his novels, but he had acquired a taste for the gratification of reading aloud much earlier, and in private. After reading his second Christmas story, *The Chimes*, to a group of friends and witnessing their reactions, he wrote to his wife, 'If you had seen Maclise last night – undisguisedly sobbing, and crying on the sofa, as I read – you would have felt (as I did) what a thing it is to have Power'.[62] Robert Louis Stevenson also found reading aloud an intensely satisfying experience. He once described how, reading poems from Walt Whitman's *Leaves of Grass* to a rapt audience,

> I was very much affected myself, never so much before, and it fetched the auditory considerable. Reading these things that I like aloud when I am painfully excited is the keenest artistic pleasure I know: it does seem strange that these dependent arts – singing, acting and in its small way, reading aloud – seem the best rewarded of all arts. I am sure it is more exciting for me to read, than it was for W[alt] W[hitman] to write: and how much more must this be so with singing![63]

There is plenty of evidence that hearing Stevenson read aloud did indeed 'fetch' his auditors. Edmund Gosse remembered the sheer 'intellectual pleasure' of listening to the novelist reading chapters from *Treasure Island* in 1881 at his cottage in Braemar, 'by the lamplight, emphasizing the purpler passages with lifted voice and gesticulating finger', and the writer S. R. Lysaght, who visited Stevenson in Samoa in 1894, vividly remembered him reading the first chapters of *Weir of Herminston* while sitting on the edge of his camp bed: 'I can hear the tone of his voice and see the changing expression on his face as he read, for he was in love with the work . . . and his reading showed his interest'.[64]

I want, finally, to reflect briefly on the place of reading aloud now, in our own society. It still happens: parents and teachers continue to read aloud to children, and religious texts are still read aloud in places of worship. But in the case of adults, apart from religious observance, is there any particular reason to read literature aloud rather than silently?

Reading silently is of course an intensely enjoyable and rewarding activity on which many of us spend a great deal of time. (You are almost certainly reading this chapter silently and alone.) Nevertheless, I want to suggest that there are many reasons why reading literature aloud, and listening to others read aloud, are also intensely enjoyable and rewarding activities. Doing it out loud adds a distinctively physical dimension to the experience of reading. As well as my eyes I have to use my tongue and my lips; I have to control my breathing; I have to think about how to give vocal expression to matters such as rhythm, intonation, pace, stress patterns. It also has a social dimension: I have to think about the people who are listening to me, how to 'connect' with them by eye, facial expression, gesture, and respond to their reactions.

In my view, reading literature aloud is such a valuable and pleasurable activity that it needs no further justification. However, there is a growing body of evidence that it also has a distinctive and useful role to play in society. The Care Homes Reading Project established in 2011 at the University of Exeter is an excellent example, where student volunteers are trained to read poetry, plays and short stories to people in residential care.[65] It is now widely accepted that for people with dementia, hearing poetry read aloud can unlock memories of the past, a phenomenon beautifully and movingly described in Gillian Clarke's poem 'Miracle on St David's Day'. The speaker is reading poetry to patients in a mental hospital, when suddenly a man who had never spoken since entering the hospital gets to his feet and begins reciting Wordsworth's 'Daffodils'.[66]

Further evidence of the beneficial health and social effects of reading aloud is provided by the work of The Reader, an organisation based in Liverpool, which promotes it as a way of improving well-being, reducing social isolation and building stronger communities by enabling ordinary people to connect with, and discuss their responses to, works of serious literature.[67] The idea is that groups meet weekly to read aloud and discuss short stories, poems and even whole novels. They are called 'shared reading groups' to highlight the fact that reading is not being undertaken silently and alone, as in traditional reading groups, but out loud with other people, so that it becomes a social activity. Each member of the group has a copy of the text that they can follow as the oral reading happens, or not, as they choose.

This model of reading and discussing literature has been astonishingly successful. Registered as a charity in 2008, The Reader now delivers over 300 shared reading groups across the UK each week. These are held mainly in community spaces, such as libraries and local community centres, but they are also held in prisons, mental health units and care homes. Research is beginning to be carried out into the social and therapeutic benefits of its 'shared reading' model, in association with the interdisciplinary Centre for Research into Reading, Literature and Society, at the University of Liverpool. So, for example, one group of researchers studied a shared reading group over six weeks. Each session was video-recorded, transcribed and analysed; individual participants were interviewed; and all participants filled in questionnaires designed to elicit their experience of the sessions. The researchers identified five key elements in how reading aloud 'worked'. The first was 'liveness': reading was something done here and now, with others, rather than alone. The second was 'creative inarticulacy': participants were encouraged to search for the best words to express personal feelings, and to follow thoughts without necessarily knowing in advance where they may be leading. The third was 'emotional engagement': reading aloud and discussing the texts enabled deeper reflection on human suffering, so that apparently negative life experiences could be engaged with in new and productive ways. The fourth was 'the personal': participants felt able to bring aspects of their lives to the text, as well as learning from it and measuring it against their own experiences. The fifth was 'the group': connections were made with other people in a dynamic and unpredictable process of open discussion.[68]

In his best-selling book *The Rights of the Reader*, the French novelist Daniel Pennac makes a passionate and witty defence of reading for sheer pleasure. One of his ten 'Rights of the Reader' is the right to read out loud. He rejects any suggestion that 'reading out loud is a dying art', and wonders what writers like Dostoevsky, or Flaubert, or Dickens, or Kafka – all famous readers-aloud – would have made of such an idea. For, as Pennac says: 'when someone reads aloud, they raise you to the level of the book. They *give* you reading, as a gift.'[69]

Notes

1. Nehemiah 8: 1–3; cited from David Norton (ed.), *The Bible: King James Version with The Apocrypha* (London: Penguin Books, 2006).
2. Simon Schama, *The Story of the Jews: Finding the Words 1000 BCE – 1492 CE* (London: Vintage Books, 2014), pp. 32–4.
3. Steven Roger Fischer, *A History of Reading* (London: Reaktion Books, 2003), pp. 150–7.
4. Saint Augustine, *Confessions*, trans. R. S. Pine-Coffin (Harmondsworth: Penguin Books, 1961), pp. 114, 178.
5. William A. Johnson, 'Toward a Sociology of Reading in Classical Antiquity', *American Journal of Philology*, 121 (2000), pp. 593–627.
6. Raymond J. Starr, 'Reading Aloud: Lectores and Roman Reading', *Classical Journal*, 86 (1991), pp. 337–43.
7. Paul Saenger, *Space Between Words: The Origins of Silent Reading* (Stanford: Stanford University Press, 1997), pp. 8, 257.
8. Paul Saenger, 'Reading in the Later Middle Ages', in Guglielmo Cavallo and Roger Chartier (eds), *A History of Reading in the West*, trans. Lydia G. Cochrane (Cambridge: Polity Press, 1999), pp. 120–48 (p. 137).
9. Roger Chartier, 'The Practical Impact of Writing', in Roger Chartier (ed.), *A History of Private Life*, trans. Arthur Goldhammer (Cambridge, MA: Belknap Press, 1989), pp. 124–5.
10. Alberto Manguel, *A History of Reading* (London: Flamingo, 1997), pp. 109–23.
11. Fischer, *A History of Reading*, pp. 159–64 (and see also pp. 274–6).
12. Rosalind Crone, Katie Halsey, W. R. Owens and Shafquat Towheed (eds), *The History of Reading*, 3 vols (Basingstoke: Palgrave Macmillan, 2011).
13. Joyce Coleman, *Public Reading and the Reading Public in Late Medieval England and France* (Cambridge: Cambridge University Press, 1996), p. 108, and passim.
14. Roger Chartier, 'Leisure and Sociability: Reading Aloud in Early Modern Europe', in Susan Zimmerman and Ronald F. E. Weissman (eds), *Urban Life in the Renaissance* (Newark: University of Delaware Press, 1989), pp. 103–20 (p. 104).
15. D. R. Woolf, *Reading History in Early Modern England* (Cambridge: Cambridge University Press, 2000), pp. 80–7.

16. Andrew Cambers, *Godly Reading: Print, Manuscript and Puritanism in England, 1580–1720* (Cambridge: Cambridge University Press, 2011), passim.
17. Elspeth Jajdelska, 'Pepys in the History of Reading', *Historical Journal*, 50 (2007), pp. 549–69.
18. Jacqueline Pearson, *Women's Reading in Britain 1750–1835: A Dangerous Recreation* (Cambridge: Cambridge University Press, 1999), pp. 170–5.
19. Abigail Williams, *The Social Life of Books: Reading Together in the Eighteenth-Century Home* (New Haven: Yale University Press, 2017), pp. 8, 77, and passim.
20. Ronald J. Zboray and Mary Saracino Zboray, *Everyday Ideas: Socio-literary Experience among Antebellum New Englanders* (Knoxville: University of Tennessee Press, 2006), pp. 127–47 (p. 130).
21. Kate Flint, *The Woman Reader 1837–1914* (Oxford: Clarendon Press, 1993), pp. 60, 83, 109, 116, 157–8, 194, 201.
22. Jonathan Rose, *The Intellectual Life of the British Working Classes* (New Haven: Yale University Press, 2002), p. 84.
23. Kevin Sharpe, *Reading Revolutions: The Politics of Reading in Early Modern England* (New Haven: Yale University Press, 2000), pp. 271–2.
24. *The Book of Margery Kempe*, trans. and ed. Anthony Bale (Oxford: Oxford University Press, 2015), p. 130.
25. On the recent growth in popularity of audiobooks, see Matthew Rubery, *The Untold Story of the Talking Book* (Cambridge, MA: Harvard University Press, 2016).
26. Guglielmo Cavallo and Roger Chartier, 'Introduction', in Cavallo and Chartier (eds), *A History of Reading in the West*, p. 32.
27. Cited in David Daniell, *The Bible in English* (New Haven: Yale University Press, 2003), p. 265.
28. *Diary of Lady Margaret Hoby 1599–1605*, ed. Dorothy M. Meads (London: Routledge, 1930), pp. 69, 73, 76, 87, 104, 130.
29. *The Memoir of 1603 and The Diary of 1616–1619: Anne Clifford*, ed. Katherine O. Acheson (Peterborough: Broadview Press, 2007), pp. 123–5, 129.
30. Ri[chard] Ro[gers], *A Garden of Spirituall Flowers* (1609; London: Robert Bird, 1635), p. 123.
31. [Lewis Bayly,] *The Practice of Pietie: Directing a Christian how to Walke that he may Please God* (1612; [London:] John Hodgets, 1624), pp. 343, 365.
32. *The Works of [. . .] Dr. John Tillotson*, 10th edition (London: James, John and Paul Knapton et al., 1735), p. 480.
33. Cited in Paul S. Seaver, *Wallington's World: A Puritan Artisan in Seventeenth-Century London* (Stanford: Stanford University Press, 1985), p. 40.
34. [Anthony Walker,] *The Vertuous Wife: or, The Holy Life of Mrs. Elizabeth Walker* (London: J. Robinson, A. and J. Churchill, J. Taylor, and J. Wyat, 1694), pp. 34, 41, 44, 71.

35. David D. Hall, *Cultures of Print: Essays in the History of the Book* (Amherst: University of Massachusetts Press, 1996), pp. 55–8.
36. John Ruskin, *Praeterita* (1885–9), in *John Ruskin: Selected Writings*, ed. Dinah Birch (Oxford: Oxford University Press, 2004), p. 280.
37. *The Correspondence of Samuel Richardson*, 6 vols, ed. Anna Letitia Barbauld (London: Richard Phillips, 1804), vol. I, p. clxxxvi.
38. Timothy Larsen, *A People of One Book: The Bible and the Victorians* (Oxford: Oxford University Press, 2011), pp. 115, 131, 153, 171.
39. Martyn Lyons and Lucy Taska, *Australian Readers Remember: An Oral History of Reading 1890–1930* (Melbourne: Oxford University Press, 1992), p. 32.
40. William Buchan, *John Buchan: A Memoir* (London: Buchan & Enright, 1982), p. 46.
41. Mary Ellen Lamb, 'Margaret Hoby's Diary: Women's Reading Practices and the Gendering of the Reformation Subject', in Sigrid King (ed.), *Pilgrimage for Love: Essays in Early Modern Literature in Honor of Josephine A. Roberts* (Tempe: Arizona Center for Medieval and Renaissance Studies, 1999), pp. 63–94 (p. 76).
42. Sharpe, *Reading Revolutions*, p. 272.
43. Chartier, 'The Practical Impact of Writing', pp. 148, 149.
44. For the Reading Experience Database, see <http://www.open.ac.uk/Arts/reading/UK> (last accessed 15 August 2019). In notes that follow, I cite the record numbers for items included in RED, as well as the original source.
45. Henry Mayhew, *London Labour and the London Poor*, 4 vols (London: Charles Griffin and Co., [1864?]), vol. I, pp. 27–8; RED record number 1257.
46. John Forster, *The Life of Charles Dickens* (London: Chapman & Hall and Humphrey Milford, n.d.), pp. 485–6.
47. Flint, *The Woman Reader*, p. 224; RED record number 4782. For fuller details, see Frances Power Cobbe, *Life of Frances Power Cobbe* (London: Swan Sonnenschein, 1904), pp. 84–5.
48. Rose, *The Intellectual Life of the British Working Classes*, p. 421; RED record number 5961. See also Howard Spring, *Heaven Lies About Us: A Fragment of Infancy* (London: Constable, 1939), pp. 7–8, 34.
49. *William Allingham: A Diary*, ed. H. Allingham and D. Radford (London: Macmillan, 1908), p. 27.
50. Hermione Lee, *Virginia Woolf* (1996; London: Vintage, 1997), pp. 112, 143.
51. Stanley Baldwin, *Our Inheritance* (1928; London: Hodder and Stoughton, 1938), p. 232.
52. Lee, *Virginia Woolf*, p. 146.
53. *Harriet Martineau's Autobiography*, 3 vols, ed. Maria Weston Chapman (Boston: Osgood, 1877), vol. I, pp. 77–8.
54. Florence Nightingale, *Cassandra* (1852; first published in 1928), in J. M.

Golby (ed.), *Culture and Society in Britain 1850–1890* (Oxford: Oxford University Press, 1986), p. 247.
55. George Acorn, *One of the Multitude* (New York: Dodd, Mead and Co., 1912), p. 35.
56. Philip Waller, *Writers, Readers, and Reputations: Literary Life in Britain 1870–1918* (Oxford: Oxford University Press, 2006), p. 21; RED record number 3101.
57. *No Priest But Love: The Journals of Anne Lister from 1824–1826*, ed. Helena Whitbread (Otley: Smith Settle, 1992), p. 114; RED record number 3018.
58. *Harriet Martineau's Autobiography*, vol. I, p. 324.
59. *Emma Darwin: A Century of Family Letters, 1792–1896*, 2 vols, ed. Henrietta Litchfield (London: John Murray, 1915), vol. I, p. 277; RED record number 29208.
60. *Journal of Katherine Mansfield*, ed. J. Middleton Murry (London: Constable, 1954), p. 251; RED record number 12087.
61. Letters from George Eliot to Harriet Beecher Stowe, 24 June 1872, and to Alexander Main, 9 August 1871, in *The George Eliot Letters, Vol. V: 1869–1873*, ed. Gordon S. Haight (New Haven: Yale University Press, 1954), pp. 281, 175.
62. Letter from Dickens to his wife Catherine, 2 December 1844, cited in Claire Tomalin, *Charles Dickens: A Life* (London: Viking, 2011), p. 159.
63. *Letters of Robert Louis Stevenson, April 1874–July 1879*, 6 vols, ed. Bradford A. Booth (New Haven: Yale University Press, 1994), vol. II, p. 31; RED record number 17357.
64. *Portraits from Life by Edmund Gosse*, ed. Ann Thwaite (Aldershot: Scolar Press, 1991), p. 19; S. R. Lysaght, 'Treasured Island', *Times Literary Supplement*, 4 December 1919; reprinted ibid., 14 April 2017.
65. See <http://readingproject.exeter.ac.uk> (accessed 15 August 2019).
66. Gillian Clarke, *Collected Poems* (Manchester: Carcanet Press, 1997), pp. 36–7.
67. See <http://www.thereader.org.uk> (accessed 15 August 2019).
68. Philip Davis, Josie Billington, Rhiannon Corcoran and others, 'Cultural Value: Assessing the Intrinsic Value of The Reader Organisation's Shared Reading Scheme' (2015), available at <https://www.thereader.org.uk/research> (accessed 2 August 2018). See also the chapter by Philip Davis and Josie Billington, '"A bolt is shot back somewhere in the breast" (Matthew Arnold, "The Buried Life"): A Methodology for Literary Reading in the Twenty-First Century', in Mary Hammond and Jonathan Rose (eds), *The Edinburgh History of Reading: Modern Readers* (Edinburgh: Edinburgh University Press, 2020).
69. Daniel Pennac, *The Rights of the Reader*, trans. Sarah Adams (London: Walker Books, 2006), pp. 96, 171–2.

Select Bibliography

The bibliography lists mostly print publications cited in the text as well as suggested further reading.

A Catalogue of the Entire and Valuable Library of the Late Rev. Michael Lort (London: Leigh and Sotheby, 1791).
A Catalogue of the Entire Library of the Reverend Conyers Middleton, D.D. [. . .] (London: Samuel Baker, 1750–1).
A Catalogue of the Libraries of . . . Mr. J. Killinghal, of Southwark; Mr. E. Bentley, of Coggeshall; and Several Other Eminent Persons Deceased (London: James Buckland, 1741).
A Catalogue of the Town-library of the Late Sir William Burrell [. . .] (London, 1786).
A Curious Collection of Choice Books, being the Library of Thomas Kirke (Leeds, 1706).
Ablow, Rachel (ed.), *The Feeling of Reading: Affective Experience and Victorian Literature* (Ann Arbor: University of Michigan Press, 2010).
Acheson, Katherine O. (ed.), *The Memoir of 1603 and The Diary of 1616–1619: Anne Clifford* (Peterborough: Broadview Press, 2007).
Achinstein, Sharon, *Literature and Dissent in Milton's England* (Cambridge: Cambridge University Press, 2003).
Açıl, Berat (ed.,) *Osmanlı Kitap Kültürü: Carullah Efendi Kütüphanesi ve Derkenar Notları* (Ankara: Nobel, 2015).
Acorn, George, *One of the Multitude* (New York: Dodd, Mead and Co., 1912).
Adam, Wolfgang, 'Privatbibliotheken im 17. und 18. Jahrhundert. Forschungsbericht 1975–1988', *Internationales Archiv für Sozialgeschichte der Deutschen Literatur*, 15:1 (1990), pp. 123–73.
Adams, Tracy, 'État Présent: Christine de Pizan', *French Studies*, 71:3 (July 2017), pp. 388–400.
Adorno, Rolena, *Colonial Latin American Literature: A Very Short Introduction* (Oxford: Oxford University Press, 2011).
Adorno, Rolena, 'Las otras fuentes de Guamán Poma: sus lecturas castellanas', *Histórica*, 2:2 (December 1978), p. 138.

Adorno, Rolena, *The Polemics of Possession in Spanish American Narrative* (New Haven: Yale University Press, 2007).
Ahern, John, 'Singing the Book: Orality in the Reception of Dante's *Comedy*', in Amilcare A. Iannucci (ed.), *Dante: Contemporary Perspectives* (Toronto: University of Toronto Press, 1997), pp. 214–39.
Ahern, John, 'The New Life of the Book: The Implied Reader of the *Vita Nuova*', *Dante Studies*, 110 (1992), pp. 1–16.
Ahern, John, 'What Did the First Copies of the *Comedy* Look Like?', in Teodolinda Barolini and H. Wayne Storey (eds), *Dante for the New Millennium* (New York: Fordham University Press, 2003), p. 9.
Alemany y Selfa, Bernardo, *Vocabulario de las obras de don Luis de Góngora y Argote* (Madrid: Revista de Archivos, Bibliotecas y Museos, 1930).
Allan, David, 'Book-Collecting and Literature in Eighteenth-Century Britain', in *The Yearbook of English of English Studies*, 45 (2015), pp. 74–92.
Allingham, H., and D. Radford (eds), *William Allingham: A Diary* (London: Macmillan, 1908).
Alston, Robin C., *Inventory of Sale Catalogues of Named and Attributed Owners of Books Sold by Retail or Auction 1676–1800: An Inventory of Sales in the British Isles, America, the United States, Canada, India* (Yeadon: privately printed for the author, 2010).
Althusser, Louis, *Lenin and Philosophy and Other Essays*, trans. Ben Brewster (New York: Monthly Review, 1971).
Álvarez, Julio Pimentel, *Francisco Javier Alegre y Diego José Abad: humanistas gemelos* (Mexico City: UNAM, 1990).
Álvarez, Natalia Maillard, 'Early Circulation of Classical Books in New Spain and Peru', in Andrew Laird and Nicola Miller (eds), *Antiquities and Classical Traditions in Latin America* (Chichester: Wiley/SLAS, 2018), pp. 26–40.
Ames, Richard, 'AN ELEGY On the Death of that Learned, Pious, and Laborious Minister of Jesus Christ Mr. Richard Baxter. . .' (London: Printed for Richard Baldwin, 1691).
Ammannati, Francesco, and Angela Nuovo, 'Investigating Book Prices in Early Modern Europe: Questions and Sources', *Italian Journal of Library, Archives and Information Science (JLIS.it)*, 8:3 (2017), pp. 1–25.
Angela of Foligno: Complete Works, trans. Paul Lachance (New York: Paulist Press, 1993).
Annand, William, 'A FUNERAL ELEGIE, Upon the Death of GEORGE SONDS. . .' (London: Printed by John Crowch, 1655).
Anon., 'A Funerall Monument: or the manner of the Herse of the most renowned *Robert Devereux*, Earl of *Essex* and *Ewe*. . .' (London: Printed for J. Hancock in Popes-head Alley, 1646).
Anon., 'A MEMORIAL on the Death of that faithful Servant of Jesus Christ, Nathanael Strange. . .' (London: 1666).
Anon., 'A MITE from Three MOURNERS: In MEMORIAL of *THOMAS GLASS*. . .' (London: 1666).

Anon., 'A PILLAR ERECTED To the Memory of that Holy, Humble, and Faithful Servant of Iesus Christ, Mr. Henry Iesse. . .' (London: 1663).

Anon., 'An Elegiack Acrostick upon The Reverend, Learned, and much to be lamented Mr. Joseph Caryl. . .' (London: Printed for Benj. Hurlock, 1672).

Anon., 'AN ELEGIE UPON . . . Lord Brooke' (printed by Robert Austin, and Andrew Coe, 1643).

Anon., 'An Elegie upon the death of the right Honourable & most renowned, ROBERT DEVEREUX. . .' (London: Printed by R. Austin, 1646).

Anon., 'AN ELEGY On the Death of the Reverend and Pious Mr. Thomas Wadsworth. . .' (London: 1676).

Anon., 'AN ELEGY On the Learned and Zealous Minister of the Gospel, Mr. Christopher Fowler. . .' (London: 1677).

Anon., 'AN ELEGY to Commemorate . . . John Micklevvaite, Kt. . .' (London: Printed for William Miller, 1682).

Anon., 'An ELEGY Upon the death of that Faithful Servant of the LORD . . . Mr. John Wells,' (London: printed for B. H., 1676).

Anon., 'An ELOGY Upon that never to be Forgotten Matron, Old Maddam Gwinn. . .' (1679).

Ansgar Kelly, Henry, and Christopher Baswell (eds), *Medieval Manuscripts: Their Makers and Users. A Special Issue of Viator in Honor of Richard and Mary Rouse* (Turnhout: Brepols, 2011).

Appadurai, A., *The Social Life of Things: Commodities in Cultural Perspective* (Cambridge: Cambridge University Press, 1996).

Arbo, Desiree, 'The Uses of Classical Learning in the Río de la Plata, c. 1750–1815', PhD thesis (University of Warwick, 2016).

Arslan, Mehmet (ed.), *Mihri Hatun Divanı* (Ankara: Kültür ve Turizm Bakanlığı, 2018).

Astorgano Abajo, Antonio (ed.), *Lorenzo Hervás y Panduro: Biblioteca jesuítico-española (1759–1799)* (Madrid: Libris, 2007).

Atalay, Mehmet, and Orhan Başaran, 'Gelibolulu Ali'nin Mecmau'l-Bahreyn Adlı Eseri – I', *Doğu Araştırmaları*, 6 (2010), p. 79.

Atalay, Mehmet, and Orhan Başaran, 'Gelibolulu Ali'nin Rebiu'l-Manzum Adlı Eseri – I', *Doğu Araştırmaları*, 9 (2012), p. 68.

Baird, Joseph L., and John R. Kane (eds and trans.), *La Querelle de la Rose: Letters and Documents* (Chapel Hill: University of North Carolina, Department of Romance Languages, 1978).

Baldini, Ugo, and Gian Paolo Brizzi, *La presenza in Italia dei gesuiti iberici espulsi: aspetti religiosi, politici, culturali* (Bologna: CLUEB, 2010).

Baldwin, Stanley, *Our Inheritance* (1928; London: Hodder and Stoughton, 1938).

Ban, G., 汉书 [*History of Han*] (111 CE; Changsha: Yue Lu Press, 1991).

Ban, Gu (comp.), 汉书 [*The History of the Former Han Dynasty*] (Beijing: Zhonghua shuju, 1962).

Barański, Zygmunt G., 'Dante's Signs: An Introduction to Medieval Semiotics and Dante', in John C. Barnes and Cormac Ó Cuilleanáin (eds), *Dante and the Middle Ages: Literary and Historical Essays* (Dublin: Irish Academic Press, 1995), pp. 150–1.

Barbauld, Anna Letitia (ed.), *The Correspondence of Samuel Richardson*, 6 vols (London: Richard Phillips, 1804).

Barbier, Frédéric, Thierry Dubois and Yann Sordet (eds), *De l'argile au nuage: une archéologie des catalogues (2e millénaire av. J-C – 21e siècle). Catalogue de l'exposition* (Paris: Bibliothèque Mazarine/Bibliothèque de Genève, Éditions des Cendres, 2015).

Barnard, John, 'London Publishing, 1640–1660: Crisis, Continuity, and Innovation', *Book History*, 4 (2001).

Barolini, Teodolinda, and H. Wayne Storey (eds), *Dante for the New Millenium* (New York: Fordham University Press, 2003).

Barthes, Roland, 'The Death of the Author', in *Image–Music–Text* (London: Fontana Press, 1977), pp. 142–8.

Bartra, Enrique (ed.), *III Concilio Provincial de Lima 1582–1583* (Lima: Facultad Pontificia y Civil de Teología de Lima, 1982).

Bayard, Pierre, *Comment parler des livres que l'on n'a pas lus* (Paris: Les Éditions de Minuit, 2007).

[Bayly, Lewis] *The Practice of Pietie: Directing a Christian how to Walke that he may Please God* (1612; [London:] John Hodgets, 1624).

Beckmann, Friedhelm, *Französische Privatbibliotheken: Untersuchungen zu Literatursystematik und Buchbesitz im 18. Jahrhundert* (Frankfurt am Main: Buchhändler Vereinigung, 1988).

Beckwith, Sarah, 'A Very Material Mysticism', in David Aers (ed.), *Medieval Literature: Criticism, Ideology, and History* (New York: St Martin's Press, 1986), p. 37.

Beckwith, Sarah, *Shakespeare and the Grammar of Forgiveness* (Ithaca: Cornell University Press, 2011).

Bedloe, William, AN ELEGIE Upon the Truly Worthy, and ever-to-be-remembred Loyal Gentleman...' (1680).

Bell, David N., *What the Nuns Read: Books and Libraries in Medieval English Nunneries* (Kalamazoo: Cistercian Publications, 1995).

Bell, Maureen, 'Mise-En-Page, Illustration, Expressive Form', in John Barnard and D. F. McKenzie (eds), *The Cambridge History of the Book in Britain* (Cambridge: Cambridge University Press, 2002), vol. IV, p. 632.

Bellomo, Saverio, 'How to Read the Early Commentaries', in Paola Nasti and Claudia Rossignoli (eds), *Interpreting Dante: Essays on the Traditions of Dante Commentary* (Notre Dame: University of Notre Dame Press, 2013), pp. 84–5.

Bergamo, Stefania, and Marco Callegari (eds), *Libri in vendita. Cataloghi librari nelle biblioteche padovane (1647–1850)* (Milan: Franco Angeli, 2009).

Berger, Günter, 'Inventare als Quelle der Sozialgeschichte des Lesens', *Romanistische Zeitschrift für Literaturgeschichte*, 5 (1981), pp. 368–80.

Bermúdez, David Tavárez, *Las guerras invisibles. Devociones indígenas, disciplina y disidencia en el México colonial* (Mexico City: El Colegio de Michoacán, CIESAS, Universidad Autónoma Metropolitana and Universidad Autónoma Benito Juárez de Oaxaca, 2012), p. 237.

Bernier, Marc André, Clorinda Donato and Hans-Jürgen Lüsebrink (eds), *Jesuit accounts of the Colonial Americas: Intercultural Transfers, Intellectual Disputes, and Textualities* (Toronto: University of Toronto Press, 2014).

Beyer, Hartmut, Katrin Schmidt, Jörn Münkner and Timo Steyer, 'Bibliotheken im Buch: Die Erschließung von privaten Büchersammlungen der Frühneuzeit über Auktionskataloge', in Hannah Busch, Franz Fischer and Patrick Sahle (eds), *Kodikologie und Paläographie im digitalen Zeitalter* (Norderstedt: Books on Demand, 2017), vol. IV, pp. 43–70.

Bibliotheca Cantiana (Leiden: Johannes Verbeek & Hermanus Verbeek, [1724]).

Birch, Dinah (ed.), *John Ruskin: Selected Writings* (Oxford: Oxford University Press, 2004).

Bland, Olivia, *The Royal Way of Death* (London: Constable, 1986).

Bléchet, Françoise, *Les ventes publiques de livres en France, 1630–1750: répertoire des catalogues conservés à la Bibliothèque Nationale* (Oxford: Voltaire Foundation, 1991).

Blogie, Jeanne, *Répertoire des catalogues de ventes de livres imprimés* (Brussels: Fl. Tulkens, 1982–2003).

Blom, Helwi, 'La présence de romans de chevalerie dans les bibliothèques privées des XVIIe et XVIIIe siècles', in Thierry Delcourt and Élisabth Parinet (eds), *La Bibliothèque bleue et les littératures de colportage* (Paris: École des Chartes/La maison du boulanger, 2000), pp. 51–67.

Blumenfeld-Kosinski, Renate, 'Christine de Pizan and the Misogynistic Tradition', in Renate Blumenfeld-Kosinski (ed.), *The Selected Writings of Christine de Pizan*, Renate Blumenfeld-Kosinski and Kevin Brownlee (trans.) (New York: Norton, 1997), p. 302.

Bogin, Meg, *The Women Troubadours* (New York: Norton, 1980).

'Book Catalogues, Tomorrow and Beyond: Proceedings of the 2008 Conference Sponsored by the Grolier Club and the Bibliographical Society', *PBSA*, 102:4 (2008), pp. 541–80.

Booth, Bradford A. (ed.), *Letters of Robert Louis Stevenson, April 1874–July 1879*, 6 vols (New Haven: Yale University Press, 1994).

Borah, Woodrow, *El Juzgado general de indios en la Nueva España* (Mexico City: Fondo de Cultura Económica, 1985).

Botterill, Steven, 'Reading, Writing, and Speech in the Fourteenth- and Fifteenth-Century Commentaries on Dante's *Comedy*', in Paola Nasti and Claudia Rossignoli (eds), *Interpreting Dante: Essays on the Traditions of Dante Commentary* (Notre Dame: University of Notre Dame Press, 2013), p. 26.

Bourdua, Louise, *The Franciscans and Art Patronage in Late Medieval Italy* (Cambridge: Cambridge University Press, 2004).

Bowra, Cecil Maurice, *From Virgil to Milton* (New York: St Martin's Press, 1967).

Boyle, L. E., *Integral Palaeography* (Turnhout: Brepols, 2001).

Brading, David, *Mexican Phoenix. Our Lady of Guadalupe: Image and Tradition Across Five Centuries* (Cambridge: Cambridge University Press, 2001).

Brayman Hackel, Heidi, *Reading Material in Early Modern England: Print, Gender, and Literacy* (Cambridge: Cambridge University Press, 2005).

Brooks, E. B., and A. Taeko Brooks, *The Original Analects: Sayings of Confucius and His Successors* (New York: Cambridge University Press, 1998).

Brown, Michelle P., *The Lindisfarne Gospels: Society, Spirituality and the Scribe* (Toronto: University of Toronto Press, 2003).

Bruckner, Matilda, 'Fictions of the Female Voice: The Women Troubadours', in Anne L. Klinck and Ann Marie Rasmussen (eds), *Medieval Woman's Song* (Philadelphia: University of Pennsylvania Press, 2002), pp. 127–51.

Bruni, Flavia, and Andrew Pettegree (eds), *Lost Books: Reconstructing the Print World of Pre-Industrial Europe* (Leiden: Brill, 2016).

Buchan, William, *John Buchan: A Memoir* (London: Buchan & Enright, 1982).

Buettner, Brigitte, 'Profane Illuminations, Secular Illusions: Manuscripts in Late Medieval Courtly Society', *Art Bulletin*, 74:1 (1992), p. 78.

Burgess, Glyn S., and Keith Busby (trans. and eds), *The Lais of Marie de France* (New York: Penguin, 1986).

Burrus, Ernest J., 'Alegre Capetillo, Francisco Javier', in Charles E. O'Neill and Joaquín María Domínguez (eds), *Diccionario Histórico de la Compañía de Jesús* (Rome/Madrid: Institutum Historicum, S.I./Universidad Pontificia Comillas, 2001), pp. 43–4.

Butler, Shane, *The Matter of the Page: Essays in Search of Ancient and Medieval Authors* (Madison: University of Wisconsin Press, 2011).

Byberg, Lis, *Brukte bøker til bymann og bonde: bokauksjonen i den norske litterære offentlighet 1750–1815* (Oslo: Det Humanistiske Fakultet, Universitetet i Oslo, 2007).

Cacho, Rodrigo, 'Balbuena's *Grandeza Mexicana* and the American Georgic', *Colonial Latin American Review*, 24:2 (2015), pp. 190–214.

Cacho, Rodrigo, 'Iberian Myths and American History in Balbuena's *El Bernardo*', in Javier Muñoz-Basols et al. (eds), *The Routledge Companion to Iberian Studies* (London: Routledge, 2017).

Cacho, Rodrigo, and Imogen Choi (eds), *The Rise of Spanish American Poetry, 1500–1700: Literary and Cultural Transmission in the New World* (Oxford: Legenda, 2019).

Cambers, Andrew, *Godly Reading: Print, Manuscript and Puritanism in England, 1580–1720* (Cambridge: Cambridge University Press, 2011).

Cañizares-Esguerra, Jorge, *How to Write the History of the New World: Histories, Epistemologies, and Identities in the Eighteenth-Century Atlantic World* (Stanford: Stanford University Press, 2001).

Cannon Willard, Charity, 'An Autograph Manuscript of Christine de Pizan?', *Studi Francesi*, 27 (1965), pp. 452–7.

Cannon Willard, Charity, *Christine de Pizan: Her Life and Works* (New York: Persea, 1984).

Cannon Willard, Charity, 'The Franco-Italian Professional Writer Christine de Pizan', in Katharina M. Wilson (ed.), *Medieval Women Writers* (Athens: University of Georgia Press, 1984), pp. 333–63.

Capron, Loïc (ed.), *Correspondance française de Guy Patin*, ed. Loïc Capron (Paris: Bibliothèque interuniversitaire de santé, 2015).

Carey, Hilary, 'Astrological Medicine and the Medieval English Folded Almanac', *Social History of Medicine*, 17:3 (2004), pp. 345–63.

Carey, Hilary, 'What Is a Folded Almanac? The Form and Function of a Key Manuscript Source for Astro-Medical Practice in Later Medieval England', *Social History of Medicine*, 16 (2003), pp. 481–509.

Casanova, Pablo González, *La literatura perseguida en la crisis de la colonia* (Mexico City: SEP, 1986).

Catálogos de libreros españoles, 1661–1840: intento bibliográfico (Madrid: Langa, 1945).

Catalogue des livres curieux, qui se vendront dans la salle de l'Hôtel de Ville le 4 de Septembre 1713. delaissez par le Trépas de Mr. de Larre, vivant Pasteur de Verlenghem (Lille, 1713) (Lille, Méd. Jean Lévy, L8–564).

Catalogue des livres de la bibliothèque de feu M.L.B.D. [. . .] (Paris: Méquignon, 1792).

Catalogus Exquisitissimorum Librorum. Juridicorum, Historicorum, & Miscellaneorum [. . .] *Heer Balthazar Boreel* (Amsterdam: Salomon Schouten, [1745]) (Amsterdam, City Archives, Bibliotheek F 526).

Cavallo, Guglielmo and Roger Chartier (eds), *A History of Reading in the West*, trans. Lydia G. Cochrane (Cambridge: Polity, 1999).

Cavallo, Guglielmo, and Roger Chartier, 'Introduction', in Cavallo and Chartier (eds), *A History of Reading in the West*, p. 32.

Cazabon, Marie-Renée, 'Catalogue', in Pascal Fouché, Daniel Péchoin and Philippe Schuwer (eds), *Dictionnaire encyclopédique du livre* (Paris: Éditions du Cercle de la Libraire, 2002), vol. I, pp. 469–79.

Ceccarelli, Maria G., *Vocis et animarum pinacothecae. Cataloghi di biblioteche private dei secoli XVII–XVIII nei fondi dell'Angelica* (Roma: Istituto poligrafico e Zecca dello Stato, 1990).

Çelebi, Aşık, *Meşairü'ş-Şuara*, ed. Filiz Kılıç (Ankara: Kültür ve Turizm Bakanlığı, 2018).

Çelebi, Evliya, *Günümüz Türkçesiyle Evliya Çelebi Seyahatnamesi: 1–6. Kitaplar*, ed. Seyit Ali Kahraman and Yücel Dağlı (Istanbul: Yapı Kredi Yayınları, 2013).

Çelebi, Evliya, *Günümüz Türkçesiyle Evliya Çelebi Seyahatnamesi: 7–10.*

Kitaplar, ed. Seyit Ali Kahraman and Yücel Dağlı (Istanbul: Yapı Kredi Yayınları, 2013).

Çelebi, Kınalızade Hasan, *Tezkiretü'ş-Şuara*, ed. Aysun Sungurhan-Eyduran (Ankara: Kültür ve Turizm Bakanlığı, 2009).

Çelebi, Lamii, *Şerh-i Dibace-i Gülistan* (MS Hacı Selim Ağa 956, Hacı Selim Ağa Manuscript Library, Istanbul).

Chang, Kang-I Sun, and Stephen Owen (eds), *The Cambridge History of Chinese Literature, Vol. I: To 1375* (Cambridge: Cambridge University Press, 2014).

Chapron, Emmanuelle, 'Circulation et usages des catalogues de bibliothèques dans l'Europe du XVIIIe siècle', in Frédéric Barbier and Andrea De Pasquale (eds), *Un'istituzione dei Lumi: la biblioteca. Teoria, gestione e pratiche biblioteconomiche nell'Europa dei Lumi* (Parma: Museo Bodoniano, 2013), pp. 29–49.

Chapron, Emmanuelle, 'Monde savant et ventes de bibliothèques en France méridionale dans la seconde moitié du XVIIIe siècle', *Annales du Midi*, 283 (2013), pp. 409–29.

Charles, John, *Allies at Odds: The Andean Church and Its Indigenous Agents, 1583–1671* (Albuquerque: University of New Mexico Press, 2010).

Charon, Annie, *Esprit des livres* (Paris: École nationale des chartes, 2015), édition électronique at <https://elec.enc.sorbonne.fr/cataloguevente> (accessed 15 August 2019).

Charon, Annie, and Élisabeth Parinet (eds), *Les ventes de livres et leurs catalogues: XVIIe–XXe siècle. Actes des journées organisées par l'Ecole nationale des chartes (Paris, 15 janvier 1998) et par l'ENSSIB (Villeurbanne, 22 janvier 1998)* (Paris: École nationale des chartes, 2000).

Chartier, Roger, 'Communities of Readers', in *The Order of Books: Readers, Authors, and Libraries in Europe*, trans. Lydia G. Cochrane (Stanford: Stanford University Press, 1994), p. 4.

Chartier, Roger, 'Labourers and Voyagers: From the Text to the Reader', in David Finkelstein and Alistair McCleery (eds), *The Book History Reader* (New York: Routledge, 2006), pp. 47–59.

Chartier, Roger, 'Leisure and Sociability: Reading Aloud in Early Modern Europe', in Susan Zimmerman and Ronald F. E. Weissman (eds), *Urban Life in the Renaissance* (Newark: University of Delaware Press, 1989), pp. 103–20.

Chartier, Roger, 'The Practical Impact of Writing', in Roger Chartier (ed.), *A History of Private Life*, trans. Arthur Goldhammer (Cambridge, MA: Belknap Press, 1989), pp. 124–5.

Chatelain, Jean-Marc, *La bibliothèque de l'honnête homme: livres, lectures et collection en France à l'âge classique* (Paris: BnF, 2003).

Chazelle, Celia, 'Painting the Voice of God: Wearmouth-Jarrow, Rome and the Tabernacle Miniature in the Codex Amiatinus', *Quintana*, 8 (2009), pp. 15–59.

Chen, Jack W., *The Poetics of Sovereignty: On Emperor Taizong of the*

Tang Dynasty (Cambridge, MA: Harvard University Asia Center for the Harvard–Yenching Institute, 2010).

Chen, P., *Modern Chinese: History and Sociolinguistics* (New York: Cambridge University Press, 1999).

Chi, X., 中国古代小学教育研究 [*A Study of Elementary Education in Ancient China*] (Shanghai: Shanghai Education Press, 1991).

Chu, Y., 'The Chinese Language', in John Meskill (ed.), *An Introduction to Chinese Civilisation* (New York: Columbia University Press, 1973), pp. 587–615.

Church of England, *Articles to be inquired of in the first trienniall visitation of the most reverend father William* (London, 1637).

Çiçekler, Mustafa, 'Kemal Paşa-zade ve Nigaristan'ı', PhD dissertation (Istanbul University, 1994).

Clanchy, Michael T., *Abelard: A Medieval Life* (Cambridge: Blackwell, 1997).

Clanchy, Michael T., *From Memory to Written Record: England, 1066–1307*, 3rd edition (Chichester: Wiley, 2013).

Clarke, Gillian, *Collected Poems* (Manchester: Carcanet Press, 1997).

Clymer, Lorna, 'The Funeral Elegy in Early Modern Britain: A Brief History', in Karen Weisman (ed.), *The Oxford Handbook of the Elegy* (Oxford: Oxford University Press, 2010), pp. 170–86.

Cobbe, Frances Power, *Life of Frances Power Cobbe* (London: Swan Sonnenschein, 1904).

Coleman, Joyce, *Public Reading and the Reading Public in Late Medieval England and France* (Cambridge: Cambridge University Press, 1996).

Colgrave, Bertram, and R. A. B. Mynors (trans. and eds), *Bede's Ecclesiastical History of the English People* (Oxford: Clarendon Press, 1969).

Colledge, Edmund, and James Walsh (eds), *A Book of Showings to the Anchoress Julian of Norwich* (Toronto: University of Toronto Press, 1978).

Colledge, Edmund, and James Walsh, 'Editing Julian of Norwich's Revelations: A Progress Report', *Medieval Studies*, 38 (1976), pp. 407–10.

'Concolocorvo' (Alonso Carrió de la Vandera), *El lazarillo de ciegos caminantes* (Barcelona: Editorial Labor, 1973).

Confucius, *The Analects* (479 BCE?; Beijing: Zhonghua Press, 1980).

Conte, Gian Biagio, *Stealing the Club from Hercules: On Imitation in Latin Poetry* (Berlin: De Gruyter, 2017).

Cornejo Polar, Antonio, *Discurso en loor de la poesía: estudio y edición* (Lima: CELACP, 2000).

Cornish, Alison, 'A Lady Asks: The Gender of Vulgarization in Late Medieval Italy', *PMLA*, 115 (2000), p. 173.

Crick, Julia C., and Alexandra Walsham (eds), *The Uses of Script and Print, 1300–1700* (Cambridge: Cambridge University Press, 2004).

Crone, Rosalind, Katie Halsey, W. R. Owens and Shafquat Towheed (eds), *The History of Reading* (Basingstoke: Palgrave, 2011).

Cunill, Caroline, *Los defensores de indios de Yucatán y el acceso de los mayas a la justicia real* (Mérida: Universidad Nacional Autónoma de México, 2012).

da Fonseca, Martinho, *Lista de alguns catálogos de bibliothecas públicas e particulares de livreiros e alfarrabistas* (Lisbon: Libanio da Silva, 1913).

Dacier, Émile, 'Des livres précieux sans en avoir l'air: les anciens catalogues de vente', *Bulletin du bibliophile*, 3 (1952), pp. 117–142.

Daems, Jim, and Holly Faith Nelson, *Eikon Basilike*, with selections from *Eikonoklastes* (Orchard Park: Broadview, 2006).

Dağlar, Abdülkadir, 'Şem'i Şem'ullah: Şerh-i Mesnevi, I. Cilt (İnceleme-Tenkitli Metin-Sözlük)', PhD dissertation (Erciyes University, 2009).

Dahl, Gina, *Book Collections of Clerics in Norway, 1650–1750* (Leiden: Brill, 2010).

Dailey, Alice, 'Beyond Typology: King Charles and the Martyrdom of Conscience', in *The English Martyr from Reformation to Revolution* (Indiana: University of Notre Dame Press, 2012).

Dallasta, Federica, *Eredità di carta. Biblioteche private e circolazione libraria nella Parma farnesiana (1545–1731)* (Milan: Franco Angeli, 2010).

Daniell, David, *The Bible in English* (New Haven: Yale University Press, 2003).

Daniels, Rhiannon, *Boccaccio and the Book: Production and Reading in Italy 1340–1520* (London: Legenda, 2009).

Darnton, Robert, 'What Is the History of Books?', *Daedalus*, 111:3 (1982), p. 67.

Davidson, Adele, '"A More Singular Mirror": Herbert, Acrostics, and the Biblical Psalms', *George Herbert Journal*, 38:1–2 (2014–15), p. 15.

Davis, Philip, and Josie Billington, '"A bolt is shot back somewhere in the breast" (Matthew Arnold, "The Buried Life"): A Methodology for Literary Reading in the Twenty-First Century', in Mary Hammond and Jonathan Rose (eds), *The Edinburgh History of Reading: Modern Readers* (Edinburgh: Edinburgh University Press, 2020).

Davis, Philip, Josie Billington, Rhiannon Corcoran and others, 'Cultural Value: Assessing the Intrinsic Value of The Reader Organisation's Shared Reading Scheme' (2015), available at <https://www.thereader.org.uk/research> (accessed 2 August 2018).

de Acosta, José, *Historia natural y moral de las Indias* (Seville: Juan de León, 1590).

de Estrada, Dorothy Tank, 'La enseñanza de la lectura y la escritura en la Nueva España, 1700–1821', in *Historia de la lectura* (Mexico City: El Colegio de México, 2010), p. 49.

de Kooker, Henk W., and Bert van Selm, *Boekcultuur in de Lage Landen, 1500–1800: bibliografie van publikaties over particulier boekenbezit in Noord- en Zuid-Nederland, verschenen voor 1991* (Utrecht: HES, 1983).

de Kruif, José, *Liefhebbers en gewoontelezers: leescultuur in Den Haag in de achttiende eeuw* (Zutphen: Walburg Pers, 1999).

de La Bruyère, Jean, *Les Caractères* [...], ed. Louis Van Delft (Paris: Imprimerie nationale, 1998), ch. 13,' De la Mode', part 2, p. 416.

de la Puente Luna, José Carlos, and Renzo Honores, 'Guardianes de la real justicia: alcaldes de indios, costumbre y justicia local en Huarochirí colonial', *Histórica*, 40:2 (December 2016), pp. 11–47.

de la Roncière, Charles, 'La vida privada de los nobles toscanos en el umbral del Renacimiento', in Philippe Ariès and Georges Duby (eds), *Historia de la vida privada. Poder privado y poder público en la Europa Feudal* (Madrid: Taurus, 1990), p. 221.

de Pizan, Christine, *The Book of the City of Ladies*, Earl Jeffrey Richards (trans.) (New York: Persea, 1982).

Deck, Allan F., *Francisco Javier Alegre: A Study in Mexican Literary Criticism* (Rome/Tucson: Jesuit Historical Institute/Kino House, 1976).

Dede, Esrar, *Tezkire-i Şuara-yı Mevleviyye*, ed. İlhan Genç (Ankara: Kültür ve Turizm Bakanlığı, 2018).

Değirmenci, Tülün, 'Bir Kitabı Kaç Kişi Okur? Osmanlı'da Okurlar ve Okuma Biçimleri Üzerine Bazı Gözlemler', *Tarih ve Toplum: Yeni Yaklaşımlar*, 13 (2011), pp. 7–43.

Değirmenci, Tülün, 'Osmanlı İstanbul'unda Hamzaname Geleneğine Göre Kamusal Okuma', in Coşkun Yılmaz (ed.), *Antik Çağ'dan XXI. Yüzyıla Büyük İstanbul Tarihi* (Istanbul: ISAM, 2015), vol. VII, pp. 634–49.

del Castillo, Francisco Fernández, *Libros y libreros en el siglo XVI* (Mexico City: Fondo de Cultura Económica, 1982).

Delsaerdt, Pierre, and Dries Vanysacker, 'Repertorium van Antwerpse boekenveilingen 1750–1800', *De Gulden Passer*, 75 (1997), pp. 5–119.

Delsaux, Olivier, *Manuscrits et practiques autographes chez les écrivains français de la fin du Moyen Âge: l'exemple de Christine de Pizan* (Geneva: Droz, 2013).

Demaitre, Luke, 'Medical Writing in Transition: Between Ars and Vulgus', *Early Science and Medicine*, 3:2 (1998), pp. 88–102.

Demaitre, Luke, 'Scholasticism in Compendia of Practical Medicine, 1250–1450', *Manuscripta*, 20 (1976), pp. 81–95.

Diego, Gerardo (ed.), *Antología poética en honor de Góngora: desde Lope de Vega a Rubén Darío* (Madrid: Revista de Occidente, 1927).

Dronke, Peter, *Abelard and Heloise in Medieval Testimonies* (Glasgow: University of Glasgow Press, 1976).

Dronke, Peter, 'The Provençal Troubairitz Castelloza', in Katharina M. Wilson (ed.), *Medieval Women Writers* (Athens: University of Georgia Press, 1984), pp. 131–52.

Dronke, Peter, *Women Writers of the Middle Ages: A Critical Study of Texts from Perpetua (203) to Marguerite Porete (1310)* (Cambridge: Cambridge University Press, 1984).

Dular, Anja, 'Problematika raziskovanja zgodovine zasebnih knjižnic – zanke in uganke [Problems Arising When Researching the History of Private Libraries – Traps and Puzzles]', *Knjižnica*, 59:3 (2015), pp. 17–32.

Duncan-Eaves, T. C., 'An Unrecorded Children's Book by Thomas Bewick', *The Library*, series 5, 4 (1951), pp. 272–3.

Duncan-Eaves, T. C., 'Graphic Illustration of the Novels of Samuel Richardson, 1740–1810', *Huntington Library Quarterly*, 14 (1951), pp. 355–6.
Dupront, Alphonse, 'Livre et culture dans la société française du XVIIIe siècle. Réflexion sur une enquête', in Furet (ed.), *Livre et société dans la France du XVIIIe siècle*, pp. 185–238.
Durling, Robert, 'The Audience(s) of the *De vulgari eloquentia* and the Petrose', *Dante Studies*, 110 (1992), pp. 25–35.
Durling, Robert M., and Ronald L. Martinez, *Time and the Crystal: Studies in Dante's* Rime Petrose (Berkeley: University of California Press, 1990).
Earl of Salisbury, 'AN ELEGY IN Commemoration of the Right Honourable James Earl of Salisbury. . .' (1683).
Egan, Caroline, and Vivien Kogut Lessa de Sá, 'Translation and Prolepsis: The Jesuit Origins of a Tupi Christian Doctrine', in Linda Newson (ed.), *The Cultural Legacy of the Jesuits in Latin America* (London: University of London Institute of Latin American Studies, forthcoming).
Eguiguren, Luis Antonio, *Diccionario histórico y cronológico de la real y pontificia universidad de San Marcos y sus colegios* (Lima: Torres Aguirre, 1940), vol. I, p. 289.
Eikon Basilike (London, 1649), Folger Shakespeare Library, E311.
Eisenstein, E. L., *The Printing Press as an Agent of Change* (Cambridge: Cambridge University Press, 1979).
Eisner, Martin, 'The Word Made Flesh in *Inferno 5*: Francesca Reading and the Figure of the Annunciation', *Dante Studies*, 131 (2013), p. 62.
Elliott, J. E., 'The Cost of Reading in Eighteenth-Century Britain: Auction Sale Catalogues and the Cheap Literature Hypothesis', *English Literary History*, 77:2 (2010), pp. 353–84.
Emre, *Terceme-i Pend-nâme-i Attar*, ed. Azmi Bilgin (Istanbul: Enderun Kitabevi, 1998).
Engelsing, Rolf, 'Die Perioden der Lesergeschichte in der Neuzeit', in *Zur Sozialgeschichte deutscher Mittel- und Unterschichten* (Gottingen: Vandenhoeck und Ruprecht, 1973), pp. 112–54.
Erünsal, İsmail E., *Osmanlı Kültür Tarihinin Bilinmeyenleri: Şahıslardan Eserlere, Kurumlardan Kimliklere*, 2nd edition (Istanbul: Timaş, 2019), pp. 69–94.
Erünsal, İsmail E., *Osmanlılarda Kütüphaneler ve Kütüphanecilik* (Istanbul: Timaş, 2015).
Erünsal, İsmail E., *Osmanlılarda Sahaflık ve Sahaflar* (Istanbul: Timaş, 2013).
Erünsal, İsmail E., *Ottoman Libraries: A Survey of the History, Development and Organization of Ottoman Foundation Libraries* (Cambridge, MA: Department of Near Eastern Languages and Literatures at Harvard University, 2008).
Espíndola, Walter Hanisch, *Juan Ignacio Molina: sabio de su tiempo* (Caracas: Universidad Católica Andrés Bello, 1974).
Fabri, Manuel, 'De Auctoris Vita Commentarius', in Francisco Xavier Alegre,

Institutionum Theologicarum (Venice: Antonio Zatta, 1789), vol. I, pp. vii–xxxi.

Farmer, Alan B., and Zachary Lesser, 'What Is Print Popularity? A Map of the Elizabethan Book Trade', in Andy Kesson and Emma Smith (eds), *The Elizabethan Top Ten* (Farnham: Ashgate Publishing, 2013), p. 36.

Fehrenbach, Robert J., and Elisabeth S. Leedham-Green (eds), *Private Libraries in Renaissance England: A Collection and Catalogue of Tudor and Early Stuart Book-Lists* (Binghamton: Medieval & Renaissance Texts & Studies, 1992–2004, and online <https://plre.folger.edu>, accessed 15 August 2019).

Feile Tomes, Maya, '"*Dejando a Italia en mucha parte*": Towards a Poetics of the New World', in Micha Lazarus and Vladimir Brljak (eds), '*Artes poeticae*': *Formations and Transformations, 1500–1650* (special issue of *Classical Receptions Journal*, forthcoming).

Feile Tomes, Maya, 'Introduction', in Matthew Duquès, Maya Feile Tomes and Adam Goldwyn (eds), *Brill's Companion to Classics in the Early Americas* (Leiden: Brill, forthcoming).

Feile Tomes, Maya, 'News of a Hitherto Unknown Neo-Latin Columbus Epic, Part I. José Manuel Peramás's *De Invento Novo Orbe Inductoque Illuc Christi Sacrificio* (1777)', *International Journal of the Classical Tradition*, 22:1 (2015), pp. 1–28; 'Part II', *International Journal of the Classical Tradition*, 22:2 (2015), pp. 223–57; 'Further Points on Peramás', *International Journal of the Classical Tradition*, 22:3 (2015), pp. 383–9.

Feile Tomes, Maya, 'Südamerika: Die spanischsprachigen Länder', in Joachim Jacob and Johannes Süßmann (eds), *Der neue Pauly – Supplementband 13. Das 18. Jahrhundert: Lexikon zur Antikerezeption in Aufklärung und Klassizismus* (Stuttgart/Weimar: J. B. Metzler, 2018), pp. 920–31.

Feile Tomes, Maya, 'The Angel and Ameri(c)a: Performing the "New World" in José Manuel Peramás's *De Invento Novo Orbe* (1777)', in Yasmin Haskell and Raphaële Garrod (eds), *Changing Hearts: Performing Jesuit Emotions between Europe, Asia and the Americas* (Leiden: Brill, 2018), pp. 121–46.

Fein, Susanna (ed.), *Poems and Carols: Oxford, Bodleian Library MS Douce 302, John the Blind Audelay* (Kalamazoo: Medieval Institute Publications, 2009).

Ferrante, Joan M., 'The Education of Women in the Middle Ages in Theory, Fact, and Fantasy', in Patricia H. Labalme (ed.), *Beyond Their Sex: Learned Women of the European Past* (New York: New York University Press, 1984), pp. 9–42.

Ferrell, Lori Anne, 'Introduction', in *Government by Polemic: James I, the King's Preachers, and the Rhetoric of Conformity, 1603–1625* (Stanford: Stanford University Press, 1998).

Fetvacı, Emine, *Picturing History at the Ottoman Court* (Bloomington: Indiana University Press, 2013).

Fincham, Kenneth, and Nicholas Tyacke, *Altars Restored: The Changing Face of English Religious Worship, 1547– c. 1700* (New York: Oxford University Press, 2007).
Fischer, Steven Roger, *A History of Reading* (London: Reaktion Books, 2003).
Fish, Stanley, 'Interpreting the Variorum', in David Finkelstein and Alistair McCleery (eds), *The Book History Reader*, 2nd edition (London: Routledge, 2006), pp. 450–8.
Flint, Kate, *The Woman Reader 1837–1914* (Oxford: Clarendon Press, 1993).
Flouret, Jean, 'La bibliothèque de Richelieu', *Revue française d'histoire du livre*, 24 (1979), p. 615.
Folkenflik, Robert, 'The Rise of the Illustrated Novel to 1832', in Alan Downie (ed.), *The Oxford Handbook to the Eighteenth-Century Novel* (Oxford: Oxford University Press, 2016), p. 316.
Ford, Richard, 'LONDON'S SIGHS For her Worthy Patriot. . .' (1678).
Forster, John, *The Life of Charles Dickens* (London: Chapman & Hall and Humphrey Milford, n.d.).
Francis, W. W., R. H. Hill and Archibald Malloch (eds), *Bibliotheca Osleriana: A Catalogue of Books Illustrating the History of Medicine and Science Collected, Arranged and Annotates by Sir William Osler, Bt., and Bequeathed to McGill University*, 2nd edition (Montreal: McGill-Queen's University Press, 1969).
François, Anne, 'Les collections privées de livres et d'instruments de musique au travers des catalogues de vente bruxellois, durant les règnes de Marie-Thérèse et Joseph II d'Autriche (1740–1790)', *Études sur le 18e siècle*, 19 (1992), pp. 79–82.
Franke, William, *Dante's Interpretive Journey* (Chicago: University of Chicago Press, 1996).
Fraschini, Alfredo Eduardo, and Luis Ángel Sánchez, *Index Librorum Bibliothecae Collegii Maximi Cordubensis Societatis Iesu* (Córdoba: Universidad Nacional de Córdoba, 2005).
Friedman, John B., *Northern English Books, Owners, and Makers in the Late Middle Ages* (Syracuse: Syracuse University Press, 1995).
Furet, François (ed.), *Livre et société dans la France du XVIIIe siècle* (Paris: Mouton, 1965).
Furlong, Guillermo, *Historia y bibliografía de las primeras imprentas rioplatenses, 1700–1850: misiones del Paraguay, Argentina, Uruguay*, 3 vols (Buenos Aires: Guaranía, 1953).
Furlong, Guillermo, *José Manuel Peramás y su Diario del Destierro (1768)* (Buenos Aires: Librería del Plata, 1952).
Galland, Antoine, *Journal d'Antoine Galland pendant son séjour à Constantinople (1672–1673)*, 2 vols, ed. Charles Schefer (Paris: Ernest Leroux, 1881).
Garatea, Carlos, *Tras una lengua de papel. El español en el Perú* (Lima: Pontificia Universidad Católica del Perú, 2010).

García, Idalia, 'Imprenta y librerías jesuitas en la Nueva España', in Pedro Rueda and Idalia García (eds), *El libro en circulación en la América colonial* (Mexico City: Ediciones Quivira, 2014), p. 224.

García-Ballester, Luis, Roger French, Jon Arrizabalaga and Andrew Cunningham (eds), *Practical Medicine from Salerno to the Black Death* (Cambridge: Cambridge University Press, 1994).

García Galán, Agustín, *El 'Oficio de Indias' de Sevilla y la organización económica y misional de la Compañía de Jesús (1566–1767)* (Seville: Fundación Fondo de Cultura Sevilla, 1995).

Gaudio, Michael, *The Bible and the Printed Image in Early Modern England: Little Gidding and the Pursuit of Scriptural Harmony* (New York: Routledge, 2017).

Gay, David, 'Prayer and the Sacred Image: Milton, Jeremy Taylor, and the *Eikon Basilike*', *Milton Quarterly*, 46:1 (2012), pp. 1–14.

Gebauer, Hans Dieter, *Bücherauktionen in Deutschland im 17. Jahrhundert* (Bonn: Bouvier, 1981)

Genette, Gérard, *Paratexts: Thresholds of Interpretation (Literature, Culture, Theory)* (Cambridge: Cambridge University Press, 2010).

Getz, Faye Marie, 'Charity, Translation, and Language of Medical Learning in Medieval England', *Bulletin of the History of Medicine*, 64 (1990).

Gibbs, Laura (trans. and ed.), *Aesop's Fables* (Oxford: Oxford University Press, 2002).

Gillespie, Vincent, 'Seek, Suffer, and Trust: "Ese" and "Disese" in Julian of Norwich', in Sarah Salih (ed.), *Studies in the Age of Chaucer* (London: New Chaucer Society, 2017), vol. XXXIX, pp. 129–58.

Gilson, Simon, 'Modes of Reading in Boccaccio's *Esposizioni sopra la Commedia*', in Paola Nasti and Claudia Rossignoli (eds), *Interpreting Dante: Essays on the Traditions of Dante Commentary* (Notre Dame: University of Notre Dame Press, 2013), p. 251.

Gitlitz, David M., *Secrecy and Deceit: The Religion of the Crypto-Jews* (Philadelphia: Jewish Publication Society, 1996).

Glasscoe, Marion, *English Medieval Mystics: Games of Faith* (London: Longman, 1993).

Glasscoe, Marion (ed.), *Julian of Norwich, Revelation of Love* (Exeter: University of Exeter, 1976, revised edition 1986).

Gobbers, Walter, *Jean-Jacques Rousseau in Holland. Een onderzoek naar de invloed van de mens en het werk (ca. 1760–ca. 1810)* (Ghent: Koninklijke Vlaamse Academie voor Taal- en Letterkunde, 1963).

Golby, J. M. (ed.), *Culture and Society in Britain 1850–1890* (Oxford: Oxford University Press, 1986).

Gómez Álvarez, Cristina, *Navegar con libros. El comercio de libros entre España y Nueva España (1750–1820)* (Madrid: Trama Editorial, 2011).

Gonzalbo, Pilar, 'La lectura de evangelización en la Nueva España', in *Historia de la lectura en México* (Mexico City: El Colegio de México, 1990), p. 37.

Goodwin, Robert, *Spain: The Centre of the World, 1519–1682* (London: Bloomsbury, 2015).
Green, Monica H., *Making Women's Medicine Masculine: The Rise of Male Authority in Pre-modern Gynaecology* (Oxford: Oxford University Press, 2008).
Green, Monica H., 'Moving from Philology to Social History: The Circulation and Uses of Albucasis's Latin *Surgery* in the Middle Ages', in Florence Eliza Glaze and Brian Nance (eds), *Between Text and Patient: The Medical Enterprise in Medieval and Early Modern Europe* (Florence: SISMEL/Edizioni del Galluzzo), pp. 331–72.
Greenblatt, Stephen, *Marvelous Possessions: The Wonder of the New World* (Oxford: Clarendon Press, 1991).
Griffin, Clive, 'La primera imprenta en México y sus oficiales', in Idalia García and Pedro Rueda (eds), *Leer en tiempos de la colonia. Imprenta, bibliotecas y lectores en la Nueva España* (Mexico City: Universidad Nacional Autónoma de México, 2010), pp. 8–9.
Gruys, J. A. (Hans), and Henk W. de Kooker (eds), *Book Sales Catalogues of the Dutch Republic, 1599–1800: Guide* (Leiden: IDC Publishers, 1997).
Guasti, Niccolò, *L'esilio italiano dei gesuiti spagnoli: identità, controllo sociale e pratiche culturali, 1767–1798* (Rome: Edizioni di Storia e Letteratura, 2006).
Guibovich Pérez, Pedro, 'Autores, censores y producción de libros en el virreinato peruano', in Pedro Rueda and Idalia García (coords), *El libro en circulación en la América colonial* (Ciudad de México: Ediciones Quivira, 2014).
Guibovich Pérez, Pedro, *Censura, libros e Inquisición en el Perú colonial, 1570–1754* (Seville: Consejo Superior de Investigaciones Científicas/ Universidad de Sevilla, 2003).
Guibovich Pérez, Pedro, *En defensa de Dios: estudios y documentos sobre la Inquisición en el Perú* (Lima: Fondo Editorial del Congreso del Perú, 1998).
Guibovich Pérez, Pedro, *Lecturas prohibidas. La censura en el Perú tardío colonial* (Lima: Pontificia Universidad Católica del Perú, 2013).
Guibovich Pérez, Pedro, 'Los espacios de los libros', *Lexis*, 27:2 (2003), p. 184.
Guibovich Pérez, Pedro, 'Los libros de los doctrineros en el virreinato del Perú, siglos XV–XVII', in Wulf Oesterreicher and Roland Schmidt-Reise (eds), *Esplendores y miserias de la evangelización de América. Antecedentes europeos y alteridad indígena* (Berlin: De Gruyter, 2010), p. 79.
Guinizelli, Guido, *Poeti del duecento*, 2 vols. ed. Gianfranco Contini (Milan: Ricciardi, 1960).
Güleç, İsmail, *Türk Edebiyatında Mesnevi Tercüme ve Şerhleri* (Istanbul: Pan Yayıncılık, 2008).
Hacker, Joseph R., 'Authors, Readers and Printers of Sixteenth-Century Hebrew Books in the Ottoman Empire', in Peggy K. Pearlstein (ed.), *Perspectives on the Hebraic Book* (Washington, DC: Library of Congress, 2012), pp. 17–63.

Haight, Gordon S. (ed.), *The George Eliot Letters, Vol. V: 1869–1873* (New Haven: Yale University Press, 1954).
Hall, David D., *Cultures of Print: Essays in the History of the Book* (Amherst: University of Massachusetts Press, 1996).
Hammond, Mary, 'Book History in the Reading Experience', in Leslie Howsam (ed.), *The Cambridge Companion to the History of the Book* (Cambridge: Cambridge University Press, 2015), p. 240.
Hammond, Paul, and Maureen Bell, 'The Restoration Poetic and Dramatic Canon', in Barnard and McKenzie (eds), *The Cambridge History of the Book in Britain*, vol. IV, p. 391.
Harriet Martineau's Autobiography, 3 vols, ed. Maria Weston Chapman (Boston: Osgood, 1877).
Haskell, Yasmin, 'Latin Writing by Jesuits During the Long Suppression Period', in Yasmin Haskell, Floris Verhaart and Laurence Brockliss (eds), *Latin Enlightenment* (Oxford: Oxford University Press, forthcoming).
Haskell, Yasmin, 'Practicing What They Preach? Vergil and the Jesuits', in Joseph Farrell and Michael Putnam (eds), *A Companion to Vergil's* Aeneid *and Its Tradition* (Malden: Wiley-Blackwell, 2010), pp. 203–16.
Haskell, Yasmin, 'Sleeping with the Enemy: Tommaso Ceva's Use and Abuse of Lucretius in the *Philosophia Novo-Antiqua* (Milan 1704)', in Juanita Feros Ruys (ed.), *What Nature Does Not Teach: Didactic Literature in the Medieval and Early-Modern Periods* (Brepols: Turnhout, 2008), pp. 497–520.
Haskell, Yasmin, 'Suppressed Emotions: The Heroic *Tristia* of Portuguese (Ex-)Jesuit, Emanuel de Azevedo', *Journal of Jesuit Studies*, 3:1 (2016), pp. 42–60.
Havely, Nick, *Dante and the Franciscans: Poverty and the Papacy in the 'Commedia'* (Cambridge: Cambridge University Press, 2004).
Havlioğlu, Didem, *Mihrî Hatun: Performance, Gender-Bending, and Subversion in Ottoman Intellectual History* (Syracuse: Syracuse University Press, 2017).
Hazen, Helen, 'The Cloistered Books of Peru', *American Scholar*, 6 March 2017, available at <https://theamericanscholar.org/the-cloistered-books-of-peru> (accessed 26 September 2019).
Helgerson, Richard, *A Sonnet from Carthage: Garcilaso de la Vega and the New Poetry of Sixteenth-Century Europe* (Philadelphia: Pennsylvania, 2007).
Helmer, Ángela, *El latín en el Perú colonial: diglosia e historia de una lengua viva* (Lima: Universidad Nacional Mayor de San Marcos, 2013).
Herrlinger, R., *History of Medical Illustration from Antiquity to A.D. 1600* (London: Medicina Rara, 1970).
Hicks, Eric (ed.), *Le débat sure le Roman de la Rose*, Bibliothèque du XVe siècle 43 (Paris: Champion, 1977).
Higgins, Antony, '(Post-)colonial Sublime: Order and Indeterminacy in Eighteenth-Century Spanish American Poetics and Aesthetics', in Álvaro

Félix Bolaños and Gustavo Verdesio (eds), *Colonialism Past and Present: Reading and Writing about Colonial Latin America Today* (Albany: State University of New York Press, 2002), pp. 119–49.

Hill, Matthew J. K., 'Intercolonial Currents: Printing Press and Book Circulation in the Spanish Philippines, 1571–1821', PhD dissertation (University of Texas, 2015).

Hindman, Sandra, 'Aesop's Cock and Marie's Hen: Gendered Authorship in Text and Image in Manuscripts of Marie's Fables', in Jane H. M. Taylor and Lesley Smith (eds), *Women and the Book: Assessing the Visual Evidence* (London: British Library, 1996), pp. 45–56.

Hollander, Robert, 'Dante and Cino da Pistoia', *Dante Studies*, 110 (1992), p. 201.

Hooker, Richard, *The Lawes of Ecclesiastical Polity* (London: 1597).

Horden, Peregrine, 'Prefatory Note: The Uses of Medical Manuscripts', in Barbara Zipser (ed.), *Medical Books in the Byzantine World* (Bologna: Eikasmós Online, 2013), p. 1.

Horden, Peregrine, 'The Millennium Bug: Health and Medicine Around the Year 1000', *Social History of Medicine*, 13:2 (2000), pp. 207–8.

Hu, Q., 中国小学史 [*A History of Chinese Grammatology*] (Shanghai: Shanghai People Press, 2005).

Hume, Robert, 'The Value of Money in Eighteenth-Century England: Incomes, Prices, Buying Power – and Some Problems in Cultural Economics', *Huntington Library Quarterly*, 77:4 (2014), pp. 373–416.

Hunt, Arnold, 'The Lord's Supper in Early Modern England', *Past and Present*, 161:1 (1998), pp. 39–83.

Hunt, Tony, *The Medieval Surgery* (Woodbridge: Boydell, 1992).

Hüseyin, Kefeli, *Razname (Süleymaniye, Hekimoğlu Ali Paşa No. 539): Çeviriyazı ve Tıpkıbasımı*, ed. İ. Hakkı Aksoyak (Cambridge, MA: Department of Near Eastern Languages and Literatures at Harvard University, 2004).

Iannucci, Amilcare A., *Dante: Contemporary Perspectives* (Toronto: University of Toronto Press, 1997).

Icazbalceta, Joaquín García (ed.), *Opúsculos inéditos latinos y castellanos del P. Francisco Xavier Alegre* (Mexico City: Díaz de León, 1889).

Ilsøe, Harald, *Biblioteker til salg. Om danske bogauktioner og kataloger 1661–1811* (Copenhagen: Museum Tusculanums Forlag, København, 2007).

Inan, Murat Umut, 'Crossing Interpretive Boundaries in Sixteenth-Century Istanbul: Ahmed Sudi on the *Divan* of Hafiz of Shiraz', *Philological Encounters*, 3:3 (2018), pp. 275–309.

Inan, Murat Umut, 'Imperial Ambitions, Mystical Aspirations: Persian Learning in the Ottoman World', in Nile Green (ed.), *The Persianate World: The Frontiers of a Eurasian Lingua Franca* (Oakland: University of California Press, 2019), pp. 75–92.

Inan, Murat Umut, 'Imperial Patronage of Literature in the Ottoman

World, 1400–1600', in Hani Khafipour (ed.), *The Empires of the Near East and India: Source Studies of the Safavid, Ottoman, and Mughal Literate Communities* (New York: Columbia University Press, 2019), pp. 493–504.

Inan, Murat Umut, 'Rethinking the Ottoman Imitation of Persian Poetry', *Iranian Studies*, 50:5 (2017), pp. 671–89.

Irmscher, Christoph, 'Reading for Our Delight', *Dante Studies*, 128 (2010), pp. 49–50.

İsen, Mustafa, *Künhü'l-Ahbar'ın Tezkire Kısmı* (Ankara: Atatürk Kültür Merkezi Yayınları, 1994).

Iser, Wolfgang, 'Interaction Between Text and Reader', in David Finkelstein and Alistair McCleery (eds), *The Book History Reader*, 2nd edition (London: Routledge, 2006), pp. 391–6.

Itier, César, 'Las cartas quechuas de Cotahuasi: el pensamiento político de un cacique del siglo XVII', in Bernard Lavalle (ed.), *Máscaras, tretas y rodeos del discurso colonial en los Andes* (Lima: Instituto Francés de Estudios Andinos and Instituto Riva-Agüero, 2005), pp. 44–5.

Jacobs, Nicole, 'Robbing His Captive Shepherdess: Princess Elizabeth, John Milton, and the Memory of Charles I in the "Eikon Basilike" and "Eikonoklastes"', *Criticism*, 54:2 (2012), pp. 227–55.

Jacquart, Danielle, and Charles Burnett (eds), *Scientia in margine: Études sur les marginalia scientifiques du moyen âge à la Renaissance* (Geneva: Droz, 2005).

Jajdelska, Elspeth, 'Pepys in the History of Reading', *Historical Journal*, 50 (2007), pp. 549–69.

Jardine, Lisa, and Anthony Grafton, '"Studied for Action:" How Gabriel Harvey Read His Livy', *Past and Present*, 129 (1990), pp. 30–78.

Jaspers, K., *The Origin and Goal of History* (New Haven: Yale University Press, 1953).

Jayne, Sears, *Library Catalogues of the English Renaissance*, 2nd edition (Godalming: St Paul's Bibliographies, 1983).

Johnson, William A., 'Toward a Sociology of Reading in Classical Antiquity', *American Journal of Philology*, 121 (2000), pp. 593–627.

Jung, Sandro, 'James Robertson's *Poems of Allan Ramsay* (1802) and the Adaptation of Other Scottish Booksellers' Book Illustrations of the Works of Ramsay', *Scottish Literary Review*, 8:1 (2018), pp. 139–58.

Jung, Sandro, *James Thomson's 'The Seasons', Print Culture, and Visual Interpretation, 1730–1842* (Bethlehem: Lehigh University Press, 2015), pp. 158–62.

Jung, Sandro, 'Reading the Romantic Vignette: Stothard Illustrates Bloomfield, Byron and Crabbe for the *Royal Engagement Pocket Atlas*', in Ian Haywood, Susan Matthews and Mary Shannon (eds), *Romanticism and Illustration* (Cambridge: Cambridge University Press, 2019), pp. 143–70.

Jung, Sandro, 'The Other *Pamela*: Readership and the Illustrated Chapbook

Abridgment', *Journal for Eighteenth-Century Studies*, 39:4 (2016), pp. 513–31.

Jung, Sandro, *The Publishing and Marketing of Illustrated Literature in Scotland, 1760–1825* (Bethlehem: Lehigh University Press, 2017).

Jung, Sandro, 'Thomas Stothard's Illustrations for *The Royal Engagement Pocket Atlas, 1779–1826*', *The Library*, 12:1 (2011), pp. 3–22.

Kaimowitz, Jeffrey H., 'Translation of the Apologetical Essay Appended to the *Alexandriad* of Francisco Javier Alegre', *Dieciocho*, 13:1–2 (1990), pp. 135–48.

Kalas Williams, Laura, 'The *Swetenesse* of Confection', *Studies in the Age of Chauce* 40 (2018), pp. 155–90.

Katherine, Acheson, *Early Modern English Marginalia* (London: Routledge, 2019).

Katouzian, Homa, *Sa'di: The Poet of Life, Love and Compassion* (London: Oneworld Publications, 2006).

Kay, Dennis, *Melodious Tears: The English Funeral Elegy from Spenser to Milton* (Oxford: Clarendon Press, 1990).

Kay, Richard, 'The Intended Readers of Dante's *Monarchia*', *Dante Studies*, 110 (1992), pp. 37–44.

Kay, Sarah, *Subjectivity in Troubadour Poetry* (Cambridge: Cambridge University Press, 1990).

Kearney, James, *The Incarnate Text: Imagining the Book in Reformation England* (Philadelphia: University of Pennsylvania Press, 2009).

Keblusek, Marika, 'Gekocht in Den Haag. Hertog August van Wolfenbüttel en de Haagse Elzeviers', in Berry Dongelmans, Paul Hoftijzer and Otto Lankhorst (eds), *Boekverkopers van Europa: het 17de-eeuwse Nederlandse uitgevershuis Elzevier* (Zutphen: Walburg Pers, 2000), pp. 211–24.

Kelly, Henry Ansgar, and Christopher Baswell (eds), *Medieval Manuscripts: Their Makers and Users. A Special Issue of* Viator *in Honor of Richard and Mary Rouse* (Turnhout: Brepols, 2011).

Kempe, Margery, *The Book of Margery Kempe*, trans. and ed. Anthony Bale (Oxford: Oxford University Press, 2015).

Kerny-Fulton, K., *Reformist Apocalypticism and 'Piers Plowman'* (Cambridge: Cambridge University Press, 1990).

Kerson, Arnold L., 'Diego José Abad, *Dissertatio Ludicro-Seria*', *Humanistica Lovaniensia*, 40 (1991), pp. 357–422.

Kerson, Arnold L., 'Francisco Javier Alegre's Translation of Boileau's *Art poétique*', *Modern Language Quarterly*, 41:2 (1981), pp. 153–65.

Kesik, Beyhan (ed.), *Selîmî (II. Selîm) Divançesi* (Ankara: Vizyon Yayınevi, 2012).

Key, Newton, 'Reporting the Rye House Plot: Treason Trial Accounts, Proceedings, and "Prints" Before the State Trials', in Brian Cowan and Scott Sowerby (eds), *Rethinking the State Trials: The Politics of Justice in Later Stuart England* (London: Boydell and Brewer, forthcoming).

Keymer, Thomas, and Peter Sabor, *'Pamela' in the Marketplace: Literary*

Controversy and Print Culture in Eighteenth-Century Britain and Ireland (Cambridge: Cambridge University Press, 2009).

Kılıç, Atabey, 'Türkçe-Farsça Manzum Sözlüklerden Tuhfe-i Şahidi (Metin)', *Turkish Studies*, 2:4 (2007), pp. 516–48.

Kılıç, Filiz (ed.), *Şahi Divanı* (Ankara: Kültür ve Turizm Bakanlığı, 2018).

Kim, Sooyong, 'An Ottoman Order of Persian Verse', in Gülru Necipoğlu, Cemal Kafadar and Cornell H. Fleischer (eds), *Treasures of Knowledge: An Inventory of the Ottoman Palace Library (1502/3–1503/4)* (Leiden: Brill, 2019), vol. I, pp. 635–56.

Knight, Sarah, and Stefan Tilg (eds), *The Oxford Handbook of Neo-Latin* (Oxford: Oxford University Press, 2015).

Knoppers, Laura Lunger, *Politicizing Domesticity from Henrietta Maria to Milton's Eve* (New York: Cambridge University Press, 2011).

Kolve, V. A., and Glending Olson (eds), *Geoffrey Chaucer: The Canterbury Tales* (New York: Norton, 1989).

Krijn, Sophie A., 'Franse lektuur in Nederland in het begin van de 18e eeuw', *De Nieuwe Taalgids*, 11 (1917), pp. 161–78.

Kuru, Selim S., 'The Literature of Rum: The Making of a Literary Tradition (1450–1600)', in Suraiya N. Faroqhi and Kate Fleet (eds), *The Cambridge History of Turkey* (Cambridge: Cambridge University Press, 2013), vol. II, pp. 548–92.

Lacey, Andrew, 'Texts to be Read: Charles I and the *Eikon Basilike*', *Prose Studies*, 29:1 (2007), p. 5.

Lacey, Barbara E., *From Sacred to Secular: Visual Images in Early American Publications* (Newark: University of Delaware Press, 2007).

Lai, Yanyuan (annot. and trans.), 韓詩外傳今注今譯 [*An Annotated Edition of Hanshi Waizhuan with Modern Translation*] (Taipei: Taiwan shangwu yinshuguan, 1972).

Laidlaw, James, 'Christine and the Manuscript Tradition', in Barbara K. Altmann and Deborah L. McGrady (eds), *Christine de Pizan: A Casebook* (New York: Routledge, 2003), pp. 119–21.

Laidlaw, James, 'Christine de Pizan as Publisher', *Modern Language Review*, 82 (1987), pp. 35–75.

Laird, Andrew, 'Classical Letters and Millenarian Madness in Post-Conquest Mexico: The *Ecstasis* of Fray Cristóbal Cabrera (1548)', *International Journal of the Classical Tradition*, 24:1 (2017), pp. 78–108.

Laird, Andrew, 'Colonial Spanish America and Brazil', in Sarah Knight and Stefan Tilg (eds), *The Oxford Handbook of Neo-Latin* (Oxford: Oxford University Press, 2015), pp. 525–40.

Laird, Andrew, 'Latin America', in Philip Ford et al. (eds), *Brill's Encylopaedia of the Neo-Latin World* (Leiden: Brill, 2014), pp. 821–32.

Laird, Andrew, 'Nahua Latinists: Classical Learning and Indigenous Legacies in Sixteenth-Century Mexico', in Matthew Duquès, Maya Feile Tomes and Adam Goldwyn (eds), *Brill's Companion to Classics in the Early Americas* (Leiden: Brill, forthcoming).

Laird, Andrew, 'Patriotism and the Rise of Latin in Eighteenth-Century New Spain: Disputes of the New World and the Jesuit Constructions of a Mexican Legacy', *Renæssanceforum*, 8 (2012), pp. 231–62.

Laird, Andrew, *The Epic of America: An Introduction to Rafael Landívar and the* Rusticatio Mexicana (London: Duckworth, 2006).

Lamb, Mary Ellen, 'Margaret Hoby's Diary: Women's Reading Practices and the Gendering of the Reformation Subject', in Sigrid King (ed.), *Pilgrimage for Love: Essays in Early Modern Literature in Honor of Josephine A. Roberts* (Tempe: Arizona Center for Medieval and Renaissance Studies, 1999), pp. 63–94.

Lambour, Ruud, 'Het boekenbezit van Amsterdamse doopsgezinden uit de Gouden Eeuw', *Doopsgezinde Bijdragen Nieuwe Reeks*, 40 (2014), pp. 135–60.

Lang, Anouk, *From Codex to Hypertext: Reading at the Turn of the Twenty-First Century* (Amherst: University of Massachusetts Press, 2012).

Lankhorst, Otto, 'Dutch Book Auctions in the Seventeenth and Eighteenth Centuries', in Robin Myers, Michael Harris and Giles Mandelbrote (eds), *Under the Hammer: Book Auctions since the Seventeenth Century* (New Castle, DE: Oak Knoll Press; and London: British Library, 2001), pp. 65–88.

Lansing, Richard, 'Dante's Intended Audience in the *Convivio*', *Dante Studies*, 110 (1992), pp. 17–24.

Lapidge, Michael, Katherine O'Brien O'Keeffe and Andy Orchard (eds), *Latin Learning and English Lore: Studies in Anglo-Saxon Literature* (Toronto: University of Toronto Press, 2005).

Larsen, Timothy, *A People of One Book: The Bible and the Victorians* (Oxford: Oxford University Press, 2011).

Latifi, Abdüllatif, *Tezkiretü'ş-Şuara ve Tabsıratü'n-Nuzama*, ed. Rıdvan Canım (Ankara: Atatürk Kültür Merkezi Başkanlığı, 2000).

Laud, William, *A speech delivered in the Starr-chamber* (London, 1637).

Lawson, Sarah, *Treasure of the City of Ladies* (New York: Penguin, 2003).

Lee, Hermione, *Virginia Woolf* (1996; London: Vintage, 1997).

Lee, T. H. C., *Education in Traditional China: A History* (Boston: Brill, 2000).

Leedham-Green, Elisabeth S., *Books in Cambridge Inventories: Book-Lists from Vice-Chancellor's Court Probate Inventories in the Tudor and Stuart Periods* (Cambridge: Cambridge University Press, 1986).

Leinsle, Ulrich G., *Introduction to Scholastic Theology*, trans. Michael J. Miller (Washington, DC: Catholic University of American Press, 2010).

L'Engle, Susan, 'The Pro-Active Reader: Learning to Learn the Law', in Henry Ansgar Kelly and Christopher Baswell (eds), *Medieval Manuscripts: Their Makers and Users. A Special Issue of* Viator *in Honor of Richard and Mary Rouse* (Turnhout: Brepols, 2011), pp. 51–75.

Leonard, Irving, *Baroque Times in Old Mexico: Seventeenth-Century*

Persons, Places, and Practices (Ann Arbor: University of Michigan Press, 1959).
Leonard, Irving, *Books of the Brave: Being an Account of Books and of Men in the Spanish Conquest and Settlement of the Sixteenth-Century New World* (Cambridge, MA: Harvard University Press, 1949).
Leonard, Irving, *Don Carlos de Sigüenza y Góngora: A Mexican Savant of the Seventeenth Century* (Berkeley: University of California Press, 1929).
Leonard, Irving, *Los libros del conquistador* (Mexico City: Fondo de Cultura Económica, 1979).
Levers, Stanley W., 'From Revelation to Dilation in Dante's *Studio*', *Dante Studies*, 134 (2016), pp. 11–12.
Lewis, Franklin D., *Rumi, Past and Present, East and West: The Life, Teachings and Poetry of Jalal al-Din Rumi* (London: Oneworld Publications, 2000).
Lewis, M. E., *Writing and Authority in Early China* (Albany: SUNY Press, 1999).
Lewis, Robert E., et al. (eds), *Middle English Dictionary*, Ann Arbor (University of Michigan Press, 1952–2001). Online edition in Middle English Compendium, ed. Frances McSparran, et al. (Ann Arbor: University of Michigan Library, 2000–18).
Lewisohn, Leonard (ed.), *Hafiz and the Religion of Love in Classical Persian Poetry* (London: I. B. Tauris, 2010).
Lewisohn, Leonard, and Christopher Shackle (eds), *Attar and the Persian Sufi Tradition: The Art of Spiritual Flight* (London: I. B. Tauris, 2006).
Li, F., and D. P. Branner (eds), *Writing and Literacy in Early China: Studies from the Columbia Early China Seminar* (Seattle: University of Washington Press, 2011).
Lisson Chaves, Emilio, *La Iglesia de España en el Perú* (Sevilla: Editorial Católica, 1943–1956).
Litchfield, Henrietta (ed.), *Emma Darwin: A Century of Family Letters, 1792–1896*, 2 vols (London: John Murray, 1915).
Lochrie, Karma, *Margery Kempe and Translations of the Flesh* (Philadelphia: University of Pennsylvania Press, 1991), pp. 100–1.
Loh, Gerhard, *Die europäischen Privatbibliotheken und Buchauktionen. Ein Verzeichnis ihrer Kataloge* (Leipzig: Universitätsbibliothek Leipzig, 1996–).
Loh, Gerhard, *Verzeichnis der Kataloge von Buchauktionen und Privatbibliotheken aus dem deutschsprachigen Raum* (Leipzig: Universitätsbibliothek Leipzig, 1995–).
Lombardi, Elena, *The Wings of the Doves: Love and Desire in Dante and Medieval Culture* (Montreal: McGill-Queen's University Press, 2012).
López, Rosalva Loreto, 'Leer, contar, cantar y escribir. Un acercamiento a las prácticas de lectura conventual. Puebla de los Ángeles, México, siglos XVII–XVIII', *Estudios de historia novohispana*, 23 (2000), p. 78.

Lyons, Martyn, and Lucy Taska, *Australian Readers Remember: An Oral History of Reading 1890–1930* (Melbourne: Oxford University Press, 1992).
Lysaght, S. R., 'Treasured Island', *Times Literary Supplement*, 4 December 1919.
Madan, Francis, *New Bibliography of the* Eikon Basilike *of King Charles the First, With a Note on the Authorship* (Oxford: Oxford University Press, 1950).
Magaloni Kerpel, Diana, *The Colors of the New World: Artists, Materials, and the Creation of the* Florentine Codex (Los Angeles: Getty Research Institute, 2014).
Maillard Álvarez, Natalia (ed.), *Books in the Catholic World During the Early Modern Period* (Leiden: Bril, 2014).
Makeham, John, 'On the Formation of Lun Yu as a Book', *Monumenta Serica*, 44 (1996), p. 1.
Makeham, John, *Transmitters and Creators: Chinese Commentators and Commentaries on the 'Analects'* (Cambridge, MA: Harvard University Press, 2003).
Mäkinen, Virpi, *Property Rights in the Late Medieval Discussion of Franciscan Poverty* (Leuven: Peeters, 2001).
Maltby, Judith, *Prayer Book and People in Elizabethan and Early Stuart England* (Cambridge: Cambridge University Press, 1998).
Maltby, Judith, 'Suffering and Surviving: The Civil Wars, the Commonwealth and the Formation of "Anglicanism"', in Christopher Durston and Judith Maltby (eds), *Religion in Revolutionary England* (Manchester: Manchester University Press, 2006), pp. 158–80.
Manguel, Alberto, *A History of Reading* (London: Penguin, 1997).
Marion, Michel, *Collections et collectionneurs de livres au XVIIIe siècle* (Paris: H. Champion, 1999).
Marion, Michel, *Les Bibliothèques privées à Paris au milieu du XVIIIe siècle* (Paris: BnF, 1978).
Marsilius of Padua, *The Defender of Peace*, trans. Alan Gewirth (New York: Columbia University Press, 1956).
Martin, Philippe, *Une religion des livres: 1640–1850* (Paris: Éditions du Cerf, 2003).
Martínez, José Luis, *El libro en Hispanoamérica. Origen y desarrollo* (Madrid: Fundación G. Sánchez-Ruipérez, 1986).
Martínez, Miguel, *Front Lines: Soldiers' Writing in the Early Modern Hispanic World* (Philadelphia: University of Pennsylvania Press, 2016).
Martínez, Miguel, 'Writing on the Edge: The Poet, the Printer, and the Colonial Frontier in Ercilla's *La Araucana* (1569–1590)', *Colonial Latin American Review*, 26:2 (2017), pp. 132–53.
Masson, Nicole, 'Typologie des catalogues de vente', in Charon and Parinet (eds), *Les ventes de livres*, pp. 119–27.
Mattingly, Harold, and Ian A. K. Burnett, *List of Catalogues of English*

Book Sales, 1676–1900, now in the British Museum (London: British Museum, Department of Printed Books, 1915).

Maurach, Gregor, 'Johannicius. Isagoge ad Techne Galieni', Sudhoffs Archiv, 62:2 (1978), pp. 148–74.

Mayhew, Henry, London Labour and the London Poor, 4 vols (London: Charles Griffin and Co., [1864?]).

McCoy, Richard, Alterations of State: Sacred Kingship in the English Reformation (New York: Columbia University Press).

McGrady, Deborah, 'Reading for Authority: Portraits of Christine de Pizan and Her Readers', in Stephen Partridge and Erik Kwakkel (eds), *Author, Reader, Book: Medieval Authorship in Theory and Practice* (Toronto: University of Toronto Press, 2012), pp. 154–77.

McGrath, Alister E., *Iustitia Dei: A History of the Christian Doctrine of Justification*, 3rd edition (Cambridge: Cambridge University Press, 2005).

McKay, George L., *American Book Auction Catalogues, 1713–1934* (New York: New York Public Library, 1937).

McKitterick, Rosamond (ed.), *The Uses of Literacy in Early Mediaeval Europe* (Cambridge: Cambridge University Press, 1990).

McManus, Stuart, 'Humanismo en la ciudad mundial: Gaspar de San Agustín', *Revista de Crítica Literaria Latinoamericana*, 88 (2018).

Meads, Dorothy M. (ed.), *Diary of Lady Margaret Hoby 1599–1605* (London: Routledge, 1930).

Means, Laurel, *Medieval Lunar Astrology: A Collection of Representative Middle English Texts* (Lewiston: Edwin Mellen Press, 1993).

Medina, José Toribio, *Bibliografía española de las Islas Filipinas, 1523–1810* (Amsterdam: N. Israel, 1966; reprint of the original 1897-8 Santiago de Chile edition).

Medina, José Toribio, *Biblioteca hispano-americana, 1492–1810* (Amsterdam: N. Israel, 1962; reprint of the original 1898 Santiago de Chile edition).

Meech Brown, Sanford, and Hope Emily Allen (eds), *The Book of Margery Kempe* (New York: Oxford University Press, 1940).

Menagiana (Paris: Florentin et Pierre Delaulne, 1693).

Mencius, 孟子 [*Mencius*] (300 BCE?; Beijing: Zhonghua Press, 2015).

Méndez Plancarte, Gabriel, *Horacio en México* (Mexico City: Universidad Nacional Autónoma de México, 1937).

Méndez Plancarte, Gabriel, *Humanistas del siglo XVIII* (Mexico City: Universidad Nacional Autónoma de México, 1941).

Mews, Constant J., *Abelard and Heloise* (Oxford: Oxford University Press, 2005).

Mews, Constant J., with Neville Chiavaroli (ed. and trans.), *The Lost Love Letters of Heloise and Abelard: Perceptions of Dialogue in Twelfth-Century France* (New York: St Martin's Press, 1999).

Middleton, Roger, 'Chrétien de Troyes at Auction: Nicolas-Joseph Foucault and Other Eighteenth-Century Collectors', in Peter Damian-Grint (ed.),

Medievalism and 'manière gothique' in Enlightenment France (Oxford: Voltaire Foundation, 2006), pp. 261–83.

Middleton Murry, J. (ed.), *Journal of Katherine Mansfield* (London: Constable, 1954).

Mignolo, Walter, *The Darker Side of the Renaissance: Literacy, Territoriality, and Colonization* (Ann Arbor: Michigan, 2003).

Miller, D. A., *The Novel and the Police* (Berkeley: University of California Press, 1988).

Mills, Kenneth, and William Taylor, *Colonial Spanish America: A Documentary History* (Wilmington: Scholarly Resources, 1998).

Minnis, A. J., *Medieval Theory of Authorship: Scholastic Literary Attitudes in the Later Middle Ages* (Philadelphia: University of Pennsylvania Press, [1984] 1988).

Mojarro Romero, Jorge, *A History of the Book in the Philippines (1521–1845)* (Quezon City: Vibal Foundation, forthcoming).

Monok, István, *Könyvkatalógusok és könyvjegyzékek Magyarországon, 1526–1720, Forrástipológia, forráskritika, forráskiadás* (Szeged: Scriptum, 1993).

Monok, István, 'Les bibliothèques privées et la lecture à l'époque moderne: un aperçu des orientations de la recherche en Europe, 1958–2008', in Dominique Varry (ed.), *50 ans d'histoire du livre: 1958–2008* (Lyon: Enssib, 2014), pp. 140–56.

Montoya, Alicia C., 'French and English Women Writers in Dutch Library Catalogues, 1700–1800: Some Methodological Considerations and Preliminary Results', in Suzan van Dijk, Petra Broomans, Janet F. van der Meulen and Pim van Oostrum (eds), *'I Have Heard About You'. Foreign Women's Writing Crossing the Dutch Border: From Sappho to Selma Lagerlöf* (Hilversum: Verloren, 2004), pp. 182–216.

Montoya, Alicia, 'Middlebrow, Religion, and The European Enlightenment: A New Bibliometric Project, MEDIATE (1665–1820)', *French History and Civilization*, 7 (2017), pp. 66–79, at <http://h-france.net/rude/vol7/montoya7> (accessed 15 August 2019).

Monumentum Regale or a tomb, erected for that incomparable and glorious monarch, Charles the First, King of Great Britane, France and Ireland (London, 1649).

Mooney, Linne, 'Manuscript Evidence for the Use of Utilitarian Writings in Late Medieval England', in Richard Firth Green and Linne R. Mooney (eds), *Interstices: Studies in Middle English and Anglo-Latin Texts in Honour of A. G. Rigg* (Toronto: University of Toronto Press, 2004), pp. 184–202.

Moretti, Franco, *Distant Reading* (London: Verso, 2013).

Mornet, Daniel, 'Les enseignements des bibliothèques privées (1750–1780)', *Revue d'histoire littéraire de la France*, 17 (1910), pp. 449–96.

Moss Quinn, Meredith, 'Books and Their Readers in Seventeenth-Century Istanbul', PhD dissertation (Harvard University, 2016).

Munby, Alan N. L., and Lenore Coral (eds), *British Book Sale Catalogues 1676–1800: A Union List* (London: Mansell, 1977).

Murray Jones, Peter, 'Harley MS 2558: A Fifteenth Century Medical Commonplace Book', in Margaret Schleissner (ed.), *Manuscript Sources of Medieval Medicine* (New York: Garland, 1995), pp. 37–40.

Murray Jones, Peter, 'Staying with the Programme: Illustrated Manuscripts of John of Arderne, c. 1380–c. 1550', *English Manuscript Studies*, 10 (2002), p. 210.

Murray Jones, Peter, 'Thomas Fayreford: An English Fifteenth-Century Practitioner', in Roger French, Jon Arrizabalaga, Andrew Cunningham and Luis Garcís Ballester (eds), *Medicine from the Black Death to the French Disease* (Cambridge: Cambridge University Press, 1998), pp. 156–63.

Murray Jones, Peter, 'Witnesses to Medieval Medical Practice in the Harley Collection', *Electronic British Library Journal* (2008), p. 2, at <http://www.bl.uk/eblj/2008articles/articles.html> (last accessed 5 August 2019).

Mustafa Ali, Gelibolulu, *Divanlar: I. Divan, II. Varidatü'l-Enika, III. Layıhatü'l-Hakika, IV. Divan*, ed. İ. Hakkı Aksoyak (Ankara: Kültür ve Turizm Bakanlığı, 2018).

Mustain, James K., 'A Rural Medical Practitioner in Fifteenth-Century England', *Bulletin of the History of Medicine*, 45:5 (1972), pp. 469–76.

Myers, Robin, Michael Harris and Giles Mandelbrote (eds), *Under the Hammer: Book Auctions since the Seventeenth Century* (New Castle, DE: Oak Knoll Press; and London: British Library, 2001).

Nasti, Paola, and Claudia Rossignoli (eds), *Interpreting Dante: Essays on the Traditions of Dante Commentary* (Notre Dame: University of Notre Dame Press, 2013).

Navarro, Bernabé (ed.), *Vidas de mexicanos ilustres del siglo XVIII – Juan Luis Maneiro y Manuel Fabri* (Mexico City: UNAM, 1956).

Nazmi, Edirneli, *Pend-name-i Nazmi (Tercüme-i Pend-name-i Attar)*, ed. Kudret Altun (Kayseri: Laçin, 2004).

Netzley, Ryan, *Reading, Desire, and the Eucharist in Early Modern Religious Poetry* (Toronto: University of Toronto Press, 2011).

Neumann, Christoph K., 'Üç Tarz-ı Mütalaa: Yeniçağ Osmanlı Dünyası'nda Kitap Yazmak ve Okumak', *Tarih ve Toplum: Yeni Yaklaşımlar*, 1 (2005), pp. 51–76.

Neveu, Valérie, 'L'inscription de la classification bibliographique dans le champ des sciences (fin XVIIe–début XVIIIe s.)', November 2010, Angers, France, at <https://halshs.archives-ouvertes.fr/halshs-00599276> (accessed 15 August 2019).

Newman, Barbara, *Making Love in the Twelfth Century: 'Letters of Two Lovers' in Context* (Philadelphia: University of Pennsylvania Press, 2016).

Nightingale, Florence, *Cassandra* (1852; first published in 1928), in J. M. Golby (ed.), *Culture and Society in Britain 1850–1890* (Oxford: Oxford University Press, 1986), p. 247.

North, Michael, *Printed Catalogues of French Book Auctions and Sales by*

Private Treaty, 1643–1830, in the Library of the Grolier Club (New York: Grolier Club, 2004).

Norton, David (ed.), *The Bible: King James Version with The Apocrypha* (London: Penguin Books, 2006).

Novikoff, Alex J., *The Medieval Culture of Disputation: Pedagogy, Practice, and Performance* (Philadelphia: University of Pennsylvania Press, 2013).

Nyström, Eva, 'Looking for the Purpose Behind a Multitext Book: The Miscellany as a Personal "One-Volume Library"', in L. Doležalová and K. Rivers (eds), *Medieval Manuscript Miscellanies: Composition, Authorship, Use* (Krems: Institut für Realienkunde des Mittelalters und der frühen Neuzeit, 2013).

O'Boyle, Cornelius, *Medieval Prognosis and Astrology. A Working Edition of the Aggregationes de crisi et creticis diebus: with Introduction and English Summary* (Cambridge: Wellcome Unit for the History of Medicine, 1991).

Oldridge, Darren, *Religion and Society in Early Stuart England* (Brookefield: Ashgate, 1998).

Olson, D. R., 'From Utterance to Text: The Bias of Language in Speech and Writing', in S. W. Beck and L. N. Olah (eds), *Perspectives on Language and Literacy: Beyond the Here and Now* (Cambridge, MA: Harvard Educational Review, 2001), pp. 137–60.

O'Neill, Charles E., and Joaquín María Domínguez (eds), *Diccionario Histórico de la Compañía de Jesús* (Rome/Madrid: Institutum Historicum, SI/Universidad Pontificia Comillas, 2001).

Ong, Walter J., *Orality and Literacy: The Technologizing of the Word* (New York: Methuen, 1982).

Onuş, Muhammed Usame, 'Bir Osmanlı Alimi Veliyyüddin Carullah Efendi'nin Terceme-i Hali', in Berat Açıl (ed.,) *Osmanlı Kitap Kültürü: Carullah Efendi Kütüphanesi ve Derkenar Notları* (Ankara: Nobel, 2015), pp. 17–43.

Ouy, Gilbert, and Christine M. Reno, 'Identification des autographes de Christine de Pizan', *Scriptorium*, 34 (1980), pp. 221–38.

Owen, Stephen, *Readings in Chinese Literary Thought* (Cambridge, MA: Council on East Asian Studies, Harvard University Press, 1992).

Öz, Yusuf, *Tarih Boyunca Farsça-Türkçe Sözlükler* (Ankara: Türk Dil Kurumu, 2010).

Özdemir, Mehmet, 'Türk Edebiyatında Gülistan Tercümeleri ve 17. Yüzyıl Yazarlarından Hocazade Esad Mehmed Efendi'nin Gül-i Handan (Terceme-i Gülistan)'ı', PhD dissertation (Gazi University, 2011).

Öztürk, Zehra, 'Osmanlı Döneminde Kıraat Meclislerinde Okunan Halk Kitapları', *Türkiye Araştırmaları Literatür Dergisi*, 5:9 (2007), pp. 401–45.

Paden, Jr, William D., 'The Poems of the Trobairitz Na Castelloza', *Romance Philology*, 35 (1981), pp. 158–82.

Padrón, Ricardo, *The Spacious Word: Cartography, Literature, and Empire in Early Modern Spain* (Chicago: University of Chicago Press, 2004).

Palacios, Felipe Reyes, and José Quiñones Melgoza (eds), *Nicolas Boileau-Despréaux, Francisco Javier Alegre: Arte Poética. Edición bilingüe* (Mexico City: UNAM, 2014).

Paladini, Mariantonietta, *Lucrezio e l'epicureismo tra Riforma e Controriforma* (Naples: Liguori, 2011).

Parada, Concepción Rodríguez, 'Los catálogos e inventarios en la historia del libro y de las bibliotecas', *BiD: textos universitaris de biblioteconomia i documentación*, 18 (2007), at <http://www.ub.edu/bid/18rodri4.htm> (accessed 15 August 2019).

Park, Dabney G., 'The Good, the Bad, and the Ugly: What Dante Says about Bonaventure of Bagnoregio, Matthew of Acquasparta, and Ubertino da Casale', *Dante Studies*, 132 (2014), p. 275.

Parkes, Malcolm B., *Pause and Effect: Punctuation in the West* (Berkeley: University of California Press, 1993).

Parsons, Kelly, 'The Red Ink Annotator', in Kathryn Kerby-Fulton and Maidie Hilmo (eds), *The Medieval Professional Reader at Work: Evidence from Manuscripts of Chaucer, Langland, Kempe, and Gower* (Victoria: University of Victoria, 2001), pp. 143–216.

Paşa, Derviş, *Murad-name*, ed. Beyhan Kesik (Giresun: Kiraz Ofis Baskı Merkezi, 2009).

Pearlstein, Peggy K. (ed.), *Perspectives on the Hebraic Book* (Washington, DC: Library of Congress, 2012).

Pearson, David, 'The English Private Library in the 17th Century', *Library*, 14:4 (2012), pp. 379–99.

Pearson, Jacqueline, *Women's Reading in Britain 1750–1835: A Dangerous Recreation* (Cambridge: Cambridge University Press, 1999), pp. 170–5.

Péligry, Christian, *Les catalogues de bibliothèques du XVIIe, XVIIIe et XIXe siècles, jusqu'en 1815: contribution à l'inventaire du Fonds ancien de la Bibliothèque Municipale de Toulouse* (Toulouse: Bibliothèque municipale de Toulouse, 1974).

Pennac, Daniel, *The Rights of the Reader*, trans. Sarah Adams (London: Walker Books, 2006).

Peramás, José Manuel, *De Invento Novo Orbe* (1777), in Yasmin Haskell and Raphaële Garrod (eds), *Changing Hearts: Performing Jesuit Emotions Between Europe, Asia and the Americas* (Leiden: Brill, 2018), pp. 121–46.

Peramás, José Manuel, *De Vita et Moribus Tredecim Virorum Paraguaycorum* (Faenza: Archi, 1793).

Pérez, Pedro Ángel Palou, 'Breve noticia de la Biblioteca Palafoxiana', *Artes de México*, 68 (2004), pp. 50–1.

Perry, Nandra, *Imitatio Christi: The Poetics of Piety in Early Modern England* (Notre Dame: University of Notre Dame Press, 2014).

Pertile, Lino, 'Does the *Stilnovo* Go to Heaven?', in Teodolinda Barolini and H. Wayne Storey (eds), *Dante for the New Millennium* (New York: Fordham University Press, 2003), pp. 104–13.

Petrucci, Armando, *Writers and Readers in Medieval Italy*, ed. and trans. Charles Radding (New Haven: Yale University Press, 1995).

Philipot, Thomas, 'AN ELEGIE OFFER'D UP TO THE Memory of His Excellencie Robert Earle of *Essex* and *Ewe*. . .' (London: Printed for William Ley at his shop, 1646).

Pimentel Álvarez, Julio, *Francisco Javier Alegre y Diego José Abad: humanistas gemelos* (Mexico City: UNAM, 1990).

Plato, *Phaedrus* (370 BCE; Indianapolis: Hackett Publishing, 1995).

Pollard, Graham, and Albert Ehrman, *The Distribution of Books by Catalogue from the Invention of Printing to A.D. 1800: Based on Material in the Broxbourne Library* (Cambridge: Printed for presentation to members of the Roxburghe Club, 1965).

Pomposo Fernández de San Salvador, Agustín, *Los jesuitas quitados y restituidos al mundo* (Mexico City: Mariano Ontiveros, 1816).

Potter, Lois, *Secret Rites and Secret Writing: Royalist Literature, 1641–60* (Cambridge: Cambridge University Press, 1989).

Power, D'Arcy (trans.), *De arte phisicali et de cirurgia of Master John Arderne, surgeon of Newark, dated 1412* (London: John Bale, Sons & Danielsson, 1922).

Prince Rupert, 'AN ELEGY ON That Illustrious and High-Born PRINCE RUPERT. . .' (1682).

Provost, William, 'The English Religious Enthusiast Margery Kempe', in Katharina M. Wilson (ed.), *Medieval Women Writers* (Athens: University of Georgia Press, 1984), p. 301.

Pseudo-Hugh of Saint Victor, *De Bestiis et Aliis Rebus*, in Jacques-Paul Migne (ed.), *Patrologia Latina* (Paris: Migne, 1844–55), vol. CLXXVII, cols 19–20.

Qiu, X., 文字学概要 [*Chinese Grammatology: An Outline*] (Beijing: Commerce Press, 2009).

Quéniart, Jean, *Culture et société urbaines dans la France de l'Ouest au XVIIIe siècle* (Paris: Klincksieck, 1978).

Rabinowitz, Peter J., *Before Reading: Narrative Conventions and the Politics of Interpretation* (Ithaca: Cornell University Press, 1987).

Radice, Betty, 'The French Scholar-Lover Heloise', in Katharina M. Wilson (ed.), *Medieval Women Writers* (Athens: University of Georgia Press, 1984), pp. 90–108.

Radice, Betty, *The Letters of Abelard and Heloise* (New York: Penguin, 1974).

Rahmi, Mehmed, *Tuhfe-i Dustan, Şerh-i Bustan* (MS A 6178, National Library, Ankara).

Rama, Angel, *La ciudad letrada* (Hannover: Ediciones del Norte, 1985).

Raymond, Joad, 'Popular Representations of Charles I', in Thomas Corns (ed.), *The Royal Image: Representations of Charles I* (New York: Cambridge University Press, 1999), p. 65.

Raytcheva, Eliana, 'Bibliomane', in Pascal Fouché, Daniel Péchoin and

Philippe Schuwer (eds), *Dictionnaire encyclopédique du livre* (Paris: Éditions du Cercle de la Libraire, 2002), vol. I, pp. 279–80.

Ricraft, Josiah, 'A Funerall Elegy upon the most Honored upon Earth, and now glorious in Heaven, His Excellency *Robert Devereux* Earl of *Essex* and *Ewe*. . .' (London: to be sold by John Hancock, 1646).

Riddle, John, 'Theory and Practice in Medieval Medicine', *Viator*, 5 (1974), pp. 157–70.

Roberts, Jane, and Trudi L. Darby (eds), *English Without Boundaries: Reading English from China to Canada* (Newcastle upon Tyne: Cambridge Scholars, 2017).

Robinson, Pamela, 'A "Very Curious Almanac": The Gift of Sir Robert Moray FRS, 1668' (a non-medical folding almanac), at <https://royalsociety publishing.org/doi/full/10.1098/rsnr.2007.0017> (last accessed 5 August 2019).

Rocafull, Gallegos, *El pensamiento mexicano en los siglos XVI y XVII* (Mexico City: Universidad Nacional Autónoma de México, 1974).

Rodríguez Moñino, Antonio, *Catálogos de libreros españoles, 1661–1798: intento bibliográfico* (Madrid: Tip. de los Sucesores de J. Sánchez Ocaña, 1942).

Rodríguez Moñino, Antonio, *Historia de los catálogos de librería españoles (1661–1840): estudio bibliográfico* (Madrid: Artes Gráficas Soler, 1966).

Ro[gers], Ri[chard], *A Garden of Spirituall Flowers* (1609; London: Robert Bird, 1635).

Romero, Ignacio Osorio, *Colegios y profesores jesuitas que enseñaron latín en Nueva España, 1572–1767* (Mexico City: UNAM, 1979).

Romero, Ignacio Osorio, *Floresta de gramática, poética y retórica en Nueva España (1521–1767)* (Mexico City: UNAM, 1980).

Romero, Ignacio Osorio, 'Latín y neolatín en México', in Ignacio Osorio Romero et al. (eds), *La tradición clásica en México* (Mexico City: UNAM, 1991), pp. 7–76.

Ronan, Charles E., *Juan Ignacio Molina, S.J. (1740–1829): The World's Window on Chile* (New York: Lang, 2002).

Rosamund, Allen S. (ed.), *Richard Rolle: The English Writings* (New York: Paulist Press, 1988).

Rose, Jonathan, 'Rereading the English Common Reader: A Preface to a History of Audiences', *Journal of the History of Ideas*, 52:1 (1992), p. 49.

Rose, Jonathan, *The Intellectual Life of the British Working Classes* (New Haven: Yale University Press, 2002).

Rotelle, John E. (ed.), *The Works of Saint Augustine: A Translation for the 21st Century* (Hyde Park: New City Press, 1990–).

Rouse, Richard, and Mary Rouse, '*Statim invenire*: Schools, Preachers, and New Attitudes to the Page', in Robert L. Benson and Giles Constable (eds), *Renaissance and Renewal in the Twelfth Century* (Cambridge, MA: Harvard University Press, 1982), pp. 201–25.

Rubery, Matthew, *The Untold Story of the Talking Book* (Cambridge, MA: Harvard University Press, 2016).
Rueda Ramírez, Pedro, 'Libros venales. Los catálogos de los libreros andaluces (siglos XVII–XVIII)', *Estudios Humanísticos. Historia*, 11 (2012), pp. 195–222.
Rueda, Pedro, 'Los catálogos de Tomás López de Haro: las redes atlánticas del negocio europeo del libro en Nueva España, 1682–1683', in Pedro Rueda and Lluis Agustí (eds), *La publicidad del libro en el mundo hispánico (Siglos XVII–XX)* (Barcelona: Calambur, 2016), pp. 44–5.
Rueda, Pedro, *Negocio e intercambio cultural. El comercio de libros con América en la carrera de Indias (Siglo XVII)* (Seville: Diputación de Sevilla, Universidad de Sevilla and Escuela de Estudios Hispano-Americanos, 2005).
Rueda Ramírez, Pedro, and Lluís Agustí (eds), *La publicidad del libro en el mundo hispánico (siglos XVII–XX): Catálogos de venta de libreros y editors* (Barcelona: Calambur, 2016).
Rust, Martha Dana, *Imaginary Worlds in Medieval Books: Exploring the Manuscript Matrix* (New York: Palgrave Macmillan, 2007).
Rycaut, Paul, *The Present State of the Ottoman Empire*, 3rd edition (London: John Starkey and Henry Brome, 1670).
Saenger, Paul, 'Reading in the Later Middle Ages', in Guglielmo Cavallo and Roger Chartier (eds), *A History of Reading in the West*, trans. Lydia G. Cochrane (Cambridge: Polity Press, 1999), pp. 120–48.
Saenger, Paul, *Space Between Words: The Origins of Silent Reading* (Stanford: Stanford University Press, 1997).
Saint Augustine, *Confessions*, trans. R. S. Pine-Coffin (Harmondsworth: Penguin Books, 1961).
Salgado, Silvia, 'La biblioteca y la librería coral de la catedral de México', in Pedro Rueda and Idalia García (eds), *El libro en circulación en la América colonial* (Mexico City: Ediciones Quivira, 2014), p. 200.
Santagata, Marco, *Dante: The Story of His Life*, trans. Richard Dixon (Cambridge, MA: Belknap Press, 2016).
Saunders, Edmund, 'AN ELEGY IN Commemoration of S^R Edmund Saunders. . .' (1683).
Schama, Simon, *The Story of the Jews: Finding the Words 1000 BCE – 1492 CE* (London: Vintage Books, 2014).
Schmandt-Besserat, Denise, *Before Writing, Vol. I: From Counting to Cuneiform* (Austin: University of Texas Press, 1992).
Schulte, Petra, Marco Mostert and Irene van Renswoude (eds), *Strategies of Writing: Studies on Text and Trust in the Middle Ages. Papers from 'Trust in Writing in the Middle Ages' (Utrecht 28–29 November 2002)* (Turnhout: Brepols, 2008).
Schwaller, John Frederick, 'The Brothers Fernando de Alva Ixtlixochitl and Bartolomé de Alva: Two Native Intellectuals of Seventeenth-Century Mexico', in Gabriela Ramos and Yanna Yannakakis (eds), *Indigenous*

Intellectuals: Knowledge, Power, and Political Culture in Mexico and the Andes (Durham, NC: Duke University Press, 2014), p. 47.

Scott, Kathleen L., *Illuminated Manuscripts and Other Remarkable Documents from the Collections of the Royal Library, Stockholm*, Catalogue of an Exhibition, June–September 1963, Kungl. Bibliotekets utställningskatalog nr. 35 (Stockholm: A. B. Björkmans Eftr, 1963).

Scott, Kathleen L., *Later Gothic Manuscripts 1390–1490*, A Survey of Manuscripts Illuminated in the British Isles 6 (London: Harvey Miller, 1998).

Scott-Warren, Jason, 'Reading Graffiti in the Early Modern Book', *Huntington Library Quarterly*, 73:3 (2010), pp. 363–81.

Scribner, S., and Michael Cole, 'Unpackaging Literacy', in E. Cushman, E. R. Kintgen, B. M. Kroll and M. Rose (eds), *Literacy: A Critical Sourcebook* (Boston: Bedford/St Martin's, 2001), pp. 123–37.

Seaver, Paul S., *Wallington's World: A Puritan Artisan in Seventeenth-Century London* (Stanford: Stanford University Press, 1985).

Şemi, Şemullah, *Saadetname* (MS Kadızade Mehmed 400, Süleymaniye Manuscript Library, Istanbul).

Serés, Guillermo, 'Presentación', in Laura Fernández et al. (eds), *Clásicos para un Nuevo Mundo. Estudios sobre la tradición clásica en la América de los siglos XVI y XVII* (Bellaterra: Universitat Autònoma de Barcelona, 2016), pp. 7–8.

Sethuraman, Jayshree, 'The Impact of the Indo-Arabic Fable Tradition on the "Esope" of Marie de France: A Literary, Historical, and Folkloristic Study', PhD dissertation (Tulane University, 1998).

Sevindik, Hakan, 'Yeni Bir Hamse Şairi: Abdi ve Manzum Bostan Tercümesi', *Selçuk Üniversitesi Edebiyat Fakültesi Dergisi*, 35 (2016), pp. 105–30.

Sharpe, Kevin, *Image Wars: Promoting Kings and Commonwealths in England, 1603–1660* (New Haven: Yale University Press, 2010).

Sharpe, Kevin, *Reading Revolutions: The Politics of Reading in Early Modern England* (New Haven: Yale University Press, 2000).

Shen, C., 中国历史：先秦史 [*China: A Pre-Qin History*] (Beijing: People's Press, 2006).

Sherman, William H., *Used Books: Marking Readers in Renaissance England* (Philadelphia: University of Pennsylvania Press, 2008).

Shuffelton, George, *Codex Ashmole 61: A Compilation of Popular Middle English Verse* (Kalamazoo: Medieval Institute Publications, 2008).

Sievert, Henning, 'Eavesdropping on the Pasha's Salon: Usual and Unusual Readings of an Eighteenth-Century Ottoman Bureaucrat', *Osmanlı Araştırmaları/ Journal of Ottoman Studies*, 41 (2013), pp. 159–95.

Sigerist, Henry E., 'Bedside Manners in the Middle Ages: The Treatise *De cautelis medicorum* Attributed to Arnold of Villanova', in *Henry E. Sigerist on the History of Medicine*, ed. Féliz Marti-Albañez (New York: MD Publications, 1960), pp. 134–40.

Sigerist, Henry E., 'The Sphere of Life and Death in Early Mediaeval Manuscripts', *Bulletin of the History of Medicine*, 11 (1942), pp. 292–303.

Sima, Q., 史记 [*The Records of the Historian*] (86 BCE; Zhengzhou: Zhongzhou Classic Press, 2003).
Skerpan-Wheeler, Elizabeth, 'Eikon Basilike and the Rhetoric of Self-Representation', in Thomas Corns (ed.), *The Royal Image: Representations of Charles I* (New York: Cambridge University Press, 1999), p. 164.
Skerpan-Wheeler, Elizabeth, 'The First "Royal": Charles I as Celebrity', *PMLA*, 126:4 (2011), pp. 912–34.
Smith, Paul J., 'La présence de la littérature française renaissante dans les catalogues des ventes aux enchères en Hollande au XVIIe siècle. Bilan et perspectives', *Renaissance and Reformation/Renaissance et Reforme*, 34:3 (2011), pp. 185–202.
Sobecki, Sebastian, '"The writyng of this tretys": Margery Kempe's Son and the Authorship of Her Book', *Studies in the Age of Chaucer*, 37 (2015), pp. 257–83.
Sordet, Yann, *L'Amour des livres au siècle des lumières. Pierre Adamoli et ses collections* (Paris: École des chartes, 2001).
Sordet, Yann, 'Pour une histoire des catalogues de livres: matérialité, formes, usages', in Barbier, Dubois and Sordet (eds), *De l'argile au nuage*, pp. 15–46.
Sordet, Yann, 'Une approche des "catalogues domestiques" de bibliothèques privées (XVIIe–XVIIIe siècle), instruments et miroirs de collections particulières', *Bulletin du bibliophile*, 1 (1997), pp. 92–123.
Spalding, Mary Caroline, 'The Middle English Charters of Christ', dissertation (Bryn Mawr College, 1912).
Speigel, Harriet (ed. and trans.), *Marie de France: Fables* (Toronto: University of Toronto Press, 1987).
Spring, Howard, *Heaven Lies About Us: A Fragment of Infancy* (London: Constable, 1939).
Staley, Lynn (trans. and ed.), *The Book of Margery Kempe* (New York: Norton: 2001).
Starr, Raymond J., 'Reading Aloud: Lectores and Roman Reading', *Classical Journal*, 86 (1991), pp. 337–43.
Steinberg, Justin, *Accounting for Dante: Urban Readers and Writers in Late Medieval Italy* (Notre Dame: University of Notre Dame Press, 2007).
Stock, Brian, *Augustine the Reader: Meditation, Self-Knowledge, and the Ethics of Interpretation* (Cambridge, MA: Harvard University Press, 1996).
Strauss, Johann, 'Who Read What in the Ottoman Empire (19th–20th Centuries)?', *Middle Eastern Literatures*, 6:1 (2003), pp. 39–76.
Streete, Adrian, *Apocalypse and Anti-Catholicism in Seventeenth-Century English Drama* (Cambridge: Cambridge University Press, 2017).
Strengers-Olde Kalter, Karin M. P., 'Boeken in Bossche boedels. De belangstelling voor lectuur in de achttiende eeuw', *Noordbrabants Historisch Jaarboek*, 14 (1998), pp. 143–79.

'Supplement au catalogue des livres de M. Huguet de Semonville, contenant Ceux de feuë Madame la Marquise de Costentin, sa Fille', in *Catalogus librorum ill. viri d. Caroli-Nicolai Huguet de Semonville, senatus parisiensis decani* (Paris: Gabriel Martin et Louis Guérin, 1732), pp. 141–56, also available at <https://books.google.nl/books?id=4jJbAAAAQAAJ&> (accessed 15 August 2019).

Sürüri, Muslihüddin, *Şerh-i Hafız* (MS Ayasofya 4056, Süleymaniye Manuscript Library, Istanbul).

Svenbro, Jesper, 'Archaic and Classical Greece: The Invention of Silent Reading', in Guglielmo Cavallo and Roger Chartier (eds), *A History of Reading in the West*, trans. Lydia G. Cochrane (Cambridge: Polity, 1999), pp. 37–63.

Swan, Mary, 'Using the Book: Cambridge, University Library, MS Ii.1.33', *New Medieval Literatures*, 13 (2011), pp. 289–97.

Taavitsainen, I., *Middle English Lunaries: A Study of the Genre* (Helsinki: Société néophilologique, 1988).

Talbot, C. H., 'A Mediaeval Physician's Vade Mecum', *Journal of the History of Medicine and Allied Sciences*, 16 (1961), pp. 213–33.

Tanyıldız, Ahmet, 'İsmail Rusuhi-yi Ankaravi: Şerh-i Mesnevi, Mecmuatü'l-Letayif ve Matmuratü'l-Maarif, I. Cilt (İnceleme-Metin-Sözlük)', PhD dissertation (Erciyes University, 2010).

Targoff, Ramie, *Common Prayer: The Language of Public Devotion in Early Modern England* (Chicago: University of Chicago Press, 2001).

Tarlan, Ali Nihat (ed.), *Necati Beg Divanı* (Ankara: Akçağ Yayınları, 1992).

Tavárez Bermúdez, David, *Las guerras invisibles. Devociones indígenas, disciplina y disidencia en el México colonial* (Mexico City: El Colegio de Michoacán, CIESAS, Universidad Autónoma Metropolitana y Universidad Autónoma Benito Juárez de Oaxaca, 2012).

Taylor, Archer, *Book Catalogues: Their Varieties and Uses*, 2nd edition, revised by Wm. P. Barlow Jr (Winchester: St Edmundsbury Press, 1986).

Taylor, Jane H. M., and Lesley Smith (eds), *Women and the Book: Assessing the Visual Evidence* (London: British Library, 1997).

Tenorio, Martha Lilia, *El gongorismo en Nueva España: ensayo de restitución* (Mexico City: Colegio de México, 2013).

Th., Tw., 'An Elegiack Memoriall of the Right Honourable Generall DEANE...' (London: Printed by M. S. for Tho. Jenner, 1653).

The Cloud of Unknowing and Other Works, trans. A. C. Spearing (London: Penguin, 2001).

The Curious Hieroglyphick Bible; or, Select Passages in the Old and New Testaments (Worcester: printed by Isaiah Thomas, 1788).

The Death of Abel (London: Dodesley, Durham, and Field, 1764).

The Death of Abel (London: printed for S. Toplis and J. Bunney et al., 1779).

The History of Pamela; or, Virtue Rewarded. Abridged from the Works *by Samuel Richardson* (Boston: printed and sold by S. Hall, 1794).

The Memoir of 1603 and The Diary of 1616–1619: Anne Clifford, ed. Katherine O. Acheson (Peterborough: Broadview Press, 2007).

'The Textuality and Materiality of Reading', *Huntington Library Quarterly*, 73:3 (2010).

The Works of [. . .] *Dr. John Tillotson*, 10th edition (London: James, John and Paul Knapton et al., 1735).

The Works of the Late Aaron Hill, 4 vols (London: printed for the benefit of the family, 1754).

Thiébaux, Marcelle, *The Writings of Medieval Women* (New York: Routledge, 1994), p. 254.

Thomas of Celano, *Vita Beati Francisci* 21.58, in *Saint Francis of Assisi*, trans. Placid Hermann (Chicago: Franciscan Herald Press, 1963), p. 53.

Thwaite, Ann (ed.), *Portraits from Life by Edmund Gosse* (Aldershot: Scolar Press, 1991).

Tolan, John, 'Mendicants and Muslims in Dante's Florence', *Dante Studies*, 125 (2007), pp. 234–8.

Tomalin, Claire, *Charles Dickens: A Life* (London: Viking, 2011).

Towheed, Shafquat, Rosalind Crone and Katie Halsey (eds), *The History of Reading: A Reader* (London: Routledge, 2011).

Trabulse, Elías, 'Los libros científicos en la Nueva España, 1550–1630', in Alicia Hernández Chávez and Manuel Miño Grijalva (eds), *Cincuenta años de Historia de México* (Mexico City: El Colegio de México, 1991), p. 17.

Tsien, Tsuen Hsuin, *Science and Civilisation in China, Volume V: Chemistry and Chemical Technology. Part 1, Paper and Printing* (Cambridge: Cambridge University Press, 1985).

Tsien, Tsuen Hsuin, *Written on Bamboo and Silk: The Beginning of Chinese Books and Inscriptions* (Chicago: Chicago University Press, 2004).

Twitchett, Denis (ed.), *The Cambridge History of China* (Cambridge: Cambridge University Press, 1979).

Üzgör, Tahir, *Türkçe Divan Dibaceleri* (Ankara: Kültür Bakanlığı Yayınları, 1990).

van der Woude, Joanne, '*La Primera Parte del Parnaso Antártico*: Print and the Politics of Translation in Early Peruvian Poetry', in Matthew Duquès, Maya Feile Tomes and Adam Goldwyn (eds), *Brill's Companion to Classics in the Early Americas* (Leiden: Brill, forthcoming).

Van Deusen, Nancy, 'El cuerpo como libro viviente, Lima 1600–1640', *Histórica*, 31:1 (July 2007), p. 33.

van Goinga, Hannie, *Alom te bekomen: veranderingen in de boekdistributie in de Republiek 1720–1800* (Amsterdam: De Buitenkant, 1999).

van Selm, Bert, *Een menighte treffelijcke boecken: Nederlandse boekhandelscatalogi in het begin van de zeventiende eeuw* (Utrecht: HES, 1987).

Vandenhole, Frans, *Inventaris van veilingcatalogi 1615–1914 met topografische, alfabetische en inhoudsindexen* (Ghent: Rijksuniversiteit te Gent, 1987).

Varry, Dominique (ed.), *50 ans d'histoire du livre: 1958–2008* (Lyon: Enssib, 2014).
Varry, Dominique, 'Aperçu sur les bibliothèques privées de l'Eure confisquées sous la Révolution', *Annales de Normandie*, 45:3 (1995), pp. 327–8.
Varry, Dominique, 'Grandes collections et bibliothèques des élites', in Claude Joly (ed.), *Histoire des bibliothèques françaises* (Paris: Electre, 2008), vol. II, pp. 295–323.
Vaticinium Votivum or, Palæmon's Prophetick Prayer (London, 1649).
Venezky, R., 'The Development of Literacy in the Industrialized Nations of the West', in R. Barr, M. L. Kamil, P. Mosenthal and P. D. Pearson (eds), *Handbook of Reading Research, Vol. II* (New York: Longman, 1991), pp. 46–67.
Vickers, Brian (ed.), *The Oxford Authors: Francis Bacon* (Oxford: Oxford University Press, 1996).
Vitale, Kyle, 'Grace of Life: Marriage, Campion's Lord Hay's Masque, and Sacraments of Conjunction', *Religion and Literature*, 48:2 (2016), pp. 21–48.
Voaden, Rosalynn, *God's Words, Women's Voices: The Discernment of Spirits in the Writing of Late-Medieval Women Visionaries* (Rochester: York Medieval Press, 1999).
[Walker, Anthony] *The Vertuous Wife: or, The Holy Life of Mrs. Elizabeth Walker* (London: J. Robinson, A. and J. Churchill, J. Taylor, and J. Wyat, 1694).
Walker Bynum, Caroline, *Jesus as Mother: Studies in Spirituality of the High Middle Ages* (Berkeley: University of California Press, 1982).
Wall, Cynthia, 'The English Auction: Narrative of Dismantlings', *Eighteenth-Century Studies*, 31:1 (1997), pp. 1–25.
Waller, Philip, *Writers, Readers, and Reputations: Literary Life in Britain 1870–1918* (Oxford: Oxford University Press, 2006).
Wallis, Faith, 'Inventing Diagnosis: Theophilus' *De urinis* in the Classroom', *Dynamis*, 20 (2000), pp. 31–73.
Wallis, Faith (trans.), *Medieval Medicine: A Reader* (Toronto: University of Toronto Press, 2010).
Wallis, Faith, 'Signs and Senses: Diagnosis and Prognosis in Early Medieval Pulse and Urine Texts', *Social History of Medicine*, 13 (2000), pp. 265–78.
Wallis, Faith, 'The Experience of the Book: Manuscripts, Texts, and the Role of Epistemology in Early Medieval Medicine', in Don G. Bates (ed.), *Knowledge and the Scholarly Medical Traditions* (Cambridge: Cambridge University Press, 1995), pp. 102–26.
Walsby, Malcolm, 'Book Lists and Their Meaning', in Malcolm Walsby and Natasha Constantinidou (eds), *Documenting the Early Modern Book World: Inventories and Catalogues in Manuscript and Print* (Leiden: Brill, 2013), pp. 1–24.
Wang, Yunwu (comp.), 叢書集成初編 [*A Compendium of Miscellaneous Books*] (Beijing: Zhonghua shuju, 1985).

Ward, Susan L., 'Fables for the Court: Illustrations of Marie de France's Fables in Paris, BN, MS Arsenal 3142', in Taylor and Smith (eds), *Women and the Book*, pp. 190–203.

Warnke, Karl, *Die Fabeln der Marie de France, mit Benutzung des von Ed. Mall hinterlassenen Materials* (Halle: M. Niemeyer, 1898).

Warnke, Karl, *Die Quellen des Esope de Marie de France* (Halle: M. Niemeyer, 1900).

Webby, Elizabeth, 'A Checklist of Early Australian Booksellers' and Auctioneers' Catalogues and Advertisements: 1800–1849' (in three parts), *Bulletin of the Bibliographical Society of Australia and New Zealand*, 3 (1978), pp. 123–148; 4:1 (1979), pp. 31–66; 4:2 (1979), pp. 95–150.

Wei, Zheng (comp.), 隋書 [*The History of Sui*] (Beijing: Zhonghua shuju, 1973).

Whitbread, Helena (ed.), *No Priest But Love: The Journals of Anne Lister from 1824–1826* (Otley: Smith Settle, 1992).

Whitehall Evening Post, 22 October 1796.

Whitmore, William, 'An ELEGIE On that Incomparable Example of Hospitality, Charity, and Generosity...' (1678).

Whittaker, Gordon, 'Aztec Hieroglyphics: A Name-Based Writing System', *Language and History*, 61:1–2 (2018), pp. 60–76.

Wickersheimer, Ernest, 'Figures médico-astrologiques des IXe, Xe et XIe siècles', *Janus*, 19 (1914), pp. 157–77.

Wilcher, Robert, '*Eikon Basilike*: The Printing, Composition, Strategy, and Impact of the King's Book', in Laura Lunger Knoppers (ed.), *The Oxford Handbook of Literature and the English Revolution* (New York: Oxford University Press, 2013), pp. 289–308.

Wilcher, Robert, *The Writing of Royalism, 1628–60* (Cambridge: Cambridge University Press, 2001).

Wilcox, Jonathan (ed.), *Scraped, Stroked and Bound: Materially Engaged Readings of Medieval Manuscripts* (Turnhout: Brepols, 2013).

Wild, Robert, 'ON THE Death of Mr Calamy, Not known to the Author of a long time after' (London: 1667).

Wilkinson, E., *Chinese History: A Manual* (Cambridge, MA: Harvard University Press, 1998).

Williams, Abigail, *The Social Life of Books: Reading Together in the Eighteenth-Century Home* (New Haven: Yale University Press, 2017).

Wilson, Robert, 'Allegory as Avoidance in Dante's Early Commentators: "bella menzogna" to "roza corteccia"', in Paola Nasti and Claudia Rossignoli (eds), *Interpreting Dante: Essays on the Traditions of Dante Commentary* (Notre Dame: University of Notre Dame Press, 2013), p. 30.

Wilson-Lee, Edward, *The Catalogue of Shipwrecked Books: Young Columbus and the Quest for a Universal Library* (London: William Collins, 2018).

Windeatt, Barry (ed.), *The Book of Margery Kempe* (Cambridge: D. S. Brewer, 2004).

Wittmann, Reinhard (ed.), *Bücherkataloge als buchgeschichtliche Quellen in der frühen Neuzeit* (Wiesbaden: O. Harrassowitz, 1984).
Wolf, Maryanne, *Proust and the Squid: The Story and Science of the Reading Brain* (New York: Harper Perennial, 2007), p. 16.
Wolters, Clifton (trans. and ed.), *Julian of Norwich: Revelations of Divine Love* (New York: Penguin, 1966).
Woodward, Jennifer, *The Theatre of Death: The Ritual Management of Royal Funerals in Renaissance England, 1570–1625* (Rochester: Boydell, 1997).
Woolf, D. R., *Reading History in Early Modern England* (Cambridge: Cambridge University Press, 2000).
Wu, Jing (comp.), 貞觀政要 [*The Essentials of the Reign of Zhenguan*] (Shanghai: Shanghai guji chubanshe, 1978).
Xu, C., 上古汉语词汇史 [*A History of Archaic Chinese Words*] (Beijing: Commerce Press, 2003).
Xun, Jiao (ed. and annot.), 孟子正義 [*Commentary on Mencius*] (Beijing: Zhonghua shuju, 1987).
Xun, K., 荀子 [*Xun Zi*] (245 BCE?; Shanghai, Shanghai People's Press, 1974).
Yakut, Emrullah, 'Feridi'nin Manzum Hafız Divanı Tercümesi (İnceleme-Metin)', PhD dissertation (Istanbul University, 2015).
Yang, Bojun (ed. and annot.), 春秋左傳注 [*An Annotated Edition of Spring and Autumn*] (Beijing: Zhonghua shuju, 1990).
Yang, K., 战国史 [*A History of Warring States*] (Taibei: Taiwan Commerce Press, 1997).
Yates, Frances A., *The Art of Memory* (Chicago: University of Chicago Press, 1966).
Yates, R. D. S., 'Soldiers, Scribes, and Women: Literacy Among the Lower Orders in Early China', in F. Li and D. P. Branner (eds), *Writing and Literacy in Early China: Studies from the Columbia Early China Seminar* (Seattle: University of Washington Press, 2011), pp. 339–69.
Yazar, Sadık, 'Anadolu Sahası Klasik Türk Edebiyatında Tercüme ve Şerh Geleneği', PhD dissertation (Istanbul University, 2011).
Yu, Y. S., 人文与理性的中国 [*A Humanitarian and Rational China*] (Taipei: Lianjing Press, 2008).
Yuan, Ruan (ed. and annot.), 十三经注疏 [*Annotated Editions of the Thirteen Classics*] (Beijing: Zhonghua shuju, 2009).
Yun, Wu, and Ji Yu (eds and annots), 唐太宗集 [*Collected Writings of Emperor Taizong*] (Xi'an: Shaanxi renmin chubanshe, 1986).
Zapata, José Eusebio Llano, *Memorias histórico, físico, crítico apologéticas de la América Meridional* (Lima: Instituto Francés de Estudios Andinos, Pontificia Universidad Católica del Perú and Universidad Nacional Mayor de San Marcos, 2005).
Zboray, Ronald J., and Mary Saracino Zboray, *Everyday Ideas: Socioliterary Experience among Antebellum New Englanders* (Knoxville: University of Tennessee Press, 2006).

Zhang, Xiumin, 中國印刷史 [*A History of Printing in China*] (Hangzhou: Zhejiang guji chubanshe, 2006).
Zhou, Xunchu (ed. and annot.), 韓非子校注 [*An Annotated Edition of Hanfei zi*] (Nanjing: Fenghuang chuban she, 2009).
Zhu, Xi (ed. and annot.), 四書章句集注 [*An Annotated Edition of the Four Books*] (Beijing: Zhonghua shuju, 1983).
Ziegler, Joseph, 'Skin and Character in Medieval and Early Renaissance Physiognomy', in *La pelle umana: The Human Skin*, Micrologus 13 (Florence: SISMEL – Edizioni del Galluzzo, 2005), pp. 511–35.

Index of Methods and Sources

Annotation (in texts): Wallis (Ch. 6); Inan (Ch. 8)
Assumed/implied readers: Steinberg (Ch. 4)
Autobiographies/biographies: Driver (Ch. 3); Inan (Ch. 8)
Buying power: Jung (Ch. 13)
Circulation (of texts): Pérez (Ch. 9); Blom et al. (Ch. 12)
Collection and acquisition habits: Driver (Ch. 3)
Copying of texts: Driver (Ch. 3)
Descriptive bibliography: Vitale (Ch. 10)
Evidence of use: Wallis (Ch. 6)
Hermeneutics: Tao and Reinking (Ch. 1); Wang (Ch. 2); Ott (Ch. 5)
Image analysis: Wallis (Ch. 6); Acheson (Ch. 7); Jung (Ch. 13)
Interpellation: Steinberg (Ch. 4)
Intertextuality: Tomes (Ch. 11)
Library records: Blom et al. (Ch. 12);
Literate/oral mentality: Tao and Reinking (Ch. 1)
Materialist analysis: Wallis (Ch. 6); Tomes (Ch. 11)
Paratexts: Tao and Reinking (Ch. 1); Inan (Ch. 8); Acheson (Ch. 7); Blom et al. (Ch. 12)
Periodical culture: Jung (Ch. 13)
Quantitative analysis/bibliometrics: Blom et al. (Ch. 12)
Reading aloud: Driver (Ch. 3); Inan (Ch. 8); Owens (Ch. 14)
Reception theory: Vitale (Ch. 10)
Shared reading: Inan (Ch. 8); Owens (Ch. 14)
Single reader history: Wang (Ch. 2); Ott (Ch.5)
Translation: Tao and Reinking (Ch. 1); Wang (Ch. 2); Driver (Ch. 3); Inan (Ch. 8); Steinberg (Ch. 4); Pérez (Ch. 9)
(Un)readability: Ott (Ch. 5)

General Index

Page numbers in italics denote illustrations; numbers preceded by p refer to plates.

Abdi Pasha, 163, 169
Abelard, Peter, 54, 55–6, 69n
Ablow, Rachel, 4
Achinstein, Sharon, 143–4, 145, 153
Acorn, George, 307
acrostics, 145–9, *148*
Adalbertus, 56
Adorno, Rolena, 200
advice literature, 163
Aesop, *Fables*, 54, 59
Ahern, John, 75–6
Ahmed (Prince), 170
Ahmed Pasha, Melek, 169
Albucasis, 129–30
  Surgery, 127–8
Alegre, Francisco Javier, 233, 234–8, 243–4
  Antonio suo, 236–7
  Arte poetica, 235–8, 242, 243
Alfonso X the Wise, *Siete partidas*, 199
Ali, Mustafa
  Kunhu'l-Ahbar, 165–6, 171
  Mecmau'l-Bahreyn, 171, 172, 175
  Rebiu'l-Manzum, 171
Allan, David, 256
Allingham, William, 306
Alonso de la Veracruz, Fray, 190
Althusser, Louis, 74, 77, 80
Alva Ixtlilxochitl, Fernando de, 201

Álvarez, Bartolomé, 199
Álvaro de Rodríguez, 197
American Repository of Useful Information, The (1795), 275
anagrams, 145–9, *148*
Analects, 15–16, 16–18, 24–6, 34
Angus, William, 273–5, 275
anonymity, 257
Argenteuil, 55–6, 60
Arminian Church, 207, 209–10, 211, 219
Arnaldo, 107–8
Arnau of Vilanova, 124
Árpide y Ulloa, Doctor Antonio de, 193
Art of Uniformity 1662, 143–4
Art of War, The, 34
Attar, Farid al-Din, *Pandnama*, 162, 162–3, 169–70, 172, 173–4
Audelay, John, 'Pope John's Passion of Our Lord', 103
August II, 256
Augustine, 91–4
  Confessions, 105–6, 298
Australia, 304
'authorial audience', 77–9
'authorial intention', 42–3
autobiography, 55, 63
Avendaño, Fernando de, 193
Axial Age, 11, 27

356

Bacon, Francis, 39
Baker, Thomas
    The Royal Engagement Pocket Atlas, 273–8, 277
Baldwin, Stanley, 306
Bale, Anthony, 100
bamboo, 35
Barthes, Roland, 43
Bartolomé de Las Casas, 200
Bayard, Pierre, 259
Bayezid, 169
Bayly, Lewis, *The Practice of Pietie*, 302
Beckwith, Sarah, 99, 104, 215
Bede, *Ecclesiatic History of the English People*, 99
Bedloe, William, 152, 154–5
Bedlow, Captain William, *151*
beginning readers, 167–8, 172–3
Bell, Maureen, 135, 156, 159n
Bellomo, Saverio, 76, 89
Bentley, Edward, 257
Benvenuto da Imola, 82–3, 87–9
Bernard of Gordon, *Lilium medicine*, 119
Bewick, Thomas, 291
Bible, 55, 211, 222, 297–8, 301–4
Biblioteca Palafoxiana, 191
bilingual author-readers, 170–1
bird images, 80–3, 84–5, 86–7, 89–90, 94
black borders, 137
Black Legend, 189
Bléchet, Françoise, 252, *253*
Blessed Angela of Foligno, *Memorial*, 107–1
Blood, Colonel Thomas, 152
Bloomfield, Robert, *Farmer's Boy*, 276
Boccaccio, 86, 89
Boethius, *Consolation of Philosophy*, 67
Boileau-Despréaux, Nicolas, *L'Art poétique*, 235
Bonagiunta da Lucca, 85

Bonaventure, 92–3
book-burning, 27
Book of Common Prayer, 147, 149, 150, 206–7, 209, 222
Book of Documents, 41–2
book trade, development of, 187–9
Bookman's Price Index, 252
books of hours, 197
Boreel, Balthazar, 258
Brazil, 229
British catalogues, 250, 253, 257
British Library, 59, 65
British Museum catalogue, 250
broadside funeral elegies, 135–59
Brown, M., 285–6
Bruckner, Matilda, 58, 69n
Buchan, John, 304
Buckingham, Joseph, 303
Buckland, James, 257
Buettner, Brigitte, 215
Bunyan, John, *The Pilgrim's Progress*, 305
Burnet, John, 275–6
Burnett, Ian, 249–50
Burrell, Sir Williams, 255
Butler, Shane, 100–1, 112
Butler, Thomas, 153

Cabezas, Alonso, 187–8
Caedmon, 99
Calamy, Edmund, 143
Calleja, Diego, 193
Calvinism, 209–10
Cambers, Andrew, 300
Campion, Henri de, *Memoirs*, 304
Capel, Lord Arthur, 219
captions, 283–6, 286–8
Care, Henry, *History of the damnable popish plot*, 154
Care Homes Reading Project, 309
Caroline Church, 209–10
Carpenter, Mary, 304
Carrió de la Vandera, Alonso, 197–8
Carta dei, 101–2
Carullah Efendi, 172

Caryl, Joseph, 145, *148*, 149
Castelloza, 57, 58
    portrait of, p2
    vida, 58
Castilian, 185, 186, 231, 240
Castillo, Don Cristóbal, 200
catalogues, 249–69, 253
Catholicism, 190, 195, 200, *see also* Christianity; Jesuits
Catton, Charles, 275, 278
Cavallo, Guglielmo, 5–6, 301
Cayetano Marcellano de Ayamonte, 192
Cecil, James, 152
Çelebi, Aşık, 164, 168–9
Çelebi, Evliya, 165
    Seyahatname, 164–5
Çelebi, Şuri, 168–9
censorship, 254–5
Centre for Research into Reading, Literature and Society, 310
Charles, John, 186
Charles I, *214*, p6
Charles V's library, 66
Charles de la Roncière, 193
Charters of Christ, 101–3
Chartier, Roger, 5–6, 156, 217, 299, 299–300, 301, 304
Chekov, Anton, 308
children, 185–6, 305–6
Chile, 231
China, 11–30
    Chia-ku-wen script on a tortoise shell, 2–3
Christianity, 83–4, 184–6, 200, 201, *see also* Catholicism
Christine de Pizan, 55, 65–8, p4
    Avision-Christine, 67
    Book of the City of Ladies, 66–7
    The Book of the Three Virtues, 67
    Epître d'Othea, 67
    Faits d'armes et de chevalerie, 68
    Le livre des fais et bonnes meurs du sage Roy Charles V, 67–8
    Livre du chemin de long estude, 67
    Mutacion de fortune, 67
    One Hundred Ballades, 67
    Sept psaumes allegorisés, 67
    'Swan Geese', 48–9
chroniclers, 200–1
Cicero, 56
Clanchy, Michael, 12, 56, 69n
Clare, John, 279
Clarke, Gillian, 'Miracle of St David's Day,' 309
Classic of Poetry, The, 32, 38–44
    'April', 48–9
    'Collecting Weeds', 48–9
    Exoteric Commentary on the Classic of Poetry by Master Han Ying, 38
    'Han edition', 38–41
    'Hatchet Handle', 50
    'Mao edition', 38, 41–4, 44
    political critique, 44–7
    quotation, 47–50
    'Winged Chariot', 48–9
Clifford, Anne, 302
Cloud of Unknowing, The, 110
Clymer, Lorna, 145, 158n
Cobbe, Frances Power, 305
Coleman, Joyce, 299
collective reading, 172–3
Collyer, J., 285
Collyer, Mary, 281–3
colonial libraries, 190–4
Columbus, Christopher, 231, 239, 242
commentaries, 76, 173, 175
Commento, L'Ottimo, 82
'community of readers', 304
Compañón, Baltasar Jaime Martínez de, 186
Confucianism, 11–30, 33–4
Confucius, 13, 16–18, 25–6, 39–40, 47
Contention of Hundred Schools of Thought, 13
Conversino da Frignano, 128
Coral, Lenore, 252, 253
Corbould, Richard, 275, 278

Cordero, Antonio, 196
Cornelius de Pauw, 230
cost-effective reprinting, 286
Council of Trent, 201
Countess of Dia, 56–8, p1
    vida, 57
Cromberger House, 187
Cuba, 234, 235, 238, 243, 299
Curious Hieroglyphic Bible, The, 282, *282*
Curtis, Langley, 153–6, *156*

Daems, Jim, 207
Daniel, Henry, 126
Dante
    Convivio, 81–2, 84–5, 87
    Divine Comedy, 67
    Inferno, 74–97
    Memoriali bolognesi, 76
    Paradiso, 90
Dante Studies journal, 78
Darnton, Robert, 135
Davidson, Adele, 146
Davies, J. D., 153
Derviş Pasha, 167, 174
Devereux, Robert, 137–43, *142*, 156
Dharani Sutra, 35
Dickens, Charles, 306
    The Chimes, 308
    David Copperfield, 307
    Dombey and Son, 305
    The Pickwick Papers, 307, 308
Dido, 87–9
Diego de la Palma, 200
disbelief, 110–13
Discourses of the States, 48
discretio spirituum, 109
dissenting ministers, 143–50, 257
Domingo de Santo Tomás, 200
Drake, William, 39
Dronke, Peter, 48–9, 56, 57
Duke Mu, of Xu, 48
Duke Wen, of Lu, 48–9
Durling, Robert, 85
Dutch catalogues, 249, 253, 256, 257

Early English Books Online, 157–8n
Ehrman, Albert, 250
Eikon Basilike, 206–26, *214*, p6
Eisener, Martin, 91
elegies, 218–21
    broadside funeral, 135–9
    for Captain Will Bedlow, *151*
    for dissenting ministers, 143–50
    featuring a skull-and-crossbones headpiece, 150–6
    for Joseph Caryl, *148*
    for Robert Devereux, 137–43, *142*
    for Thomas Glass, *147*
Eliot, George, 308
el-Kefevi, Hüseyin, *Razname*, 164–5
Emperor Fei, 39
Emperor Taizong of Tang, 31–53
Emre, 169
English Short Title Catalogue, 153
engravings, 273, 273–8, 281–3, 286–91
Enlightenment, 198, 249, 251
epics, 229, 231, 236–7, *237*
epitaphs, 141, 144–5, 155, 212, 218
Ercilla, Alonso de, 236
    La Araucana, 231, 233, 241–2
'Esprit des livres', 252
Essex group, 137–43, *142*, 144, 156
Estrada, Dorothy Tank de, 184
Europeanising reading culture, 227–48
Exoteric Commentary on the Classic of Poetry by Master Han Ying, 38

Fabri, Manuel, 235, 237
Farewell sermons of the late London Ministers, The, 143
Farmer, Alan B., 155, 159n
Father Johannes, 119–20, 128–9
Fayreford, Thomas, 116–18, 120, 127
Ferrel, Lori Anne, 209
Finch, Heneage, 152
Fincham, Kenneth, 208, 210
Firdavsi, *Shahnama*, 161

First Provincial Council of Mexico, 201
first-person, 74–5
Fischer, Steven R., *A History of Reading*, 4, 299
Fish, Stanley, 2
Flint, Kate, 300
folding medical almanac, 124
Folger Shakespeare Library, 208
Ford, Richard, 152
Forster, John, 305
Francesca (character), 74, 75, 80–1, 85–6, 89–91
Francesco da Buti, 88–9
Franciscans, 92–4, 232
Francisco de Toledo, 185–6
Franke, William, 79
French catalogues, 250, 252, *253*, 255, 257
French language, 54–5, 57, 59–60, 65–8, 89, 91, 116
French literature, 198–9
Friedman, John, 101
frontispieces
  Christine de Pizan, 65
  The Death of Abel, 281–3, 285–8, 285, 287, 295n
  Devereux, Robert, 138
  Eikon Basilike, 206–8, 215–16
  Pamela, 289–92, *289*, *291*, *292*
  The Seasons, 273–5, *274*, 279–81, *280*
  The Sugar Plumb, 293, *294*
Frugard, Roger, *Surgery*, 130
Fry, Elizabeth, 304
Furet, François, 250
fushi duanzhang, 48, 49

Gabriel de Monterroso, *Práctica civil y criminal e instrucción de escribanos*, 199
Galland, Antoine, 173
Galt, John, *Laurie Todd*, 306
Garden of Spirituall Flowers, A, 302–3

Gauden, John, *214*, p5
Gay, David, 207, 208
Genette, Gérard, 1
Genius, 66–7
Gerard of Cremona, 127
Gessner, Salomon, *The Death of Abel*, 271, 281–8, *284*, *285*, 293, 295n
Ghibellines, 84, 86, 89
Gil, Manuel, 197
Gillespie, Vincent, 63
Gilson, Simon, 76
Glass, Thomas, 146–9, *147*
Godfrey, Edmund Berry, 152
'godly reading', 300
Gong Sunchou, 42
Góngora, Luis de, 233–4, 236, 240–1
  Canción XIV, 227, 229
Gonzalbo, Pilar, 184–5
Goodrich, Samuel, 303
Gosse, Edmund, 309
grammatical reading, 174
Gravelot, Hubert-François, 288–90
Green, Monica, 127–8
Gregory, Francis, 219–20, 221
Greville, Robert, Baron Brooke, 136
Griffin, Clive, 187
Gruys, Hans, *253*, 256
Guamán Poma de Ayala, Felipe, 200, 201
  Nueva Coronica, 200
Guaraní language, 239, 240–1
Guelphs, 84, 87
guidebooks, 32–7
Guinizelli, Guido, 84–5, 86
Guittone d'Arezzo, 84

Hafiz of Shiraz, 168, 175
  Divan, 160–1, 162, 164–6, 169, 170–2, 174–6
Hall, David D., 303
Hall, Samuel, 293
Hammond, Mary, 195
Hammond, Paul, 159n
Han Fei, 34

Han Feizi, 34
Han Ying, 38–9
handwriting, 103–4, 106
Haro, Tomás Lopéz de, 188
Harvey, Gabriel, 39
Havely, Nick, 93
Hayali Bey, 164
Hayman, Francis, 288–90
heard reading, 54, 62–4, 195–6
Helaki, 165, 172
Heloise, 54, 55–6, 69n
   Problemata Heloissae, 55
Henri de Mondeville, *Surgery*, 118
Heptinstall, T., 286
Herbert, George, *The Temple*, 146
Herrera, Luis Antonio Oviedo de, 237
Herringman, Henry, 159n
Herzog August Bibliothek, 256
Hill, Aaron, 290
Hilton, Walter, *Scale of Perfection*, 64
History of Reading, The, 5, 299
Hoby, Elizabeth, 304
Hoby, Margaret, 302
Holbach, Baron, 198
Holdsworth, Richard, of Cambridge, 213
Hook, Theodore, 307
Hooker, Richard, *Of the Laws of Ecclesiastical Polity*, 210–11
Horden, Peregrine, 125, 126
Howell, James, 212, 213, 220, 221
Huang lan, 46
Huguet de Sémonville, Charles-Nicolas, 256
Huguet de Sémonville, Charlotte-Madeleine, 256
Hume, Robert, 270
Hunt, Arnold, 211, 214
Hunt, Tony, 130
hyperbole, 136, 138

Iberian world, 227–48
illustrated literary text, 270–96

Inés de la Cruz, Juana, 193, 196
Inquisition, 195, 197, 198, 237–8
'interpretive communities', 2
intertextuality, 227–48
Iser, Wolfgang, 2
Islam, 163–4, 165, 298
Italian language, 235
Italy, 234, 239, 243

Jackson, B., 285–6
Jajdelska, Elspeth, 300
James I
   Basilikon Doron, 211
   Works, 211, 216
Jami, Abd al-Rahman, *Nafahat al-Uns*, 172
Jean de Meun, 55
Jerónimo de Loayza, 185–6
Jerónimo de San Francisco, 196
Jesuits, 230, 232–5, 238, 239, 242
   colleges, 191–2, 243–4
   see also Catholicism
Ji Wenzi, 48–9
John of Arderne, *Practica*, 118–19
Johnson, Kimberly, 210
Jones, Peter Murray, 117, 118–19, 126
José de Anchieta, *De Gestis Mendi de Saa*, 229
José Eusebio de Llano Zapata, 192
Juan de Dueñas, *El Espejo de Consolación*, 197
Juan de Grijalva, Fray, 190
Juan de Matienzo, 185
Juan de Sarria, 188
Judaism, 298
Julian of Norwich, 55, 61–3, 71n
   Revelations of Divine Love, 55, 61
Julius, 256

Kay, Dennis, 155
Kearney, James, 209, 221
Kemmish, W., 295n
Kempe, Margery, 55, 63–5, 71–2n, 301
   Book, 63–5, 98–114

Kendrew, James, 292–3
Killinghal, John, 257
Knoppers, Laura, 206
Krijn, Sophie A., 249

Lacey, Andrew, 216–17, 217
Laideguive de Becheville, 255
Lamb, Mary Ellen, 304
lan, 36
Landívar, Rafael, 238
Lang, Anouk, 3
Latin
    Arderne, 119
    Arte poetica, 235–6
    Blessed Angela of Foligno, 107
    Dante, 76
    Iberian world, 228
    Jesuits, 184–5
    Julian of Norwich, 71n
    Marie de France, 54–6, 59–62
    Peramás, 239–40
    practical medicine books, 116, 120
    Ratio Studiorum, 232–3
Laud, Archbishop William, 209–10, 213
    Articles . . . in the first trienniall visitation, 209–10
legibilis, 100
legibility of Christ, 102–3
Leonard, Irving, 187
Lepautre, Jean, 254
Lesser, Zachary, 155, 159n
lettered cities, 182
lettered Indians, 199–201
Lettres de Julie à Eulalie ou Tableau du libertinage de Paris, 198–9
Li, 13, 19
Liber Passionalis, 126
Lindisfarne Gospels, 121
Lister, Anne, 307
literacy, 12–13
    among Confucian scholars in ancient China, 11–30
    evidence of through analysis, 16–24

Persian, 161–2, 167, 172
Spanish, 186
visual, 270–96
literary reading, 175
literate culture, 12–13
literate mentality, 12–13, 24–6
literature
    advice, 163
    French, 198–9
Lobo, Eugenio Gerado, *Selva de las Musas*, 237
Lochrie, Karma, 104–5
Lodge, John, 289–90
Lombardi, Elena, 90–1
Long Charter of Christ, The, 101–2
'lore', 123
Lort, Michael, 253
Love, Nicholas, *Meditationes vita Christi*, 64
Lu Buwei, 26
Luís de Camões, *Os Lusíadas*, 236
Lysaght, S. R., 309

Mackenzie & Co., J., 279–81
Madame Xumu, of Wei, 48–9
Madan, Francis, 212–13, 216
Mahmud, 165
Maldon, William, 301
Malet, Gilles, 66
Maltby, Judith, 207, 214, 217
Manguel, Alberto
    A History of Reading, 4, 299
Mansfield, Katherine, 308
marginalia, 121–3, 124, 149–50, 172, 258–9
Mariano Arbites, 198
Marie de France, 58–60, p3
    Fables, 59–60
    Lais, 54, 59–60
    St Patrick's Purgatory, 59, 60
Marion, Michel, 253
Marsilius of Padua, 83–4, 87
Martí, Manuel, 230
Martin, Philippe, 259
Martineau, Harriet, 306–7, 308

Mary of Oignies, 111
Masson, Nicole, 252
Master, 16-4, 24-6, 26-7, 39-40
materiality of the book, 115-34
Mattingly, Harold, 249-50
Mayhew, Henry, *London Labour and the London Poor*, 305
McCoy, Richard, 211
MEDIATE project, 251, 259-60
medical manuscripts, 121-3
medicina practica, 115-34
medieval women writers, 54-73
Mehmed, Esad, 165, 174
memorisation, 16, 32, 62, 167-8, 173, 185
Menacho, Juan Pérez, 196
Ménage, Gilles, 254
Menagiana, 254
Mencius, 19-20, 26, 42-3
  Mencius, 15-16, 18-20, 24-6
Mendes, Antonio, 197
Méndez, Miguel, 188
Merced convent library, La, 191
Mews, Constant, 55
Mexico, 232-3, 234, 235, 237, 243
Mexico City, 187, 229, 231, 243
Mi ritrovai per un poema sacro, 74-97
Micklethwaite, John, 153
Middle English, 57, 60, 65, 101, 116
Middleton, Ann, 254
Mihiri Hatun, *Divan*, 170-1
Miller, D. A., 4
Milton, John, 208, 236-7
minatures, 213-14, 215, 216-17
minimalists and motivationists, 123-5
Minnis, Alastair, 105
Mollinedo y Angulo, Manuel de, 193-5
Monumentum Regale, 218-19
Mooney, Linne, 123-4
'more open' text, 105-9
Moretti, Franco, 4

Morison, Robert, 275, 278
Mornet, Daniel, 'Les enseignements des bibliothèques privées (1750-80)', 249, 253
Munby, Alan, 252, 253
Murad III, 170
Murry, Middleton, 308
Muscio, 127-128
  Gynecia, 118
mystical reading, 175

Nahuatl language, 201
Nazmi, Edirneli, 163, 174
Nelson, Holly Faith, 207
Netzley, Ryan, 208, 210-11, 212
neuroscientists, 2
New Spain, 182-205
Newbery, Francis, 289-91
newssheets, 140
niao-chong, 13
Nicholas of Lyra, *Postilla in Iob*, 119-20, 127
Nightingale, Florence, 303-4, 307
Nisari, 165-6, 170, 175
Northern Ireland, 304
Notre Dame Cathedral Library, 56

Occitan language, 57
Oldridge, Darren, 210
Opie, Amelia, *Temper, or, Domestic Scenes*, 308
ornate lettering, 214-15, 216-17
orthodoxy, 83-6, 88-9, 90-2, 94
Ortiz, Pero, 187-8
Osler, Sir William, 119-20
Ottoman Empire, 160-81
Ottoman Turkish, 165
Ovid, 67, 100-1, 229
  Heroides, 56, 57
Ovide moralisé, 67
Owen, John, 236
Owen, Stephen, 42

Palafox Seminary library in Puebla, Mexico, 191, *191*

Palafox y Mendoza, Bishop Juan de, 191
Palomares de Vargas, Juan, 195
Panama, 241–2
Paolo (character), 74, 80–1, 85–6, 89
paper, 35–6
Paraclete, 56
Paraguay, 229, 238, 238–9, 240–1, 243
paratextual material, 1, 279–80, 294
Parsons, Kelly, 101
Pashazade, Kemal, *Nigaristan*, 171
Pearson, Jacqueline, 300
Pennac, Daniel, *The Rights of the Reader*, 310–11
Pepwell, Henry, 100
Pepys, Samuel, 300
Peramás, José Manuel, 238–43, 243–4
    De Administratione Guaranica Comparata ad Rempublicam Platonis Commentarius, 239
    De Invento Novo Orbe Inductoque Illuc Christi Sacrificio, 239–43
Pérez, Christóbal, accent, 188
Pérez de Guzmán, Fernán, *Cancionerio*, 195
Perry, Nandra, 209
Persian bestsellers, 162–3
Persian classics, 160–81
Persian literacy, 161–2, 167, 172
Pertile, Lino, 89
Peru, 182–205, 229, 231
Peter the Venerable, 55
Philipot, Thomas, *139*, *141*
philological reading, 174–5
pictographic tablets, Mesopotamia, 2–3
pictures, 118–19, 127–8, 129–30
Placcius, Vincentius, *Atlantis Retecta*, 242
plates, 275, 290

plurilingual poetry, 227–48
Pollard, Graham, 250
Poma, Guamán, 199
Popish Plot, 152–4
portraits, 57, 58, 59, 140, 207–8
Portugal, 229
Portuguese *conversos*, 196–7
Potter, Lois, 214
Poynings, Lady, 117–18
practical medicine books, 115–34, *129*
priest-scribe, 103–9, 111–12
printed private library catalogues, 249–69
private libraries, 193–5, 249–69
private reading, 172
'privitization' of reading, 299
professional readers, 166–7, 172
'pseudo-utilitarian texts', 123
public libraries, 192
Puritans, 300

Qin, China, 13
Qin dynasty, 15
Qin Shi Huang, 27
Quechua language, 200
Queen Zhangsun, 35
Qunshu zhiyao, 31–53
Qur'an, 163–4, 165, 298

Rabinowitz, Peter, 77–8
Rahmi, Mehmed, 174
Raimbaut III d'Orange, 57
Rama, Angel, *La ciudad letrada*, 182, 201–2
Ratio Studiorum, 232–3, 238, 243
'read for action', 39
Reader, The, 310
reader-reciters, 161
readers
    beginning, 167–8, 172–3
    'community of', 304
    elite, 169
    professional, 166–7, 172
    Sufis, 168–9, 175

reading
  aloud, 297–314
  beneficial to health, 309–10
  Catholic books, 196–7
  collective, 172–3
  communities, 135–59
  as devotion and sacrament, 209–12
  'distant', 4
  diverse modes of, 171–5
  and doing, 115–34
  Europeanising culture, 227–48
  experiences, 195–9
  to the family, 301–4
  'godly', 300
  grammatical, 174
  heard, 54, 62–4, 195–6
  ideological, 74–97
  by listening, 301–5
  literary, 175
  at mealtimes, 195–6
  mystical, 175
  philological, 174–5
  private, 172
  'privitization' of, 299
  public, 183–6
  sacramental, 206–26
  shared, 310
  silent, 54, 297–9
  by special grace, 100–5
  in translation, 173–4
'readness', 230–4
'receptive fallacy', 272
recommended reading, 196, 302
Red Ink Annotator, 101
Reed, John, 124
Reilly, Charles H., 307
Reinking, David, 31
Requerimiento, 227–8
Rhodes, Richard, 302
Richardson, Samuel, 303
  Pamela, 271, 288–293, *291*, *292*
Richter, Henry James, 286–8
River Plate, 231
Robertson, James, 287–8

Rolle, Richard, of Hampole
  Incendium amoris, 64
  Meditations on the Passion, 101–3
Roman de Renart, 59, 66–7
Romance of the Rose, 55
Romulus, 59
Rose, Jonathan, 272
  The Intellectual Life of the British Working Classes, 300
Royalists, 206–26
Rueda, Pedro, 188–9
Rumi, Jalal al-Din, *Masnavi*, 161–5, 167–9, 170, 172, 172–3, 175
Rupert (Prince), 152
Ruskin, John, 303
Russell, William, 153–4
Rusuhi, Ismail, 163–4, 172–3
Rycaut, Sir Paul, 167
Rye House Plot, 152–4

sacramental reading, 206–26
Sadi of Shiraz
  Bustan, 162, 164–5, 169, 172, 173–4
  Gulistan, 162, 164–5, 166, 171, 172, 173, 174
Saenger, Paul, 298–9
Şahidi, Ibrahim, 167–8
Saint, Thomas, 291
Salduendo, Francisco Xavier, 196
San Jerónimo of Puebla convent, 196
San Pablo Augustinian college library, 190, 192, 196
Santa Teresa convent, Puebla, 195–6
Santa Teresa of Ávila, 196
Santo Domingo, 231
Sarmiento, Agustin, *194*
Sarria-Méndez, 188
Schama, Simon, 298
Scholasticism, 81–4, 86–9, 90, 94, 119–20, 120–1, 122–3, 126
Schoolmen, 83

Schwaller, John Frederick, 201
Scott, Kathleen, 119
Scott, Robert, 275–6
Scott, Sir Walter, 306
scrolls, 35–7, 118–19
Seaman, Lazarus, 152
Second volumne of the farewel se[r]mons, preached by some London and country ministers, The, 144
self-promotion, 117
Selim II, 169
Şemi, Şemullah, 162–4, 166, 170
   Saadetname, 169
Seneca, 56
Seville, 187, 188
Shao Jingbang, *Hongjian lu*, 35
'shared reading', 310
Sharpe, Kevin, 211, 301
Shi, 13
Shizhou, 13–14
Short Charter of Christ, The, 101–2
Shuffelton, George, 101–2
Sigüenza y Góngora, Carlos de, 192
silent reading, 54, 297–9
silk, 35–6
Sitz in Leben, 125
Skerpan-Wheeler, Elizabeth, 206
Smith, Horace, *Brambletye House*, 306
Sobecki, Sebastian, 103
Sonds, George, 136
songs, 44–5
Spanish language, 235, 240
Spanish literacy, 186
'special grace', 99–100, 107
Spiritual Franciscans, 93
Spring, Howard, 305–6
Spryngolde, Robert, 99
St Bridget, *Revelations*, 64–5
St Patrick's Purgatory, 54
Stafford's memoires, 154
Statius, 79, 91, 92
Steinberg, Justin, 75–6, 84
Stephen, Leslie, 306

Stevenson, Robert Louis, 308–9
   Treasure Island, 309
   Weir of Herminston, 309
stilnovistic poetry, 84–5, 86–7, 89, 90, 94
Stimulus amoris, 64
Stockdale, John, 273–4
Stothard, Thomas, 273–8, 286
Stowe, Harriet Beecher, 308
Strange, Nathaniel, 146–50
Streete, Adrian, 208
Sudi, Ahmed, 166–7, 168, 172, 173, 174–5
Sufis, 160–9, 175
Sui Dynasty, 44–5, 50
Süleyman the Magnificent, 169–70
Sürurî, Muslihüddin, 160–1, 166, 168, 172, 174, 175
Svenbro, Jesper, 'Archaic and Classical Greece', 6

T. Osborn and J. Mozley, 283
tabulae, 117
Tang Dynasty, 35, 37
Tao, 31
Targoff, Ramie, 207, 210
Taylor, Archer, 250
textual autonomy, 12t
Third Council of Lima, 185–6, 199, 200
Third Provincial Council of Mexico, 201
Thomas, Isaiah, 282
   The Sugar Plumb, 293, 294
Thomas de Pizan, 65–6
Thomas of Celano, 94
Thomson, James, *The Seasons*, 271, 273–81, 274, 277, 280, 294
Tillotson, John, 302
Titian, 281–3
title page, 214–15
Tomkins, Peltro William, 281
Tonson, Jacob, 159n
travellers, 195
True Protestant Mercury, 154

Turkish, 171
Turriana library, 192
Tyacke, Nicholas, 208, 210
Tyndale, William, 301

UK Reading Experience Database (RED), 305
United States catalogues, 250
University of Exeter, 309
University of Liverpool, 310
University of Paris, 56
University of San Marcos, 193
unreadable, 98–114
Urquizu, Santiago, 198
'use', 120–1, 121–3, 125–9
utilitarian texts, 123

van Selm, Bert, 'Book Sales Catalogues of the Dutch Republic', 252
Varry, Dominique, 250, 251
Vaticinium Votivum, 218–19
Vernor & Hood, 286–8
Viceroy Toledo, 199
vicesimo-quarto size, 213–14, 216–17
vignettes, 273, 275, 277, 278, 283, 291
Virgil, 79, 87–9, 91
   Aeneid, 233
   Georgics, 240–1
visual form, 135–59
visual literacy, 270–96
Voaden, Rosalynn, 109
Voltaire, 198

Wadsworth, Thomas, 145, 150
Walker, Elizabeth, 303
Wallington, Nehemiah, 302–3
Wang Shi, 39
Warring States period, 11
Wedgwood, Emma, 308
Wei Zheng, 33, 35–6, 38–9, 41, 44–6, 49–50
Wenman, Joseph, 273–5
Western Han Dynasty, 39
Western Zhou, 41
   Western Zhou Dynasty, 44
Whitefield, C., 290
Whitman, Walt, *Leaves of Grass*, 308
Wild, Robert, 152–3
Willard, Charity Cannon, 66
Williams, Abigail, 300
Williams, John, 213
Wilson, Spencer, & Mawman, 291
Windeatt, B. A., 107
Wolf, Maryanne, 2
women troubadours, 56–61, 68, 69n
women writers, 54–73
woodblock printing, 35
woodcuts, 275–8, 277, 283, 290–1
Woolf, D. R., 300
Woolf, Virginia, 306
Wynkyn de Worde, 99, 100

Xun Zi, 21–4, 26
   Xun Zi, 15–16, 21–4, 25–6

You Zi, 17–18

Zaifi, Muhammed, 170
Zboary, Mary Saracino, 300
Zboray, Ronald J., 300
Zeyrek Agha Pasha, 169
Zheng, 41, 48–9
zhi, 42–3
Zhou court, 14
Zhou Dynasty, 47–8, 49
Zigong, 39–40
Zijia, 48–9
Zixia, 40
Zou Tradition, 48

EU representative:
Easy Access System Europe
Mustamäe tee 50, 10621 Tallinn, Estonia
Gpsr.requests@easproject.com

www.ingramcontent.com/pod-product-compliance
Lightning Source LLC
Chambersburg PA
CBHW052055300426
44117CB00013B/2139